D1555914

Toyota
Corolla &
Geo Prizm
Automotive
Repair
Manual

by Jay Storer
and John H Haynes
Member of the Guild of Motoring Writers

Models covered:
All Toyota Corolla and Geo Prizm models
1993 through 1997

(5A1 - 92036)

ABCDE
FGHIJ
KLMNO
PQ

Haynes Publishing Group
Sparkford Nr Yeovil
Somerset BA22 7JJ England

Haynes North America, Inc
861 Lawrence Drive
Newbury Park
California 91320 USA

Acknowledgements

Technical writers who contributed to this project include Rob Maddox, Mike Stubblefield and Larry Warren.

A book in the Haynes Automotive Repair Manual Series

Printed in the U.S.A.

ISBN 1 56392 322 X

Library of Congress Catalog Card Number 98-85020

Contents

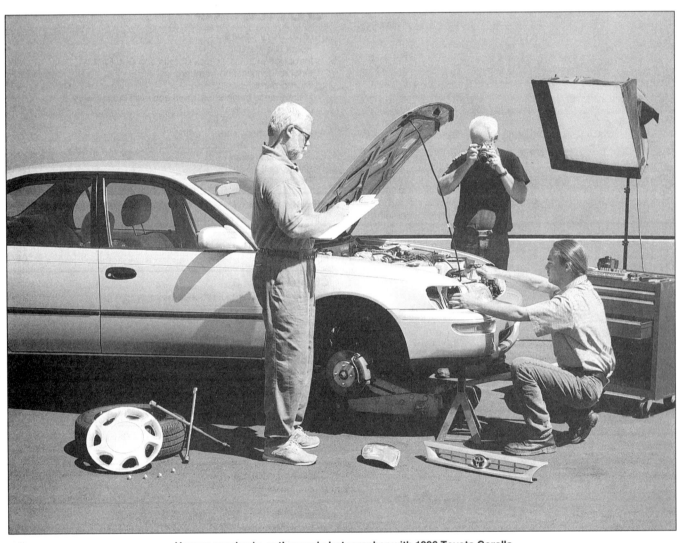

Haynes mechanic, author and photographer with 1996 Toyota Corolla

About this manual

Its purpose

The purpose of this manual is to help you get the best value from your vehicle. It can do so in several ways. It can help you decide what work must be done, even if you choose to have it done by a dealer service department or a repair shop; it provides information and procedures for routine maintenance and servicing; and it offers diagnostic and repair procedures to follow when trouble occurs.

We hope you use the manual to tackle the work yourself. For many simpler jobs, doing it yourself may be quicker than arranging an appointment to get the vehicle into a shop and making the trips to leave it and pick it up. More importantly, a lot of money can be saved by avoiding the expense the shop must pass on to you to cover its labor and overhead costs. An added benefit is the sense of satisfaction and accomplishment that you feel after doing the job yourself.

Using the manual

The manual is divided into Chapters. Each Chapter is divided into numbered Sections, which are headed in bold type between horizontal lines. Each Section consists of consecutively numbered paragraphs.

At the beginning of each numbered Section you will be referred to any illustrations which apply to the procedures in that Section. The reference numbers used in illustration captions pinpoint the pertinent Section and the Step within that Section. That is, illustration 3.2 means the illustration refers to Section 3 and Step (or paragraph) 2 within that Section.

Procedures, once described in the text, are not normally repeated. When it's necessary to refer to another Chapter, the reference will be given as Chapter and Section number. Cross references given without use of the word "Chapter" apply to Sections and/or paragraphs in the same Chapter. For example, "see Section 8" means in the same Chapter.

References to the left or right side of the vehicle assume you are sitting in the driver's seat, facing forward.

Even though we have prepared this manual with extreme care, neither the publisher nor the author can accept responsibility for any errors in, or omissions from, the information given.

NOTE

A **Note** provides information necessary to properly complete a procedure or information which will make the procedure easier to understand.

CAUTION

A **Caution** provides a special procedure or special steps which must be taken while completing the procedure where the Caution is found. Not heeding a Caution can result in damage to the assembly being worked on.

WARNING

A **Warning** provides a special procedure or special steps which must be taken while completing the procedure where the Warning is found. Not heeding a Warning can result in personal injury.

Introduction to the Toyota Corolla and Geo Prizm

Toyota Corolla models are available in two-and four-door sedan and station wagon body styles. Geo Prizm models are available as four-door sedans only.

The transversely mounted inline four-cylinder engines used in these vehicles are equipped with electronic fuel injection.

The engine drives the front wheels through either a five-speed manual or a three-or four-speed automatic transaxle via independent driveaxles.

Independent suspension, featuring coil spring/strut damper units, is used on all four wheels. The rack-and-pinion steering unit is mounted behind the engine with power-assist available as an option.

The brakes are disc at the front and drums at the rear, with power assist standard. An Anti-lock Brake System (ABS) became available on some models.

Vehicle identification numbers

Modifications are a continuing and unpublicized process in vehicle manufacturing. Since spare parts manuals and lists are compiled on a numerical basis, the individual vehicle numbers are essential to correctly identify the component required.

Vehicle Identification Number (VIN)

This very important identification number is stamped on the firewall in the engine compartment and on a plate attached to the dashboard inside the windshield on the driver's side of the vehicle and on some models the end of the driver's door **(see illustration)**. The VIN also appears on the Vehicle Certificate of Title and Registration. It contains information such as where and when the vehicle was manufactured, the model year and the body style.

Manufacturer's Certification Regulation label

The manufacturer's Certification Regulation label is attached to the driver's side door end or post. The plate contains the name of the manufacturer, the month and year of production, the Gross Vehicle Weight Rating (GVWR), the Gross Axle Weight Rating (GAWR) and the certification statement.

VIN engine and model year codes

Two particularly important pieces of information found in the VIN are the engine code (Geo models only) and the model year code. Counting from the left, the engine code letter designation is the 8th digit and the model year code letter designation is the 10th digit.

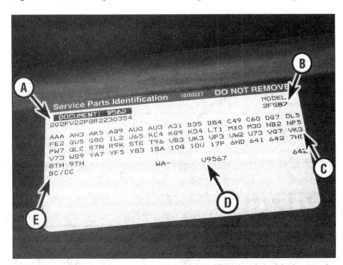

On Geo models, the service parts identification label is located on the spare tire cover

A	Vehicle identification number
B	Body type and style
C	Options
D	Paint codes
E	Paint type

On the Geo models covered by this manual the engine codes are:

6	1.6L
8	1.8L

On all models covered by this manual the model year codes are:

P	1993
R	1994
S	1995
T	1996

Service parts identification label (Geo models only)

This label is located on the spare tire cover **(see illustration)**. It lists the VIN, paint number, options and other information specific to the vehicle. Always refer to this label when you order parts.

Engine number

The engine code number can be found on a pad on the front (radiator) side of the cylinder block **(see illustration)**.

Locations of the Vehicle Identification Number (VIN) (A) which is visible through the driver's side of the windshield and the Certification Regulation label (B)

Location of the engine identification number

Buying parts

Replacement parts are available from many sources, which generally fall into one of two categories - authorized dealer parts departments and independent retail auto parts stores. Our advice concerning these parts is as follows:

Retail auto parts stores: Good auto parts stores will stock frequently needed components which wear out relatively fast, such as clutch components, exhaust systems, brake parts, tune-up parts, etc. These stores often supply new or reconditioned parts on an exchange basis, which can save a considerable amount of money. Discount auto parts stores are often very good places to buy materials and parts needed for general vehicle maintenance such as oil, grease, filters, spark plugs, belts, touch-up paint, bulbs, etc. They also usually sell tools and general accessories, have convenient

hours, charge lower prices and can often be found not far from home.

Authorized dealer parts department: This is the best source for parts which are unique to the vehicle and not generally available elsewhere (such as major engine parts, transmission parts, trim pieces, etc.).

Warranty information: If the vehicle is still covered under warranty, be sure that any replacement parts purchased - regardless of the source - do not invalidate the warranty!

To be sure of obtaining the correct parts, have engine and chassis numbers available and, if possible, take the old parts along for positive identification.

Maintenance techniques, tools and working facilities

Maintenance techniques

There are a number of techniques involved in maintenance and repair that will be referred to throughout this manual. Application of these techniques will enable the home mechanic to be more efficient, better organized and capable of performing the various tasks properly, which will ensure that the repair job is thorough and complete.

Fasteners

Fasteners are nuts, bolts, studs and screws used to hold two or more parts together. There are a few things to keep in mind when working with fasteners. Almost all of them use a locking device of some type, either a lockwasher, locknut, locking tab or thread adhesive. All threaded fasteners should be clean and straight, with undamaged threads and undamaged corners on the hex head where the wrench fits. Develop the habit of replacing all damaged nuts and bolts with new ones. Special locknuts with nylon or fiber inserts can only be

used once. If they are removed, they lose their locking ability and must be replaced with new ones.

Rusted nuts and bolts should be treated with a penetrating fluid to ease removal and prevent breakage. Some mechanics use turpentine in a spout-type oil can, which works quite well. After applying the rust penetrant, let it work for a few minutes before trying to loosen the nut or bolt. Badly rusted fasteners may have to be chiseled or sawed off or removed with a special nut breaker, available at tool stores.

If a bolt or stud breaks off in an assembly, it can be drilled and removed with a special tool commonly available for this purpose. Most automotive machine shops can perform this task, as well as other repair procedures, such as the repair of threaded holes that have been stripped out.

Flat washers and lockwashers, when removed from an assembly, should always be replaced exactly as removed. Replace any damaged washers with new ones. Never use a lockwasher on any soft metal surface (such as aluminum), thin sheet metal or plastic.

Fastener sizes

For a number of reasons, automobile manufacturers are making wider and wider use of metric fasteners. Therefore, it is important to be able to tell the difference between standard (sometimes called U.S. or SAE) and metric hardware, since they cannot be interchanged.

All bolts, whether standard or metric, are sized according to diameter, thread pitch and length. For example, a standard 1/2 - 13 x 1 bolt is 1/2 inch in diameter, has 13 threads per inch and is 1 inch long. An M12 - 1.75 x 25 metric bolt is 12 mm in diameter, has a thread pitch of 1.75 mm (the distance between threads) and is 25 mm long. The two bolts are nearly identical, and easily confused, but they are not interchangeable.

In addition to the differences in diameter, thread pitch and length, metric and standard bolts can also be distinguished by examining the bolt heads. To begin with, the distance across the flats on a standard bolt head is measured in inches, while the same dimension on a metric bolt is sized in millimeters (the same is true for nuts). As a result, a standard wrench should not be used on a metric bolt and a metric wrench should not be used on a standard bolt. Also, most standard bolts have slashes radiating out from the center of the head to denote the grade or strength of the bolt, which is an indication of the amount of torque that can be applied to it. The greater the number of slashes, the greater the strength of the bolt. Grades 0 through 5 are commonly used on automobiles. Metric bolts have a property class (grade) number, rather than a slash, molded into their heads to indicate bolt strength. In this case, the higher the number, the stronger the bolt. Property class numbers 8.8, 9.8 and 10.9 are commonly used on automobiles.

Strength markings can also be used to distinguish standard hex nuts from metric hex nuts. Many standard nuts have dots stamped into one side, while metric nuts are marked with a number. The greater the number of dots, or the higher the number, the greater the strength of the nut.

Metric studs are also marked on their ends according to property class (grade). Larger studs are numbered (the same as metric bolts), while smaller studs carry a geometric code to denote grade.

Bolt strength markings (top - standard/SAE/USS; bottom - metric)

Standard hex nut strength markings

Metric hex nut strength markings

Metric stud strength markings

It should be noted that many fasteners, especially Grades 0 through 2, have no distinguishing marks on them. When such is the case, the only way to determine whether it is standard or metric is to measure the thread pitch or compare it to a known fastener of the same size.

Standard fasteners are often referred to as SAE, as opposed to metric. However, it should be noted that SAE technically refers to a non-metric fine thread fastener only. Coarse thread non-metric fasteners are referred to as USS sizes.

Since fasteners of the same size (both standard and metric) may have different strength ratings, be sure to reinstall any bolts, studs or nuts removed from your vehicle in their original locations. Also, when replacing a fastener with a new one, make sure that the new one has a strength rating equal to or greater than the original.

Tightening sequences and procedures

Most threaded fasteners should be tightened to a specific torque value (torque is the twisting force applied to a threaded component such as a nut or bolt). Overtightening the fastener can weaken it and cause it to break, while undertightening can cause it to eventually come loose. Bolts, screws and studs, depending on the material they are made of and their thread diameters, have specific torque values, many of which are noted in the Specifications at the beginning of each Chapter. Be sure to follow the torque recommendations closely. For fasteners not assigned a specific torque, a general torque value chart is presented here as a guide. These torque values are for dry (unlubricated) fasteners threaded into steel or cast iron (not aluminum). As was previously mentioned, the size and grade of a fastener determine the amount of torque that can safely be applied to it. The figures listed

Metric thread sizes	Ft-lbs	Nm
M-6	6 to 9	9 to 12
M-8	14 to 21	19 to 28
M-10	28 to 40	38 to 54
M-12	50 to 71	68 to 96
M-14	80 to 140	109 to 154
Pipe thread sizes		
1/8	5 to 8	7 to 10
1/4	12 to 18	17 to 24
3/8	22 to 33	30 to 44
1/2	25 to 35	34 to 47
U.S. thread sizes		
1/4 - 20	6 to 9	9 to 12
5/16 - 18	12 to 18	17 to 24
5/16 - 24	14 to 20	19 to 27
3/8 - 16	22 to 32	30 to 43
3/8 - 24	27 to 38	37 to 51
7/16 - 14	40 to 55	55 to 74
7/16 - 20	40 to 60	55 to 81
1/2 - 13	55 to 80	75 to 108

Standard (SAE and USS) bolt dimensions/grade marks

G   Grade marks (bolt strength)
L   Length (in inches)
T   Thread pitch (number of threads per inch)
D   Nominal diameter (in inches)

Metric bolt dimensions/grade marks

P   Property class (bolt strength)
L   Length (in millimeters)
T   Thread pitch (distance between threads in millimeters)
D   Diameter

here are approximate for Grade 2 and Grade 3 fasteners. Higher grades can tolerate higher torque values.

Fasteners laid out in a pattern, such as cylinder head bolts, oil pan bolts, differential cover bolts, etc., must be loosened or tightened in sequence to avoid warping the component. This sequence will normally be shown in the appropriate Chapter. If a specific pattern is not given, the following procedures can be used to prevent warping.

Initially, the bolts or nuts should be assembled finger-tight only. Next, they should be tightened one full turn each, in a criss-cross or diagonal pattern. After each one has been tightened one full turn, return to the first one and tighten them all one-half turn, following the same pattern. Finally, tighten each of them one-quarter turn at a time until each fastener has been tightened to the proper torque. To loosen and remove the fasteners, the procedure would be reversed.

Component disassembly

Component disassembly should be done with care and purpose to help ensure that the parts go back together properly. Always keep track of the sequence in which parts are removed. Make note of special characteristics or marks on parts that can be installed more than one way, such as a grooved thrust washer on a shaft. It is a good idea to lay the disassembled parts out on a clean surface in the order that they were removed. It may also be helpful to make sketches or take instant photos of components before removal.

When removing fasteners from a component, keep track of their locations. Sometimes threading a bolt back in a part, or putting the washers and nut back on a stud, can prevent mix-ups later. If nuts and bolts cannot be returned to their original locations, they should be kept in a compartmented box or a series of small boxes. A cupcake or muffin tin is ideal for this purpose, since each cavity can hold the bolts and nuts from a particular area (i.e. oil pan bolts, valve cover bolts, engine mount bolts, etc.). A pan of this type is especially helpful when working on assemblies with very small parts, such as the carburetor, alternator, valve train or interior dash and trim pieces. The cavities can be marked with paint or tape to identify the contents.

Whenever wiring looms, harnesses or connectors are separated, it is a good idea to identify the two halves with numbered pieces of masking tape so they can be easily reconnected.

Gasket sealing surfaces

Throughout any vehicle, gaskets are used to seal the mating surfaces between two parts and keep lubricants, fluids, vacuum or pressure contained in an assembly.

Many times these gaskets are coated with a liquid or paste-type gasket sealing compound before assembly. Age, heat and pressure can sometimes cause the two parts to stick together so tightly that they are very difficult to separate. Often, the assembly can be loosened by striking it with a soft-face hammer near the mating surfaces. A regular hammer can be used if a block of wood is placed between the hammer and the part. Do not hammer on cast parts or parts that could be easily damaged. With any particularly stubborn part, always recheck to make sure that every fastener has been removed.

Avoid using a screwdriver or bar to pry apart an assembly, as they can easily mar the gasket sealing surfaces of the parts, which must remain smooth. If prying is absolutely necessary, use an old broom handle, but keep in mind that extra clean up will be necessary if the wood splinters.

After the parts are separated, the old gasket must be carefully scraped off and the gasket surfaces cleaned. Stubborn gasket material can be soaked with rust penetrant or treated with a special chemical to soften it so it can be easily scraped off. A scraper can be fashioned from a piece of copper tubing by flattening and sharpening one end. Copper is recommended because it is usually softer than the surfaces to be scraped, which reduces the chance of gouging the part. Some gaskets can be removed with a wire brush, but regardless of the method used, the mating surfaces must be left clean and smooth. If for some reason the gasket surface is gouged, then a gasket sealer thick enough to fill scratches will have to be used during reassembly of the components. For most applications, a non-drying (or semi-drying) gasket sealer should be used.

Hose removal tips

Warning: *If the vehicle is equipped with air conditioning, do not disconnect any of the A/C hoses without first having the system depressurized by a dealer service department or a service station.*

Hose removal precautions closely parallel gasket removal precautions. Avoid scratching or gouging the surface that the hose mates against or the connection may leak. This is especially true for radiator hoses. Because of various chemical reactions, the rubber in hoses can bond itself to the metal spigot that the hose fits over. To remove a hose, first loosen the hose clamps that secure it to the spigot. Then, with slip-joint pliers, grab the hose at the clamp and rotate it around the spigot. Work it back and forth until it is completely free, then pull it off. Silicone or other lubricants will ease removal if they can be applied between the hose and the outside of the spigot. Apply the same lubricant to the inside of the hose and the outside of the spigot to simplify installation.

As a last resort (and if the hose is to be replaced with a new one anyway), the rubber can be slit with a knife and the hose peeled from the spigot. If this must be done, be careful that the metal connection is not damaged.

If a hose clamp is broken or damaged, do not reuse it. Wire-type clamps usually weaken with age, so it is a good idea to replace them with screw-type clamps whenever a hose is removed.

Tools

A selection of good tools is a basic requirement for anyone who plans to maintain and repair his or her own vehicle. For the owner who has few tools, the initial investment might seem high, but when compared to the spiraling costs of professional auto maintenance and repair, it is a wise one.

Micrometer set

Dial indicator set

Dial caliper

Hand-operated vacuum pump

Timing light

Compression gauge with spark plug hole adapter

Damper/steering wheel puller

General purpose puller

Hydraulic lifter removal tool

Valve spring compressor

Valve spring compressor

Ridge reamer

Piston ring groove cleaning tool

Ring removal/installation tool

Ring compressor

Cylinder hone

Brake hold-down spring tool

Brake cylinder hone

Clutch plate alignment tool

Tap and die set

To help the owner decide which tools are needed to perform the tasks detailed in this manual, the following tool lists are offered: *Maintenance and minor repair, Repair/overhaul* and *Special.*

The newcomer to practical mechanics should start off with the *maintenance and minor repair* tool kit, which is adequate for the simpler jobs performed on a vehicle. Then, as confidence and experience grow, the owner can tackle more difficult tasks, buying additional tools as they are needed. Eventually the basic kit will be expanded into the *repair and overhaul* tool set. Over a period of time, the experienced do-it-yourselfer will assemble a tool set complete enough for most repair and overhaul procedures and will add tools from the special category when it is felt that the expense is justified by the frequency of use.

Maintenance and minor repair tool kit

The tools in this list should be considered the minimum required for performance of routine maintenance, servicing and minor repair work. We recommend the purchase of combination wrenches (box-end and open-end combined in one wrench). While more expensive than open end wrenches, they offer the advantages of both types of wrench.

Combination wrench set (1/4-inch to 1 inch or 6 mm to 19 mm)
Adjustable wrench, 8 inch
Spark plug wrench with rubber insert
Spark plug gap adjusting tool
Feeler gauge set
Brake bleeder wrench
Standard screwdriver (5/16-inch x 6 inch)
Phillips screwdriver (No. 2 x 6 inch)
Combination pliers - 6 inch
Hacksaw and assortment of blades
Tire pressure gauge
Grease gun

Oil can
Fine emery cloth
Wire brush
Battery post and cable cleaning tool
Oil filter wrench
Funnel (medium size)
Safety goggles
Jackstands (2)
Drain pan

Note: *If basic tune-ups are going to be part of routine maintenance, it will be necessary to purchase a good quality stroboscopic timing light and combination tachometer/dwell meter. Although they are included in the list of special tools, it is mentioned here because they are absolutely necessary for tuning most vehicles properly.*

Repair and overhaul tool set

These tools are essential for anyone who plans to perform major repairs and are in addition to those in the maintenance and minor repair tool kit. Included is a comprehensive set of sockets which, though expensive, are invaluable because of their versatility, especially when various extensions and drives are available. We recommend the 1/2-inch drive over the 3/8-inch drive. Although the larger drive is bulky and more expensive, it has the capacity of accepting a very wide range of large sockets. Ideally, however, the mechanic should have a 3/8-inch drive set and a 1/2-inch drive set.

Socket set(s)
Reversible ratchet
Extension - 10 inch
Universal joint
Torque wrench (same size drive as sockets)
Ball peen hammer - 8 ounce
Soft-face hammer (plastic/rubber)
Standard screwdriver (1/4-inch x 6 inch)

Standard screwdriver (stubby - 5/16-inch)
Phillips screwdriver (No. 3 x 8 inch)
Phillips screwdriver (stubby - No. 2)
Pliers - vise grip
Pliers - lineman's
Pliers - needle nose
Pliers - snap-ring (internal and external)
Cold chisel - 1/2-inch
Scribe
Scraper (made from flattened copper tubing)
Centerpunch
Pin punches (1/16, 1/8, 3/16-inch)
Steel rule/straightedge - 12 inch
Allen wrench set (1/8 to 3/8-inch or 4 mm to 10 mm)
A selection of files
Wire brush (large)
Jackstands (second set)
Jack (scissor or hydraulic type)

Note: *Another tool which is often useful is an electric drill with a chuck capacity of 3/8-inch and a set of good quality drill bits.*

Special tools

The tools in this list include those which are not used regularly, are expensive to buy, or which need to be used in accordance with their manufacturer's instructions. Unless these tools will be used frequently, it is not very economical to purchase many of them. A consideration would be to split the cost and use between yourself and a friend or friends. In addition, most of these tools can be obtained from a tool rental shop on a temporary basis.

This list primarily contains only those tools and instruments widely available to the public, and not those special tools produced by the vehicle manufacturer for distribution to dealer service departments. Occasionally, references to the manufacturer's special tools are included in the text of this manual. Generally, an alternative method of doing the job without the special tool is offered. However, sometimes there is no alternative to their use. Where this is the case, and the tool cannot be purchased or borrowed, the work should be turned over to the dealer service department or an automotive repair shop.

Valve spring compressor
Piston ring groove cleaning tool
Piston ring compressor
Piston ring installation tool
Cylinder compression gauge
Cylinder ridge reamer
Cylinder surfacing hone
Cylinder bore gauge
Micrometers and/or dial calipers
Hydraulic lifter removal tool
Balljoint separator
Universal-type puller
Impact screwdriver
Dial indicator set
Stroboscopic timing light (inductive pick-up)
Hand operated vacuum/pressure pump
Tachometer/dwell meter
Universal electrical multimeter
Cable hoist
Brake spring removal and installation tools
Floor jack

Buying tools

For the do-it-yourselfer who is just starting to get involved in vehicle maintenance and repair, there are a number of options available when purchasing tools. If maintenance and minor repair is the extent of the work to be done, the purchase of individual tools is satisfactory. If,

on the other hand, extensive work is planned, it would be a good idea to purchase a modest tool set from one of the large retail chain stores. A set can usually be bought at a substantial savings over the individual tool prices, and they often come with a tool box. As additional tools are needed, add-on sets, individual tools and a larger tool box can be purchased to expand the tool selection. Building a tool set gradually allows the cost of the tools to be spread over a longer period of time and gives the mechanic the freedom to choose only those tools that will actually be used.

Tool stores will often be the only source of some of the special tools that are needed, but regardless of where tools are bought, try to avoid cheap ones, especially when buying screwdrivers and sockets, because they won't last very long. The expense involved in replacing cheap tools will eventually be greater than the initial cost of quality tools.

Care and maintenance of tools

Good tools are expensive, so it makes sense to treat them with respect. Keep them clean and in usable condition and store them properly when not in use. Always wipe off any dirt, grease or metal chips before putting them away. Never leave tools lying around in the work area. Upon completion of a job, always check closely under the hood for tools that may have been left there so they won't get lost during a test drive.

Some tools, such as screwdrivers, pliers, wrenches and sockets, can be hung on a panel mounted on the garage or workshop wall, while others should be kept in a tool box or tray. Measuring instruments, gauges, meters, etc. must be carefully stored where they cannot be damaged by weather or impact from other tools.

When tools are used with care and stored properly, they will last a very long time. Even with the best of care, though, tools will wear out if used frequently. When a tool is damaged or worn out, replace it. Subsequent jobs will be safer and more enjoyable if you do

Working facilities

Not to be overlooked when discussing tools is the workshop. If anything more than routine maintenance is to be carried out, some sort of suitable work area is essential.

It is understood, and appreciated, that many home mechanics do not have a good workshop or garage available, and end up removing an engine or doing major repairs outside. It is recommended, however, that the overhaul or repair be completed under the cover of a roof.

A clean, flat workbench or table of comfortable working height is an absolute necessity. The workbench should be equipped with a vise that has a jaw opening of at least four inches.

As mentioned previously, some clean, dry storage space is also required for tools, as well as the lubricants, fluids, cleaning solvents, etc. which soon become necessary.

Sometimes waste oil and fluids, drained from the engine or cooling system during normal maintenance or repairs, present a disposal problem. To avoid pouring them on the ground or into a sewage system, pour the used fluids into large containers, seal them with caps and take them to an authorized disposal site or recycling center. Plastic jugs, such as old antifreeze containers, are ideal for this purpose.

Always keep a supply of old newspapers and clean rags available. Old towels are excellent for mopping up spills. Many mechanics use rolls of paper towels for most work because they are readily available and disposable. To help keep the area under the vehicle clean, a large cardboard box can be cut open and flattened to protect the garage or shop floor.

Whenever working over a painted surface, such as when leaning over a fender to service something under the hood, always cover it with an old blanket or bedspread to protect the finish. Vinyl covered pads, made especially for this purpose, are available at auto parts stores.

Jacking and towing

Jacking

Warning: *The jack supplied with the vehicle should only be used for changing a tire or placing jackstands under the frame. Never work under the vehicle or start the engine while this jack is being used as the only means of support.*

The vehicle should be on level ground. Place the shift lever in Park, if you have an automatic, or Reverse if you have a manual transaxle. Block the wheel diagonally opposite the wheel being changed. Set the parking brake.

Remove the spare tire and jack from stowage. Remove the wheel cover and trim ring (if so equipped) with the tapered end of the lug nut wrench by inserting and twisting the handle and then prying against the back of the wheel cover. Loosen, but do not remove, the lug nuts (one-half turn is sufficient).

Place the scissors-type jack under the side of the vehicle and adjust the jack height until it fits between the notches in the vertical rocker panel flange nearest the wheel to be changed. There is a front and rear jacking point on each side of the vehicle **(see illustration)**.

Turn the jack handle clockwise until the tire clears the ground. Remove the lug nuts and pull the wheel off. Replace it with the spare.

Install the lug nuts with the beveled edges facing in. Tighten them snugly. Don't attempt to tighten them completely until the vehicle is lowered or it could slip off the jack. Turn the jack handle counterclockwise to lower the vehicle. Remove the jack and tighten the lug nuts in a diagonal pattern.

Install the cover (and trim ring, if used) and be sure it's snapped into place all the way around.

Stow the tire, jack and wrench. Unblock the wheels.

Towing

The manufacturer does not recommend towing except with a towing dolly under the front wheels. In an emergency the vehicle can be towed a short distance with a cable or chain attached to one of the towing eyelets located under the front or rear bumpers following the precautions above. The driver must remain in the vehicle to operate the steering and brakes (remember that power steering and power brakes will not work with the engine off).

The jack fits over the rocker panel flange, between the two notches (there are two jacking points on each side of the vehicle)

Anti-theft audio system

General information

1   Some models are equipped with the anti-theft audio system which includes an anti-theft feature that will render the stereo inoperative if stolen. If the power source to the stereo is cut with the anti-theft feature activated, the stereo will be inoperative. Even if the power source is immediately re-connected, the stereo will not function. If your vehicle is equipped with this anti-theft system, do not disconnect the battery, remove the stereo or disconnect related components unless you have either turned off the feature or have the individual ID (code) number for the stereo.

2   Refer to your vehicle's owner's manual for more complete information on this audio system and its anti-theft feature.

Disabling the anti-theft feature

3   Press the stereo's 1 and 4 buttons at the same time for five seconds with the ignition on and the radio power off. The display will show SEC, indicating the unit is in the secure mode (anti-theft feature enabled).

4   Press the SEEK left arrow until the first digit of your code appears.

5   Press the SEEK right arrow until the second digit of your code appears.

6   Press the TUNE left arrow until the third digit of your code appears.

7   Press the TUNE right arrow until the fourth digit of your code appears.

8   Press the AM/FM knob. "0000" will be displayed if you entered the correct code.

9   If Err is displayed, the code you entered was incorrect and the anti-theft feature is still enabled.

Unlocking the stereo after a power loss

10   When power is restored to the stereo, the stereo won't turn on and LOC will appear on the display. Enter your ID code as follows; pause no more than 15 seconds between Steps.

11   Turn the ignition switch to ON, but leave the stereo off.

12   Press the SEEK left arrow until the first digit of your code appears.

13   Press the SEEK right arrow until the second digit of your code appears.

14   Press the TUNE left arrow until the third digit of your code appears.

15   Press the TUNE right arrow until the fourth digit of your code appears.

16   Press the AM/FM knob. If the time of day appears, the numbers you entered were correct and the stereo will work. If Err appears, the numbers you entered were not correct and the stereo is still inoperative.

Booster battery (jump) starting

Observe these precautions when using a booster battery to start a vehicle:

a)   Before connecting the booster battery, make sure the ignition switch is in the Off position.

b)   Turn off the lights, heater and other electrical loads.

c)   Your eyes should be shielded. Safety goggles are a good idea.

d)   Make sure the booster battery is the same voltage as the dead one in the vehicle.

e)   The two vehicles MUST NOT TOUCH each other!

f)   Make sure the transaxle is in Neutral (manual) or Park (automatic).

g)   If the booster battery is not a maintenance-free type, remove the vent caps and lay a cloth over the vent holes.

Connect the red jumper cable to the positive (+) terminals of each battery (see illustration).

Connect one end of the black jumper cable to the negative (-) terminal of the booster battery. The other end of this cable should be connected to a good ground on the vehicle to be started, such as a bolt or bracket on the body.

Start the engine using the booster battery, then, with the engine running at idle speed, disconnect the jumper cables in the reverse order of connection.

Make the booster battery cable connections in the numerical order shown (note that the negative cable of the booster battery is NOT attached to the negative terminal of the dead battery)

Automotive chemicals and lubricants

A number of automotive chemicals and lubricants are available for use during vehicle maintenance and repair. They include a wide variety of products ranging from cleaning solvents and degreasers to lubricants and protective sprays for rubber, plastic and vinyl.

Cleaners

Carburetor cleaner and choke cleaner is a strong solvent for gum, varnish and carbon. Most carburetor cleaners leave a dry-type lubricant film which will not harden or gum up. Because of this film it is not recommended for use on electrical components.

Brake system cleaner is used to remove grease and brake fluid from the brake system, where clean surfaces are absolutely necessary. It leaves no residue and often eliminates brake squeal caused by contaminants.

Electrical cleaner removes oxidation, corrosion and carbon deposits from electrical contacts, restoring full current flow. It can also be used to clean spark plugs, carburetor jets, voltage regulators and other parts where an oil-free surface is desired.

Demoisturants remove water and moisture from electrical components such as alternators, voltage regulators, electrical connectors and fuse blocks. They are non-conductive, non-corrosive and non-flammable.

Degreasers are heavy-duty solvents used to remove grease from the outside of the engine and from chassis components. They can be sprayed or brushed on and, depending on the type, are rinsed off either with water or solvent.

Lubricants

Motor oil is the lubricant formulated for use in engines. It normally contains a wide variety of additives to prevent corrosion and reduce foaming and wear. Motor oil comes in various weights (viscosity ratings) from 5 to 80. The recommended weight of the oil depends on the season, temperature and the demands on the engine. Light oil is used in cold climates and under light load conditions. Heavy oil is used in hot climates and where high loads are encountered. Multi-viscosity oils are designed to have characteristics of both light and heavy oils and are available in a number of weights from 5W-20 to 20W-50.

Gear oil is designed to be used in differentials, manual transmissions and other areas where high-temperature lubrication is required.

Chassis and wheel bearing grease is a heavy grease used where increased loads and friction are encountered, such as for wheel bearings, balljoints, tie-rod ends and universal joints.

High-temperature wheel bearing grease is designed to withstand the extreme temperatures encountered by wheel bearings in disc brake equipped vehicles. It usually contains molybdenum disulfide (moly), which is a dry-type lubricant.

White grease is a heavy grease for metal-to-metal applications where water is a problem. White grease stays soft under both low and high temperatures (usually from -100 to +190-degrees F), and will not wash off or dilute in the presence of water.

Assembly lube is a special extreme pressure lubricant, usually containing moly, used to lubricate high-load parts (such as main and rod bearings and cam lobes) for initial start-up of a new engine. The assembly lube lubricates the parts without being squeezed out or washed away until the engine oiling system begins to function.

Silicone lubricants are used to protect rubber, plastic, vinyl and nylon parts.

Graphite lubricants are used where oils cannot be used due to contamination problems, such as in locks. The dry graphite will lubricate metal parts while remaining uncontaminated by dirt, water, oil or acids. It is electrically conductive and will not foul electrical contacts in locks such as the ignition switch.

Moly penetrants loosen and lubricate frozen, rusted and corroded fasteners and prevent future rusting or freezing.

Heat-sink grease is a special electrically non-conductive grease that is used for mounting electronic ignition modules where it is essential that heat is transferred away from the module.

Sealants

RTV sealant is one of the most widely used gasket compounds. Made from silicone, RTV is air curing, it seals, bonds, waterproofs, fills surface irregularities, remains flexible, doesn't shrink, is relatively easy to remove, and is used as a supplementary sealer with almost all low and medium temperature gaskets.

Anaerobic sealant is much like RTV in that it can be used either to seal gaskets or to form gaskets by itself. It remains flexible, is solvent resistant and fills surface imperfections. The difference between an anaerobic sealant and an RTV-type sealant is in the curing. RTV cures when exposed to air, while an anaerobic sealant cures only in the absence of air. This means that an anaerobic sealant cures only after the assembly of parts, sealing them together.

Thread and pipe sealant is used for sealing hydraulic and pneumatic fittings and vacuum lines. It is usually made from a Teflon compound, and comes in a spray, a paint-on liquid and as a wrap-around tape.

Chemicals

Anti-seize compound prevents seizing, galling, cold welding, rust and corrosion in fasteners. High-temperature ant-seize, usually made with copper and graphite lubricants, is used for exhaust system and exhaust manifold bolts.

Anaerobic locking compounds are used to keep fasteners from vibrating or working loose and cure only after installation, in the absence of air. Medium strength locking compound is used for small nuts, bolts and screws that may be removed later. High-strength locking compound is for large nuts, bolts and studs which aren't removed on a regular basis.

Oil additives range from viscosity index improvers to chemical treatments that claim to reduce internal engine friction. It should be noted that most oil manufacturers caution against using additives with their oils.

Gas additives perform several functions, depending on their chemical makeup. They usually contain solvents that help dissolve gum and varnish that build up on carburetor, fuel injection and intake parts. They also serve to break down carbon deposits that form on the inside surfaces of the combustion chambers. Some additives contain upper cylinder lubricants for valves and piston rings, and others contain chemicals to remove condensation from the gas tank.

Miscellaneous

Brake fluid is specially formulated hydraulic fluid that can withstand the heat and pressure encountered in brake systems. Care must be taken so this fluid does not come in contact with painted surfaces or plastics. An opened container should always be resealed to prevent contamination by water or dirt.

Weatherstrip adhesive is used to bond weatherstripping around doors, windows and trunk lids. It is sometimes used to attach trim pieces.

Undercoating is a petroleum-based, tar-like substance that is designed to protect metal surfaces on the underside of the vehicle from corrosion. It also acts as a sound-deadening agent by insulating the bottom of the vehicle.

Waxes and polishes are used to help protect painted and plated surfaces from the weather. Different types of paint may require the use of different types of wax and polish. Some polishes utilize a chemical or abrasive cleaner to help remove the top layer of oxidized (dull) paint on older vehicles. In recent years many non-wax polishes that contain a wide variety of chemicals such as polymers and silicones have been introduced. These non-wax polishes are usually easier to apply and last longer than conventional waxes and polishes.

Conversion factors

Length (distance)

Inches (in)	X	25.4	= Millimetres (mm)	X 0.0394	= Inches (in)
Feet (ft)	X	0.305	= Metres (m)	X 3.281	= Feet (ft)
Miles	X	1.609	= Kilometres (km)	X 0.621	= Miles

Volume (capacity)

Cubic inches (cu in; in³)	X	16.387	= Cubic centimetres (cc; cm³)	X 0.061	= Cubic inches (cu in; in³)
Imperial pints (Imp pt)	X	0.568	= Litres (l)	X 1.76	= Imperial pints (Imp pt)
Imperial quarts (Imp qt)	X	1.137	= Litres (l)	X 0.88	= Imperial quarts (Imp qt)
Imperial quarts (Imp qt)	X	1.201	= US quarts (US qt)	X 0.833	= Imperial quarts (Imp qt)
US quarts (US qt)	X	0.946	= Litres (l)	X 1.057	= US quarts (US qt)
Imperial gallons (Imp gal)	X	4.546	= Litres (l)	X 0.22	= Imperial gallons (Imp gal)
Imperial gallons (Imp gal)	X	1.201	= US gallons (US gal)	X 0.833	= Imperial gallons (Imp gal)
US gallons (US gal)	X	3.785	= Litres (l)	X 0.264	= US gallons (US gal)

Mass (weight)

Ounces (oz)	X	28.35	= Grams (g)	X 0.035	Ounces (oz)
Pounds (lb)	X	0.454	= Kilograms (kg)	X 2.205	= Pounds (lb)

Force

Ounces-force (ozf; oz)	X	0.278	= Newtons (N)	X 3.6	= Ounces-force (ozf; oz)
Pounds-force (lbf; lb)	X	4.448	= Newtons (N)	X 0.225	= Pounds-force (lbf; lb)
Newtons (N)	X	0.1	= Kilograms-force (kgf; kg)	X 9.81	= Newtons (N)

Pressure

Pounds-force per square inch (psi; lbf/in²; lb/in²)	X	0.070	= Kilograms-force per square centimetre (kgf/cm²; kg/cm²)	X 14.223	= Pounds-force per square inch (psi; lbf/in²; lb/in²)
Pounds-force per square inch (psi; lbf/in²; lb/in²)	X	0.068	= Atmospheres (atm)	X 14.696	= Pounds-force per square inch (psi; lbf/in²; lb/in²)
Pounds-force per square inch (psi; lbf/in²; lb/in²)	X	0.069	= Bars	X 14.5	= Pounds-force per square inch (psi; lbf/in²; lb/in²)
Pounds-force per square inch (psi; lbf/in²; lb/in²)	X	6.895	= Kilopascals (kPa)	X 0.145	= Pounds-force per square inch (psi; lbf/in²; lb/in²)
Kilopascals (kPa)	X	0.01	= Kilograms-force per square centimetre (kgf/cm²; kg/cm²)	X 98.1	= Kilopascals (kPa)

Torque (moment of force)

Pounds-force inches (lbf in; lb in)	X	1.152	= Kilograms-force centimetre (kgf cm; kg cm)	X 0.868	= Pounds-force inches (lbf in; lb in)
Pounds-force inches (lbf in; lb in)	X	0.113	= Newton metres (Nm)	X 8.85	= Pounds-force inches (lbf in; lb in)
Pounds-force inches (lbf in; lb in)	X	0.083	= Pounds-force feet (lbf ft; lb ft)	X 12	= Pounds-force inches (lbf in; lb in)
Pounds-force feet (lbf ft; lb ft)	X	0.138	= Kilograms-force metres (kgf m; kg m)	X 7.233	= Pounds-force feet (lbf ft; lb ft)
Pounds-force feet (lbf ft; lb ft)	X	1.356	= Newton metres (Nm)	X 0.738	= Pounds-force feet (lbf ft; lb ft)
Newton metres (Nm)	X	0.102	= Kilograms-force metres (kgf m; kg m)	X 9.804	= Newton metres (Nm)

Power

Horsepower (hp)	X	745.7	= Watts (W)	X 0.0013	= Horsepower (hp)

Velocity (speed)

Miles per hour (miles/hr; mph)	X	1.609	= Kilometres per hour (km/hr; kph)	X 0.621	= Miles per hour (miles/hr; mph)

Fuel consumption*

Miles per gallon, Imperial (mpg)	X	0.354	= Kilometres per litre (km/l)	X 2.825	= Miles per gallon, Imperial (mpg)
Miles per gallon, US (mpg)	X	0.425	= Kilometres per litre (km/l)	X 2.352	= Miles per gallon, US (mpg)

Temperature

Degrees Fahrenheit = (°C x 1.8) + 32   Degrees Celsius (Degrees Centigrade; °C) = (°F - 32) x 0.56

*It is common practice to convert from miles per gallon (mpg) to litres/100 kilometres (l/100km), where mpg (Imperial) x l/100 km = 282 and mpg (US) x l/100 km = 235

Safety first!

Regardless of how enthusiastic you may be about getting on with the job at hand, take the time to ensure that your safety is not jeopardized. A moment's lack of attention can result in an accident, as can failure to observe certain simple safety precautions. The possibility of an accident will always exist, and the following points should not be considered a comprehensive list of all dangers. Rather, they are intended to make you aware of the risks and to encourage a safety conscious approach to all work you carry out on your vehicle.

Essential DOs and DON'Ts

DON'T rely on a jack when working under the vehicle. Always use approved jackstands to support the weight of the vehicle and place them under the recommended lift or support points.

DON'T attempt to loosen extremely tight fasteners (i.e. wheel lug nuts) while the vehicle is on a jack - it may fall.

DON'T start the engine without first making sure that the transmission is in Neutral (or Park where applicable) and the parking brake is set.

DON'T remove the radiator cap from a hot cooling system - let it cool or cover it with a cloth and release the pressure gradually.

DON'T attempt to drain the engine oil until you are sure it has cooled to the point that it will not burn you.

DON'T touch any part of the engine or exhaust system until it has cooled sufficiently to avoid burns.

DON'T siphon toxic liquids such as gasoline, antifreeze and brake fluid by mouth, or allow them to remain on your skin.

DON'T inhale brake lining dust - it is potentially hazardous (see *Asbestos* below).

DON'T allow spilled oil or grease to remain on the floor - wipe it up before someone slips on it.

DON'T use loose fitting wrenches or other tools which may slip and cause injury.

DON'T push on wrenches when loosening or tightening nuts or bolts. Always try to pull the wrench toward you. If the situation calls for pushing the wrench away, push with an open hand to avoid scraped knuckles if the wrench should slip.

DON'T attempt to lift a heavy component alone - get someone to help you.

DON'T rush or take unsafe shortcuts to finish a job.

DON'T allow children or animals in or around the vehicle while you are working on it.

DO wear eye protection when using power tools such as a drill, sander, bench grinder, etc. and when working under a vehicle.

DO keep loose clothing and long hair well out of the way of moving parts.

DO make sure that any hoist used has a safe working load rating adequate for the job.

DO get someone to check on you periodically when working alone on a vehicle.

DO carry out work in a logical sequence and make sure that everything is correctly assembled and tightened.

DO keep chemicals and fluids tightly capped and out of the reach of children and pets.

DO remember that your vehicle's safety affects that of yourself and others. If in doubt on any point, get professional advice.

Asbestos

Certain friction, insulating, sealing, and other products - such as brake linings, brake bands, clutch linings, torque converters, gaskets, etc. - contain asbestos. Extreme care must be taken to avoid inhalation of dust from such products, since it is hazardous to health. If in doubt, assume that they do contain asbestos.

Fire

Remember at all times that gasoline is highly flammable. Never smoke or have any kind of open flame around when working on a vehicle. But the risk does not end there. A spark caused by an electrical short circuit, by two metal surfaces contacting each other, or even by static electricity built up in your body under certain conditions, can ignite gasoline vapors, which in a confined space are highly explosive. Do not, under any circumstances, use gasoline for cleaning parts. Use an approved safety solvent.

Always disconnect the battery ground (-) cable at the battery before working on any part of the fuel system or electrical system. Never risk spilling fuel on a hot engine or exhaust component. It is strongly recommended that a fire extinguisher suitable for use on fuel and electrical fires be kept handy in the garage or workshop at all times. Never try to extinguish a fuel or electrical fire with water.

Fumes

Certain fumes are highly toxic and can quickly cause unconsciousness and even death if inhaled to any extent. Gasoline vapor falls into this category, as do the vapors from some cleaning solvents. Any draining or pouring of such volatile fluids should be done in a well ventilated area.

When using cleaning fluids and solvents, read the instructions on the container carefully. Never use materials from unmarked containers.

Never run the engine in an enclosed space, such as a garage. Exhaust fumes contain carbon monoxide, which is extremely poisonous. If you need to run the engine, always do so in the open air, or at least have the rear of the vehicle outside the work area.

If you are fortunate enough to have the use of an inspection pit, never drain or pour gasoline and never run the engine while the vehicle is over the pit. The fumes, being heavier than air, will concentrate in the pit with possibly lethal results.

The battery

Never create a spark or allow a bare light bulb near a battery. They normally give off a certain amount of hydrogen gas, which is highly explosive.

Always disconnect the battery ground (-) cable at the battery before working on the fuel or electrical systems.

If possible, loosen the filler caps or cover when charging the battery from an external source (this does not apply to sealed or maintenance-free batteries). Do not charge at an excessive rate or the battery may burst.

Take care when adding water to a non maintenance-free battery and when carrying a battery. The electrolyte, even when diluted, is very corrosive and should not be allowed to contact clothing or skin.

Always wear eye protection when cleaning the battery to prevent the caustic deposits from entering your eyes.

Household current

When using an electric power tool, inspection light, etc., which operates on household current, always make sure that the tool is correctly connected to its plug and that, where necessary, it is properly grounded. Do not use such items in damp conditions and, again, do not create a spark or apply excessive heat in the vicinity of fuel or fuel vapor.

Secondary ignition system voltage

A severe electric shock can result from touching certain parts of the ignition system (such as the spark plug wires) when the engine is running or being cranked, particularly if components are damp or the insulation is defective. In the case of an electronic ignition system, the secondary system voltage is much higher and could prove fatal.

Troubleshooting

Contents

This section provides an easy reference guide to the more common problems which may occur during the operation of your vehicle. These problems and their possible causes are grouped under headings denoting various components or systems, such as Engine, Cooling system, etc. They also refer you to the chapter and/or section which deals with the problem.

Remember that successful troubleshooting is not a mysterious black art practiced only by professional mechanics. It is simply the result of the right knowledge combined with an intelligent, systematic approach to the problem. Always work by a process of elimination, starting with the simplest solution and working through to the most complex - and never overlook the obvious. Anyone can run the gas tank dry or leave the lights on overnight, so don't assume that you are exempt from such oversights.

Finally, always establish a clear idea of why a problem has occurred and take steps to ensure that it doesn't happen again. If the electrical system fails because of a poor connection, check the other connections in the system to make sure that they don't fail as well. If a particular fuse continues to blow, find out why - don't just replace one fuse after another. Remember, failure of a small component can often be indicative of potential failure or incorrect functioning of a more important component or system.

Engine

1   Engine will not rotate when attempting to start

1   Battery terminal connections loose or corroded (Chapter 1).
2   Battery discharged or faulty (Chapter 1).
3   Automatic transaxle not completely engaged in Park (Chapter 7) or clutch pedal not completely depressed (Chapter 8).
4   Broken, loose or disconnected wiring in the starting circuit (Chapters 5 and 12).
5   Starter motor pinion jammed in flywheel ring gear (Chapter 5).
6   Starter solenoid faulty (Chapter 5).
7   Starter motor faulty (Chapter 5).
8   Ignition switch faulty (Chapter 12).
9   Starter pinion or flywheel teeth worn or broken (Chapter 5).

2   Engine rotates but will not start

1   Fuel tank empty.
2   Battery discharged (engine rotates slowly) (Chapter 5).
3   Battery terminal connections loose or corroded (Chapter 1).
4   Leaking fuel injector(s), faulty fuel pump, pressure regulator, etc. (Chapter 4).
5   Broken or stripped timing belt (Chapter 2).
6   Ignition components damp or damaged (Chapter 5).
7   Worn, faulty or incorrectly gapped spark plugs (Chapter 1).
8   Broken, loose or disconnected wiring in the starting circuit (Chapter 5).
9   Loose distributor is changing ignition timing (Chapter 5).
10   Broken, loose or disconnected wires at the ignition coil or faulty coil (Chapter 5).

3   Engine hard to start when cold

1   Battery discharged or low (Chapter 1).
2   Malfunctioning fuel system (Chapter 4).
3   Faulty coolant temperature sensor or intake air temperature sensor (Chapter 6).
4   Injector(s) leaking (Chapter 4).
5   Faulty ignition system (Chapter 5).

4   Engine hard to start when hot

1   Air filter clogged (Chapter 1).
2   Fuel not reaching the fuel injection system (Chapter 4).
3   Corroded battery connections, especially ground (Chapter 1).
4   Faulty coolant temperature sensor or intake air temperature sensor (Chapter 6).

5   Starter motor noisy or excessively rough in engagement

1   Pinion or flywheel gear teeth worn or broken (Chapter 5).
2   Starter motor mounting bolts loose or missing (Chapter 5).

6   Engine starts but stops immediately

1   Loose or faulty electrical connections at distributor, coil or alternator (Chapter 5).
2   Insufficient fuel reaching the fuel injector(s) (Chapters 1 and 4).
3   Vacuum leak at the gasket between the intake manifold/plenum and throttle body (Chapter 4).
4   Idle speed incorrect (Chapter 1).

7   Oil puddle under engine

1   Oil pan gasket and/or oil pan drain bolt washer leaking (Chapter 2).
2   Oil pressure sending unit leaking (Chapter 2).
3   Cylinder head covers leaking (Chapter 2).
4   Engine oil seals leaking (Chapter 2).
5   Oil pump housing leaking (Chapter 2).

8   Engine lopes while idling or idles erratically

1   Vacuum leakage (Chapters 2 and 4).
2   Leaking EGR valve (Chapter 6).
3   Air filter clogged (Chapter 1).
4   Malfunction in the fuel injection or engine control system (Chapters 4 and 6).
5   Leaking head gasket (Chapter 2).
6   Timing belt and/or pulleys worn (Chapter 2).
7   Camshaft lobes worn (Chapter 2).

9   Engine misses at idle speed

1   Spark plugs worn or not gapped properly (Chapter 1).
2   Faulty spark plug wires (Chapter 1).
3   Vacuum leaks (Chapter 1).
4   Incorrect ignition timing (Chapter 1).
5   Uneven or low compression (Chapter 2).
6   Problem with the fuel injection system (Chapter 4).

10   Engine misses throughout driving speed range

1   Fuel filter clogged and/or impurities in the fuel system (Chapter 1).
2   Low fuel output at the injector(s) (Chapter 4).
3   Faulty or incorrectly gapped spark plugs (Chapter 1).

4 Incorrect ignition timing (Chapter 5).
5 Cracked distributor cap, disconnected distributor wires or damaged distributor components (Chapters 1 and 5).
6 Leaking spark plug wires (Chapters 1 or 5).
7 Faulty emission system components (Chapter 6).
8 Low or uneven cylinder compression pressures (Chapter 2).
9 Weak or faulty ignition system (Chapter 5).
10 Vacuum leak in fuel injection system, intake manifold, air control valve or vacuum hoses (Chapter 4).

11 Engine stumbles on acceleration

1 Spark plugs fouled (Chapter 1).
2 Problem with fuel injection or engine control system (Chapters 4 and 6).
3 Fuel filter clogged (Chapters 1 and 4).
4 Incorrect ignition timing (Chapter 5).
5 Intake manifold air leak (Chapters 2 and 4).
6 Problem with the emissions control system (Chapter 6).

12 Engine surges while holding accelerator steady

1 Intake air leak (Chapter 4).
2 Fuel pump or fuel pressure regulator faulty (Chapter 4).
3 Problem with fuel injection system (Chapter 4).
4 Problem with the emissions control system (Chapter 6).

13 Engine stalls

1 Idle speed incorrect (Chapter 1).
2 Fuel filter clogged and/or water and impurities in the fuel system (Chapters 1 and 4).
3 Distributor components damp or damaged (Chapter 5).
4 Faulty emissions system components (Chapter 6).
5 Faulty or incorrectly gapped spark plugs (Chapter 1).
6 Faulty spark plug wires (Chapter 1).
7 Vacuum leak in the fuel injection system, intake manifold or vacuum hoses (Chapters 2 and 4).
8 Valve clearances incorrectly set (Chapter 1).

14 Engine lacks power

1 Incorrect ignition timing (Chapter 5).
2 Excessive play in distributor shaft (Chapter 5).
3 Worn rotor, distributor cap, spark plug wires or faulty coil (Chapters 1 and 5).
4 Faulty or incorrectly gapped spark plugs (Chapter 1).
5 Problem with the fuel injection system (Chapter 4).
6 Plugged air filter (Chapter 1).
7 Brakes binding (Chapter 9).
8 Automatic transaxle fluid level incorrect (Chapter 1).
9 Clutch slipping (Chapter 8).
10 Fuel filter clogged and/or impurities in the fuel system (Chapters 1 and 4).
11 Emission control system not functioning properly (Chapter 6).
12 Low or uneven cylinder compression pressures (Chapter 2).
13 Obstructed exhaust system (Chapter 4).

15 Engine backfires

1 Emission control system not functioning properly (Chapter 6).

2 Ignition timing incorrect (Chapter 5).
3 Faulty secondary ignition system (cracked spark plug insulator, faulty plug wires, distributor cap and/or rotor) (Chapters 1 and 5).
4 Problem with the fuel injection system (Chapter 4).
5 Vacuum leak at fuel injector(s), intake manifold, air control valve or vacuum hoses (Chapters 2 and 4).
6 Valve clearances incorrectly set and/or valves sticking (Chapter 1).

16 Pinging or knocking engine sounds during acceleration or uphill

1 Incorrect grade of fuel.
2 Ignition timing incorrect (Chapter 5).
3 Fuel injection system faulty (Chapter 4).
4 Improper or damaged spark plugs or wires (Chapter 1).
5 Worn or damaged distributor components (Chapter 5).
6 EGR valve not functioning (Chapter 6).
7 Vacuum leak (Chapters 2 and 4).

17 Engine runs with oil pressure light on

1 Low oil level (Chapter 1).
2 Idle rpm below specification (Chapter 1).
3 Short in wiring circuit (Chapter 12).
4 Faulty oil pressure sender (Chapter 2).
5 Worn engine bearings and/or oil pump (Chapter 2).

18 Engine diesels (continues to run) after switching off

1 Idle speed too high (Chapter 1).
2 Excessive engine operating temperature (Chapter 3).
3 Ignition timing in need of adjustment (Chapter 5).

Engine electrical system

19 Battery will not hold a charge

1 Alternator drivebelt defective or not adjusted properly (Chapter 1).
2 Battery electrolyte level low (Chapter 1).
3 Battery terminals loose or corroded (Chapter 1).
4 Alternator not charging properly (Chapter 5).
5 Loose, broken or faulty wiring in the charging circuit (Chapter 5).
6 Short in vehicle wiring (Chapter 12).
7 Internally defective battery (Chapters 1 and 5).

20 Alternator light fails to go out

1 Faulty alternator or charging circuit (Chapter 5).
2 Alternator drivebelt defective or out of adjustment (Chapter 1).
3 Alternator voltage regulator inoperative (Chapter 5).

21 Alternator light fails to come on when key is turned on

1 Warning light bulb defective (Chapter 12).
2 Fault in the printed circuit, dash wiring or bulb holder (Chapter 12).

Fuel system

22 Excessive fuel consumption

1 Dirty or clogged air filter element (Chapter 1).
2 Incorrectly set ignition timing (Chapter 5).
3 Emissions system not functioning properly (Chapter 6).
4 Fuel injection system not functioning properly (Chapter 4).
5 Low tire pressure or incorrect tire size (Chapter 1).

23 Fuel leakage and/or fuel odor

1 Leaking fuel feed or return line (Chapters 1 and 4).
2 Tank overfilled.
3 Evaporative canister filter clogged (Chapters 1 and 6).
4 Problem with fuel injection system (Chapter 4).

Cooling system

24 Overheating

1 Insufficient coolant in system (Chapter 1).
2 Water pump drivebelt defective or out of adjustment (Chapter 1).
3 Radiator core blocked or grille restricted (Chapter 3).
4 Thermostat faulty (Chapter 3).
5 Electric coolant fan inoperative or blades broken (Chapter 3).
6 Radiator cap not maintaining proper pressure (Chapter 3).
7 Ignition timing incorrect (Chapter 5).

25 Overcooling

1 Faulty thermostat (Chapter 3).
2 Inaccurate temperature gauge sending unit (Chapter 3).

26 External coolant leakage

1 Deteriorated/damaged hoses; loose clamps (Chapters 1 and 3).
2 Water pump defective (Chapter 3).
3 Leakage from radiator core or coolant reservoir bottle (Chapter 3).
4 Engine drain or water jacket core plugs leaking (Chapter 2).

27 Internal coolant leakage

1 Leaking cylinder head gasket (Chapter 2).
2 Cracked cylinder bore or cylinder head (Chapter 2).

28 Coolant loss

1 Too much coolant in reservoir (Chapter 1).
2 Coolant boiling away because of overheating (Chapter 3).
3 Internal or external leakage (Chapter 3).
4 Faulty radiator cap (Chapter 3).

29 Poor coolant circulation

1 Inoperative water pump (Chapter 3).
2 Restriction in cooling system (Chapters 1 and 3).

3 Water pump drivebelt defective/out of adjustment (Chapter 1).
4 Thermostat sticking (Chapter 3).

Clutch

30 Pedal travels to floor - no pressure or very little resistance

1 Master or release cylinder faulty (Chapter 8).
2 Hose/pipe burst or leaking (Chapter 8).
3 Connections leaking (Chapter 8).
4 No fluid in reservoir (Chapter 8).
5 If fluid level in reservoir rises as pedal is depressed, master cylinder center valve seal is faulty (Chapter 8).
6 If there is fluid on dust seal at master cylinder, piston primary seal is leaking (Chapter 8).
7 Broken release bearing or fork (Chapter 8).

31 Fluid in area of master cylinder dust cover and on pedal

Rear seal failure in master cylinder (Chapter 8).

32 Fluid on release cylinder

Release cylinder plunger seal faulty (Chapter 8).

33 Pedal feels spongy when depressed

Air in system (Chapter 8).

34 Unable to select gears

1 Faulty transaxle (Chapter 7).
2 Faulty clutch disc or pressure plate (Chapter 8).
3 Faulty release lever or release bearing (Chapter 8).
4 Faulty shift lever assembly or control cables (Chapter 8).

35 Clutch slips (engine speed increases with no increase in vehicle speed)

1 Clutch plate worn (Chapter 8).
2 Clutch plate is oil soaked by leaking rear main seal (Chapter 8).
3 Clutch plate not seated (Chapter 8).
4 Warped pressure plate or flywheel (Chapter 8).
5 Weak diaphragm springs (Chapter 8).
6 Clutch plate overheated. Allow to cool.

36 Grabbing (chattering) as clutch is engaged

1 Oil on clutch plate lining, burned or glazed facings (Chapter 8).
2 Worn or loose engine or transaxle mounts (Chapters 2 and 7).
3 Worn splines on clutch plate hub (Chapter 8).
4 Warped pressure plate or flywheel (Chapter 8).
5 Burned or smeared resin on flywheel or pressure plate (Chapter 8).

37 Transaxle rattling (clicking)

1   Release lever loose (Chapter 8).
2   Clutch plate damper spring failure (Chapter 8).
3   Low engine idle speed (Chapter 1).

38 Noise in clutch area

1   Fork shaft improperly installed (Chapter 8).
2   Faulty bearing (Chapter 8).

39 Clutch pedal stays on floor

1   Clutch master cylinder piston binding in bore (Chapter 8).
2   Broken release bearing or fork (Chapter 8).

40 High pedal effort

1   Piston binding in bore (Chapter 8).
2   Pressure plate faulty (Chapter 8).
3   Incorrect size master or release cylinder (Chapter 8).

Manual transaxle

41 Knocking noise at low speeds

1   Worn driveaxle constant velocity (CV) joints (Chapter 8).
2   Worn side gear shaft counterbore in differential case (Chapter 7A).*

42 Noise most pronounced when turning

Differential gear noise (Chapter 7A).*

43 Clunk on acceleration or deceleration

1   Loose engine or transaxle mounts (Chapters 2 and 7A).
2   Worn differential pinion shaft in case.*
3   Worn side gear shaft counterbore in differential case (Chapter 7A).*
4   Worn or damaged driveaxle inboard CV joints (Chapter 8).

44 Clicking noise in turns

Worn or damaged outboard CV joint (Chapter 8).

45 Vibration

1   Rough wheel bearing (Chapters 1 and 10).
2   Damaged driveaxle (Chapter 8).
3   Out of round tires (Chapter 1).
4   Tire out of balance (Chapters 1 and 10).
5   Worn CV joint (Chapter 8).

46 Noisy in neutral with engine running

1   Damaged input gear bearing (Chapter 7A).*
2   Damaged clutch release bearing (Chapter 8).

47 Noisy in one particular gear

1   Damaged or worn constant mesh gears (Chapter 7A).*
2   Damaged or worn synchronizers (Chapter 7A).*
3   Bent reverse fork (Chapter 7A).*
4   Damaged fourth speed gear or output gear (Chapter 7A).*
5   Worn or damaged reverse idler gear or idler bushing (Chapter 7A).*

48 Noisy in all gears

1   Insufficient lubricant (Chapter 7A).
2   Damaged or worn bearings (Chapter 7A).*
3   Worn or damaged input gear shaft and/or output gear shaft (Chapter 7A).*

49 Slips out of gear

1   Worn or improperly adjusted linkage (Chapter 7A).
2   Transaxle loose on engine (Chapter 7A).
3   Shift linkage does not work freely, binds (Chapter 7A).
4   Input gear bearing retainer broken or loose (Chapter 7A).*
5   Dirt between clutch cover and engine housing (Chapter 7A).
6   Worn shift fork (Chapter 7A).*

50 Leaks lubricant

1   Side gear shaft seals worn (Chapter 7).
2   Excessive amount of lubricant in transaxle (Chapters 1 and 7A).
3   Loose or broken input gear shaft bearing retainer (Chapter 7A).*
4   Input gear bearing retainer O-ring and/or lip seal damaged (Chapter 7A).*

51 Locked in gear

Lock pin or interlock pin missing (Chapter 7A).*
* Although the corrective action necessary to remedy the symptoms described is beyond the scope of this manual, the above information should be helpful in isolating the cause of the condition so that the owner can communicate clearly with a professional mechanic.

Automatic transaxle

Note: Due to the complexity of the automatic transaxle, it is difficult for the home mechanic to properly diagnose and service this component. For problems other than the following, the vehicle should be taken to a dealer or transaxle shop.

52 Fluid leakage

1   Automatic transaxle fluid is a deep red color. Fluid leaks should not be confused with engine oil, which can easily be blown onto the transaxle by air flow.

2   To pinpoint a leak, first remove all built-up dirt and grime from the transaxle housing with degreasing agents and/or steam cleaning. Then drive the vehicle at low speeds so air flow will not blow the leak far from its source. Raise the vehicle and determine where the leak is coming from. Common areas of leakage are:

a) *Pan (Chapters 1 and 7)*
b) *Dipstick tube (Chapters 1 and 7)*
c) *Transaxle oil lines (Chapter 7)*
d) *Speed sensor (Chapter 7)*
e) *Driveaxle oil seals (Chapter 7).*

53   Transaxle fluid brown or has a burned smell

Transaxle fluid overheated (Chapter 1).

54   General shift mechanism problems

1   Chapter 7, Part B, deals with checking and adjusting the shift linkage on automatic transaxles. Common problems which may be attributed to poorly adjusted linkage are:

a) *Engine starting in gears other than Park or Neutral.*
b) *Indicator on shifter pointing to a gear other than the one actually being used.*
c) *Vehicle moves when in Park.*

2   Refer to Chapter 7B for the shift linkage adjustment procedure.

55   Transaxle will not downshift with accelerator pedal pressed to the floor

Throttle valve cable out of adjustment (Chapter 7B).

56   Engine will start in gears other than Park or Neutral

Neutral start switch malfunctioning (Chapter 7B).

57   Transaxle slips, shifts roughly, is noisy or has no drive in forward or reverse gears

There are many probable causes for the above problems, but the home mechanic should be concerned with only one possibility - fluid level. Before taking the vehicle to a repair shop, check the level and condition of the fluid as described in Chapter 1. Correct the fluid level as necessary or change the fluid and filter if needed. If the problem persists, have a professional diagnose the cause.

Driveaxles

58   Clicking noise in turns

Worn or damaged outboard CV joint (Chapter 8).

59   Shudder or vibration during acceleration

1   Excessive toe-in (Chapter 10).
2   Incorrect spring heights (Chapter 10).
3   Worn or damaged inboard or outboard CV joints (Chapter 8).
4   Sticking inboard CV joint assembly (Chapter 8).

60   Vibration at highway speeds

1   Out of balance front wheels and/or tires (Chapters 1 and 10).
2   Out of round front tires (Chapters 1 and 10).
3   Worn CV joint(s) (Chapter 8).

Brakes

Note: *Before assuming that a brake problem exists, make sure that:*
a) *The tires are in good condition and properly inflated (Chapter 1).*
b) *The front end alignment is correct (Chapter 10).*
c) *The vehicle is not loaded with weight in an unequal manner.*

61   Vehicle pulls to one side during braking

1   Incorrect tire pressures (Chapter 1).
2   Front end out of alignment (have the front end aligned).
3   Front, or rear, tire sizes not matched to one another.
4   Restricted brake lines or hoses (Chapter 9).
5   Malfunctioning drum brake or caliper assembly (Chapter 9).
6   Loose suspension parts (Chapter 10).
7   Loose calipers (Chapter 9).
8   Excessive wear of brake shoe or pad material or disc/drum on one side.

62   Noise (high-pitched squeal when the brakes are applied)

Front and/or rear disc brake pads worn out. The noise comes from the wear sensor rubbing against the disc (does not apply to all vehicles). Replace pads with new ones immediately (Chapter 9).

63   Brake roughness or chatter (pedal pulsates)

1   Excessive lateral runout (Chapter 9).
2   Uneven pad wear (Chapter 9).
3   Defective disc (Chapter 9).

64   Excessive brake pedal effort required to stop vehicle

1   Malfunctioning power brake booster (Chapter 9).
2   Partial system failure (Chapter 9).
3   Excessively worn pads or shoes (Chapter 9).
4   Piston in caliper or wheel cylinder stuck or sluggish (Chapter 9).
5   Brake pads or shoes contaminated with oil or grease (Chapter 9).
6   Brake disc grooved and/or glazed (Chapter 1).
7   New pads or shoes installed and not yet seated. It will take a while for the new material to seat against the disc or drum.

65   Excessive brake pedal travel

1   Partial brake system failure (Chapter 9).
2   Insufficient fluid in master cylinder (Chapters 1 and 9).
3   Air trapped in system (Chapters 1 and 9).

66   Dragging brakes

1   Incorrect adjustment of brake light switch (Chapter 9).
2   Master cylinder pistons not returning correctly (Chapter 9).
3   Restricted brakes lines or hoses (Chapters 1 and 9).
4   Incorrect parking brake adjustment (Chapter 9).

67 Grabbing or uneven braking action

1   Malfunction of proportioning valve (Chapter 9).
2   Malfunction of power brake booster unit (Chapter 9).
3   Binding brake pedal mechanism (Chapter 9).

68 Brake pedal feels spongy when depressed

1   Air in hydraulic lines (Chapter 9).
2   Master cylinder mounting bolts loose (Chapter 9).
3   Master cylinder defective (Chapter 9).

69 Brake pedal travels to the floor with little resistance

1   Little or no fluid in the master cylinder reservoir caused by leaking caliper piston(s) (Chapter 9).
2   Loose, damaged or disconnected brake lines (Chapter 9).

70 Parking brake does not hold

Parking brake linkage improperly adjusted (Chapters 1 and 9).

Suspension and steering systems

Note: *Before attempting to diagnose the suspension and steering systems, perform the following preliminary checks:*
a) Tires for wrong pressure and uneven wear.
b) Steering universal joints from the column to the rack and pinion for loose connectors or wear.
c) Front and rear suspension and the rack and pinion assembly for loose or damaged parts.
d) Out-of-round or out-of-balance tires, bent rims and loose and/or rough wheel bearings.

71 Vehicle pulls to one side

1   Mismatched or uneven tires (Chapter 10).
2   Broken or sagging springs (Chapter 10).
3   Wheel alignment out-of-specifications (Chapter 10).
4   Front brake dragging (Chapter 9).

72 Abnormal or excessive tire wear

1   Wheel alignment out-of-specifications (Chapter 10).
2   Sagging or broken springs (Chapter 10).
3   Tire out-of-balance (Chapter 10).
4   Worn strut damper (Chapter 10).
5   Overloaded vehicle.
6   Tires not rotated regularly.

73 Wheel makes a thumping noise

1   Blister or bump on tire (Chapter 10).
2   Improper strut damper action (Chapter 10).

74 Shimmy, shake or vibration

1   Tire or wheel out-of-balance or out-of-round (Chapter 10).

2   Loose or worn wheel bearings (Chapters 1, 8 and 10).
3   Worn tie-rod ends (Chapter 10).
4   Worn balljoints (Chapters 1 and 10).
5   Excessive wheel runout (Chapter 10).
6   Blister or bump on tire (Chapter 10).

75 Hard steering

1   Lack of lubrication at balljoints, tie-rod ends and rack and pinion assembly (Chapter 10).
2   Front wheel alignment out-of-specifications (Chapter 10).
3   Low tire pressure(s) (Chapters 1 and 10).

76 Poor returnability of steering to center

1   Lack of lubrication at balljoints and tie-rod ends (Chapter 10).
2   Binding in balljoints (Chapter 10).
3   Binding in steering column (Chapter 10).
4   Lack of lubricant in steering gear assembly (Chapter 10).
5   Front wheel alignment out-of-specifications (Chapter 10).

77 Abnormal noise at the front end

1   Lack of lubrication at balljoints and tie-rod ends (Chapters 1 and 10).
2   Damaged strut mounting (Chapter 10).
3   Worn control arm bushings or tie-rod ends (Chapter 10).
4   Loose stabilizer bar (Chapter 10).
5   Loose wheel nuts (Chapters 1 and 10).
6   Loose suspension bolts (Chapter 10).

78 Wander or poor steering stability

1   Mismatched or uneven tires (Chapter 10).
2   Lack of lubrication at balljoints and tie-rod ends (Chapters 1 and 10).
3   Worn strut assemblies (Chapter 10).
4   Loose stabilizer bar (Chapter 10).
5   Broken or sagging springs (Chapter 10).
6   Wheels out of alignment (Chapter 10).

79 Erratic steering when braking

1   Wheel bearings worn (Chapter 10).
2   Broken or sagging springs (Chapter 10).
3   Leaking wheel cylinder or caliper (Chapter 10).
4   Warped rotors or drums (Chapter 10).

80 Excessive pitching and/or rolling around corners or during braking

1   Loose stabilizer bar (Chapter 10).
2   Worn strut dampers or mountings (Chapter 10).
3   Broken or sagging springs (Chapter 10).
4   Overloaded vehicle.

81 Suspension bottoms

1   Overloaded vehicle.

2   Worn strut dampers (Chapter 10).
3   Incorrect, broken or sagging springs (Chapter 10).

82   Cupped tires

1   Front wheel or rear wheel alignment out-of-specifications (Chapter 10).
2   Worn strut dampers (Chapter 10).
3   Wheel bearings worn (Chapter 10).
4   Excessive tire or wheel runout (Chapter 10).
5   Worn balljoints (Chapter 10).

83   Excessive tire wear on outside edge

1   Inflation pressures incorrect (Chapter 1).
2   Excessive speed in turns.
3   Front end alignment incorrect (excessive toe-in). Have professionally aligned.
4   Suspension arm bent or twisted (Chapter 10).

84   Excessive tire wear on inside edge

1   Inflation pressures incorrect (Chapter 1).

2   Front end alignment incorrect (toe-out). Have professionally aligned.
3   Loose or damaged steering components (Chapter 10).

85   Tire tread worn in one place

1   Tires out-of-balance.
2   Damaged or buckled wheel. Inspect and replace if necessary.
3   Defective tire (Chapter 1).

86   Excessive play or looseness in steering system

1   Wheel bearing(s) worn (Chapter 10).
2   Tie-rod end loose (Chapter 10).
3   Steering gear loose (Chapter 10).
4   Worn or loose steering intermediate shaft (Chapter 10).

87   Rattling or clicking noise in rack and pinion

1   Steering gear loose (Chapter 10).
2   Steering gear defective.

Chapter 1
Tune-up and routine maintenance

Contents

1

Specifications

Recommended lubricants and fluids

Engine oil	
Type	API grade SG, SH, or SG/CD or SH/CD multigrade and fuel efficient oil
Viscosity	See accompanying chart
Fuel	Unleaded gasoline, 87 octane or higher
Automatic transaxle	
Fluid	DEXRON II automatic transmission fluid
Differential lubricant	DEXRON II automatic transmission fluid
Manual transaxle lubricant	API GL-5 75W-90 gear oil
Brake fluid	DOT 3 brake fluid
Clutch fluid	DOT 3 brake fluid
Power steering system	DEXRON II automatic transmission fluid

Recommended engine oil viscosity

Capacities*

Engine oil (including filter)
    1.6L engine.. 3.0 qts
    1.8L engine.. 3.7 qts
Coolant .... 6.0 qts
Transaxle
    Automatic (drain and refill)
        Three-speed .... 2.6 qts
            Differential .... 1.5 qts
        Four-speed .... 3.3 qts
    Manual.. 2.7 qts

* All capacities approximate. Add as necessary to bring up to appropriate level.

Ignition system

Spark plug type and gap
    Type.. NGK BKR5EYA or equivalent
    Gap.. 0.031 inch
Spark plug wire resistance .... 10,000 to 25,000 ohms
Engine firing order 1-3-4-2

**Cylinder location and
distributor rotation**

Valve clearances (engine hot)

Intake valve... 0.006 to 0.010 inch
Exhaust valve.. 0.0010 to 0014 inch

Cooling system

Thermostat rating
    Starts to open... 190-degrees F
    Fully open.. 212-degrees F
Accessory drivebelt tension (with Burroughs or Nippondenso tension gauge)
    Used belt
        Alternator .... 95 to 135 lbs
        Power steering pump.. 60 to 100 lbs
        Air conditioning compressor............................. 80 to 120 lbs
    New belt (a belt which has been used less than 5 minutes)
        Alternator .... 170 to 180 lbs
        Power steering pump.. 100 to 150 lbs
        Air conditioning compressor............................. 140 to 180 lbs

Clutch pedal

Freeplay .... 3/16 to 5/8 inch
Height .... 6 inches

Brakes

Disc brake pad lining thickness (minimum) .... 1/16 inch
Drum brake shoe lining thickness (minimum)...................... 1/16 inch
Parking brake adjustment... 4 to 7 clicks

Suspension and steering

Steering wheel freeplay limit.. 1-3/16 inch
Balljoint allowable movement .... 0 inch

Torque specifications

                                                 Ft-lbs (unless otherwise indicated)

Automatic transaxle
    Three-speed
        Pan bolts.. 48 in-lbs
        Filter bolts .... 48 in-lbs
        Drain plug.. 13
    Four-speed
        Pan bolts.. 48 in-lbs
        Filter bolts .... 84 in-lbs
        Drain plug.. 36
Manual transaxle drain and filler plugs 29
Spark plugs.. 13
Seat bolts/nuts 27
Wheel lug nuts 76

Typical engine compartment components

1	Engine oil dipstick	7	Air cleaner assembly	13	Radiator cap
2	Power steering fluid reservoir	8	Coolant reservoir	14	Spark plug
3	Brake fluid reservoir	9	Automatic transaxle dipstick	15	Oil filler cap
4	Fuse block	10	Distributor	16	Drivebelt
5	Relay block	11	Radiator hose	17	Windshield washer fluid reservoir
6	Battery	12	PCV valve		

1

Typical engine compartment underside components

1	Driveaxle boot	4	Steering gear boot	7	Radiator drain fitting
2	Automatic transaxle drain plug	5	Engine oil drain plug	8	Engine oil filter
3	Exhaust system catalytic converter	6	Front suspension strut unit	9	Front disc brake caliper

Typical rear underside components

1	Gas tank filler pipe	3	Suspension strut	5	Gas tank
2	Muffler	4	Exhaust system	6	Rear brake assembly

1 Toyota Corolla and Geo Prizm Maintenance schedule

The maintenance intervals in this manual are provided with the assumption that you, not the dealer, will be doing the work. These are the minimum maintenance intervals recommended by the factory for vehicles that are driven daily. If you wish to keep your vehicle in peak condition at all times, you may wish to perform some of these procedures even more often. Because frequent maintenance enhances the efficiency, performance and resale value of your car, we encourage you to do so. If you drive in dusty areas, tow a trailer, idle or drive at low speeds for extended periods or drive for short distances (less than four miles) in below freezing temperatures, shorter intervals are also recommended.

When your vehicle is new, it should be serviced by a factory authorized dealer service department to protect the factory warranty. In many cases, the initial maintenance check is done at no cost to the owner.

Every 250 miles or weekly, whichever comes first

Check the engine oil level (Section 4)
Check the engine coolant level (Section 4)
Check the windshield washer fluid level (Section 4)
Check the brake fluid level (Section 4)
Check the tires and tire pressures (Section 5)

Every 3000 miles or 3 months, whichever comes first

All items listed above plus:
Check the power steering fluid level (Section 6)
Check the automatic transaxle fluid level (Section 7)
Change the engine oil and oil filter (Section 8)

Every 7500 miles or 6 months, whichever comes first

Inspect and replace if necessary the windshield wiper blades (Section 9)
Check the clutch pedal for proper freeplay (Section 10)
Check and service the battery (Section 11)
Check and adjust if necessary the engine drivebelts (Section 12)
Inspect and replace if necessary all underhood hoses (Section 13)
Check the cooling system (Section 14)
Rotate the tires (Section 15)

Every 15,000 miles or 12 months, whichever comes first

All items listed above plus:
Inspect the brake system (Section 16)*
Replace the air filter (Section 17)
Inspect the fuel system (Section 18)
Check the three-speed automatic transaxle lubricant level (Section 19)
Check the manual transaxle lubricant level (Section 20)
Inspect the suspension and steering components (Section 21)*
Check the driveaxle boots (Section 22)

Every 30,000 miles or 24 months, whichever comes first

All items listed above plus:
Replace the fuel filter (Section 23)
Check and replace if necessary the spark plugs (Section 24)
Inspect and replace if necessary the spark plug wires, distributor cap and rotor (Section 25)
Service the cooling system (drain, flush and refill) (Section 26)
Inspect the evaporative emissions control system (Section 27)
Inspect the exhaust system (Section 28)
Change the automatic transaxle fluid and filter and differential lubricant (Section 29)**
Change the manual transaxle lubricant (Section 30)**
Check and replace if necessary the PCV valve (Section 31)

Every 60,000 miles or 48 months, whichever comes first

Check and adjust the valve clearances (Section 32)
Replace the timing belt (Chapter 2A)

* This item is affected by "severe" operating conditions as described below. If your vehicle is operated under "severe" conditions, perform all maintenance indicated with an asterisk (*) at 3000 mile/3 month intervals. Severe conditions are indicated if you mainly operate your vehicle under one or more of the following conditions:

Operating in dusty areas
Towing a trailer
Idling for extended periods and/or low speed operation
Operating when outside temperatures remain below freezing and when most trips are less than 4 miles

** If operated under one or more of the following conditions, change the manual or automatic transaxle fluid and differential lubricant every 15,000 miles:

In heavy city traffic where the outside temperature regularly reaches 90-degrees F (32-degrees C) or higher
In hilly or mountainous terrain
Frequent trailer pulling

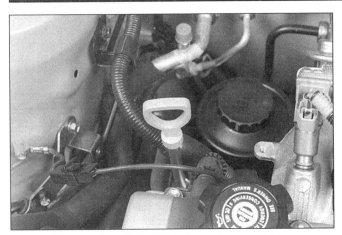

4.2 The engine oil dipstick is located on the right rear side of the engine

4.4 The oil level should be at or near the F mark - if it isn't, add enough oil to bring the level to near the F mark (it takes one full quart to raise the level from the L to the F mark)

2   Introduction

This chapter is designed to help the home mechanic maintain the Toyota Corolla or Geo Prizm for peak performance, economy, safety and long life.

On the following pages is a master maintenance schedule, followed by sections dealing specifically with each item on the schedule. Visual checks, adjustments, component replacement and other helpful items are included. Refer to the **accompanying illustrations** of the engine compartment and the underside of the vehicle for the location of various components.

Servicing your Corolla or Prizm in accordance with the mileage/time maintenance schedule and the following Sections will provide it with a planned maintenance program that should result in a long and reliable service life. This is a comprehensive plan, so maintaining some items but not others at the specified service intervals will not produce the same results.

As you service your Corolla or Prizm, you will discover that many of the procedures can - and should - be grouped together because of the nature of the particular procedure you're performing or because of the close proximity of two otherwise unrelated components to one another.

For example, if the vehicle is raised for any reason, you should inspect the exhaust, suspension, steering and fuel systems while you're under the vehicle. When you're rotating the tires, it makes good sense to check the brakes and wheel bearings since the wheels are already removed.

Finally, let's suppose you have to borrow or rent a torque wrench. Even if you only need to tighten the spark plugs, you might as well check the torque of as many critical fasteners as time allows.

The first step of this maintenance program is to prepare yourself before the actual work begins. Read through all sections pertinent to the procedures you're planning to do, then make a list of and gather together all the parts and tools you will need to do the job. If it looks as if you might run into problems during a particular segment of some procedure, seek advice from your local parts man or dealer service department.

3   Tune-up general information

The term tune-up is used in this manual to represent a combination of individual operations rather than one specific procedure.

If, from the time the vehicle is new, the routine maintenance schedule is followed closely and frequent checks are made of fluid levels and high wear items, as suggested throughout this manual, the engine will be kept in relatively good running condition and the need for additional work will be minimized.

More likely than not, however, there will be times when the engine is running poorly due to lack of regular maintenance. This is even more

likely if a used vehicle, which has not received regular and frequent maintenance checks, is purchased. In such cases, an engine tune-up will be needed outside of the regular routine maintenance intervals.

The first step in any tune-up or engine diagnosis to help correct a poor running engine would be a cylinder compression check. A check of the engine compression (Chapter 2 Part B) will give valuable information regarding the overall performance of many internal components and should be used as a basis for tune-up and repair procedures. If, for instance, a compression check indicates serious internal engine wear, a conventional tune-up will not help the running condition of the engine and would be a waste of time and money.

The following series of operations are those most often needed to bring a generally poor running engine back into a proper state of tune.

Minor tune-up

Clean, inspect and test the battery (Section 11)
Check all engine related fluids (Section 4)
Check and adjust the drivebelts (Section 12)
Replace the spark plugs (Section 24)
Inspect the distributor cap and rotor (Section 25)
Inspect the spark plug and coil wires (Section 25)
Check all underhood hoses (Section 13)
Check the cooling system (Section 14)
Check the air filter (Section 17)

Major tune-up

All items listed under Minor tune-up, plus . . .
Check the ignition system (Section 25)
Check the charging system (Chapter 5)
Check the fuel system (Section 18)
Replace the air filter (Section 17)
Replace the distributor cap and rotor (Section 25)
Replace the spark plug wires (Section 25)

4   Fluid level checks (every 250 miles or weekly)

1   Fluids are an essential part of the lubrication, cooling, brake, clutch and other systems. Because these fluids gradually become depleted and/or contaminated during normal operation of the vehicle, they must be periodically replenished. See *Recommended lubricants and fluids* and *Capacities* at the beginning of this Chapter before adding fluid to any of the following components. **Note:** *The vehicle must be on level ground before fluid levels can be checked.*

Engine oil

Refer to illustrations 4.2, 4.4 and 4.6
2   The engine oil level is checked with a dipstick located at the back side of the engine **(see illustration)**. The dipstick extends through a metal tube from which it protrudes down into the engine oil pan.
3   The oil level should be checked before the vehicle has been driven, or about 15 minutes after the engine has been shut off. If the oil is checked immediately after driving the vehicle, some of the oil will remain in the upper engine components, producing an inaccurate reading on the dipstick.
4   Pull the dipstick from the tube and wipe all the oil from the end with a clean rag or paper towel. Insert the clean dipstick all the way back into its metal tube and pull it out again. Observe the oil at the end of the dipstick. At its highest point, the level should be between the L and F marks **(see illustration)**.
5   It takes one quart of oil to raise the level from the L mark to the

4.6 The threaded oil filler cap is located on the valve cover - always make sure the area around the opening is clean before unscrewing the cap to prevent dirt from contaminating the engine

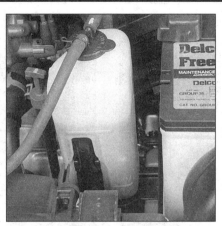

4.8 The coolant reservoir is located next to the battery - make sure the level is between Low and Full marks on the reservoir

4.14 The windshield washer fluid reservoir tank is located on the right front corner of the engine compartment

F mark on the dipstick. Do not allow the level to drop below the L mark or oil starvation may cause engine damage. Conversely, overfilling the engine (adding oil above the F mark) may cause oil fouled spark plugs, oil leaks or oil seal failures.

6   Remove the threaded cap from the valve cover to add oil **(see illustration)**. Use a funnel to prevent spills. After adding the oil, install the filler cap hand tight. Start the engine and look carefully for any small leaks around the oil filter or drain plug. Stop the engine and check the oil level again after it has had sufficient time to drain from the upper block and cylinder head galleys.

7   Checking the oil level is an important preventive maintenance step. A continually dropping oil level indicates oil leakage through damaged seals, from loose connections, or past worn rings or valve guides. If the oil looks milky in color or has water droplets in it, a cylinder head gasket may be blown. The engine should be checked immediately. The condition of the oil should also be checked. Each time you check the oil level, slide your thumb and index finger up the dipstick before wiping off the oil. If you see small dirt or metal particles clinging to the dipstick, the oil should be changed (Section 8).

Engine coolant

Refer to illustration 4.8

Warning: *Do not allow antifreeze to come in contact with your skin or painted surfaces of the vehicle. Flush contaminated areas immediately with plenty of water. Don't store new coolant or leave old coolant lying around where it's accessible to children or pets - they're attracted by its sweet smell and may drink it. Ingestion of even a small amount of coolant can be fatal! Wipe up garage floor and drip pan spills immediately. Keep antifreeze containers covered and repair cooling system leaks as soon as they're noticed.*

8   All vehicles covered by this manual are equipped with a pressurized coolant recovery system. A white coolant reservoir located in the left front corner of the engine compartment is connected by a hose to the base of the coolant filler cap **(see illustration)**. If the coolant heats up during engine operation, coolant can escape through a pressurized filler cap, then through a connecting hose into the reservoir. As the engine cools, the coolant is automatically drawn back into the cooling system to maintain the correct level.

9   The coolant level should be checked regularly. It must be between the Full and Low lines on the tank. The level will vary with the temperature of the engine. When the engine is cold, the coolant level should be at or slightly above the Low mark on the tank. Once the engine has warmed up, the level should be at or near the Full mark. If it isn't, allow the fluid in the tank to cool, then remove the cap from the reservoir and add coolant to bring the level up to the Full line. Use only ethylene/glycol type coolant and water in the mixture ratio recommended by your owner's manual. Do not use supplemental inhibitor additives. If only a

small amount of coolant is required to bring the system up to the proper level, water can be used. However, repeated additions of water will dilute the recommended antifreeze and water solution. In order to maintain the proper ratio of antifreeze and water, it is advisable to top up the coolant level with the correct mixture. Refer to your owner's manual for the recommended ratio.

10   If the coolant level drops within a short time after replenishment, there may be a leak in the system. Inspect the radiator, hoses, engine coolant filler cap, drain plugs, air bleeder plugs and water pump. If no leak is evident, have the radiator cap pressure tested by your dealer. **Warning:** *Never remove the radiator cap or the coolant recovery reservoir cap when the engine is running or has just been shut down, because the cooling system is hot. Escaping steam and scalding liquid could cause serious injury.*

11   If it is necessary to open the radiator cap, wait until the system has cooled completely, then wrap a thick cloth around the cap and turn it to the first stop. If any steam escapes, wait until the system has cooled further, then remove the cap.

12   When checking the coolant level, always note its condition. It should be relatively clear. If it is brown or rust colored, the system should be drained, flushed and refilled. Even if the coolant appears to be normal, the corrosion inhibitors wear out with use, so it must be replaced at the specified intervals.

13   Do not allow antifreeze to come in contact with your skin or painted surfaces of the vehicle. Flush contacted areas immediately with plenty of water.

Windshield washer fluid

Refer to illustration 4.14

14   Fluid for the windshield washer system is stored in a plastic reservoir which is located on the right side of the engine compartment **(see illustration)**. In milder climates, plain water can be used to top up the reservoir, but the reservoir should be kept no more than two-thirds full to allow for expansion should the water freeze. In colder climates, the use of a specially designed windshield washer fluid, available at your dealer and any auto parts store, will help lower the freezing point of the fluid. Mix the solution with water in accordance with the manufacturer's directions on the container. Do not use regular antifreeze. It will damage the vehicle's paint.

Battery electrolyte

15   On models not equipped with a sealed battery, unscrew the filler/vent cap and check the electrolyte level. It must be between the upper and lower levels. If the level is low, and add distilled water. Install and securely retighten the cap. **Caution:** *Overfilling the cells may cause electrolyte to spill over during periods of heavy charging, causing corrosion or damage.*

4.17 The brake fluid level should be kept between the MIN and MAX marks on the translucent plastic reservoir - lift up the cap to add fluid

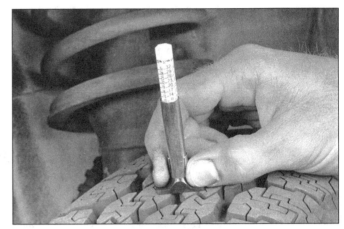

5.2 A tire tread depth indicator should be used to monitor tire wear - they are available at auto parts stores and service stations and cost very little

Brake and clutch fluid

Refer to illustration 4.17

16   The brake master cylinder is mounted on the front of the power booster unit in the engine compartment. The clutch cylinder used on vehicles with manual transaxles is located next to the master cylinder.

17   To check either the fluid level of the brake master cylinder or clutch reservoir, simply look at the MAX and MIN marks on the reservoirs **(see illustration)**. The level should be at or near the maximum fill line for both reservoirs.

18   If the level is low for either reservoir, wipe the top of the reservoir cover with a clean rag to prevent contamination of the brake or clutch system before lifting the cover.

19   Add only the specified brake fluid to the brake or clutch reservoir (refer to *Recommended lubricants and fluids* at the front of this chapter or to your owner's manual). Mixing different types of brake fluid can damage the system. Fill the brake master cylinder reservoir only to the dotted line - this brings the fluid to the correct level when you put the cover back on. **Warning:** *Use caution when filling either reservoir- brake fluid can harm your eyes and damage painted surfaces. Do not use brake fluid that has been opened for more than one year (even if the cap has been on) or has been left open. Brake fluid absorbs moisture from the air. Excess moisture can cause a dangerous loss of braking.*

20   While the reservoir cap is removed, inspect the master cylinder reservoir for contamination. If deposits, dirt particles or water droplets are present, the system should be drained and refilled (see Chapter 8 for clutch reservoir or Chapter 9 for brake reservoir).

21   After filling the reservoir to the proper level, make sure the lid is properly seated to prevent fluid leakage and/or system pressure loss.

22   The brake fluid in the master cylinder will drop slightly as the brake pads at each wheel wear down during normal operation. If the master cylinder requires repeated replenishing to keep it at the proper level, this is an indication of leakage in the brake system, which should be corrected immediately. Check all brake lines and connections, along with the wheel cylinders and booster (see Section 16 for more information).

23   If, upon checking the master cylinder fluid level, you discover one or both reservoirs empty or nearly empty, the brake system must be diagnosed immediately (see Chapter 9).

UNDERINFLATION

INCORRECT TOE-IN OR EXTREME CAMBER

CUPPING

UNDERINFLATION AND/OR MECHANICAL IRREGULARITIES SUCH AS OUT-OF-BALANCE CONDITION OF WHEEL AND/OR TIRE, AND BENT OR DAMAGED WHEEL.
POSSIBLE LOOSE OR WORN STEERING TIE-ROD OR STEERING IDLER ARM.
POSSIBLE LOOSE, DAMAGED OR WORN FRONT SUSPENSION PARTS.

OVERINFLATION

FEATHERING DUE TO MISALIGNMENT

1-b HAYNES

5.3 This chart will help you determine the condition of your tires, the probable cause(s) of abnormal wear and the corrective action necessary

5.4a If a tire loses air on a steady basis, check the valve core first to make sure it's snug (special inexpensive wrenches are commonly available at auto parts stores)

5.4b If the valve core is tight, raise the corner of the vehicle with the low tire and spray a soapy water solution onto the tread as the tire is turned slowly - slow leaks will cause small bubbles to appear

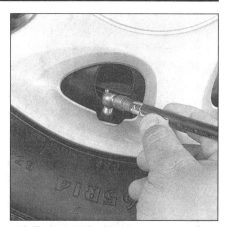

5.8 To extend the life of your tires, check the air pressure at least once a week with an accurate gauge (don't forget the spare!)

5 Tire and tire pressure checks (every 250 miles or weekly)

Refer to illustrations 5.2, 5.3, 5.4a, 5.4b and 5.8

1   Periodic inspection of the tires may spare you from the inconvenience of being stranded with a flat tire. It can also provide you with vital information regarding possible problems in the steering and suspension systems before major damage occurs.

2   Normal tread wear can be monitored with a simple, inexpensive device known as a tread depth indicator **(see illustration)**. When the tread depth reaches the specified minimum, replace the tire(s).

3   Note any abnormal tread wear **(see illustration)**. Tread pattern irregularities such as cupping, flat spots and more wear on one side than the other are indications of front end alignment and/or balance problems. If any of these conditions are noted, take the vehicle to a tire shop or service station to correct the problem.

4   Look closely for cuts, punctures and embedded nails or tacks. Sometimes a tire will hold its air pressure for a short time or leak down very slowly even after a nail has embedded itself into the tread. If a slow leak persists, check the valve stem core to make sure it is tight **(see illustration)**. Examine the tread for an object that may have embedded itself into the tire or for a "plug" that may have begun to leak (radial tire punctures are repaired with a plug that is installed in a puncture). If a puncture is suspected, it can be easily verified by

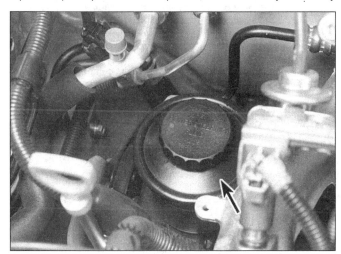

6.2 The power steering fluid reservoir (arrow) is located in the right rear corner of the engine compartment

spraying a solution of soapy water onto the puncture area **(see illustration)**. The soapy solution will bubble if there is a leak. Unless the puncture is inordinately large, a tire shop or gas station can usually repair the punctured tire.

5   Carefully inspect the inner sidewall of each tire for evidence of brake fluid leakage. If you see any, inspect the brakes immediately.

6   Correct tire air pressure adds miles to the lifespan of the tires, improves mileage and enhances overall ride quality. Tire pressure cannot be accurately estimated by looking at a tire, particularly if it is a radial. A tire pressure gauge is therefore essential. Keep an accurate gauge in the glovebox. The pressure gauges fitted to the nozzles of air hoses at gas stations are often inaccurate.

7   Always check tire pressure when the tires are cold. "Cold," in this case, means the vehicle has not been driven over a mile in the three hours preceding a tire pressure check. A pressure rise of four to eight pounds is not uncommon once the tires are warm.

8   Unscrew the valve cap protruding from the wheel or hubcap and push the gauge firmly onto the valve **(see illustration)**. Note the reading on the gauge and compare this figure to the recommended tire pressure shown on the tire placard on the left door. Be sure to reinstall the valve cap to keep dirt and moisture out of the valve stem mechanism. Check all four tires and, if necessary, add enough air to bring them up to the recommended pressure levels.

9   Don't forget to keep the spare tire inflated to the specified pressure (consult your owner's manual). Note that the air pressure specified for the compact spare is significantly higher than the pressure of the regular tires.

6 Power steering fluid level check (every 3000 miles or 3 months)

Refer to illustrations 6.2 and 6.6

1   Unlike manual steering, the power steering system relies on fluid which may, over a period of time, require replenishing.

2   The fluid reservoir for the power steering pump is located on the inner fender panel near the front of the engine **(see illustration)**.

3   For the check, the front wheels should be pointed straight ahead and the engine should be off.

4   Use a clean rag to wipe off the reservoir cap and the area around the cap. This will help prevent any foreign matter from entering the reservoir during the check.

5   Twist off the cap and check the temperature of the fluid at the end of the dipstick with your finger.

6   Wipe off the fluid with a clean rag, reinsert it, then withdraw it and read the fluid level. The level should be at the HOT mark if the fluid was hot to the touch. It should be at the COLD mark if the fluid was cool to

1

6.6 The power steering fluid is checked with a dipstick which is part of the cap - the fluid level varies with temperature, so the fluid can be checked hot or cold

7.4a The automatic transaxle dipstick (arrow) is located in a tube which extends forward from the transaxle toward the radiator

7.4b If the automatic transaxle fluid is cold, the level should be between the two lower notches; if it's at operating temperature, the level should be between the two upper notches

the touch. Note that the marks (HOT and COLD) are on opposite sides of the dipstick **(see illustration)**. At no time should the fluid level drop below the upper mark for each heat range.

7   If additional fluid is required, pour the specified type directly into the reservoir, using a funnel to prevent spills.

8   If the reservoir requires frequent fluid additions, all power steering hoses, hose connections, the power steering pump and the rack and pinion assembly should be carefully checked for leaks.

7   Automatic transaxle fluid level check (every 3000 miles or 3 months)

Refer to illustrations 7.4a and 7.4b

1   The level of the automatic transaxle fluid should be carefully maintained. Low fluid level can lead to slipping or loss of drive, while overfilling can cause foaming, loss of fluid and transaxle damage.

2   The transaxle fluid level should only be checked when the transaxle is hot (at its normal operating temperature). If the vehicle has just been driven over 10 miles (15 miles in a frigid climate), and the fluid temperature is 160 to 175-degrees F, the transaxle is hot. **Caution:** *If the vehicle has just been driven for a long time at high speed or in city traffic in hot weather, or if it has been pulling a trailer, an accurate fluid level reading cannot be obtained. Allow the fluid to cool down for about 30 minutes.*

3   If the vehicle has not just been driven, park the vehicle on level ground, set the parking brake and start the engine. While the engine is idling, depress the brake pedal and move the selector lever through all the gear ranges, beginning and ending in Park.

4   With the engine still idling, remove the dipstick from its tube **(see illustration)**. Check the level of the fluid on the dipstick **(see illustration)** and note its condition.

5   Wipe the fluid from the dipstick with a clean rag and reinsert it back into the filler tube until the cap seats.

6   Pull the dipstick out again and note the fluid level. If the transaxle is cold, the level should be in the COLD or COOL range on the dipstick. If it is hot, the fluid level should be in the HOT range. If the level is at the low side of either range, add the specified automatic transmission fluid through the dipstick tube with a funnel.

7   Add just enough of the recommended fluid to fill the transaxle to the proper level. It takes about one pint to raise the level from the low mark to the high mark when the fluid is hot, so add the fluid a little at a time and keep checking the level until it is correct.

8   The condition of the fluid should also be checked along with the level. If the fluid at the end of the dipstick is black or a dark reddish brown color, or if it emits a burned smell, the fluid should be changed (see Section 29). If you are in doubt about the condition of the fluid, purchase some new fluid and compare the two for color and smell.

8   Engine oil and oil filter change (every 3000 miles or 3 months)

Refer to illustrations 8.2, 8.7, 8.13 and 8.15

1   Frequent oil changes are the best preventive maintenance the home mechanic can give the engine, because aging oil becomes diluted and contaminated, which leads to premature engine wear.

2   Make sure that you have all the necessary tools before you begin this procedure **(see illustration)**. You should also have plenty of rags or newspapers handy for mopping up any spills.

3   Access to the underside of the vehicle is greatly improved if the vehicle can be lifted on a hoist, driven onto ramps or supported by jackstands. **Warning:** *Do not work under a vehicle which is supported only by a bumper, hydraulic or scissors-type jack.*

4   If this is your first oil change, get under the vehicle and familiarize yourself with the location of the oil drain plug. The engine and exhaust components will be warm during the actual work, so try to anticipate any potential problems before the engine and accessories are hot.

5   Park the vehicle on a level spot. Start the engine and allow it to reach its normal operating temperature (the needle on the temperature gauge should be at least above the bottom mark). Warm oil and sludge will flow out more easily. Turn off the engine when it's warmed up. Remove the filler cap in the rear cam cover.

6   Raise the vehicle and support it on jackstands. **Warning:** *To avoid personal injury, never get beneath the vehicle when it is supported by only by a jack. The jack provided with your vehicle is designed solely for raising the vehicle to remove and replace the wheels. Always use jackstands to support the vehicle when it becomes necessary to place your body underneath the vehicle.*

7   Being careful not to touch the hot exhaust components, place the drain pan under the drain plug in the bottom of the pan and remove the plug **(see illustration)**. You may want to wear gloves while unscrewing the plug the final few turns if the engine is really hot.

8   Allow the old oil to drain into the pan. It may be necessary to move the pan farther under the engine as the oil flow slows to a trickle. Inspect the old oil for the presence of metal shavings and chips.

9   After all the oil has drained, wipe off the drain plug with a clean rag. Even minute metal particles clinging to the plug would immediately contaminate the new oil.

10   Clean the area around the drain plug opening, reinstall the plug and tighten it securely, but do not strip the threads.

11   Move the drain pan into position under the oil filter.

12   Remove all tools, rags, etc. from under the vehicle, being careful not to spill the oil in the drain pan, then lower the vehicle.

13   Loosen the oil filter **(see illustration)** by turning it counterclockwise with the filter wrench. Any standard filter wrench should work.

8.2 These tools are required when changing the engine oil and filter

1   **Drain pan -** *It should be fairly shallow in depth, but wide in order to prevent spills*
2   **Rubber gloves -** *When removing the drain plug and filter, it is inevitable that you will get oil on your hands (the gloves will prevent burns)*
3   **Breaker bar -** *Sometimes the oil drain plug is pretty tight and a long breaker bar is needed to loosen it*
4   **Socket –** *To be used with the breaker bar or a ratchet (must be the correct size to fit the drain plug)*
5   **Filter wrench -** *This is a metal band-type wrench, which requires clearance around the filter to be effective*
6   **Filter wrench -** *This type fits on the bottom of the filter and can be turned with a ratchet or beaker bar (different size wrenches are available for different types of filters)*

Once the filter is loose, use your hands to unscrew it from the block. Just as the filter is detached from the block, immediately tilt the open end up to prevent the oil inside the filter from spilling out. **Warning:** *The engine exhaust manifold may still be hot, so be careful.*

14   With a clean rag, wipe off the mounting surface on the block. If a residue of old oil is allowed to remain, it will smoke when the block is

heated up. It will also prevent the new filter from seating properly. Also make sure that the none of the old gasket remains stuck to the mounting surface. It can be removed with a scraper if necessary.

15   Compare the old filter with the new one to make sure they are the same type. Smear some engine oil on the rubber gasket of the new filter and screw it into place **(see illustration)**. Because overtightening the filter will damage the gasket, do not use a filter wrench to tighten the filter. Tighten it by hand until the gasket contacts the seating surface. Then seat the filter by giving it an additional 3/4-turn.

16   Add new oil to the engine through the oil filler cap in the valve cover. Use a spout or funnel to prevent oil from spilling onto the top of the engine. Pour three quarts of fresh oil into the engine. Wait a few minutes to allow the oil to drain into the pan, then check the level on the oil dipstick (see Section 4 if necessary). If the oil level is at or near the F mark, install the filler cap hand tight, start the engine and allow the new oil to circulate.

17   Allow the engine to run for about a minute. While the engine is running, look under the vehicle and check for leaks at the oil pan drain plug and around the oil filter. If either is leaking, stop the engine and tighten the plug or filter slightly.

18   Wait a few minutes to allow the oil to trickle down into the pan, then recheck the level on the dipstick and, if necessary, add enough oil to bring the level to the F mark.

19   During the first few trips after an oil change, make it a point to check frequently for leaks and proper oil level.

20   The old oil drained from the engine cannot be reused in its present state and should be discarded. Check with your local refuse disposal company, disposal facility or environmental agency to see if they will accept the oil for recycling. Don't pour used oil into drains or onto the ground. After the oil has cooled, it can be drained into a suitable container (capped plastic jugs, topped bottles, milk cartons, etc.) for transport to one of these disposal sites.

---

9   Windshield wiper blade inspection and replacement (every 7500 miles or 6 months)

Refer to illustrations 9.5, 9.6 and 9.7

1   The windshield wiper and blade assembly should be inspected periodically for damage, loose components and cracked or worn blade elements.

2   Road film can build up on the wiper blades and affect their efficiency, so they should be washed regularly with a mild detergent solution.

3   The action of the wiping mechanism can loosen bolts, nuts and fasteners, so they should be checked and tightened, as necessary, at the same time the wiper blades are checked.

4   If the wiper blade elements are cracked, worn or warped, or no longer clean adequately, they should be replaced with new ones.

1

8.7 Use a proper size box-end wrench or socket to remove the oil drain plug and avoid rounding it off

8.13 The oil filter is usually on very tight, so you'll need a special wrench for removal - DO NOT use the wrench to tighten the new filter

8.15 Lubricate the oil filter gasket with clean engine oil before installing the filter on the engine

9.5 Push on the release lever and slide the wiper assembly down out of the hook in the end of the wiper arm

9.6 After detaching the end of the element, slide it out of the end of the frame

9.7 Insert the end of the element with the protrusions in first

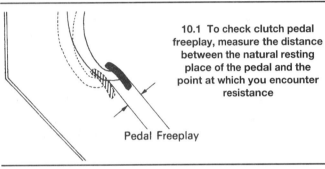

10.1 To check clutch pedal freeplay, measure the distance between the natural resting place of the pedal and the point at which you encounter resistance

Pedal Freeplay

Push Rod Play and Freeplay Adjust Point

Pedal Height Adjust Point

Push Rod Play

10.2 The clutch pedal pushrod play, pedal height and freeplay adjustments are made by loosening the locknut and turning the threaded adjuster

Pedal Height

5   Remove the wiper blade assembly from the arm by pushing on the release lever, then sliding the assembly down and out of the hook in the end of the arm **(see illustration)**.
6   Detach the blade insert element and pull it out of the right end of the wiper frame **(see illustration)**.
7   Insert the new element end with the small protrusions into the right side of the wiper frame **(see illustration)**. Slide the element fully into place, then seat the protrusions in the end of the frames to secure it.

10   Clutch pedal freeplay check and adjustment (every 7500 miles or 6 months)

Refer to illustrations 10.1 and 10.2
1   Press down lightly on the clutch pedal and, with a small steel ruler, measure the distance that it moves freely before the clutch resistance is felt **(see illustration)**. The freeplay should be within the specified limits. If it isn't, it must be adjusted.
2   Loosen the locknut on the pedal end of the clutch pushrod **(see illustration)**.
3   Turn the pushrod until pedal freeplay and pushrod freeplay are correct.
4   Tighten the locknut.
5   After adjusting the pedal freeplay, check the pedal height.
6   If pedal height is incorrect, loosen the locknut and turn the stopper bolt until the height is correct. Tighten the locknut.

11   Battery check, maintenance and charging (every 7500 miles or 6 months)

Refer to illustrations 11.1, 11.6a, 11.6b, 11.7a, 11.7b and 11.8
Warning: *Certain precautions must be followed when checking and servicing the battery. Hydrogen gas, which is highly flammable, is always present in the battery cells, so keep lighted tobacco and all other open flames and sparks away from the battery. The electrolyte inside the battery is actually dilute sulfuric acid, which will cause injury if splashed on your skin or in your eyes. It will also ruin clothes and painted surfaces. When removing the battery cables, always detach the negative cable first and hook it up last!*
1   A routine preventive maintenance program for the battery in your

vehicle is the only way to ensure quick and reliable starts. But before performing any battery maintenance, make sure that you have the proper equipment necessary to work safely around the battery **(see illustration)**.
2   There are also several precautions that should be taken whenever battery maintenance is performed. Before servicing the battery, always turn the engine and all accessories off and disconnect the cable from the negative terminal of the battery.
3   The battery produces hydrogen gas, which is both flammable and explosive. Never create a spark, smoke or light a match around the battery. Always charge the battery in a ventilated area.
4   Electrolyte contains poisonous and corrosive sulfuric acid. Do not allow it to get in your eyes, on your skin on your clothes. Never ingest it. Wear protective safety glasses when working near the battery. Keep children away from the battery.
5   Note the external condition of the battery. If the positive terminal and cable clamp on your vehicle's battery is equipped with a rubber protector, make sure that it's not torn or damaged. It should completely cover the terminal. Look for any corroded or loose connections, cracks in the case or cover or loose hold-down clamps. Also check the entire length of each cable for cracks and frayed conductors.
6   If corrosion, which looks like white, fluffy deposits **(see illustration)** is evident, particularly around the terminals, the battery should be removed for cleaning. Loosen the cable clamp bolts with a wrench, being careful to remove the ground cable first, and slide them off the terminals **(see illustration)**. Then disconnect the hold-down clamp bolt and nut, remove the clamp and lift the battery from the engine compartment.
7   Clean the cable clamps thoroughly with a battery brush or a terminal cleaner and a solution of warm water and baking soda **(see illustration)**. Wash the terminals and the top of the battery case with the same solution but make sure that the solution doesn't get into the battery. When cleaning the cables, terminals and battery top, wear safety

11.6a Battery terminal corrosion usually appears as light, fluffy powder

11.1 Tools and materials required for battery maintenance

1 **Face shield/safety goggles** - *When removing corrosion with a brush, the acidic particles can easily fly up into your eyes*
2 **Baking soda** - *A solution of baking soda and water can be used to neutralize corrosion*
3 **Petroleum jelly** - *A layer of this on the battery posts will help prevent corrosion*
4 **Battery post/cable cleaner** - *This wire brush cleaning tool will remove all traces of corrosion from the battery posts and cable clamps*
5 **Treated felt washers** - *Placing one of these on each post, directly under the cable clamps, will help prevent corrosion*
6 **Puller** - *Sometimes the cable clamps are very difficult to pull off the posts, even after the nut/bolt has been completely loosened. This tool pulls the clamp straight up and off the post without damage*
7 **Battery post/cable cleaner** - *Here is another cleaning tool which is a slightly different version of number 4 above, but it does the same thing*
8 **Rubber gloves** - *Another safety item to consider when servicing the battery; remember that's acid inside the battery*

11.6b Removing a cable from the battery post with a wrench - sometimes a pair of special battery pliers are required for this procedure if corrosion has caused deterioration of the nut hex (always remove the ground (-) cable first and hook it up last!)

goggles and rubber gloves to prevent any solution from coming in contact with your eyes or hands. Wear old clothes too - even diluted, sulfuric acid splashed onto clothes will burn holes in them. If the terminals have been extensively corroded, clean them up with a terminal cleaner **(see illustration)**. Thoroughly wash all cleaned areas with plain water.
8   Make sure that the battery tray is in good condition and the hold-down nut and bolt are tight **(see illustration)**. If the battery is removed

11.7a When cleaning the cable clamps, all corrosion must be removed (the inside of the clamp is tapered to match the taper on the post, so don't remove too much material)

11.7b Regardless of the type of tool used to clean the battery posts, a clean, shiny surface should be the result

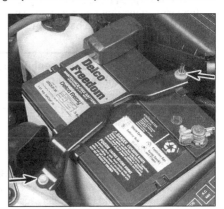

11.8 Make sure the battery clamp nut and bolt (arrows) are tight

12.3 Check the multi-ribbed belt for signs of wear like these – if the belt looks worn, replace it

12.4 If you are able to borrow either a Nippondenso or Burroughs belt tension gauge, this is how it's installed on the belt - compare the reading on the scale with the specified drivebelt tension

from the tray, make sure no parts remain in the bottom of the tray when the battery is reinstalled. When reinstalling the hold-down clamp bolt or nut, do not overtighten it.

9   Information on removing and installing the battery can be found in Chapter 5. Information on jump starting can be found at the front of this manual. For more detailed battery checking procedures, refer to the *Haynes Automotive Electrical Manual*.

Cleaning

10   Corrosion on the hold-down components, battery case and surrounding areas can be removed with a solution of water and baking soda. Thoroughly rinse all cleaned areas with plain water.

11   Any metal parts of the vehicle damaged by corrosion should be covered with a zinc-based primer, then painted.

Charging

Warning: *When batteries are being charged, hydrogen gas, which is very explosive and flammable, is produced. Do not smoke or allow open flames near a charging or a recently charged battery. Wear eye protection when near the battery during charging. Also, make sure the charger is unplugged before connecting or disconnecting the battery from the charger.*

12   Slow-rate charging is the best way to restore a battery that's discharged to the point where it will not start the engine. It's also a good way to maintain the battery charge in a vehicle that's only driven a few miles between starts. Maintaining the battery charge is particularly important in the winter when the battery must work harder to start the engine and electrical accessories that drain the battery are in greater use.

13   It's best to use a one or two-amp battery charger (sometimes called a "trickle" charger). They are the safest and put the least strain on the battery. They are also the least expensive. For a faster charge, you can use a higher amperage charger, but don't use one rated more than 1/10th the amp/hour rating of the battery. Rapid boost charges that claim to restore the power of the battery in one to two hours are hardest on the battery and can damage batteries not in good condition. This type of charging should only be used in emergency situations.

14   The average time necessary to charge a battery should be listed in the instructions that come with the charger. As a general rule, a trickle charger will charge a battery in 12 to 16 hours.

12   Drivebelt check, adjustment and replacement (every 7500 miles or 6 months)

Refer to illustrations 12.3, 12.4, 12.5, 12.6 and 12.10

Check

1   The alternator, power steering pump and air conditioning compressor drivebelts, also referred to as simply "fan" belts, are located at the right end of the engine. The good condition and proper adjustment of the alternator belt is critical to the operation of the engine. Because of their composition and the high stresses to which they are subjected, drivebelts stretch and deteriorate as they get older. They must therefore be periodically inspected.

2   The number of belts used on a particular vehicle depends on the accessories installed. One belt transmits power from the crankshaft to the alternator and air conditioning. If the vehicle is equipped with

12.5 Measuring drivebelt deflection with a straightedge and ruler

power steering, the pump is driven by it's own belt.

3   With the engine off, open the hood and locate the drivebelts. With a flashlight, check each belt for separation of the adhesive rubber on both sides of the core, core separation from the belt side, a severed core, separation of the ribs from the adhesive rubber, cracking or separation of the ribs, and torn or worn ribs or cracks in the inner ridges of the ribs **(see illustration)**. Also check for fraying and glazing, which gives the belt a shiny appearance. Both sides of the belt should be inspected, which means you will have to twist the belt to check the underside. Use your fingers to feel the belt where you can't see it. If any of the above conditions are evident, replace the belt (go to Step 8).

4   To check the tension of each belt in accordance with factory specifications, install either a Nippondenso or Burroughs belt tension gauge on the belt **(see illustration)**. Measure the tension in accordance with the manufacturer's instructions and compare your measurement to the specified drivebelt tension for either a used or new belt. **Note:** *A "used" belt is defined as any belt which has been operated more than five minutes on the engine; a "new" belt is one that has been used for less than five minutes.*

5   If you don't have either of the above tools, and cannot borrow one, the following rule of thumb method is recommended: Push firmly on the belt with your thumb at a distance halfway between the pulleys and note how far the belt can be pushed (deflected). Measure this deflection with a ruler **(see illustration)**. The belt should deflect 1/4-inch if the distance from pulley center to pulley center is between 7 and 11 inches; the belt should deflect 1/2-inch if the distance from pulley center to pulley center is between 12 and 16 inches.

Adjustment

6   If the alternator/air conditioning compressor belt must be adjusted, loosen the alternator pivot bolt located on the front left corner of the block. Loosen the idle pulley lock nut and turn the adjusting bolt **(see illustration)**. Measure the belt tension in accordance with one of the above methods. Repeat this step until the air conditioning compressor drivebelt is adjusted.

12.6 After loosening the idler pulley lock nut, turn the adjusting bolt

Adjusting Bolt

Compressor Drive Belt

Idle Pulley Lock Nut

12.10 When installing a multi-ribbed belt, make sure that it is centered - it must not overlap either edge of the pulley

CORRECT

WRONG

7   Adjust the power steering pump belt by loosening adjustment bolt that secures the pump to the slotted bracket and pivot the pump (away from the engine to tighten the belt, toward it to loosen it). Repeat the procedure until the drivebelt tension is correct and tighten the bolt.

Replacement

8   To replace a belt, follow the above procedures for drivebelt adjustment but slip the belt off the crankshaft pulley and remove it. If you are replacing the power steering pump belt, you will have to remove the air conditioning compressor belt first because of the way they are arranged on the crankshaft pulley. Because of this and because belts tend to wear out more or less together, it is a good idea to replace both belts at the same time. Mark each belt and its appropriate pulley groove so the replacement belts can be installed in their proper positions.
9   Take the old belts to the parts store in order to make a direct comparison for length, width and design.
10   After replacing the drivebelt, make sure that it fits properly in the ribbed grooves in the pulleys (see illustration). It is essential that the belt be properly centered.
11   Adjust the belt(s) in accordance with the procedure outlined above.

13 Underhood hose check and replacement (every 7500 miles or 6 months)

Caution: *Replacement of air conditioning hoses must be left to a dealer service department or air conditioning shop that has the equipment to depressurize the system safely. Never remove air conditioning components or hoses until the system has been depressurized.*

General

1   High temperatures in the engine compartment can cause the deterioration of the rubber and plastic hoses used for engine, accessory and emission systems operation. Periodic inspection should be made for cracks, loose clamps, material hardening and leaks.
2   Information specific to the cooling system hoses can be found in Section 14.
3   Some, but not all, hoses are secured to the fittings with clamps. Where clamps are used, check to be sure they haven't lost their tension, allowing the hose to leak. If clamps aren't used, make sure the hose has not expanded and/or hardened where it slips over the fitting, allowing it to leak.

Vacuum hoses

4   It's quite common for vacuum hoses, especially those in the emissions system, to be color coded or identified by colored stripes molded into them. Various systems require hoses with different wall thickness, collapse resistance and temperature resistance. When replacing hoses, be sure the new ones are made of the same material.
5   Often the only effective way to check a hose is to remove it completely from the vehicle. If more than one hose is removed, be sure to label the hoses and fittings to ensure correct installation.
6   When checking vacuum hoses, be sure to include any plastic T-fittings in the check. Inspect the fittings for cracks and the hose where

it fits over the fitting for distortion, which could cause leakage.
7   A small piece of vacuum hose (1/4-inch inside diameter) can be used as a stethoscope to detect vacuum leaks. Hold one end of the hose to your ear and probe around vacuum hoses and fittings, listening for the "hissing" sound characteristic of a vacuum leak. **Warning:** *When probing with the vacuum hose stethoscope, be very careful not to come into contact with moving engine components such as the drivebelts, cooling fan, etc.*

Fuel hose

Warning: *There are certain precautions which must be taken when inspecting or servicing fuel system components. Work in a well ventilated area and do not allow open flames (cigarettes, appliance pilot lights, etc.) or bare light bulbs near the work area. Mop up any spills immediately and do not store fuel soaked rags where they could ignite.*
8   Check all rubber fuel lines for deterioration and chafing. Check especially for cracks in areas where the hose bends and just before fittings, such as where a hose attaches to the fuel filter.
9   High quality fuel line, specifically designed for fuel injection systems, must be used for fuel line replacement. **Warning:** *Never use anything other than the proper fuel line for fuel line replacement.*
10   Spring-type clamps are commonly used on fuel lines. These clamps often lose their tension over a period of time, and can be "sprung" during removal. Replace all spring-type clamps with screw clamps whenever a hose is replaced.

Metal lines

11   Sections of metal line are often used for fuel line between the fuel pump and fuel injection unit. Check carefully to be sure the line has not been bent or crimped and that cracks have not started in the line.
12   If a section of metal fuel line must be replaced, only seamless steel tubing should be used, since copper and aluminum tubing don't have the strength necessary to withstand normal engine vibration.
13   Check the metal brake lines where they enter the master cylinder and brake proportioning unit (if used) for cracks in the lines or loose fittings. Any sign of brake fluid leakage calls for an immediate thorough inspection of the brake system.

14 Cooling system check (every 7500 miles or 6 months)

Refer to illustration 14.4

1   Many major engine failures can be attributed to a faulty cooling system. If the vehicle is equipped with an automatic transaxle, the cooling system also cools the transaxle fluid and thus plays an important role in prolonging transaxle life.
2   The cooling system should be checked with the engine cold. Do this before the vehicle is driven for the day or after the engine has been shut off for at least three hours.
3   Remove the radiator cap by turning it to the left until it reaches a stop. If you hear a hissing sound (indicating there is still pressure in the system), wait until it stops. Now press down on the cap with the palm of your hand and continue turning to the left until the cap can be removed. Thoroughly clean the cap, inside and out, with clean water. Also clean the filler neck on the radiator. All traces of corrosion should be removed. The coolant inside the radiator should be relatively

ALWAYS CHECK FOR CHAFED
OR BURNED AREAS THAT MAY CAUSE AN
UNTIMELY AND COSTLY FAILURE.

SOFT HOSE INDICATES INSIDE DETERIORATION.
THIS DETERIORATION CAN CONTAMINATE THE
COOLING SYSTEM AND CAUSE PARTICLES TO
CLOG THE RADIATOR.

HARDENED HOSE CAN FAIL AT ANY TIME.
TIGHTENING HOSE CLAMPS WILL NOT SEAL THE
CONNECTION OR STOP LEAKS.

SWOLLEN HOSE OR OIL SOAKED ENDS
INDICATE DANGER AND POSSIBLE FAILURE
FROM OIL OR GREASE CONTAMINATION. SQUEEZE
THE HOSE TO LOCATE CRACKS AND BREAKS
THAT CAUSE LEAKS.

1-m HAYNES

14.4 Hoses, like drivebelts, have a habit of failing at the worst possible time - to prevent the inconvenience of a blown radiator or heater hose, inspect them carefully as shown here

15.2 The recommended tire rotation pattern for these vehicles

1-AJ HAYNES

15   Tire rotation (every 7500 miles or 6 months)

Refer to illustration 15.2

1   The tires should be rotated at the specified intervals and whenever uneven wear is noticed. Since the vehicle will be raised and the tires removed anyway, check the brakes (see Section 16) at this time.
2   Radial tires must be rotated in a specific pattern **(see illustration)**.
3   Refer to the information in *Jacking and towing* at the front of this manual for the proper procedures to follow when raising the vehicle and changing a tire. If the brakes are to be checked, do not apply the parking brake as stated. Make sure the tires are blocked to prevent the vehicle from rolling.
4   Preferably, the entire vehicle should be raised at the same time. This can be done on a hoist or by jacking up each corner and then lowering the vehicle onto jackstands placed under the frame rails. Always use four jackstands and make sure the vehicle is firmly supported.
5   After rotation, check and adjust the tire pressures as necessary and be sure to check the lug nut tightness.
6   For further information on the wheels and tires, refer to Chapter 10.

16   Brake check (every 15,000 miles or 12 months)

Note: *For detailed photographs of the brake system, refer to Chapter 9.*
1   In addition to the specified intervals, the brakes should be inspected every time the wheels are removed or whenever a defect is suspected. Any of the following symptoms could indicate a potential brake system defect: The vehicle pulls to one side when the brake pedal is depressed; the brakes make squealing or dragging noises when applied; brake travel is excessive; the pedal pulsates; brake fluid leaks, usually onto the inside of the tire or wheel.
2   The disc brake pads have built-in wear indicators which should make a high-pitched squealing or scraping noise when they are worn to the replacement point. When you hear this noise, replace the pads immediately or expensive damage to the discs can result.
3   Loosen the wheel lug nuts.
4   Raise the vehicle and place it securely on jackstands.
5   Remove the wheels (see *Jacking and towing* at the front of this book, or your owner's manual, if necessary).

Disc brakes

Refer to illustration 16.6

6   There are two pads - an outer and an inner - in each caliper. The pads are visible through small inspection holes in each caliper **(see illustration)** .
7   Check the pad thickness by looking at each end of the caliper and through the inspection hole in the caliper body. If the lining material is less than the thickness listed in this Chapter's Specifications, replace the pads. **Note:** *Keep in mind that the lining material is riveted or bonded to a metal backing plate and the metal portion is not included in this measurement.*
8   If it is difficult to determine the exact thickness of the remaining

transparent. If it's rust colored, the system should be drained and refilled (see Section 26). If the coolant level isn't up to the top, add additional antifreeze/coolant mixture (see Section 4).
4   Carefully check the large upper and lower radiator hoses along with the smaller diameter heater hoses which run from the engine to the firewall. Inspect each hose along its entire length, replacing any hose which is cracked, swollen or shows signs of deterioration. Cracks may become more apparent if the hose is squeezed **(see illustration)**. Regardless of condition, it's a good idea to replace hoses with new ones every two years.
5   Make sure that all hose connections are tight. A leak in the cooling system will usually show up as white or rust colored deposits on the areas adjoining the leak. If wire-type clamps are used at the ends of the hoses, it may be a good idea to replace them with more secure screw-type clamps.
6   Use compressed air or a soft brush to remove bugs, leaves, etc. from the front of the radiator or air conditioning condenser. Be careful not to damage the delicate cooling fins or cut yourself on them.
7   Every other inspection, or at the first indication of cooling system problems, have the cap and system pressure tested. If you don't have a pressure tester, most gas stations and repair shops will do this for a minimal charge.

16.6 You will find an inspection hole like this in each caliper - placing a steel ruler across the hole should enable you to determine the thickness of remaining pad material for both inner and outer pads

16.15 If the lining is bonded to the brake shoe, measure the lining thickness from the outer surface to the metal shoe, as shown here; if the lining is riveted to the shoe, measure from the lining outer surface to the rivet head

16.12 A quick check of the remaining drum brake shoe lining material can be made by removing the rubber plug in the backing plate and looking through the inspection hole

16.17 Carefully peel back the wheel cylinder boot and check for leaking fluid indicating that the cylinder must be replaced or rebuilt

pad material by the above method, or if you are at all concerned about the condition of the pads, remove the caliper(s), then remove the pads from the calipers for further inspection (refer to Chapter 9).

9   Once the pads are removed from the calipers, clean them with brake cleaner and re-measure them with a small steel pocket ruler or a vernier caliper.

10   Measure the disc thickness with a micrometer to make sure that it still has service life remaining. If any disc is thinner than the specified minimum thickness, replace it (refer to Chapter 9). Even if the disc has service life remaining, check its condition. Look for scoring, gouging and burned spots. If these conditions exist, remove the disc and have it resurfaced (see Chapter 9).

11   Before installing the wheels, check all brake lines and hoses for damage, wear, deformation, cracks, corrosion, leakage, bends and twists, particularly in the vicinity of the rubber hoses at the calipers. Check the clamps for tightness and the connections for leakage. Make sure that all hoses and lines are clear of sharp edges, moving parts and the exhaust system. If any of the above conditions are noted, repair, reroute or replace the lines and/or fittings as necessary (see Chapter 9).

Rear drum brakes

Refer to illustrations 16.12, 16.15 and 16.17

12   To check the brake shoe lining thickness without removing the brake drums, remove the rubber plug from the backing plate and use a flashlight to inspect the linings **(see illustration)**. For a more thorough brake inspection, follow the procedure below.

13   Refer to Chapter 9 and remove the rear brake drums.

14   **Warning:** *Brake dust produced by lining wear and deposited on brake components contains asbestos, which is hazardous to your health. DO NOT blow it out with compressed air and DO NOT inhale it! DO NOT use gasoline or solvents to remove the dust. Brake system cleaner should be used to flush the dust into a drain pan. After the brake components are wiped clean with a damp rag,, dispose of the contaminated rag(s) and solvent in a covered and labeled container. Try to use non-asbestos replacement parts whenever possible.*

15   Note the thickness of the lining material on the rear brake shoes **(see illustration)** and look for signs of contamination by brake fluid and grease. If the lining material is within 1/16-inch of the recessed rivets or metal shoes, replace the brake shoes with new ones. The shoes should also be replaced if they are cracked, glazed (shiny lining surfaces) or contaminated with brake fluid or grease. See Chapter 9 for the replacement procedure.

16   Check the shoe return and hold-down springs and the adjusting mechanism to make sure they're installed correctly and in good condition. Deteriorated or distorted springs, if not replaced, could allow the linings to drag and wear prematurely.

17   Check the wheel cylinders for leakage by carefully peeling back the rubber boots **(see illustration)**. If brake fluid is noted behind the boots, the wheel cylinders must be replaced (see Chapter 9).

18   Check the drums for cracks, score marks, deep scratches and hard spots, which will appear as small discolored areas. If imperfections cannot be removed with emery cloth, the drums must be resurfaced by an automotive machine shop (see Chapter 9 for more detailed information).

19   Refer to Chapter 9 and install the brake drums.

20   Install the wheels and lug nuts.

21   Remove the jackstands and lower the vehicle.

22   Tighten the wheel lug nuts to the torque listed in this Chapter's Specifications.

1

17.2a Detach the clips and separate the cover from the air cleaner housing

17.2b Hold the cover up out of the way and lift the element out

18.2 Use a small screwdriver to carefully pry out the old gasket - take car not to damage the cap

Brake booster check

23   Sit in the driver's seat and perform the following sequence of tests.

24   With the engine stopped, depress the brake pedal several times-the travel distance should not change.

25   With the brake fully depressed, start the engine - the pedal should move down a little when the engine starts.

26   Depress the brake, stop the engine and hold the pedal in for about 30 seconds - the pedal should neither sink nor rise.

27   Restart the engine, run it for about a minute and turn it off. Then firmly depress the brake several times - the pedal travel should decrease with each application.

28   If your brakes do not operate as described above when the preceding tests are performed, the brake booster is either in need of repair or has failed. Refer to Chapter 9 for the removal procedure.

Parking brake

29   Slowly pull up on the parking brake and count the number of clicks you hear until the handle is up as far as it will go. The adjustment is correct if you hear the specified number of clicks. If you hear more or fewer clicks, it's time to adjust the parking brake (refer to Chapter 9).

30   An alternative method of checking the parking brake is to park the vehicle on a steep hill with the parking brake set and the transaxle in Neutral. If the parking brake cannot prevent the vehicle from rolling, it is in need of adjustment (see Chapter 9).

17   Air filter replacement
       (every 15,000 miles or 12 months)

Refer to illustrations 17.2a and 17.2b

1   The air filter is located inside a housing at the left (driver's) side of the engine compartment.

2   To remove the air filter, release the four spring clips that keep the two halves of the air cleaner housing together, then lift the cover up and remove the air filter element **(see illustrations)**.

3   Inspect the outer surface of the filter element. If it is dirty, replace it. If it is only moderately dusty, it can be reused by blowing it clean from the back to the front surface with compressed air. Because it is a pleated paper type filter, it cannot be washed or oiled. If it cannot be cleaned satisfactorily with compressed air, discard and replace it. While the cover is off, be careful not to drop anything down into the housing. **Caution:** *Never drive the vehicle with the air cleaner removed. Excessive engine wear could result and backfiring could even cause a fire under the hood.*

4   Wipe out the inside of the air cleaner housing.

5   Place the new filter into the air cleaner housing, making sure it seats properly.

6   Installation of the cover is the reverse of removal.

18.5 Inspect the filler hose for cracks and make sure the clamps are tight

18   Fuel system check (every 15,000 miles or 12 months)

Refer to illustrations 18.2 and 18.5

Warning: *Certain precautions should be observed when inspecting or servicing the fuel system components. Work in a well ventilated area and do not allow open flames (cigarettes, appliance pilot lights, etc.) near the work area. Mop up spills immediately and do not store fuel soaked rags where they could ignite. It is a good idea to keep a dry chemical (Class B) fire extinguisher near the work area any time the fuel system is being serviced.*

1   If you smell gasoline while driving or after the vehicle has been sitting in the sun, inspect the fuel system immediately.

2   Remove the gas filler cap and inspect if for damage and corrosion. The gasket should have an unbroken sealing imprint. If the gasket is damaged or corroded, remove it and install a new one **(see illustration)**.

3   Inspect the fuel feed and return lines for cracks. Make sure that the threaded flare-nut type connectors which secure the metal fuel lines to the fuel injection system and the banjo bolts which secure the banjo fittings to the in-line fuel filter are tight.

4   Since some components of the fuel system - the fuel tank and part of the fuel feed and return lines, for example - are underneath the vehicle, they can be inspected more easily with the vehicle raised on a hoist. If that's not possible, raise the vehicle and support it securely on jackstands.

5   With the vehicle raised and safely supported, inspect the gas tank

19.2 Differential filler and drain plug details (three-speed automatic transaxle)

and filler neck for punctures, cracks and other damage. The connection between the filler neck and the tank is particularly critical. Sometimes a rubber filler neck will leak because of loose clamps or deteriorated rubber **(see illustration)**. These are problems a home mechanic can usually rectify. **Warning:** *Do not, under any circumstances, try to repair a fuel tank (except rubber components). A welding torch or any open flame can easily cause fuel vapors inside the tank to explode.*

6   Carefully check all rubber hoses and metal lines leading away from the fuel tank. Check for loose connections, deteriorated hoses, crimped lines and other damage. Carefully inspect the lines from the tank to the fuel injection system. Repair or replace damaged sections as necessary (see Chapter 4).

19   Automatic transaxle differential lubricant level check (three-speed only) (15,000 miles or 12 months)

Refer to illustration 19.2

1   The three-speed automatic transaxle differential has a separate lubricant supply with a check/fill plug which must be removed to check the level. If the vehicle is raised to gain access to the plug, be sure to support it safely on jackstands - DO NOT crawl under the vehicle when it's supported only by the jack.

2   Remove the filler plug from the front of the differential **(see illustration)**.

3   Use your little finger as a dipstick to make sure the lubricant level is even with the bottom of the plug hole. If not, use a syringe or a gear oil pump to add the recommended lubricant (see this Chapter's Specifications) until it just starts to run out of the opening.

4   Install the plug and tighten it securely.

20   Manual transaxle lubricant level check (every 15,000 miles or 12 months)

Refer to illustration 20.1

1   The manual transaxle does not have a dipstick. To check the fluid level, raise the vehicle and support it securely on jackstands. On the lower front side of the transaxle housing, you will see a plug **(see illustration)**. Remove It. If the lubricant level is correct, it should be up to

the lower edge of the hole.

2   If the transaxle needs more lubricant (if the level is not up to the hole), use a syringe or a gear oil pump to add more. Stop filling the transaxle when the lubricant begins to run out the hole.

3   Install the plug and tighten it securely. Drive the vehicle a short distance, then check for leaks.

21   Steering and suspension check (every 15,000 miles or 12 months)

Refer to illustrations 21.1, 21.7 and 21.8
Note: *For detailed illustrations of the steering and suspension components, refer to Chapter 10.*

With the wheels on the ground

1   With the vehicle stopped and the front wheels pointed straight ahead, rock the steering wheel gently back and forth. If freeplay **(see illustration)** is excessive , a front wheel bearing, main shaft yoke, intermediate shaft yoke, lower arm balljoint or steering system joint is worn or the steering gear is out of adjustment or broken. Refer to Chapter 10 for the appropriate repair procedure.

2   Other symptoms, such as excessive vehicle body movement over rough roads, swaying (leaning) around corners and binding as the steering wheel is turned, may indicate faulty steering and/or suspension components.

3   Check the shock absorbers by pushing down and releasing the vehicle several times at each corner. If the vehicle does not come back to a level position within one or two bounces, the shocks/struts are worn and must be replaced. When bouncing the vehicle up and down, listen for squeaks and noises from the suspension components. Additional Information on suspension components can be found in Chapter 10.

Under the vehicle

4   Raise the vehicle with a floor jack and support it securely on jackstands. See *Jacking and towing* at the front of this book for the proper jacking points.

5   Check the tires for irregular wear patterns and proper inflation. See Section 5 in this Chapter for information regarding tire wear and Chapter 10 for the wheel bearing replacement procedures.

6   Inspect the universal joint between the steering shaft and the steering gear housing. Check the steering gear housing for grease leakage or oozing. Make sure that the dust seals and boots are not damaged and that the boot clamps are not loose. Check the steering linkage for looseness or damage. Check the tie-rod ends for excessive play. Look for loose bolts, broken or disconnected parts and deteriorated rubber bushings on all suspension and steering components. While an assistant turns the steering wheel from side to side, check the steering components for free movement, chafing and binding. If the steering components do not seem to be reacting with the movement of the steering wheel, try to determine where the slack is located.

20.1 Use your finger as a dipstick to check the manual transaxle lubricant level

LOOSEN

Freeplay

21.1 Steering wheel freeplay is the amount of travel between an initial steering input and the point at which the front wheels begin to turn (indicated by a slight resistance)

21.7 To check a balljoint for wear, raise the vehicle and support it on jackstands, place a 7-inch thick block of wood under the tire, block the wheel with chocks and lower the jack until there is about half a load on the coil spring - then move the lower arm up and down with a prybar to make sure there is no play in the balljoint (if there is, replace it)

7   Check the balljoints for wear by placing a 7-inch thick wooden block under each tire. Lower the jack until there is about half a load on the coil spring. Make sure that the front wheels are in a straight forward position and block the wheel with chocks. Move each lower arm up and down with a pry bar **(see illustration)** to ensure that its balljoint has no play. If any balljoint does have play, replace it. See Chapter 10 for the front balljoint replacement procedure.

8   Inspect the balljoint boots for damage and leaking grease **(see illustration)**. Replace the balljoints with new ones if they are damaged (see Chapter 10).

---

22   Driveaxle boot check (every 15,000 miles or 12 months)

Refer to illustration 22.2

1   The driveaxle boots are very important because they prevent dirt, water and foreign material from entering and damaging the constant velocity (CV) joints. Oil and grease can cause the boot material to deteriorate prematurely, so it's a good idea to wash the boots with soap and water. Because it constantly pivots back and forth following the steering action of the front hub, the outer CV boot wears out sooner and should be inspected regularly.

2   Inspect the boots for tears and cracks as well as loose clamps **(see illustration)**. If there is any evidence of cracks or leaking lubricant, they must be replaced as described in Chapter 8.

21.8 Push on the balljoint boot to check for damage

---

23   Fuel filter replacement (every 30,000 miles or 24 months)

Refer to illustrations 23.4a and 23.4b

1   Disconnect the negative battery cable.

2   The canister filter is mounted in a bracket on the firewall near the brake master cylinder.

3   Remove any components that would interfere with access to the top of the filter.

4   Using a backup wrench to steady the filter, remove the threaded banjo bolt at the top and loosen the fitting at the bottom of the fuel filter (use a flare-nut wrench if possible) **(see illustrations).**

5   Remove both bracket bolts from the firewall and remove the old filter and the filter support bracket assembly.

6   Note that the inlet and outlet pipes are clearly labeled on their respective ends of the filter and that the flanged end of the filter faces down. Make sure the new filter is installed so that it's facing the proper direction as noted above. When correctly installed, the filter should be installed so that the outlet pipe faces up and the inlet pipe faces down.

7   Using the new crush washers provided by the filter manufacturer, install the inlet and outlet fittings and tighten them securely.

8   The remainder of installation is the reverse of the removal procedure.

---

24   Spark plug check and replacement (every 30,000 miles or 24 months)

Refer to illustrations 24.1, 24.4a, 24.4b, 24.6, 24.8, 24.10a and 24.10b

1   Spark plug replacement requires a spark plug socket which fits

22.2 Flex the driveaxle boots by hand to check for cracks and/or leaking grease

23.4a Using a backup wrench, remove the banjo bolt at the top and . . .

23.4b . . . loosen the fitting at the bottom of the filter

24.1 Tools required for changing spark plugs

1   **Spark plug socket** - *This will have special padding inside to protect the spark plug porcelain insulator*
2   **Torque wrench** - *Although not mandatory, use of this tool is the best way to ensure that the plugs are tightened properly*
3   **Ratchet** - *Standard hand tool to fit the plug socket*
4   **Extension** - *Depending on model and accessories, you may need special extensions and universal joints to reach one or more of the plugs*
5   **Spark plug gap gauge** - *This gauge for checking the gap comes in a variety of styles. Make sure the gap for your engine is included*

24.4a Spark plug manufacturers recommend using a wire-type gauge when checking the gap - if the wire does not slide between the electrodes with a slight drag, adjustment is required

onto a ratchet wrench. This socket is lined with a rubber grommet to protect the porcelain insulator of the spark plug and to hold the plug while you insert it into the spark plug hole. You will also need a wire-type feeler gauge to check and adjust the spark plug gap and a torque wrench to tighten the new plugs to the specified torque **(see illustration)**.

2   If you are replacing the plugs, purchase the new plugs, adjust them to the proper gap and then replace each plug one at a time. **Note:** *When buying new spark plugs, it's essential that you obtain the correct plugs for your specific vehicle. This information can be found in the Specifications Section at the beginning of this Chapter, on the Vehicle Emissions Control Information (VECI) label located on the underside of the hood or in the owner's manual. If these sources specify different plugs, purchase the spark plug type specified on the VECI label because that information is provided specifically for your engine.*

3   Inspect each of the new plugs for defects. If there are any signs of cracks in the porcelain insulator of a plug, don't use it.

4   Check the electrode gaps of the new plugs. Check the gap by inserting the wire gauge of the proper thickness between the electrodes at the tip of the plug **(see illustration)**. The gap between the electrodes should be identical to that listed in this Chapter's Specifications or on the VECI label. If the gap is incorrect, use the notched adjuster on the feeler gauge body to bend the curved side electrode slightly **(see illustration)**.

5   If the side electrode is not exactly over the center electrode, use the notched adjuster to align them. **Caution:** *If the gap of a new plug must be adjusted, bend only the base of the ground electrode – do not touch the tip.*

Removal

6   To prevent the possibility of mixing up spark plug wires, work on one spark plug at a time. Remove the wire and boot from one spark plug. Grasp the boot - not the cable - as shown, give it a half twisting motion and pull straight up **(see illustration)**.

7   If compressed air is available, blow any dirt or foreign material away from the spark plug area before proceeding (a common bicycle pump will also work).

8   Remove the spark plug **(see illustration)**.

9   Whether you are replacing the plugs at this time or intend to reuse the old plugs, compare each old spark plug with the chart on the inside back cover of this manual to determine the overall running condition of the engine.

24.4b To change the gap, bend the side electrode only, as indicated by the arrows, and be very careful not to crack or chip the porcelain insulator surrounding the center electrode

24.6 When removing the spark plug wires, pull only on the boot and use a twisting/pulling motion

24.8 Use a spark plug socket with a long extension to unscrew the spark plug

24.10a Apply a thin coat of anti-seize compound to the spark plug threads

24.10b A length of 3/8-inch ID rubber hose will save time and prevent damaged threads when installing the spark plugs

25.8 Use a small screwdriver to lift the lock claw up when detaching the spark plug boot from the distributor

25.11a Remove the two screws (arrows) and detach the distributor cap

25.11b Inspect the distributor cap for carbon tracks, charred or eroded terminals and other damage (if in doubt about its condition, install a new one)

25.12 Check the rotor for damage, wear and corrosion (if in doubt about its condition, buy a new one)

Installation

10   Prior to installation, it's a good idea to coat the spark plug threads with anti-seize compound **(see illustration)**. Also, it's often difficult to insert spark plugs into their holes without cross-threading them. To avoid this possibility, fit a short piece of 3/8-inch ID rubber hose over the end of the spark plug **(see illustration)**. The flexible hose acts as a universal joint to help align the plug with the plug hole. Should the plug begin to cross-thread, the hose will slip on the spark plug, preventing thread damage. Tighten the plug to the torque listed in this Chapter's Specifications.

11   Attach the plug wire to the new spark plug, again using a twisting motion on the boot until it is firmly seated on the end of the spark plug.

12   Follow the above procedure for the remaining spark plugs, replacing them one at a time to prevent mixing up the spark plug wires.

25 Spark plug wire, distributor cap and rotor check and replacement (every 30,000 miles or 24 months)

Refer to illustrations 25.8, 25.11a, 25.11b, 25.12 and 25.13

1   The spark plug wires should be checked whenever new spark plugs are installed.

2   Begin this procedure by making a visual check of the spark plug wires while the engine is running. In a darkened garage (make sure there is ventilation) start the engine and observe each plug wire. Be careful not to come into contact with any moving engine parts. If there is a break in the wire, you will see arcing or a small spark at the damaged area. If arcing is noticed, make a note to obtain new wires, then allow the engine to cool and check the distributor cap and rotor.

3   The spark plug wires should be inspected one at a time to prevent mixing up the order, which is essential for proper engine operation. Each original plug wire should be numbered to help identify its location. If the number is illegible, a piece of tape can be marked with the correct number and wrapped around the plug wire.

4   Disconnect the plug wire from the spark plug. A removal tool can be used for this purpose or you can grasp the rubber boot, twist the boot half a turn and pull the boot free. Do not pull on the wire itself.

5   Check inside the boot for corrosion, which will look like a white crusty powder.

6   Push the wire and boot back onto the end of the spark plug. It should fit tightly onto the end of the plug. If it doesn't, remove the wire and use pliers to carefully crimp the metal connector inside the wire boot until the fit is snug.

7   Using a clean rag, wipe the entire length of the wire to remove built-up dirt and grease. Once the wire is clean, check for burns, cracks and other damage. Do not bend the wire sharply, because the conductor might break.

8   Disconnect the wire from the distributor cap, using a small screwdriver to lift up on the lock claw **(see illustration)**. Check for corrosion and a tight fit. Replace the wire in the distributor cap.

9   Inspect the remaining spark plug wires, making sure that each one is securely fastened at the distributor and spark plug when the check is complete.

10   If new spark plug wires are required, purchase a set for your specific engine model. Pre-cut wire sets with the boots already installed are available. Remove and replace the wires one at a time to avoid mix-ups in the firing order.

25.13 Measure the resistance value of the distributor cap and the spark plug wires - if it exceeds the specified maximum value, replace either the cap, or the wires, or both

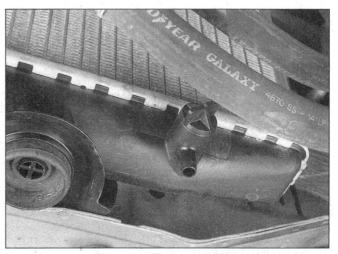

26.4 On most models you will have to remove a cover for access to the radiator drain fitting located at the bottom of the radiator - before opening the valve, push a short section of 3/8-inch ID hose onto the plastic fitting to prevent the coolant from splashing

1

11   Detach the distributor cap by removing the two retaining screws **(see illustration)**. Look inside it for cracks, carbon tracks and worn, burned or loose contacts **(see illustration)**.
12   Pull the rotor off the distributor shaft and examine it for cracks and carbon tracks **(see illustration)**. Replace the cap and rotor if any damage or defects are noted.
13   It is common practice to install a new cap and rotor whenever new spark plug wires are installed, but if you wish to continue using the old cap, check the resistance between the spark plug wires and the cap first **(see illustration)**. If the indicated resistance is more than the maximum value listed in this Chapter's Specifications, replace the cap and/or wires.
14   When installing a new cap, remove the wires from the old cap one at a time and attach them to the new cap in the exact same location – do not simultaneously remove all the wires from the old cap or firing order mix-ups may occur.

---

26   Cooling system servicing (draining, flushing and refilling) (every 30,000 miles or 24 months)

Warning: *Do not allow engine coolant (antifreeze) to come in contact with your skin or painted surfaces of the vehicle. Rinse off spills immediately with plenty of water. Antifreeze is highly toxic if ingested. Never leave antifreeze laying around in an open container or in puddles on the floor; children and pets are attracted by it's sweet smell and may drink it. Check with local authorities about disposing of used antifreeze. Many communities have collection centers which will see that antifreeze is disposed of safely.*

1   Periodically, the cooling system should be drained, flushed and refilled to replenish the antifreeze mixture and prevent formation of rust and corrosion, which can impair the performance of the cooling system and cause engine damage. When the cooling system is serviced, all hoses and the radiator cap should be checked and replaced if necessary.

Draining

Refer to illustrations 26.4 and 26.5

2   Apply the parking brake and block the wheels. If the vehicle has just been driven, wait several hours to allow the engine to cool down before beginning this procedure.
3   Once the engine is completely cool, remove the radiator cap.
4   Move a large container under the radiator drain to catch the coolant. Attach a 3/8-inch inner diameter hose to the drain fitting to direct the coolant into the container (some models are already

26.5 After draining the radiator, be sure to fully drain the cooling system by removing the block drain plug (arrow) located on the side of the engine block

equipped with a hose), then open the drain fitting (a pair of pliers may be required to turn it) **(see illustration)**.
5   After the coolant stops flowing out of the radiator, move the container under the engine block drain plug **(see illustration)**. Loosen the plug and allow the coolant in the block to drain.
6   While the coolant is draining, check the condition of the radiator hoses, heater hoses and clamps (refer to Section 13 if necessary).
7   Replace any damaged clamps or hoses (see Chapter 3).

Flushing

8   Once the system is completely drained, flush the radiator with fresh water from a garden hose until water runs clear at the drain. The flushing action of the water will remove sediments from the radiator but will not remove rust and scale from the engine and cooling tube surfaces.
9   These deposits can be removed by the chemical action of a cleaner. Follow the procedure outlined in the manufacturer's instructions. If the radiator is severely corroded, damaged or leaking, it should be removed (see Chapter 3) and taken to a radiator repair shop.
10   Remove the overflow hose from the coolant recovery reservoir. Drain the reservoir and flush it with clean water, then reconnect the hose.

27.2 Check the evaporative emissions control canister for damage and the hose connections for cracks and damage (arrows)

28.4 Be sure to check each exhaust system rubber hanger (arrow) for damage

29.7 On three-speed models, you'll need an Allen wrench to remove the transaxle drain plug

Refilling

11   Close and tighten the radiator drain. Install and tighten the block drain plug.

12   Place the heater temperature control in the maximum heat position.

13   Slowly add new coolant (a 50/50 mixture of water and antifreeze) to the radiator until it's full. Add coolant to the reservoir up to the lower mark.

14   Leave the radiator cap off and run the engine in a well-ventilated area until the thermostat opens (coolant will begin flowing through the radiator and the upper radiator hose will become hot).

15   Turn the engine off and let it cool. Add more coolant mixture to bring the level back up to the lip on the radiator filler neck.

16   Squeeze the upper radiator hose to expel air, then add more coolant mixture if necessary. Replace the radiator cap.

17   Start the engine, allow it to reach normal operating temperature and check for leaks.

27   Evaporative emissions control system check (every 30,000 miles or 24 months)

Refer to illustration 27.2

1   The function of the evaporative emissions control system is to draw fuel vapors from the gas tank and fuel system, store them in a charcoal canister and then burn them during normal engine operation.

2   The most common symptom of a fault in the evaporative emissions system is a strong fuel odor in the engine compartment. If a fuel odor is detected, inspect the charcoal canister, located at the front of the engine compartment. Check the canister and all hoses for damage and deterioration **(see illustration)**.

3   The evaporative emissions control system is explained in more detail in Chapter 6.

28   Exhaust system check (every 30,000 miles or 24 months)

Refer to illustration 28.4

1   With the engine cold (at least three hours after the vehicle has been driven), check the complete exhaust system from its starting point at the engine to the end of the tailpipe. This should be done on a hoist where unrestricted access is available.

2   Check the pipes and connections for evidence of leaks, severe corrosion or damage. Make sure that all brackets and hangers are in good condition and tight.

3   At the same time, inspect the underside of the body for holes, corrosion, open seams, etc. which may allow exhaust gases to enter

the passenger compartment. Seal all body openings with silicone or body putty.

4   Rattles and other noises can often be traced to the exhaust system, especially the mounts and hangers. Try to move the pipes, muffler and catalytic converter. If the components can come in contact with the body or suspension parts, secure the exhaust system with new mounts **(see illustration)**.

5   Check the running condition of the engine by inspecting inside the end of the tailpipe. The exhaust deposits here are an indication of engine state-of-tune. If the pipe is black and sooty or coated with white deposits, the engine is in need of a tune-up, including a thorough fuel system inspection.

29   Automatic transaxle/differential fluid and filter change (every 30,000 miles or 24 months)

Refer to illustrations 29.7, 29.8a, 29.8b, 29.9, 29.11, 29.13a and 29.13b

1   At the specified time intervals, the automatic transaxle and differential fluid should be drained and replaced.

2   Before beginning work, purchase the specified transmission fluid (see *Recommended fluids and lubricants* at the front of this chapter).

3   Other tools necessary for this job include jackstands to support the vehicle in a raised position, wrenches, drain pan capable of holding at least four quarts, newspapers and clean rags.

4   The fluid should be drained immediately after the vehicle has been driven. Hot fluid is more effective than cold fluid at removing built up sediment. **Warning:** *Fluid temperature can exceed 350-degrees F in a hot transaxle. Wear protective gloves.*

5   After the vehicle has been driven to warm up the fluid, raise it and place it on jackstands for access to the transaxle and differential drain plugs.

6   Move the necessary equipment under the vehicle, being careful not to touch any of the hot exhaust components.

7   Place the drain pan under the drain plug in the transaxle pan and remove the drain plug with the Allen wrench **(see illustration)**. Be sure the drain pan is in position, as fluid will come out with some force. Once the fluid is drained, reinstall the drain plug securely.

8   Remove the front transaxle pan bolts, then loosen the rear bolts and carefully pry the pan loose with a screwdriver and allow the remaining fluid to drain **(see illustrations)**. Once the fluid had drained, remove the bolts and lower the pan.

9   Remove the filter retaining bolts, disconnect the clip (some models) and lower the filter from the transaxle **(see illustration)**. Be careful when lowering the filter as it contains residual fluid.

10   Place the new filter in position, connect the clip (if equipped) and install the bolts. Tighten the bolts to the torque listed in the Specifications Section at the beginning of this Chapter.

29.8a After loosening the front bolts, remove the rear transaxle pan bolts and . . .

29.8b . . . allow the remaining fluid to drain out

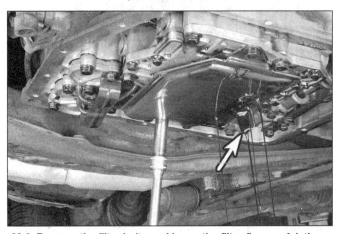

29.9 Remove the filter bolts and lower the filter (be careful, there will be some residual fluid) - note that here one of the pan magnets is stuck to the filter (arrow); be sure to clean any magnets and return them to the pan

13   Locate the differential drain plug. Place the drain pan underneath the plug, remove it with the Allen wrench and drain the fluid **(see illustrations)**. When the differential fluid has drained, reinstall the plug securely.
14   Referring to Section 19, add new fluid to the differential until it begins to run out of the filler hole (see *Recommended lubricants and fluids* at the beginning of this Chapter for the specified fluid type and capacity). **Caution:** *Do not overfill. The automatic transaxle and the differential are separate units.*
15   Lower the vehicle.
16   With the engine off, add new fluid to the transaxle through the dipstick tube (see *Recommended fluids and lubricants* for the recommended fluid type and capacity). Use a funnel to prevent spills. It is best to add a little fluid at a time, continually checking the level with the dipstick (see Section 7). Allow the fluid time to drain into the pan.
17   Start the engine and shift the selector into all positions from P through L, then shift into P and apply the parking brake.
18   With the engine idling, check the fluid level. Add fluid up to the Cool level on the dipstick.

30   Manual transaxle lubricant change (every 30,000 miles or 24 months)

1   Remove the drain plug(s) and drain the fluid.
2   Reinstall the drain plug(s) securely.
3   Add new fluid until it is even with the lower edge of the filler hole (Section 20). See *Recommended lubricants and fluids* for the specified lubricant type.

11   Carefully clean the gasket surfaces of the fluid pan, removing all traces of old gasket material. Noting their location, remove the magnets, wash the pan in clean solvent and dry it with compressed air. Be sure to clean and reinstall any magnets **(see illustration)**.
12   Install a new gasket, place the fluid pan in position and install the bolts in their original positions. Tighten the bolts to the torque listed in this Chapter's Specifications.

29.11 Noting their locations, remove any magnets and wash them and the pan in solvent before reinstalling them

29.13a Use an Allen wrench to remove the differential drain plug (three-speed models)

29.13b Be careful when removing the plug because the fluid usually comes out with some force

31.2 Grasp the hose securely and pull the PCV valve
out of the cover

31   Positive Crankcase Ventilation (PCV) valve and hose check and replacement (every 30,000 miles or 24 months)

Refer to illustrations 31.2 and 31.4

1   The PCV valve and hose is located in the valve cover.
2   Pull the PCV valve from the cover **(see illustration)**.
3   With the engine idling at normal operating temperature, place your finger over the end of the valve. If there's no vacuum at the valve, check for a plugged hose or valve. Replace any plugged or deterio-rated hoses.
4   Turn off the engine. Remove the PCV valve from the hose. Con-nect a clean piece of hose and blow through the valve from the valve cover (cylinder head) end. If air will not pass through the valve in this direction, replace it with a new one **(see illustration)**.
5   When purchasing a replacement PCV valve, make sure it's for your particular vehicle and engine size. Compare the old valve with the new one to make sure they're the same.

32   Valve clearance check and adjustment (every 60,000 miles or 48 months)

Refer to illustrations 32.6a, 32.6b, 32.7, 32.9a, 32.9b, 32.9c, 32.10 and 32.11

Note: *The following procedure requires the use of a special valve lifter tool. It is impossible to perform this task without it.*
1   Disconnect the negative cable from the battery. **Warning:** *These*

32.6b Check the clearance for each valve with a feeler gauge of
the specified thickness - if the clearance is correct, you should
feel a slight drag on the gauge as you pull it out

31.4 To check the PVC valve, first attach a clean section of hose to the cylinder head side of the valve and blow through it - air should pass through easily - then blow through the intake manifold side of the valve and verify that air passes through with difficulty

Cylinder Head Side

Clean Hose

32.6a When the no. 1 piston is at TDC on the compression stroke, the valve clearance for the no. 1 and no. 3 cylinder exhaust valves and the no. 1 and no. 2 cylinder intake valves can be measured

models are equipped with airbags. The airbag is armed and can deploy (inflate) anytime the battery is connected. To prevent accidental deploy-ment (and possible injury), turn the ignition key to LOCK and disconnect the negative battery cable whenever working near airbag components. After the battery is disconnected, wait at least two minutes before begin-ning work (the system has a back-up capacitor that must fully discharge). For more information on the airbag system see Chapter 12.
Caution: *If the stereo in your vehicle is equipped with an anti-theft sys-tem, make sure you have the correct activation code before discon-necting the battery.*
2   Disconnect the spark plug wires (Section 25) and remove any other components that will interfere with valve cover removal.
3   Blow out the recessed area around the spark plug openings with compressed air, if available, to remove any debris that might fall into the cylinders, then remove the spark plugs (see Section 24).
4   Remove the valve cover (refer to Chapter 2).
5   Refer to Chapter 2 and position the number 1 piston at TDC on the compression stroke.
6   Measure the clearances of the indicated valves with feeler gauges **(see illustrations)**. Record the measurements which are out of specifi-cation. They will be used later to determine the required replacement shims.
7   Turn the crankshaft one complete revolution and realign the tim-ing marks. Measure the remaining valves **(see illustration)**.

32.7 When the no. 4 piston is at TDC on the compression stroke, the valve clearance for the no. 2 and no. 4 exhaust valves and the no. 3 and no. 4 intake valves can be measured

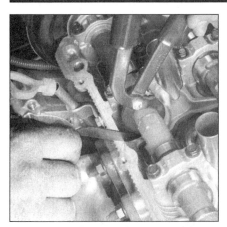

32.9a Install the valve lifter tool as shown and squeeze the handles together to depress the valve lifter, then hold the lifter down with the smaller tool so the shim can be removed

32.9b Keep pressure on the lifter with the smaller tool and remove the shim with a small screwdriver . . .

32.9c . . . a pair of tweezers or a magnet as shown here

32.10 Measure the shim thickness with a micrometer

New shim thickness		mm (in.)	
Shim No.	Thickness	Shim No.	Thickness
1	2.55 (0.1004)	9	2.95 (0.1161)
2	2.60 (0.1024)	10	3.00 (0.1181)
3	2.65 (0.1043)	11	3.05 (0.1201)
4	2.70 (0.1063)	12	3.10 (0.1220)
5	2.75 (0.1083)	13	3.15 (0.1240)
6	2.80 (0.1102)	14	3.20 (0.1260)
7	2.85 (0.1122)	15	3.25 (0.1280)
8	2.90 (0.1142)	16	3.30 (0.1299)

32.11 Valve adjusting shim thickness chart

8   After all the valves have been measured, turn the crankshaft pulley until the camshaft lobe above the first valve which you intend to adjust is pointing upward, away from the shim.

9   Position the notch in the valve lifter toward the spark plug. Then depress the valve lifter with the special valve lifter tools **(see illustration)**. Place the special valve lifter tool in position as shown, with the longer jaw of the tool gripping the lower edge of the cast lifter boss and the upper, shorter jaw gripping the upper edge of the lifter itself. Depress the valve lifter by squeezing the handles of the valve lifter tool together, then hold the lifter down with the smaller tool and remove the larger one. Remove the adjusting shim with a small screwdriver or a pair of tweezers **(see illustrations)**. Note that the wire hook on the end of some valve lifter tool handles can be used to clamp both handles together to keep the lifter depressed while the shim is removed.

10   Measure the thickness of the shim with a micrometer **(see illustration)**. To calculate the correct thickness of a replacement shim that will place the valve clearance within the specified value, use the following formula:

$$N = T + (A - V)$$

T = thickness of the old shim
A = valve clearance measured
N = thickness of the new shim
V = desired valve clearance (see this Chapters Specifications)

11   Select a shim with a thickness as close as possible to the valve clearance calculated. Shims, which are available in 17 sizes in increments of 0.0020-inch (0.050 mm), range in size from 0.0984-inch (2.500 mm) to 0.1299-inch (3.300 mm) **(see illustration)**. **Note:** *Through careful analysis of the shim sizes needed to bring the out-of-specification valve clearance within specification, it is often possible to simply move a shim that has to come out anyway to another valve lifter requiring a shim of that particular size, thereby reducing the number of new shims that must be purchased.*

12   Place the special valve lifter tool in position as shown in illustration 32.9a, with the longer jaw of the tool gripping the lower edge of the cast lifter boss and the upper, shorter jaw gripping the upper edge of the lifter itself, press down the valve lifter by squeezing the handles of the valve lifter tool together and install the new adjusting shim (note that the wire hook on the end of one valve lifter tool handle can be used to clamp the handles together to keep the lifter depressed while the shim is inserted. Measure the clearance with a feeler gauge to make sure that your calculations are correct.

13   Repeat this procedure until all the valves which are out of clearance have been corrected.

14   Installation of the spark plugs, valve cover, spark plug wires and boots, etc. is the reverse of removal.

Notes

Chapter 2 Part A Engines

Contents

2A

Specifications

General

Engine type	DOHC, inline four-cylinder, four valves per cylinder
Cylinder numbers (drivebelt end-to-transaxle end)	1-2-3-4
Firing order	1-3-4-2
Displacement	
4A-FE (VIN 6)	1.6L (97 cu. in.)
7A-FE (VIN 8)	1.8L (108 cu. in.)

920036 1-specs HAYNES

Cylinder location and distributor rotation

Timing belt

Tensioner spring free length	
1.6L	1.717 inches
1.8L	1.480 inches
Timing belt deflection	0.20 to 0.24 inch

Camshaft

Journal diameter	
Exhaust camshaft, no. 1 journal	0.9822 to 0.9829 inch
All others	0.9035 to 0.9041 inches
Bearing oil clearance	
Standard	0.0014 to 0.0028 inch
Service limit	0.0039 inch
Runout limit	0.0016 inch
Lobe height	
Intake camshaft	
1993 and 1994	
Standard	1.650 to 1.6539 inches
Service limit, minimum	1.6338 inches
1995	
Corolla	
1.6L	
Standard	1.650 to 1.6539 inches
Service limit, minimum	1.6338 inches
1.8L	
Standard	1.6421 to 1.6461 inches
Service limit, minimum	1.6260 inches

Camshaft (continued)

Prizm	
Standard	1.650 to 1.6539 inches
Service limit, minimum	1.6338 inches
1996 and later	
Standard	1.6421 to 1.6461 inches
Service limit, minimum	1.6260 inches
Exhaust camshaft	
Standard	1.6520 to 1.6560 inches
Service limit, minimum..	1.6358 inches
Camshaft thrust clearance (endplay)	
Intake camshaft	
Standard	0.0012 to 0.0033 inch
Service limit, maximum...	0.0043 inch
Exhaust camshaft	
Standard	0.0014 to 0.0035 inch
Service limit, maximum...	0.0043 inch
Camshaft gear spring free length	0.669 to 0.693 inch
Camshaft gear backlash	
Standard..	0.0008 to 0.0079 inch
Service limit	0.0188 inch
Valve lifter	
Diameter	1.2191 to 1.2195 inches
Bore diameter	1.2205 to 1.2215 inches
Lifter oil clearance	
Standard..	0.0009 to 0.0023 inch
Service limit	0.0028 inch

Oil pump

Rotor-to-body clearance	
Standard..	0.0031 to 0.0071 inch
Service limit	0.0079 inch
Rotor tip clearance	
Standard..	0.0010 to 0.0033 inch
Service limit	0.0079 inch
Rotor-to-cover clearance	
Standard..	0.0010 to 0.0033 inch
Service limit	0.0039 inch

Torque specifications

Ft-lbs (unless otherwise indicated)

Intake manifold bolts	
At EGR port	108 in-lbs
Others..	168 in-lbs
Intake manifold brace bolts	
At manifold	168 in-lbs
At block	29
Intake air chamber cover	168 in-lbs
Exhaust manifold nuts/bolts	25
Exhaust manifold brace bolts	46
Crankshaft pulley-to-crankshaft bolt..	87
Flywheel/driveplate bolts	
Flywheel (manual transaxle)	58
Driveplate (automatic transaxle)	47
Idler pulley bolts	27
Cylinder head bolts	
Step 1	22
Step 2	Tighten an additional 90-degrees
Step 3	Tighten an additional 90-degrees
Camshaft bearing cap bolts	108 in-lbs
Camshaft sprocket bolt	43
Oil pump bolts	16
Oil pick-up/strainer nuts/bolts	82 in-lbs
Oil pan bolts	
1.6L	43 in-lbs
1.8L	
Reinforcement section-to-block	144 in-lbs
Pan-to-reinforcement section	43 in-lbs
Center chassis brace bolts	45
Engine/transaxle stiffener bolts (1.6L)	17
Rear crankshaft oil seal retainer bolts	82 in-lbs

1   General information

This Part of Chapter 2 is devoted to in-vehicle repair procedures for the four-cylinder engines. All information concerning engine removal and installation and engine block and cylinder head overhaul can be found in Part B of this Chapter.

The following repair procedures are based on the assumption that the engine is installed in the vehicle. If the engine has been removed from the vehicle and mounted on a stand, many of the steps outlined in this Part of Chapter 2 will not apply.

The Specifications included in this Part of Chapter 2 apply only to the procedures contained in this Part. Part B of Chapter 2 contains the Specifications necessary for cylinder head and engine block rebuilding.

During the years covered by this manual, the four-cylinder engines in the Corolla are designated the 4A-FE (1.6L) and the 7A-FE (1.8L). The two engines are almost identical, and incorporate dual overhead camshafts (DOHC) and four valves per cylinder. In the Geo Prizm models, the 1.6L engine is designated VIN 6, and the 1.8L is the VIN 8.

2   Repair operations possible with the engine in the vehicle

Many major repair operations can be accomplished without removing the engine from the vehicle.

Clean the engine compartment and the exterior of the engine with some type of degreaser before any work is done. It will make the job easier and help keep dirt out of the internal areas of the engine.

Depending on the components involved, it may be helpful to remove the hood to improve access to the engine as repairs are performed (refer to Chapter 11 if necessary). Cover the fenders to prevent damage to the paint. Special pads are available, but an old bedspread or blanket will also work.

If vacuum, exhaust, oil or coolant leaks develop, indicating a need for gasket or seal replacement, the repairs can generally be made with the engine in the vehicle. The intake and exhaust manifold gaskets, oil pan gasket, crankshaft oil seals and cylinder head gasket are all accessible with the engine in place.

Exterior engine components, such as the intake and exhaust manifolds, the oil pan, the oil pump, the water pump, the starter motor, the alternator, the distributor and the fuel system components can be removed for repair with the engine in place, although when replacing the oil pump an engine hoist is required to support the engine from above, while the right engine mount is removed.

Since the cylinder head can be removed without pulling the engine, camshaft and valve component servicing can also be accomplished with the engine in the vehicle. Replacement of the timing belt and pulleys is also possible with the engine in the vehicle.

In extreme cases caused by a lack of necessary equipment, repair or replacement of piston rings, pistons, connecting rods and rod bearings is possible with the engine in the vehicle. However, this practice is not recommended because of the cleaning and preparation work that must be done to the components involved.

3   Top Dead Center (TDC) for number one piston - locating

Refer to illustration 3.8

Note: *The following procedure is based on the assumption that the distributor is correctly installed. If you are trying to locate TDC to install the distributor correctly, piston position must be determined by feeling for compression at the number one spark plug hole, then aligning the ignition timing marks as described in Step 8.*

1   Top Dead Center (TDC) is the highest point in the cylinder that each piston reaches as it travels up the cylinder bore. Each piston reaches TDC on the compression stroke and again on the exhaust stroke, but TDC generally refers to piston position on the compression stroke.

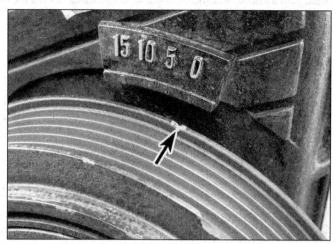

3.8 Align the crankshaft drivebelt pulley notch (arrow) with the 0 (zero) on the timing plate

2   Positioning the piston(s) at TDC is an essential part of many procedures such as camshaft and timing belt/pulley removal and distributor removal.

3   Before beginning this procedure, be sure to place the transmission in Neutral and apply the parking brake or block the rear wheels. Also, disable the ignition system by detaching the coil wire from the center terminal of the distributor cap and grounding it on the block with a jumper wire. Remove the spark plugs (see Chapter 1).

4   In order to bring any piston to TDC, the crankshaft must be turned using one of the methods outlined below. When looking at the timing belt end of the engine, normal crankshaft rotation is clockwise.

  a) *The preferred method is to turn the crankshaft with a socket and ratchet attached to the bolt threaded into the front of the crankshaft. Apply pressure on the bolt in a clockwise direction only. Never turn the bolt counterclockwise.*

  b) *A remote starter switch, which may save some time, can also be used. Follow the instructions included with the switch. Once the piston is close to TDC, use a socket and ratchet as described in the previous paragraph.*

  c) *If an assistant is available to turn the ignition switch to the Start position in short bursts, you can get the piston close to TDC without a remote starter switch. Make sure your assistant is out of the vehicle, away from the ignition switch, then use a socket and ratchet as described in Paragraph a) to complete the procedure.*

5   Note the position of the terminal for the number one spark plug wire on the distributor cap. If the terminal isn't marked, follow the plug wire from the number one cylinder spark plug to the cap.

6   Use a felt-tip pen or chalk to make a mark on the distributor body directly under the number one terminal.

7   Detach the cap from the distributor and set it aside (see Chapter 1 if necessary).

8   Turn the crankshaft until the notch in the crankshaft pulley is aligned with the 0 on the timing plate located at the front of the engine **(see illustration)**.

9   Look at the distributor rotor - it should be pointing directly at the mark you made on the distributor body. If so, you are at TDC for number 1.

10   If the rotor is 180-degrees off, the number one piston is at TDC on the exhaust stroke.

11   To get the piston to TDC on the compression stroke, turn the crankshaft one complete turn (360-degrees) clockwise. The rotor should now be pointing at the mark on the distributor. When the rotor is pointing at the number one spark plug wire terminal in the distributor cap and the ignition timing marks are aligned, the number one piston is at TDC on the compression stroke. **Note:** *If it's impossible to align the ignition timing marks when the rotor is pointing at the mark on the distributor body, the timing belt may have jumped the teeth on the pulleys or may have been installed incorrectly.*

2A

4.4 Remove the two harness-cover mounting bolts at the right end of the valve cover, allowing the wiring harness to be pulled up and clear of the valve cover

4.5 The valve cover is held in place by four nuts (arrows)

4.6 The valve cover gasket (left arrow) is a rubber O-ring-like seal - it can be reused if it hasn't hardened - make sure the spark plug tube seals (arrow) are in place before replacing the valve cover

4.7 Apply sealant to the five points indicated by the shaded areas before installing the valve cover

cover and gasket from the cylinder head **(see illustration)**. If the valve cover is stuck to the cylinder head, bump the end with a wood block and a hammer to jar it loose. If that doesn't work, try to slip a flexible putty knife between the cylinder head and valve cover to break the seal. **Caution:** *Don't pry at the valve cover-to-cylinder head joint or damage to the sealing surfaces may occur, leading to oil leaks after the valve cover is reinstalled.*

Installation

Refer to illustrations 4.6 and 4.7

6   The mating surfaces of the housing or cylinder head and valve cover must be clean when the valve cover is installed. The rubber sealing gasket can be reused unless it has high mileage and the rubber has hardened or cracked, then pull out the rubber seal and clean the mating surfaces with lacquer thinner or acetone. Install a new rubber gasket, pressing it evenly into the groove around the underside of the valve cover. If there's residue or oil on the mating surfaces when the valve cover is installed, oil leaks may develop. **Note:** *Make sure that the spark plug tube gaskets are in place on the underside of the valve cover before reinstalling it* **(see illustration)**.

7   Apply RTV sealant near the rubber plug, cam seal cap and distributor **(see illustration)**.

8   Position a new gasket on the cylinder head, then install the valve cover and nuts.

9   Tighten the nuts to the torque listed in this Chapter's Specifications in three or four equal steps.

10   Reinstall the remaining parts, run the engine and check for oil leaks.

12   After the number one piston has been positioned at TDC on the compression stroke, TDC for any of the remaining pistons can be located by turning the crankshaft and following the firing order. Mark the remaining spark plug wire terminal locations on the distributor body just like you did for the number one terminal, then number the marks to correspond with the cylinder numbers. As you turn the crankshaft, the rotor will also turn. When it's pointing directly at one of the marks on the distributor, the piston for that particular cylinder is at TDC on the compression stroke.

---

4   Valve cover - removal and installation

Removal

Refer to illustrations 4.4 and 4.5

1   Disconnect the negative cable from the battery.
Caution: *If the stereo in your vehicle is equipped with an anti-theft system, make sure you have the correct activation code before disconnecting the battery.*

2   Detach the PCV hoses from the valve cover.

3   Remove the spark plug wires from the spark plugs, handling them by the boots, not pulling on the wires.

4   Remove two bolts at the timing-belt end of the valve cover, then pull up the wiring harness cover and wiring **(see illustration)**.

5   Remove the valve cover mounting nuts, then detach the valve

---

5   Intake manifold - removal and installation

Removal

Refer to illustrations 5.3, 5.6a, 5.6b, 5.7a and 5.7b

Note: *If the intake manifold is to be unbolted only for removal of the cylinder head, then the intake manifold can simply be unbolted from the cylinder head and pushed toward the firewall, without disconnecting any hoses, wires or linkage. The following procedure is for complete removal of the manifold from the vehicle.*

5.3 The various hoses should be marked to insure correct reinstallation

5.6a From underneath the vehicle, remove the bolt retaining this brace (arrow) to the intake manifold (intake manifold removed for clarity)

5.6b On 1993 through 1995 models, unbolt this intake manifold brace from the cylinder head

6   Unbolt the upper end of the intake manifold-to-block brace (accessible from under the vehicle), and on 1993 through 1995 models, remove the intake manifold-to-cylinder head brace from the cylinder head **(see illustrations)**.
7   Remove the ground strap and mounting nuts/bolts, then detach the manifold from the engine **(see illustrations)**. **Note:** *From under the vehicle, it will be necessary to unbolt the wiring harness, the lower intake manifold bolts, and the two nuts securing the pair of steel lines to the underside of the intake manifold.*

Installation

8   Clean the mating surfaces of the intake manifold and the cylinder head mounting surface with lacquer thinner or acetone. If the gasket shows signs of leaking, have the manifold checked for warpage at an automotive machine shop and resurfaced if necessary.
9   The manifold is a two piece design, and a new gasket set may include the gasket for the air chamber cover. Unless the engine has high mileage or you suspect a vacuum leak at the mating surfaces, don't unbolt the air chamber cover. If it's necessary to replace the gasket, unbolt the cover, clean the surfaces, position the new gasket and reinstall the cover, tightening it to Specifications (see Chapter 4).
10   Install a new gasket, then position the manifold on the cylinder head and install the nuts/bolts.
11   Tighten the nuts/bolts in three or four equal steps to the torque listed in this Chapter's Specifications. Work from the center out towards the ends to avoid warping the manifold.

1   Disconnect the negative cable from the battery. **Caution:** *If the stereo in your vehicle is equipped with an anti-theft system, make sure you have the correct activation code before disconnecting the battery.*
2   Refer to Chapter 4 to remove the throttle body and linkages, and safely relieve the fuel system pressure.
3   Label and detach the PCV and vacuum hoses connected to the intake manifold, including those from the MAP sensor, brake booster and the air conditioning idle-up actuator **(see illustration)**.
4   The intake manifold can be removed with the injectors and fuel rail in place. If the injectors are to be removed from the intake manifold, refer to Chapter 4.
5   Disconnect the electrical connector from the EGR valve, label and disconnect the vacuum hose, and unbolt the EGR pipe from the intake manifold (see Chapter 4). Set the EGR assembly aside.

2A

5.7a From underneath the vehicle, unbolt the wiring harness (right arrow) from the water neck and cylinder head, then remove the lower manifold bolts (left arrow indicates one, of the four bolts)

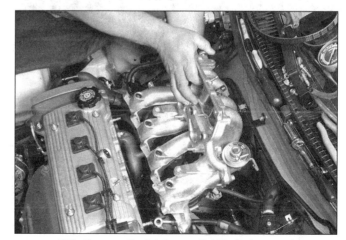

5.7b Remove the intake manifold bolts/nuts and remove the intake manifold

6.2 Remove the five upper heat insulator bolts (arrows)

6.4 Remove the upper bolt retaining the exhaust brace to the manifold (top arrow), and loosen the two bolts retaining the brace to the block (lower arrows)

6.5 Remove the bolts and nuts and remove the exhaust manifold

12   Install the remaining parts in the reverse order of removal.
13   Before starting the engine, check the throttle linkage for smooth operation.
14   Run the engine and check for coolant and vacuum leaks.
15   Road test the vehicle and check for proper operation of all accessories, including the cruise control system, if equipped.

6   Exhaust manifold - removal and installation

Warning: *The engine must be completely cool before beginning this procedure.*

Removal

Refer to illustrations 6.2, 6.4 and 6.5

1   Disconnect the negative cable from the battery. **Caution:** *If the stereo in your vehicle is equipped with an anti-theft system, make sure you have the correct activation code before disconnecting the battery.*
2   Remove the upper heat insulator from the manifold **(see illustration)**. **Note:** *There is also a lower heat insulator, but is attached to the manifold from underneath and does not need to be removed.*
3   Apply penetrating oil to the exhaust manifold mounting nuts/bolts, and the nuts retaining the exhaust pipe to the manifold. After the nuts have soaked, remove the nuts retaining the exhaust pipe to the manifold (see Chapter 4).

7.7 With the belts removed, unbolt and remove the air conditioning idler pulley (arrow, shown from below through the right fenderwell)

4   Unbolt the exhaust manifold brace **(see illustration)**.
5   Remove the nuts/bolts and detach the manifold and gasket **(see illustration)**.

Installation

6   Use a scraper to remove all traces of old gasket material and carbon deposits from the manifold and cylinder head mating surfaces. If the gasket was leaking, have the manifold checked for warpage at an automotive machine shop and resurfaced if necessary.
7   Position a new gasket over the cylinder head studs. **Note:** *The marks on the gasket should face out (away from the cylinder head) and the arrow should point toward the rear (transaxle end) of the engine.*
8   Install the manifold and thread the mounting nuts/bolts into place.
9   Working from the center out, tighten the nuts/bolts to the torque listed in this Chapter's Specifications in three or four equal steps.
10   Reinstall the remaining parts in the reverse order of removal.
11   Run the engine and check for exhaust leaks.

7   Timing belt and sprockets - removal, inspection and installation

Removal

Refer to illustrations 7.7, 7.12, 7.13, 7.14, 7.17a, 7.17b, 7.17c and 7.19

1   Disconnect the negative cable from the battery. **Caution:** *If the stereo in your vehicle is equipped with an anti-theft system, make sure you have the correct activation code before disconnecting the battery.*
2   Block the rear wheels and set the parking brake.
3   Loosen the lug nuts on the right front wheel and raise the vehicle. Support the front of the vehicle securely on jackstands.
4   Remove the right front wheel and fender apron seal.
5   Remove the coolant overflow tank (see Chapter 3).
6   Remove the spark plugs and drivebelts (see Chapter 1).
7   Remove the air conditioning compressor belt idler pulley **(see illustration)**.
8   Unbolt the cruise control actuator (if equipped) and set it aside.
9   Refer to Section 4 and remove the valve cover.
10   Support the engine from underneath with a jack (use a wood block on the jack but don't place the block under the oil pan drain plug. **Note:** *If you're planning on removing the oil pan in addition to the timing belt, support the engine with a hoist from above* (see Chapter 2, Part B).
11   Position the number one piston at TDC on the compression stroke (see Section 3).
12   Pry the flywheel inspection cover out (see Chapter 7A) and wedge a large screwdriver into the flywheel teeth to hold the engine while an assistant loosens the crankshaft pulley bolt **(see illustration)**.

7.12 Use a pry bar wedged into the flywheel (arrow) to keep the engine from rotating while loosening the crankshaft pulley bolt

7.13 After removing the center bolt, remove the crankshaft pulley

13   The crankshaft pulley should slide off the crankshaft without a puller **(see illustration)**.
14   Remove the three timing belt covers **(see illustration)**.
15   Remove the timing belt guide, noting that the cupped side faces out and the smooth side is next to the belt.
16   If you plan to re-use the timing belt, apply match marks on the sprocket and belt and an arrow indicating direction of rotation on the belt.
17   Loosen the belt tensioner adjustment bolt, pry the tensioner to the left and retighten the bolt in this position **(see illustration)**. Slip the timing belt off the sprocket. If you're removing the belt for camshaft seal replacement or cylinder head removal, it isn't necessary to detach the belt from the crankshaft sprocket, or unbolt the right engine mount. If you are removing the belt completely, remove the two nuts from the right engine mount (from underneath) and the bolt from above **(see illustrations)**.
18   If the camshaft sprocket is worn or damaged, hold the front (exhaust) camshaft with a large wrench and remove the bolt, then detach the sprocket (see Section 9).
19   Slip the timing belt off the crankshaft sprocket and remove it. If the sprocket is worn or damaged, or if you need to replace the crankshaft front oil seal, remove the sprocket from the crankshaft. Before removing it, paint matching marks on the crankshaft sprocket and the oil pump case, so that you can find the TDC position without the crankshaft pulley in place **(see illustration)**.

7.14 Timing belt cover details

2A

7.17a Loosen the center bolt on the belt tensioner, pry it to the rear of the car, then retighten to keep tension off the belt for removal/installation

7.17b With the engine supported by a jack, remove these two nuts (arrows) from the right engine mount

7.17c Remove the upper engine mount bolt (arrow) and lower the engine, then pull the upper part of the mount up (the rubber will allow movement) until the belt can be slipped out between the upper and lower sections of the mount - this saves removing the mount completely

7.19 The crankshaft sprocket should slide off the crankshaft easily - If its stuck, protect the oil pump case with rags and pry the sprocket off with two screwdrivers. While the engine is at TDC, paint marks (arrows) on the crankshaft sprocket and oil pump case, so you can find TDC without the crankshaft pulley in place

Inspection

Refer to illustrations 7.21, 7.22, 7.23 and 7.25

Caution: *Do not bend, twist or turn the timing belt inside out. Do not allow it to come in contact with oil, coolant or fuel. Do not utilize timing belt tension to keep the camshaft or crankshaft from turning when installing the sprocket bolts. Do not turn the crankshaft or camshaft more than a few degrees (if necessary for tooth alignment) while the timing belt is removed.*

20   If the timing belt broke during engine operation, the belt may have been contaminated or over-tightened. **Caution:** *If the timing belt broke during engine operation, the valves may have come in contact with the pistons, causing damage. Check the valve clearance (see Chapter 1) - bent valves usually will have excessive clearance, indicating damage that will require cylinder head removal to repair.*

21   If the belt teeth are cracked or missing **(see illustration)**, the distributor, oil pump or camshafts may have seized.

22   If there is noticeable wear or cracks on the face of the belt, check to see if there are nicks or burrs on the idler pulleys **(see illustration)**.

23   If there is wear or damage on only one side of the belt, check the belt guide and the alignment of the sprockets **(see illustration)**.

24   Replace the timing belt with a new one if obvious wear or damage is noted or if it is the least bit questionable. Correct any problems which contributed to belt failure prior to belt installation. **Note:** *Professionals recommend replacing the belt whenever it is removed, since belt failure can lead to expensive engine damage. The manufacturer recommends replacing the belt at 60,000-mile intervals.*

25   Release the bolt on the belt tensioner, then remove the tensioner and its spring. Check the idler for free rotation and measure the

7.21 Check the timing belt for cracked and missing teeth

7.22 If the face of the belt is cracked or worn, check the idler pulleys for nicks or burrs

7.23 Wear on one side of the belt indicates sprocket misalignment problems

spring's free length **(see illustration)**. Replace the spring if it doesn't meet Specifications. reinstall the tensioner and spring.

Installation

Refer to illustration 7.27

26   Remove all dirt, oil and grease from the timing belt area at the front of the engine.

27   Recheck the camshaft and crankshaft timing marks to be sure they are properly aligned **(see illustration)**. If the camshaft sprocket had been removed, reinstall it with the timing mark hole in the sprocket aligned with the notch in the front bearing cap of the exhaust camshaft. Make sure the crankshaft sprocket is still aligned at the TDC marks you made in Step 19.

28   Install the timing belt on the crankshaft and camshaft sprockets. If the original belt is being reinstalled, align the marks made during removal.

29   Slip the belt guide onto the crankshaft with the cupped side facing out.

30   Reinstall the lower timing belt cover and crankshaft pulley and recheck the TDC marks.

31   Keeping tension on the side of the belt nearest the front of the vehicle, loosen the idler pulley bolt 1/2-turn, allowing the spring to apply pressure to the idler pulley.

32   Slowly turn the crankshaft clockwise two complete revolutions (720-degrees), then tighten the idler pulley mounting bolt to the torque listed in this Chapter's Specifications. Measure the deflection of the belt on the radiator side, halfway between the camshaft and crankshaft sprockets, and compare it to this Chapter's Specifications.

7.25 Check the idler pulley bearing for smooth operation and measure the free length of the tension spring for comparison to this Chapter's Specifications

7.27 The camshaft sprocket is at TDC when the hole in the sprocket lines up with the notch in the front bearing cap

8.2a Wrap tape around the screwdriver tip and carefully work the crankshaft front oil seal out of the bore - DO NOT nick or scratch the crankshaft in the process!

8.2b The seal may be removed more easily by carefully cutting the lip as indicated

8.4 Gently drive the new seal into place with the spring side installed toward the engine

33   Recheck the timing marks. With the crankshaft at TDC for number one cylinder, the hole in the camshaft sprocket must align with the timing mark **(see illustration 7.27)**. If the marks are not aligned exactly, repeat the belt installation procedure. **Caution:** *DO NOT start the engine until you're absolutely certain that the timing belt is installed correctly. Serious and costly engine damage could occur if the belt is installed out-of-time.*

34   Reinstall the remaining parts in the reverse order of removal.

35   Run the engine and check for proper operation.

8   Crankshaft front oil seal - replacement

Refer to illustrations 8.2a, 8.2b and 8.4

1   Remove the timing belt and crankshaft sprocket (see Section 7).

2   Note how far the seal is recessed in the bore, then carefully pry it out of the oil pump housing with a screwdriver or seal removal tool **(see illustration)**. Don't scratch the housing bore or damage the crankshaft in the process (if the crankshaft is damaged, the new seal will end up leaking). **Note:** *The seal may be easier to remove if the old seal lip is cut with a sharp utility knife first* **(see illustration)**.

3   Clean the bore in the housing and coat the outer edge of the new seal with engine oil or multi-purpose grease. Apply moly-base grease to the seal lip.

4   Using a socket with an outside diameter slightly smaller than the outside diameter of the seal, carefully drive the new seal into place with a seal driver or large socket **(see illustration)**. Make sure it's installed squarely and driven in to the same depth as the original. If a socket isn't available, a short section of large diameter pipe will also work. Check the seal after installation to make sure the spring didn't pop out

of place.

5   Reinstall the crankshaft sprocket and timing belt (see Section 7).

6   Run the engine and check for oil leaks at the front seal.

9   Camshaft oil seal - replacement

Refer to illustrations 9.2, 9.3 and 9.5

1   Refer to Section 4 and remove the valve cover, then remove the timing belt.

2   Use a large wrench to hold the exhaust camshaft at its hex portion, while removing the bolt from the camshaft sprocket **(see illustration)**, then pull off the sprocket.

3   Note how far the seal is seated in the bore, then carefully pry it out with a small screwdriver **(see illustration)**. Don't scratch the bore or damage the camshaft in the process (if the camshaft is damaged, the new seal will end up leaking).

4   Clean the bore and coat the outer edge of the new seal with engine oil or multi-purpose grease. Apply multi-purpose grease to the seal lip.

5   Using a socket with an outside diameter slightly smaller than the outside diameter of the seal, carefully drive the new seal into place with a seal installer or large socket. Make sure it's installed squarely and driven in to the same depth as the original. If a socket isn't available, a short section of pipe will also work. **Note:** *There isn't much room for a hammer, so you can also pry between the engine mount and the socket to press the seal in* **(see illustration)**.

6   Reinstall the camshaft sprocket and timing belt (see Section 7). Refer to Section 4 and reinstall the valve cover.

7   Run the engine and check for oil leaks at the camshaft seal.

9.2 Use an end wrench to hold the camshaft while removing the camshaft sprocket bolt

9.3 Carefully pry the camshaft seal out of the bore - DO NOT nick or scratch the camshaft journal

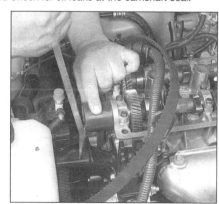

9.5 The new camshaft seal can be pressed into place squarely with an appropriate-size socket and a pry bar working against the engine mount

2A

10.4 Mount a dial indicator as shown to measure camshaft endplay - with the dial zeroed, pry the camshaft forward and back and read the endplay on the dial

10.6 Remove the two bolts and the front camshaft bearing cap from the intake camshaft

10.5 Place the EXHAUST camshaft knock pin between the 9 o'clock and 10 o'clock position

10.7 Install a service bolt through the sub-gear and thread it into the main gear (arrow)

10.10 Turn the exhaust camshaft until the knock pin is pointed at about the 5 o'clock position

10   Camshafts and valve lifters - removal, inspection and installation

Note: *Before beginning this procedure, obtain two 6 x 1.0 mm bolts 16 to 20 mm long. They will be referred to as service bolts in the text.*

Removal

Refer to illustrations 10.4, 10.5, 10.6, 10.7, 10.10, 10.14a, 10.14b, 10.15, 10.16a and 10.16b

1   Remove the valve cover as described in Section 4.
2   Refer to Section 3 and place the engine on TDC for number 1 cylinder. Apply a dab of paint to the camshaft gear TDC alignment marks (the marks where the gears mesh just at the valve cover/head interface line). **Note:** *There are two sets of marks on the camshaft gears. The marks that align at TDC are for TDC reference only, the other two marks are used to align the camshafts during installation.*
3   Remove the distributor (see Chapter 5). Remove the timing belt and camshaft sprocket (see Sections 7 and 9).
4   Measure the camshaft thrust clearance (endplay) with a dial indicator **(see illustration)**. If the clearance is greater than the service limit, replace the camshaft and/or the cylinder head.

Intake camshaft

5   Position the knock pin in the EXHAUST camshaft just above the top of the cylinder head **(see illustration)**. This will position the intake camshaft lobes so the camshaft will be pushed up evenly by valve spring pressure. **Caution:** *This positioning is important to avoid damaging the cylinder head or camshaft as the camshaft is removed.*
6   Remove the two bolts and the front bearing cap from the intake camshaft **(see illustration)**.
7   Secure the intake camshaft sub-gear to the main gear by installing one of the service bolts into the threaded hole **(see illustration)**.
8   Following the reverse of the tightening sequence **(see illustration 10.40)**, loosen the remaining intake camshaft bearing cap bolts in 1/4-turn increments until the bolts can be removed by hand. Lift the bearing caps straight up and off.
9   Lift the camshaft straight up and out of the cylinder head.

Exhaust camshaft

10   Position the knock pin in the exhaust camshaft at approximately the 5 o'clock position **(see illustration)**.
11   Remove the front (timing belt end) exhaust camshaft bearing cap bolts and detach the bearing cap and oil seal. **Caution:** *Do not pry the cap off. If it doesn't come loose easily, leave it in place without bolts.*
12   Following the reverse of the tightening sequence **(see illustration 10.30)**, loosen the remaining exhaust camshaft bearing cap bolts in 1/4-turn increments until the bolts can be removed by hand. Lift off the

10.14a Mark the lifters/shims (I for intake, E for exhaust, and number their location) and remove them with a magnetic retrieval tool

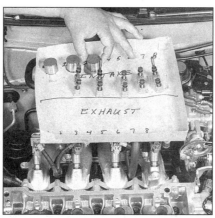

10.14b Mark up a cardboard box to store the lifters/shims and bearing caps

10.15 With the hex portion of the intake camshaft clamped in a vise, use a spanner to relieve the tension on the service bolt, remove the bolt, then release the tension on the subgear

2A

10.16a Remove the snap-ring with a pair of snap-ring pliers

10.16b Remove the wave washer (1), the camshaft subgear (2) and the gear spring (3)

bearing caps. **Caution:** *As the center bearing cap bolts are being loosened, make sure the camshaft is moving up evenly. If one end·or the other stops moving and the cam gets cocked, start over by reinstalling the bearing caps and resetting the knock pin. DO NOT try to pry or force the camshaft out.*

13   Lift the camshaft straight up and out of the cylinder head.
14   Clean the oil off the valve lifter shims, mark them with a felt-tip marker and remove the lifters, keeping the shims with their lifters **(see illustration)**. Store the camshaft bearing caps, lifters and shims so they can be reinstalled without mixing them up **(see illustration)**.
15   Position the intake camshaft in a vise, clamping it on the hex portion. Using a two-pin spanner, rotate the sub-gear clockwise and remove the service bolt from the threaded hole, then allow the subgear to rotate back until all tension is relieved **(see illustration)**.

16   Remove the sub-gear snap-ring **(see illustration)**. The wave washer, sub-gear and camshaft gear spring can now be removed from the camshaft **(see illustration)**.

Inspection

Refer to illustrations 10.17, 10.18, 10.21, 10.22, 10.23a, 10.23b and 10.24

17   Measure the free length (distance between the ends) of the camshaft gear spring **(see illustration)** and compare it to this Chapter's Specifications. If not as specified, replace the spring.
18   Inspect each lifter for scuffing and score marks **(see illustration)**.

10.18 Wipe off the oil and inspect each lifter for wear and scuffing

10.17 Measure the distance between the ends of the camshaft gear spring

10.21 Measure the lobe heights on each camshaft - if any lobe height is less than the specified allowable minimum, replace that camshaft

10.22 Measure each journal diameter with a micrometer (if any journal measures less than the specified limit, replace the camshaft)

10.23a The camshaft bearing caps are numbered and have an arrow that should face the timing belt end of the engine

10.23b Compare the width of the crushed Plastigage to the scale on the envelope to determine the oil clearance

10.24 Position a dial indicator as shown here to measure gear backlash - hold one camshaft steady with a wrench while moving the other camshaft with another wrench

10.28 Apply sealer to the shaded areas of the front exhaust camshaft bearing cap

19   Measure the outside diameter of each lifter and the corresponding lifter bore inside diameter. Subtract the lifter diameter from the lifter bore diameter to determine the oil clearance. Compare it to this Chapter's Specifications. If the oil clearance is excessive, a new cylinder head and/or new lifters will be required.

20   Visually examine the cam lobes and bearing journals for score marks, pitting, galling and evidence of overheating (blue, discolored areas). Look for flaking away of the hardened surface layer of each lobe.

21   Using a micrometer, measure the height of each camshaft lobe **(see illustration)**. Compare your measurements with this Chapter's Specifications. If the height for any one lobe is less than the specified minimum, replace the camshaft.

22   Using a micrometer, measure the diameter of each journal at several points **(see illustration)**. Compare your measurements with this Chapter's Specifications. If the diameter of any one journal is less than specified, replace the camshaft.

23   Check the oil clearance for each camshaft journal as follows:

a) *Clean the bearing caps and the camshaft journals with lacquer thinner or acetone.*

b) *Carefully lay the camshaft(s) in place in the cylinder head. Don't install the lifters or intake camshaft subgear and don't use any lubrication.*

c) *Lay a strip of Plastigage on each journal.*

d) *Install the bearing caps with the arrows pointing toward the front (timing belt end) of the engine* **(see illustration)**.

e) *Tighten the bolts to the torque listed in this Chapter's Specifications in 1/4-turn increments.* **Note:** *Don't turn the camshaft while the Plastigage is in place.*

f) *Remove the bolts and detach the caps.*

g) *Compare the width of the crushed Plastigage (at its widest point) to the scale on the Plastigage envelope* **(see illustration)**.

h) *If the clearance is greater than specified, replace the camshaft and/or cylinder head.*

i) *Scrape off the Plastigage with your fingernail or the edge of a credit card - don't scratch or nick the journals or bearing caps.*

24   With the caps reinstalled temporarily, use a dial indicator to measure the backlash between the two camshaft gears. Hold one camshaft from turning (using a wrench on the hex portion) while measuring the movement in the other camshaft gear, and compare the results to Specifications **(see illustration)**. If the backlash is beyond Specifications, replace both camshafts.

Installation

Refer to illustrations 10.28, 10.30, 10.37 and 10.40

Exhaust camshaft

25   Apply moly-base grease or engine assembly lube to the lifters, then install them in their original locations. Make sure the valve adjustment shims are on place on the lifters.

26   Apply moly-base grease or engine assembly lube to the camshaft lobes and bearing journals.

10.30 Exhaust camshaft bearing cap bolt TIGHTENING sequence

10.40 INTAKE camshaft bearing cap bolt tightening sequence

10.37 Align the camshaft gears as shown here - use the installation marks, NOT the TDC marks

27   Position the exhaust camshaft in the cylinder head with the knock pin at approximately the 5 o'clock position (see illustration 10.10).

28   Apply a thin coat of RTV sealant to the outer edge of the front bearing-cap-to-cylinder-head mating surface (see illustration). Note: The cap must be installed immediately or the sealer will dry prematurely.

29   Install the bearing caps in numerical order with the arrows pointing toward the timing belt end of the engine.

30   Following the recommended tightening sequence (see illustration), tighten the bearing cap bolts in 1/4-turn increments to the torque listed in this Chapter's Specifications.

31   Refer to Section 9 and install a new camshaft oil seal.

Intake camshaft

32   Reassemble the intake camshaft subgear. Install the camshaft gear spring, sub-gear and wave washer. Secure them with the snap-ring (see illustrations 10.16a and 10.16b).

33   Refer to Step 15 and install a service bolt.

34   Apply moly-base grease or engine assembly lube to the lifters, then install them in their original locations. Make sure the valve adjustment shims are in place on the lifters.

35   Apply moly-base grease or engine assembly lube to the camshaft lobes and bearing journals.

36   Rotate the EXHAUST camshaft until the knock pin is positioned between the 9 o'clock and 10 o'clock position (see illustration 10.5).

37   Align the intake camshaft gear with the exhaust camshaft gear by matching up the "installation" marks on the gears (see illustration). Caution: There are two sets of marks. Do not use the TDC marks you applied paint to in Step 2. The camshaft installation marks are the only marks that are duplicated on both front and rear sides of the two camshaft gears.

38   Roll the intake camshaft down into position. Turn the exhaust camshaft back and forth a little until the intake camshaft sits in the bearings evenly.

39   Install the intake camshaft bearing caps in numerical order with the arrows pointing toward the timing belt end of the engine.

40   Following the recommended sequence (see illustration), tighten the bearing cap bolts in 1/4-turn increments to the torque listed in this Chapter's Specifications.

41   Remove the service bolt from the intake camshaft gear.

42   Install the timing belt pulley on the exhaust camshaft and tighten the bolt to the torque listed in this Chapter's Specifications. Prevent the camshaft from turning by holding it with a wrench on the large hex.

43   Install the timing belt (see Section 7).

44   The remainder of installation is the reverse of the removal procedure.

11   Cylinder head - removal and installation

Note: The engine must be completely cool before beginning this procedure.

Removal

Refer to illustration 11.14

1   Disconnect the negative cable from the battery. **Caution:** If the stereo in your vehicle is equipped with an anti-theft system, make sure you have the correct activation code before disconnecting the battery.

2   Drain the coolant from the engine block and radiator (see Chapter 1).

3   Drain the engine oil and remove the oil filter (see Chapter 1).

4   Remove the throttle body, fuel injectors and fuel rail (see Chapter 4).

5   Remove the intake manifold (see Section 5).

6   Remove the exhaust manifold (see Section 6). **Note:** It is possible to leave the intake and exhaust manifolds attached to the cylinder head, to be removed along with the cylinder head for disassembly on the bench.

7   Remove the timing belt and camshaft sprocket (see Sections 7 and 9).

8   Remove the camshafts and lifters (see Section 10).

9   Remove the alternator and distributor (see Chapter 5).

10   Unbolt the upper bracket of the power steering pump and set the pump aside without disconnecting the hoses.

11   Label and remove any remaining items, such as coolant fittings, tubes, cables, hoses or wires.

12   Refer to Chapter 3 and detach the water necks from each end of the cylinder head. At this point the cylinder head should be ready for removal.

13   Using an 8 mm hex-head socket bit and a breaker bar, loosen the cylinder head bolts in 1/4-turn increments until they can be removed by hand. Loosen the cylinder head bolts opposite of the recommended tightening sequence (see illustration 11.25) to avoid warping or cracking the cylinder head.

2A

11.14 If the cylinder head is stuck, pry only at the overhang, not between the mating surfaces

11.17 Remove all traces of old gasket material - the cylinder head and block mating surfaces must be perfectly clean to ensure a good gasket seal

INTAKE SIDE

EXHAUST SIDE

11.25 Cylinder head bolt TIGHTENING sequence

11.22 Place the new cylinder head gasket over the dowels in the block, noting the markings for UP on the gasket

14   Lift the cylinder head off the engine block. If it's stuck, very carefully pry up at the transaxle end, beyond the gasket surface **(see illustration)**.

15   Remove all external components from the cylinder head to allow for thorough cleaning and inspection. See Chapter 2, Part B, for cylinder head servicing procedures.

Installation

Refer to illustrations 11.17, 11.22 and 11.25

16   The mating surfaces of the cylinder head and block must be perfectly clean when the cylinder head is installed.

17   Use a gasket scraper to remove all traces of carbon and old gasket material **(see illustration)**, then clean the mating surfaces with lacquer thinner or acetone. If there's oil on the mating surfaces when the cylinder head is installed, the gasket may not seal correctly and leaks could develop. When working on the block, stuff the cylinders with clean shop rags to keep out debris. Use a vacuum cleaner to remove material that falls into the cylinders.

18   Check the block and cylinder head mating surfaces for nicks, deep scratches and other damage. If damage is slight, it can be removed with a file; if it's excessive, machining may be the only alternative.

19   Use a tap of the correct size to chase the threads in the cylinder head bolt holes, then clean the holes with compressed air - make sure that nothing remains in the holes. **Warning:** *Wear eye protection when using compressed air!*

20   Mount each bolt in a vise and run a die down the threads to remove corrosion and restore the threads. Dirt, corrosion, sealant and damaged threads will affect torque readings.

21   Install the components that were removed from the cylinder head.

22   Position the new gasket over the dowel pins in the block **(see illustration)**.

23   Carefully set the cylinder head on the block without disturbing the gasket.

24   Before installing the cylinder head bolts, apply a small amount of clean engine oil to the threads and under the bolt heads.

25   Install the bolts in their original locations and tighten them finger tight. Install the shorter bolts along the intake side of the cylinder head and the longer bolts along the exhaust side. Following the recommended sequence, tighten the bolts in three steps to the torque listed in this Chapter's Specifications **(see illustration)**. Steps 2 and 3 of the tightening sequence each require the bolts to be tightened an additional 90 degrees. If you don't have an angle-torque attachment for your torque wrench, simply apply a paint mark at one edge of each cylinder head bolt and tighten the bolt until that mark is 90 degrees from where you started (Step 2). After Step 3, the marks will be 180 degrees from where they started.

26   The remaining installation steps are the reverse of removal. **Note:** *If the semi-circular rubber plug had been removed from the cylinder head (ahead of the intake camshaft), reinstall it with some RTV sealant.*

27   Check and adjust the valves as necessary (see Chapter 1).

28   Refill the cooling system, install a new oil filter and add oil to the engine (see Chapter 1).

29   Run the engine and check for leaks. Set the ignition timing (see Chapter 5) and road test the vehicle.

12 Oil pan - removal and installation

Removal

Refer to illustration 12.8

1   Disconnect the negative cable from the battery. **Caution:** *If the stereo in your vehicle is equipped with an anti-theft system, make sure you have the correct activation code before disconnecting the battery.*

12.8 Remove the front bolts of the chassis brace (arrows) - for better access for oil pan removal, you'll have to insert a large pry bar between the brace and the chassis to pry the brace down

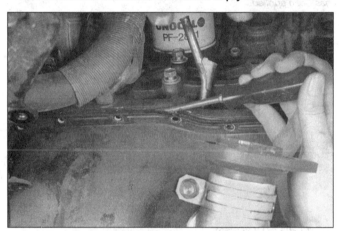

12.10 Carefully pry the oil pan away from the block - if the mating surfaces are damaged, oil leaks could develop

2   Set the parking brake and block the rear wheels.
3   Raise the front of the vehicle and support it securely on jack-stands.
4   Remove the two plastic splash shields under the engine.
5   Drain the engine oil and remove the oil filter (see Chapter 1). Remove the oil dipstick.
6   Disconnect the electrical connector to the oxygen sensor (see Chapter 6).
7   Remove the two nuts retaining the front exhaust pipe to the exhaust manifold, then the two bolts/nuts connecting the pipe to the rear of the exhaust system (see Chapter 4).
8   Remove the two front bolts of the longitudinal chassis brace and the two nuts securing the radiator-side engine mount **(see illustration)**.

1.6L engine
Refer to illustrations 12.9 and 12.10
9   Unbolt and remove the block-to-transaxle brace **(see illustration)**.
10   Remove the bolts and detach the oil pan. If it's stuck, pry it loose very carefully with a small screwdriver or putty knife **(see illustration)**. Don't damage the mating surfaces of the pan and block or oil leaks could develop.

1.8L engine
Refer to illustrations 12.12, 12.13, 12.15a and 12.15b
11   The 1.8L engine uses a steel oil pan mounted to a large cast aluminum reinforcement section that stiffens the block/transaxle mounting.

12.9 Unbolt the block-to-transaxle brace on 1.6L models

12.12 Remove the bolts and nuts securing the oil pan to the reinforcement section, then break its seal with a putty knife

12.13 Remove the oil baffle plate and the pick-up tube/strainer

There is no separate engine/transaxle brace as on the 1.6L engine.
Note: *The manufacturer uses a very tough sealant on the oil pan flange which make the steel and aluminum components difficult to separate. Take your time and use a putty knife rather than a screwdriver to break the seal.*
12   Remove the bolts and stud nuts around the perimeter of the oil pan, then carefully pry between the steel and aluminum sections to loosen the oil pan **(see illustration)**. Be careful not to gouge the softer aluminum or distort the flange of the steel pan.
13   Remove the two bolts and two nuts retaining the oil baffle and remove the baffle **(see illustration)**.
14   Unbolt the pick-up tube/oil strainer assembly and remove it for cleaning.

2A

12.15a Unbolt the six fasteners inside the area concealed by the oil pan - one is an Allen-head bolt (arrow)

12.15b To access the bolts between the reinforcement section and the transaxle (arrows), you'll need to bend the exhaust pipe down at its flex joint and pry the longitudinal chassis brace down

15   If necessary, remove the bolts and nuts retaining the aluminum reinforcement section to the block and transaxle **(see illustrations)**. Carefully pry the aluminum section down without gouging the sealing surface. Six of the fasteners are inside the area originally covered by the oil pan. **Caution:** *Do not pry on the reinforcement section until you are certain all fasteners are removed. There are two Allen bolts near the right front which will require using a ball-hex wrench to remove. If you don't have this type wrench (which allows you to turn an Allen bolt from a slight angle), you will have to remove the air conditioning compressor and bracket to allow using a L-shaped Allen wrench.*

Installation

Refer to illustrations 12.20a, 12.20b and 12.20c

16   Use a scraper to remove all traces of old gasket material and sealant from the block and oil pan. Clean the mating surfaces with lacquer thinner or acetone.
17   Make sure the threaded bolt holes in the block are clean.
18   Check the oil pan flange for distortion, particularly around the bolt holes. If necessary, place the oil pan on a wood block and use a hammer to flatten and restore the gasket surface.
19   Inspect the oil pump pick-up tube assembly for cracks and a blocked strainer. On 1.6L models, if the pick-up was removed, clean it thoroughly and install it now, using a new O-ring or gasket. Tighten the nuts/bolts to the torque listed in this Chapter's Specifications.
20   Apply a 5 mm wide bead of RTV sealant to the oil pan flange (1.6L engine) or reinforcement section (1.8L engine) **(see illustrations)**. **Note:** *Installation must be completed within 5 minutes once the sealer*

has been applied.
21   Carefully position the oil pan or reinforcement section on the engine block and install the bolts. Working from the center out. Tighten the bolts to the torque listed in this Chapter's Specifications in three or four steps.

12.20a RTV sealant application details - 1.6L engine oil pan

12.20b RTV sealant application details - 1.8L engine oil pan

12.20c RTV sealant application details - 1.8L engine aluminum reinforcement section

13.3 Remove the bolt (arrow) and withdraw the crankshaft position sensor from the oil pump body

13.4 Remove the oil pump body-to-block bolts (arrows)

On 1.8L engines, reinstall the oil baffle plate and the pick-up tube/strainer. Be sure to use a new gasket on the pick-up tube. On 1.8L engines, apply RTV to the oil pan flange and install it after the aluminum reinforcement section has been sealed and tightened to specifications.

22   The remainder of installation is the reverse of removal. Be sure to add oil and install a new oil filter. Use new gasket/seals on the front exhaust pipe.

23   Run the engine and check for oil pressure and leaks.

13   Oil pump - removal, inspection and installation

Removal

Refer to illustrations 13.3, 13.4 and 13.6

1   Remove the oil dipstick, oil pan, baffle plate (1.8L only) and the oil pick-up/strainer assembly (see Section 12).

2   Support the engine securely from above and remove the timing belt, crankshaft pulley and sprocket (see Section 7).

3   On 1996 and some 1995 models, remove the crankshaft position sensor **(see illustration)**. Unbolt and remove the oil dipstick pipe (see Chapter 3).

4   Remove the seven bolts and detach the oil pump body from the engine **(see illustration)**. You may have to pry carefully between the front main bearing cap and the pump body with a screwdriver, or tap behind the oil pump with a soft-faced hammer.

5   Use a scraper to remove all traces of sealant and old gasket material from the pump body and engine block, then clean the mating surfaces with lacquer thinner or acetone.

6   Remove the five Torx screws and separate the pump cover from the body. Lift out the drive and driven rotors **(see illustration)**.

7   Remove the oil pressure relief valve snap-ring retainer, spring and piston. **Warning:** *The spring is tightly compressed - be careful and wear eye protection.*

2A

13.6 Oil pump components

13.10a Measure the driven rotor-to-body clearance with a feeler gauge

13.10b Using a straightedge and feeler gauge, measure the rotor-to-cover clearance

Inspection

Refer to illustrations 13.10a, 13.10b and 13.10c

8   Clean all components with solvent, inspect them for wear and damage.

9   Check the oil pressure relief valve piston sliding surface and valve spring. If either the spring or the valve is damaged, they must be replaced as a set.

10   Check the driven rotor-to-body clearance, rotor-to-cover clearance and drive rotor tip clearance with a feeler gauge **(see illustrations)** and compare the results to this Chapter's Specifications. If any clearance is excessive, replace the rotors as a set. If necessary, replace the oil pump body.

Installation

Refer to illustration 13.15

11   Lubricate the drive and driven rotors with clean engine oil and place them in the pump body with the marks facing out **(see illustration13.10c)**.

12   Pack the pump cavity with petroleum jelly and attach the pump cover, tighten the screws to the torque listed in this Chapter's Specifications.

13   Lubricate the oil pressure relief valve piston with clean engine oil and reinstall the valve components in the pump body.

14   Place a new gasket on the engine block (the dowel pins should hold it in place).

15   Position the pump assembly against the block and install the mounting bolts. Make sure that the flats on the oil pump drive rotor aligns with the flats on the crankshaft **(see illustration)**.

16   Tighten the bolts to the torque listed in this Chapter's Specifications in three or four steps. Follow a criss-cross pattern to avoid warping the body.

17   Reinstall the remaining parts in the reverse order of removal.

18   Using a new gasket, install the oil pick-up tube/strainer assembly and baffle plate (see Section 12). Tighten the fasteners to the torque listed in this Chapter's Specifications. When reinstalling the dipstick tube, use a new O-ring on the oil-pump end.

19   Add oil, start the engine and check for oil pressure and leaks.

20   Recheck the engine oil level.

---

14   Flywheel/driveplate - removal and installation

Removal

Refer to illustrations 14.3 and 14.5

1   Raise the vehicle and support it securely on jackstands, then refer

13.10c Measure the rotor tip clearance with a feeler gauge - install the rotors with the marks facing out, against the cover (arrows)

to Chapter 7 and remove the transaxle.

2   Remove the pressure plate and clutch disc (Chapter 8) (manual transaxle equipped vehicles).

3   Use a center punch or paint to make alignment marks on the flywheel/driveplate and crankshaft to ensure correct alignment during reinstallation **(see illustration)**.

4   Remove the bolts that secure the flywheel/driveplate to the crankshaft. If the crankshaft turns, wedge a screwdriver in the ring gear teeth to jam the flywheel **(see illustration 7.12)**.

5   Remove the flywheel/driveplate from the crankshaft. Since the flywheel is fairly heavy, be sure to support it while removing the last bolt. Automatic transaxle equipped vehicles have spacers on both sides of the driveplate **(see illustration)**. Keep them with the driveplate. **Warning:** *The ring-gear teeth may be sharp, wear gloves to protect your hands.*

Installation

6   Clean the flywheel to remove grease and oil. Inspect the surface for cracks, rivet grooves, burned areas and score marks. Light scoring can be removed with emery cloth. Check for cracked and broken ring gear teeth. Lay the flywheel on a flat surface and use a straightedge to check for warpage.

7   Clean and inspect the mating surfaces of the flywheel/driveplate and the crankshaft. If the crankshaft rear seal is leaking, replace it

13.15 When installing the oil pump, align the flats in the pump rotor with the flats on the crankshaft (arrows)

14.3 Mark the flywheel/driveplate and the crankshaft so they can be reassembled in the same relative positions

14.5 On vehicles equipped with a spacer plate, note the position of the locating pin (arrow)

15.2 The quick way to replace the rear crankshaft oil seal is to simply pry the old one out with a screwdriver, lubricate the crankshaft journal and the lip of the new seal with moly-base grease and push the new seal into place - the seal lip is very stiff and can be easily damaged during installation if you're not careful

15.5 After removing the retainer assembly from the block, support it between two wooden blocks and drive out the old seal with a screwdriver and hammer

2A

15.6 Drive the new seal into the retainer with a wood block or a section of pipe - make sure that you don't cock the seal in the retainer bore

before reinstalling the flywheel/driveplate (see Section 15).

8   Position the flywheel/driveplate against the crankshaft. Be sure to align the marks made during removal. Note that some engines have an alignment dowel or staggered bolt holes to ensure correct installation. Before installing the bolts, apply thread-locking compound to the threads.

9   Wedge a screwdriver in the ring gear teeth to keep the flywheel/driveplate from turning and tighten the bolts to the torque listed in this Chapter's Specifications. Follow a criss-cross pattern and work up to the final torque in three or four steps.

10   The remainder of installation is the reverse of the removal procedure.

15   Rear main oil seal - replacement

Refer to illustrations 15.2, 15.5 and 15.6

1   Remove the transaxle (see Chapter 7). Remove the rear end plate.

2   The seal can be replaced without removing the oil pan or seal retainer. However, this method is not recommended because the lip of the seal is quite stiff and it's possible to cock the seal in the retainer bore or damage it during installation. If you want to take the chance, pry out the old seal with a screwdriver **(see illustration)**. Apply multi-purpose grease to the crankshaft seal journal and the lip of the new seal and carefully push the new seal into place. The lip is stiff so carefully work it onto the seal journal of the crankshaft with a smooth object like the end of an extension as you tap the seal into place. Don't rush it or you may damage the seal.

3   The following method is recommended but requires resealing the rear of the oil pan (see Section 12) and removing the seal retainer.

4   After removing the two rearmost oil pan bolts that go into the seal retainer, break the seal between the rear of the oil pan and the bottom of the seal retainer with a putty knife. Remove the bolts, detach the seal retainer and remove all the old gasket material. remove the sealant from the top of the oil pan flange. **Note:** *Cover the open area of the oil pan with clean rags to keep debris out while bracing the pan flange.*

5   Position the seal and retainer assembly between two wood blocks on a workbench and drive the old seal out from the back side with a screwdriver **(see illustration)**.

6   Drive the new seal into the retainer with a wood block **(see illustration)** or a section of pipe slightly smaller in diameter than the outside diameter of the seal.

7   Lubricate the crankshaft seal journal and the lip of the new seal with multi-purpose grease. Position a new gasket on the engine block. Apply a bead of RTV sealant to the exposed portion of oil pan flange and particularly at the pan-to-block mating surface.

8   Slowly and carefully push the seal and retainer onto the crankshaft. The seal lip is stiff, so work it onto the crankshaft with a

smooth object such as the end of an extension as you push the retainer against the block.

9   Install and tighten the retainer bolts to the torque listed in this Chapter's Specifications.

10   The remainder of installation is the reverse of removal.

16   Engine mounts - check and replacement

1   Engine mounts seldom require attention, but broken or deteriorated mounts should be replaced immediately or the added strain placed on the driveline components may cause damage or wear.

Check

Refer to illustration 16.4

2   During the check, the engine must be raised slightly to remove the weight from the mounts.

3   Raise the vehicle and support it securely on jackstands, then position a jack under the engine oil pan. Place a large wood block between the jack head and the oil pan, then carefully raise the engine just enough to take the weight off the mounts. Do not position the wood block under the drain plug. **Warning:** *DO NOT place any part of your body under the engine when it's supported only by a jack!*

4   Check the mounts **(see illustration)** to see if the rubber is cracked, hardened or separated from the metal plates. Sometimes the rubber will split right down the center.

5   Check for relative movement between the mount plates and the engine or frame (use a large screwdriver or pry bar to attempt to move the mounts). If movement is noted, lower the engine and tighten the mount fasteners.

6   Rubber preservative should be applied to the mounts to slow deterioration.

Replacement

7   Disconnect the negative battery cable from the battery, then raise the vehicle and support it securely on jackstands (if not already done). Support the engine as described in Step 3. **Caution:** *If the stereo in your vehicle is equipped with an anti-theft system, make sure you have the correct activation code before disconnecting the battery.*

8   To remove the right engine mount, remove the two nuts from underneath, one bolt from above, and the upper section will separate from the engine bracket **(see illustrations 7.17b and 7.17c)**.

9   Remove the mount-to-chassis nuts and detach the mount.

10   To remove the rear engine mount, pull the rubber plugs from the longitudinal chassis brace to access the two nuts.

11   To remove the front engine mount, remove the two nuts retaining the insulator to the longitudinal chassis brace **(see illustration 12.8)**, then the three nuts retaining the insulator to the chassis.

12   Installation is the reverse of removal. Use thread locking compound on the mount bolts/nuts and be sure to tighten them securely.

13   See Chapter 7 for transaxle mount replacement.

16.4 Typical engine mount components

Chapter 2 Part B
General engine overhaul procedures

Contents

Specifications

General

Displacement	
1.6L	97 cubic inches
1.8L	108 cubic inches
Cylinder compression pressure @ 250 rpm	
Standard..	191 psi
Minimum...	142 psi
Oil pressure (engine warm)	
At idle	4.3 psi minimum
At 3000 rpm...	36 to 71 psi

Cylinder head

Warpage limits	
Block surface	0.0020 inch
Manifold surfaces..	0.0039 inch

Valves and related components

Valve margin width	
Standard..	0.031 to 0.047 inch
Minimum...	0.020 inch
Valve stem diameter	
Intake..	0.2350 to 0.2356 inch
Exhaust..	0.2348 to 0.2354 inch
Valve stem-to-guide clearance	
Intake	
Standard	0.0010 to 0.0024 inch
Service limit..	0.0031 inch
Exhaust	
Standard	0.0012 to 0.0026 inch
Service limit..	0.0039 inch

Valves and related components (continued)

Valve spring
    Out-of-square limit .... 0.079 inch
    Free length .... 1.669 inches
    Installed height .... 1.248 inches
Valve lifter
    Diameter .... 1.2191 to 1.2195 inches
    Lifter bore diameter .... 1.2205 to 1.2215 inch
    Lifter-to-bore clearance
        Standard .... 0.0009 to 0.0023 inch
        Service limit .... 0.0028 inch

Crankshaft and connecting rods

Connecting rod journal
    Diameter
        1.6L .... 1.5742 to 1.5748 inches
        1.8L .... 1.8893 to 1.8898 inches
    Taper and out-of-round limits .... 0.0002 inch
Bearing oil clearance
    Standard
        1.6L .... 0.0008 to 0.0020 inch
        1.8L .... 0.0008 to 0.0017 inches
    Service limit .... 0.0031 inch
Connecting rod side clearance (endplay)
    Standard... 0.0059 to 0.0098 inch
    Service limit .... 0.0118 inch
Main bearing journal
    Diameter .... 1.8891 to 1.8898 inches
    Taper and out-of-round limits .... 0.0002 inch
    Runout limit .... 0.0012 inch
    Bearing oil clearance
        Standard .... 0.0006 to 0.0013 inch
        Service limit... 0.0039 inch
Crankshaft endplay
    Standard... 0.0008 to 0.0087 inch
    Service limit .... 0.0118 inch
    Thrust washer thickness .... 0.0961 to 0.0980 inch

Engine block

Deck warpage limit .... 0.0020 inch
Cylinder bore diameter
    Standard
        Mark 1 .... 3.1890 to 3.1894 inches
        Mark 2 .... 3.1894 to 3.1898 inches
        Mark 3 .... 3.1898 to 3.1902 inches
    Service limit .... 3.1982 inches
Taper and out-of-round limits... 0.0008 inch

Pistons and rings

Piston diameter
    Mark 1 .... 3.1852 to 3.1856 inches
    Mark 2 .... 3.1856 to 3.1860 inches
    Mark 3 .... 3.1860 to 3.1864 inches
Piston-to-bore clearance
    Standard... 0.0033 to 0.0041 inch
    Service limit .... 0.009 inch
Piston ring end gap
    No. 1 (top) compression ring
        Standard .... 0.0098 to 0.0138 inch
        Service limit... 0.0413 inch
    No. 2 (middle) compression ring
        Standard .... 0.0138 to 0.0197 inch
        Service limit... 0.0472 inch
    Oil ring
        Standard .... 0.0039 to 0.0157 inch
        Service limit... 0.0413 inch
Piston ring groove clearance
    No. 1 (top) compression ring.. 0.0018 to 0.0033 inch
    No. 2 (middle) compression ring .... 0.0012 to 0.0028 inch

Torque specifications*

	Ft-lbs (unless otherwise indicated)
Main bearing cap bolts	44
Connecting rod cap nuts/bolts	
Step 1	
1.6L	22
1.8L	18
Step 2	Turn an additional 90-degrees (1/4-turn)

* **Note:** *Refer to Part A for additional torque specifications.*

2.4a The oil pressure can be checked by removing the sending unit and installing a pressure gauge in its place

2.4b The oil pressure sending unit (arrow) is located in the right front corner of the engine block, near the oil filter

1 General information

Included in this portion of Chapter 2 are the general overhaul procedures for the cylinder head(s) and internal engine components.

The information ranges from advice concerning preparation for an overhaul and the purchase of replacement parts to detailed, step-by-step procedures covering removal and installation of internal engine components and the inspection of parts.

The following Sections have been written based on the assumption that the engine has been removed from the vehicle. For information concerning in-vehicle engine repair, as well as removal and installation of the external components necessary for the overhaul, see Chapter 2A and Section 8 of this Chapter.

The Specifications included in this Part are only those necessary for the inspection and overhaul procedures which follow. Refer to Part A for additional Specifications.

2 Engine overhaul - general information

Refer to illustrations 2.4a and 2.4b

It's not always easy to determine when, or if, an engine should be completely overhauled, as a number of factors must be considered.

High mileage is not necessarily an indication that an overhaul is needed, while low mileage doesn't preclude the need for an overhaul. Frequency of servicing is probably the most important consideration. An engine that's had regular and frequent oil and filter changes, as well as other required maintenance, will most likely give many thousands of miles of reliable service. Conversely, a neglected engine may require an overhaul very early in its life.

Excessive oil consumption is an indication that piston rings, valve seals and/or valve guides are in need of attention. Make sure that oil leaks aren't responsible before deciding that the rings and/or guides are bad. Perform a cylinder compression check to determine the extent of the work required (see Section 4). Also check the vacuum readings under various conditions (see Section 3).

Check the oil pressure with a gauge installed in place of the oil pressure sending unit **(see illustrations)** and compare it to this Chap-

ter's Specifications. If it's extremely low, the bearings and/or oil pump are probably worn out.

Loss of power, rough running, knocking or metallic engine noises, excessive valve train noise and high fuel consumption rates may also point to the need for an overhaul, especially if they're all present at the same time. If a complete tune-up doesn't remedy the situation, major mechanical work is the only solution.

An engine overhaul involves restoring the internal parts to the specifications of a new engine. During an overhaul, the piston rings are replaced and the cylinder walls are reconditioned (rebored and/or honed). If a rebore is done by an automotive machine shop, new oversize pistons will also be installed. The main bearings, connecting rod bearings and camshaft bearings are generally replaced with new ones and, if necessary, the crankshaft may be reground to restore the journals. Generally, the valves are serviced as well, since they're usually in less-than-perfect condition at this point. While the engine is being overhauled, other components, such as the distributor, starter and alternator, can be rebuilt as well. The end result should be a like new engine that will give many trouble free miles. **Note:** *Critical cooling system components such as the hoses, drivebelts, thermostat and water pump should be replaced with new parts when an engine is overhauled. The radiator should be checked carefully to ensure that it isn't clogged or leaking (see Chapter 3). If you purchase a rebuilt engine or short block, some rebuilders will not warranty their engines unless the radiator has been professionally flushed. Also, we don't recommend overhauling the oil pump - always install a new one when an engine is rebuilt.*

Before beginning the engine overhaul, read through the entire procedure to familiarize yourself with the scope and requirements of the job. Overhauling an engine isn't difficult, but it is time-consuming. Plan on the vehicle being tied up for a minimum of two weeks, especially if parts must be taken to an automotive machine shop for repair or reconditioning. Check on availability of parts and make sure that any necessary special tools and equipment are obtained in advance. Most work can be done with typical hand tools, although a number of precision measuring tools are required for inspecting parts to determine if they must be replaced. Often an automotive machine shop will handle the inspection of parts and offer advice concerning reconditioning and replacement. **Note:** *Always wait until the engine has been completely disassembled and all components, especially the engine block, have been inspected* *before deciding what service and repair operations must be performed by an automotive machine shop.* Since the block's condition will be the major factor to consider when determining whether to overhaul the original engine or buy a rebuilt one, never purchase parts or have machine work done on other components until the block has been thoroughly inspected. As a general rule, time is the primary cost of an overhaul, so it doesn't pay to install worn or substandard parts.

As a final note, to ensure maximum life and minimum trouble from a rebuilt engine, everything must be assembled with care in a spotlessly-clean environment.

3   Vacuum gauge diagnostic checks

Refer to illustration 3.4

A vacuum gauge provides valuable information about what is going on in the engine at a low-cost. You can check for worn rings or cylinder walls, leaking head or intake manifold gaskets, incorrect carburetor adjustments, restricted exhaust, stuck or burned valves, weak valve springs, improper ignition or valve timing and ignition problems.

Unfortunately, vacuum gauge readings are easy to misinterpret, so they should be used in conjunction with other tests to confirm the diagnosis.

Both the absolute readings and the rate of needle movement are important for accurate interpretation. Most gauges measure vacuum in inches of mercury (in-Hg). As vacuum increases (or atmospheric pressure decreases), the reading will increase. Also, for every 1,000 foot increase in elevation above sea level, the gauge readings will decrease about one inch of mercury.

Connect the vacuum gauge directly to intake manifold vacuum, not to ported (above the throttle plate) vacuum **(see illustration)**. Be sure no hoses are left disconnected during the test or false readings will result.

Before you begin the test, allow the engine to warm up completely. Block the wheels and set the parking brake. With the transmission in neutral (or Park, on automatics), start the engine and allow it to run at normal idle speed. **Warning:** *Carefully inspect the fan blades for cracks or damage before starting the engine. Keep your hands and the vacuum tester clear of the fan and do not stand in front of the vehicle or in line with the fan when the engine is running.*

Read the vacuum gauge; an average, healthy engine should normally produce between 17 and 22 inches of vacuum with a fairly steady needle.

Refer to the following vacuum gauge readings and what they indicate about the engines condition:

1   A low steady reading usually indicates a leaking gasket between the intake manifold and carburetor or throttle body, a leaky vacuum hose, late ignition timing or incorrect camshaft timing. Check ignition timing with a timing light and eliminate all other possible causes, utilizing the tests provided in this Chapter before you remove the timing belt cover to check the timing marks.

2   If the reading is three to eight inches below normal and it fluctuates at that low reading, suspect an intake manifold gasket leak at an intake port or a faulty injector.

3   If the needle has regular drops of about two to four inches at a steady rate the valves are probably leaking. Perform a compression or leak-down test to confirm this.

4   An irregular drop or down-flick of the needle can be caused by a sticking valve or an ignition misfire. Perform a compression or leak-down test and read the spark plugs.

5   A rapid vibration of about four in-Hg vibration at idle combined with exhaust smoke indicates worn valve guides. Perform a leak-down test to confirm this. If the rapid vibration occurs with an increase in engine speed, check for a leaking intake manifold gasket or head gasket, weak valve springs, burned valves or ignition misfire.

6   A slight fluctuation, say one inch up and down, may mean ignition problems. Check all the usual tune-up items and, if necessary, run the engine on an ignition analyzer.

7   If there is a large fluctuation, perform a compression or leak-down test to look for a weak or dead cylinder or a blown head gasket.

8   If the needle moves slowly through a wide range, check for a clogged PCV system, incorrect idle fuel mixture, throttle body or intake manifold gasket leaks.

9   Check for a slow return after revving the engine by quickly snapping the throttle open until the engine reaches about 2,500 rpm and let it shut. Normally the reading should drop to near zero, rise above normal idle reading (about 5 in.-Hg over) and then return to the previous idle reading. If the vacuum returns slowly and doesn't peak when the throttle is snapped shut, the rings may be worn. If there is a long delay, look for a restricted exhaust system (often the muffler or catalytic converter). An easy way to check this is to temporarily disconnect the exhaust ahead of the suspected part and redo the test.

4   Cylinder compression check

Refer to illustration 4.6

1   A compression check will tell you what mechanical condition the upper end (pistons, rings, valves, head gasket[s]) of your engine is in. Specifically, it can tell you if the compression is down due to leakage caused by worn piston rings, defective valves and seats or a blown head gasket. **Note:** *The engine must be at normal operating temperature and the battery must be fully charged for this check.*

2   Begin by cleaning the area around the spark plugs before you remove them (compressed air should be used, if available, otherwise a small brush or even a bicycle tire pump will work). The idea is to prevent dirt from getting into the cylinders as the compression check is being done.

3   Remove all of the spark plugs from the engine (see Chapter 1).

4   Block the throttle wide open.

5   Detach the coil wire from the center of the distributor cap and ground it on the engine block. Use a jumper wire with alligator clips on each end to ensure a good ground. It is also a good idea to pull the EFI fuse from the fuse panel to disable the fuel pump during the compression test.

6   Install the compression gauge in the spark plug hole **(see illustration)**.

7   Crank the engine over at least seven compression strokes and watch the gauge. The compression should build up quickly in a healthy engine. Low compression on the first stroke, followed by gradually increasing pressure on successive strokes, indicates worn piston rings. A low compression reading on the first stroke, which doesn't build up during successive strokes, indicates leaking valves or a blown head gasket (a cracked head could also be the cause). Deposits on the undersides of the valve heads can also cause low compression. Record the highest gauge reading obtained.

8   Repeat the procedure for the remaining cylinders and compare the results to this Chapter's Specifications.

9   Add some engine oil (about three squirts from a plunger-type oil can) to each cylinder, through the spark plug hole, and repeat the test.

10   If the compression increases after the oil is added, the piston rings are definitely worn. If the compression doesn't increase significantly, the leakage is occurring at the valves or head gasket. Leakage past the valves may be caused by burned valve seats and/or faces or warped, cracked or bent valves.

11   If two adjacent cylinders have equally low compression, there's a strong possibility that the head gasket between them is blown. The appearance of coolant in the combustion chambers or the crankcase would verify this condition.

12   If one cylinder is 20-percent lower than the others, and the engine has a slightly rough idle, a worn exhaust lobe on the camshaft could be the cause.

13   If the compression is unusually high, the combustion chambers are probably coated with carbon deposits. If that's the case, the cylinder head(s) should be removed and decarbonized.

14   If compression is way down or varies greatly between cylinders, it would be a good idea to have a leak-down test performed by an automotive repair shop. This test will pinpoint exactly where the leakage is occurring and how severe it is.

3.4 The vacuum gauge is easily attached to this unused port (arrow) on the intake manifold

4.6 A compression gauge with a threaded fitting for the spark plug hole is preferred over the type that requires hand pressure to maintain the seal - be sure to block open the throttle valve as far as possible during the compression check!

6.7 Label both ends of each wire and hose before disconnecting it

5 Engine removal - methods and precautions

If you've decided that an engine must be removed for overhaul or major repair work, several preliminary steps should be taken.

Locating a suitable place to work is extremely important. Adequate work space, along with storage space for the vehicle, will be needed. If a shop or garage isn't available, at the very least a flat, level, clean work surface made of concrete or asphalt is required.

Cleaning the engine compartment and engine before beginning the removal procedure will help keep tools clean and organized.

An engine hoist or A-frame will also be necessary. Make sure the equipment is rated in excess of the combined weight of the engine and transaxle. Safety is of primary importance, considering the potential hazards involved in lifting the engine out of the vehicle.

If the engine is being removed by a novice, a helper should be available. Advice and aid from someone more experienced would also be helpful. There are many instances when one person cannot simultaneously perform all of the operations required when lifting the engine out of the vehicle.

Plan the operation ahead of time. Arrange for or obtain all of the tools and equipment you'll need prior to beginning the job. Some of the equipment necessary to perform engine removal and installation safely and with relative ease are (in addition to an engine hoist) a heavy duty floor jack, complete sets of wrenches and sockets as described in the front of this manual, wooden blocks and plenty of rags and cleaning solvent for mopping up spilled oil, coolant and gasoline. If the hoist must be rented, make sure that you arrange for it in advance and perform all of the operations possible without it beforehand. This will save you money and time.

Plan for the vehicle to be out of use for quite a while. A machine shop will be required to perform some of the work which the do-it-yourselfer can't accomplish without special equipment. These shops often have a busy schedule, so it would be a good idea to consult them before removing the engine in order to accurately estimate the amount of time required to rebuild or repair components that may need work.

Always be extremely careful when removing and installing the engine. Serious injury can result from careless actions. Plan ahead, take your time and a job of this nature, although major, can be accomplished successfully.

6 Engine - removal and installation

Refer to illustrations 6.7, 6.26 and 6.27

Note: *Read through the entire Section before beginning this procedure. The factory recommends removing the engine and transaxle from* the top as a unit, then separating the engine from the transaxle on the shop floor. If the transaxle is not being serviced, it is possible to leave the transaxle in the vehicle and remove the engine from the top by itself, by removing the crankshaft pulley and tilting up the timing belt end of the engine for clearance.

Removal

Warning: *These models are equipped with airbags. The airbag is armed and can deploy (inflate) anytime the battery is connected. To prevent accidental deployment (and possible injury), turn the ignition key to LOCK and disconnect the negative battery cable whenever working near airbag components. After the battery is disconnected, wait at least two minutes before beginning work (the system has a back-up capacitor that must fully discharge). For more information see Chapter 12.*

1 Relieve the fuel system pressure (see Chapter 4).

2 Disconnect the negative cable from the battery. **Caution:** *If the stereo in your vehicle is equipped with an anti-theft system, make sure you have the correct activation code before disconnecting the battery.*

3 Remove the battery and battery tray.

4 Place protective covers on the fenders and cowl and remove the hood (see Chapter 11).

5 Remove the air cleaner assembly (see Chapter 4).

6 Raise the vehicle and support it securely on jackstands. Drain the cooling system and engine oil and remove the drivebelts (see Chapter 1).

7 Clearly label, then disconnect all vacuum lines, coolant and emissions hoses, wiring harness connectors, ground straps and fuel lines. Masking tape and/or a touch up paint applicator work well for marking items **(see illustration)**. Take instant photos or sketch the locations of components and brackets.

8 Remove the windshield washer tank and coolant reservoir tank.

9 Remove the cooling fan(s) and radiator (see Chapter 3).

10 Disconnect the heater hoses.

11 Release the residual fuel pressure in the tank by removing the gas cap, then detach the fuel lines connecting the engine to the chassis (see Chapter 4). Plug or cap all open fittings.

12 Disconnect the throttle linkage, transmission Throttle Valve (TV) linkage and speed control cable, if equipped, from the engine (see Chapter 4).

13 Remove the battery and battery tray (see Chapter 5).

14 Refer to Part A of this Chapter and remove the intake and exhaust manifolds.

15 On power steering-equipped vehicles, unbolt the power steering pump. If clearance allows, tie the pump aside without disconnecting the hoses. If necessary, remove the pump (see Chapter 10).

16 On air-conditioned models, unbolt the compressor and set it aside. Do not disconnect the refrigerant hoses. **Note:** *Wire the com-*

6.26 Lift the engine high enough to clear the vehicle, then move it away and lower the hoist - this engine is being removed with the transaxle still attached

6.27 Lower the engine outside of the vehicle, remove the driveplate, and attach the engine to a suitable workstand

pressor out of the way with a coat hanger, don't let the compressor hang on the hoses.

17   Attach a lifting sling to the engine. Position a hoist and connect the sling to it. Take up the slack until there is slight tension on the hoist.

18   Refer to Chapter 8 and remove the driveaxles.

19   Remove the through-bolt holding the rear (firewall side) engine mount to its engine bracket, then pull the rubber access plugs from the longitudinal engine brace and remove the four nuts and five bolts (see Chapter 7A).

20   Refer to Part A of this Chapter and remove the drivebelts, water pump pulley and crankshaft pulley.

21   Remove the bolt securing the radiator-side engine mount to the chassis.

22   On automatic transaxle-equipped models, pry out the plastic torque converter dust shield from the lower bellhousing. Remove the torque converter-to-driveplate fasteners (see Chapter 7B) and push the converter back slightly into the bellhousing.

23   Remove the engine-to-transaxle bolts and separate the engine from the transaxle (see Chapter 7A). The torque converter should remain in the transaxle. **Note:** *If the transaxle is to be removed at the same time, the driver's side engine mount should be disconnected, along with any wires, cables or hoses connected to the transaxle. The engine-to-transaxle bolts should remain in place at this time.*

24   Recheck to be sure nothing except the mounts are still connecting the engine to the vehicle or to the transaxle. Disconnect and label anything still remaining.

25   Support the transaxle with a floor jack. Place a block of wood on the jack head to prevent damage to the transaxle. Remove the bolts from the engine mounts, leaving those attached to the transaxle in place. **Warning:** *Do not place any part of your body under the engine/transaxle when it's supported only by a hoist or other lifting device.*

26   Slowly lift the engine (or engine/transaxle) out of the vehicle **(see illustration)**. It may be necessary to pry the mounts away from the frame brackets. **Note:** *When removing the engine from a stick-shift vehicle and the transaxle is to remain in the vehicle, you may have to use the jack supporting the transaxle to tilt the transaxle enough to allow the engine to be angled forward and up out of the vehicle.*

27   Move the engine away from the vehicle and carefully lower the hoist until the engine can be set on the floor; or remove the flywheel/driveplate and mount the engine on an engine stand **(see illustration)**. **Note:** *On automatic transaxle-equipped models, mark the front and rear spacer plates and keep them with the driveplate.*

Installation

28   Check the engine/transaxle mounts. If they're worn or damaged, replace them.

29   On manual transaxle-equipped models, inspect the clutch components (see Chapter 8) and on automatic models inspect the converter seal and bushing.

30   On automatic transaxle-equipped models, apply a dab of grease to the nose of the converter.

31   Carefully guide the transaxle into place, following the procedure outlined in Chapter 7. **Caution:** *Do not use the bolts to force the engine and transaxle into alignment. It may crack or damage major components.*

32   Install the engine-to-transaxle bolts and tighten them to the torque listed in the Chapter 7 Specifications.

33   Attach the hoist to the engine and carefully lower the engine/transaxle assembly into the engine compartment. **Note:** *If the engine was removed with the transaxle remaining in the car, lower the engine into the car until an assistant can help you line up the dowel pins on the block with the transaxle. Some twisting and angling of the engine and/or the transaxle will be necessary to secure proper alignment of the two.*

34   Install the mount bolts and tighten them securely.

35   Reinstall the remaining components and fasteners in the reverse order of removal.

36   Add coolant, oil, power steering and transmission fluids as needed (see Chapter 1).

37   Run the engine and check for proper operation and leaks. Shut off the engine and recheck the fluid levels.

7   Engine rebuilding alternatives

The do-it-yourselfer is faced with a number of options when performing an engine overhaul. The decision to replace the engine block, piston/connecting rod assemblies and crankshaft depends on a number of factors, with the number one consideration being the condition of the block. Other considerations are cost, access to machine shop facilities, parts availability, time required to complete the project and the extent of prior mechanical experience on the part of the do-it-yourselfer.

Some of the rebuilding alternatives include:

Individual parts - If the inspection procedures reveal that the engine block and most engine components are in reusable condition, purchasing individual parts may be the most economical alternative. The block, crankshaft and piston/connecting rod assemblies should all be inspected carefully. Even if the block shows little wear, the cylinder bores should be surface honed.

Short block - A short block consists of an engine block with a crankshaft and piston/connecting rod assemblies already installed. All new bearings are incorporated and all clearances will be correct. The existing camshafts, valve train components, cylinder head and external

Piston Ring (No.1 Compression)
Piston Ring (Side Rail)

4A-FE

Piston Ring (No.2 Compression)
Piston Ring (Expander)
Piston Pin
Connecting Rod
Connecting Rod Bearing
Connecting Rod Cap

Piston Ring (No.1 Compression)
Piston Ring (Side Rail)
Piston Pin

A/T
Front Spacer
Rear Plate
Drive Plate
Rear End Plate

8.5 Four-cylinder engine lower end components - exploded view

O-Ring
Knock Sensor
Water Pump
RH Engine Mounting Bracket
Gasket
Oil Pump
Crankshaft Front Oil Seal
Gasket
Crank Shaft
Main Bearing
Crankshaft Thrust Washer
Main Bearing Cap
Crankshaft Rear Oil Seal
Flywheel
Rear End Plate
Rear Oil Seal Retainer
Oil Filter
Oil Pressure Switch
Alternator Bracket

parts can be bolted to the short block with little or no machine shop work necessary.

Long block - A long block consists of a short block plus an oil pump, oil pan, cylinder head, valve cover, camshaft and valve train components, timing sprockets and chain or gears and timing cover. All components are installed with new bearings, seals and gaskets incorporated throughout. The installation of manifolds and external parts is all that's necessary.

Give careful thought to which alternative is best for you and discuss the situation with local automotive machine shops, auto parts dealers and experienced rebuilders before ordering or purchasing replacement parts.

8 Engine overhaul - disassembly sequence

Refer to illustration 8.5

1   It's much easier to disassemble and work on the engine if it's mounted on a portable engine stand. A stand can often be rented quite cheaply from an equipment rental yard. Before the engine is mounted on a stand, the flywheel/driveplate and rear oil seal retainer should be removed from the engine.

2   If a stand isn't available, it's possible to disassemble the engine with it blocked up on the floor. Be extra careful not to tip or drop the engine when working without a stand.

3   If you're going to obtain a rebuilt engine, all external components must come off first, to be transferred to the replacement engine, just as they will if you're doing a complete engine overhaul yourself. These include:

Alternator and brackets
Emissions control components
Distributor, spark plug wires and spark plugs

Thermostat and housing cover
Water pump
EFI components
Intake/exhaust manifolds
Oil filter
Engine mounts
Clutch and flywheel/driveplate
Engine rear plate

Note: *When removing the external components from the engine, pay close attention to details that may be helpful or important during installation. Note the installed position of gaskets, seals, spacers, pins, brackets, washers, bolts and other small items.*

4   If you're obtaining a short block, which consists of the engine block, crankshaft, pistons and connecting rods all assembled, then the cylinder head, oil pan and oil pump will have to be removed as well from your engine so that your short block can be turned in to the rebuilder as a core. See *Engine rebuilding alternatives* for additional information regarding the different possibilities to be considered.

5   If you're planning a complete overhaul, the engine must be disassembled and the internal components removed in the following order **(see illustration)**.

Intake and exhaust manifolds
Valve cover
Timing belt covers
Timing belt and sprockets
Cylinder head
Oil pan
Oil pump
Piston/connecting rod assemblies
Crankshaft rear oil seal retainer
Crankshaft and main bearings

6   Before beginning the disassembly and overhaul procedures,

9.2 A small plastic bag, with an appropriate label, can be used to store the valve train components so they can be kept together and reinstalled in the correct guide

9.3 Compress the spring until the keepers can be removed with a small magnetic screwdriver or needle-nose pliers

make sure the following items are available. Also, refer to Section 21 for a list of tools and materials needed for engine reassembly.

> *Common hand tools*
> *Small cardboard boxes or plastic bags for storing parts*
> *Gasket scraper*
> *Ridge reamer*
> *Micrometers*
> *Telescoping gauges*
> *Dial indicator set*
> *Valve spring compressor*
> *Cylinder surfacing hone*
> *Piston ring groove-cleaning tool*
> *Electric drill motor*
> *Tap and die set*
> *Wire brushes*
> *Oil gallery brushes*
> *Cleaning solvent*

9   Cylinder head - disassembly

Refer to illustrations 9.2 and 9.3
Note: *New and rebuilt cylinder heads are commonly available for most engines at dealerships and auto parts stores. Due to the fact that some specialized tools are necessary for the disassembly and inspection procedures, and replacement parts may not be readily available, it may be more practical and economical for the home mechanic to purchase a replacement head rather than taking the time to disassemble, inspect and recondition the original.*

1   Cylinder head disassembly involves removal of the intake and exhaust valves and related components. It's assumed that the lifters and camshafts have already been removed (see Part A as needed).

2   Before the valves are removed, arrange to label and store them, along with their related components, so they can be kept separate and reinstalled in the same valve guides they are removed from **(see illustration)**.

3   Compress the springs on the first valve with a spring compressor and remove the keepers **(see illustration)**. Carefully release the valve spring compressor and remove the retainer, the spring and the spring seat (if used). **Caution:** *Be very careful not to nick or otherwise damage the lifter bores when compressing the valve springs.* **Note:** *If your spring compressor does not have an end (such as the one shown) with cutouts on the side, an adapter is available to use with a standard spring compressor.*

4   Pull the valve out of the head, then remove the oil seal from the guide. If the valve binds in the guide (won't pull through), push it back

into the head and deburr the area around the keeper groove with a fine file or whetstone.

5   Repeat the procedure for the remaining valves. Remember to keep all the parts for each valve together so they can be reinstalled in the same locations.

6   Once the valves and related components have been removed and stored in an organized manner, the head should be thoroughly cleaned and inspected. If a complete engine overhaul is being done, finish the engine disassembly procedures before beginning the cylinder head cleaning and inspection process.

10   Cylinder head - cleaning and inspection

Refer to illustrations 10.12, 10.14, 10.16, 10.17 and 10.18
1   Thorough cleaning of the cylinder head(s) and related valve train components, followed by a detailed inspection, will enable you to decide how much valve service work must be done during the engine overhaul. **Note:** *If the engine was severely overheated, the cylinder head is probably warped (see Step 12).*

Cleaning

2   Scrape all traces of old gasket material and sealing compound off the head gasket, intake manifold and exhaust manifold sealing surfaces. Be very careful not to gouge the cylinder head. Special gasket-removal solvents that soften gaskets and make removal much easier are available at auto parts stores.

3   Remove all built up scale from the coolant passages.

4   Run a stiff wire brush through the various holes to remove deposits that may have formed in them. If there are heavy rust deposits in the water passages, the bare head should be professionally cleaned at a machine shop.

5   Run an appropriate-size tap into each of the threaded holes to remove corrosion and thread sealant that may be present. If compressed air is available, use it to clear the holes of debris produced by this operation. **Warning:** *Wear eye protection when using compressed air!*

6   Clean the exhaust and intake manifold stud threads with a wire brush.

7   Clean the cylinder head with solvent and dry it thoroughly. Compressed air will speed the drying process and ensure that all holes and recessed areas are clean. **Note:** *Decarbonizing chemicals are available and may prove very useful when cleaning cylinder heads and valve train components. They are very caustic and should be used with caution. Be sure to follow the instructions on the container.*

8   Clean the lifters with solvent and dry them thoroughly. Compressed air will speed the drying process and can be used to clean out the oil passages. Don't mix them up during the cleaning process; keep

10.12 Check the cylinder head gasket surfaces for warpage by trying to slip a feeler gauge under the precision straightedge (see the Specifications for the maximum warpage allowed and use a feeler gauge of that thickness)

them in a box with numbered compartments.

9   Clean all the valve springs, spring seats, keepers and retainers with solvent and dry them thoroughly. Work on the components from one valve at a time to avoid mixing up the parts.

10   Scrape off any heavy deposits that may have formed on the valves, then use a motorized wire brush to remove deposits from the valve heads and stems. Again, make sure the valves don't get mixed up.

Inspection

Note: *Be sure to perform all of the following inspection procedures before concluding that machine shop work is required. Make a list of the items that need attention. The inspection procedures for the lifters and camshafts, can be found in Part A.*

Cylinder head

11   Inspect the head very carefully for cracks, evidence of coolant leakage and other damage. If cracks are found, check with an automotive machine shop concerning repair. If repair isn't possible, a new cylinder head should be obtained.

12   Using a straightedge and feeler gauge, check the head gasket mating surface for warpage **(see illustration)**. If the warpage exceeds the limit found in this Chapter's Specifications, it can be resurfaced at an automotive machine shop.

13   Examine the valve seats in each of the combustion chambers. If they're pitted, cracked or burned, the head will require valve service that's beyond the scope of the home mechanic.

10.16 The margin width on each valve must be as specified (if no margin exists, the valve cannot be re-used)

10.14 Use a small dial bore gauge to determine the inside diameter of the valve guides

14   Check the valve stem-to-guide clearance with a small hole gauge and micrometer, or a small dial bore gauge **(see illustration)**. Also, check the valve stem deflection with a dial indicator attached securely to the head. The valve must be in the guide and approximately 1/16-inch off the seat. The total valve stem movement indicated by the gauge needle must be noted, then divided by two to obtain the actual clearance value. If it exceeds the stem-to-guide clearance limit found in this Chapter's Specifications, the valve guides should be replaced. After this is done, if there's still some doubt regarding the condition of the valve guides they should be checked by an automotive machine shop (the cost should be minimal). **Note:** *Most home mechanics will not have a precision small bore gauge, but your local machine shop can measure the guides for you.*

Valves

15   Carefully inspect each valve face for uneven wear, deformation, cracks, pits and burned areas. Check the valve stem for scuffing and galling and the neck for cracks. Rotate the valve and check for any obvious indication that it's bent. Look for pits and excessive wear on the end of the stem. The presence of any of these conditions indicates the need for valve service by an automotive machine shop.

16   Measure the margin width on each valve **(see illustration)**. Any valve with a margin narrower than that listed in this Chapter's Specifications will have to be replaced with a new one.

Valve components

17   Check each valve spring for wear (on the ends) and pits. Measure the free length and compare it to this Chapter's Specifications **(see illustration)**. Any springs that are shorter than specified have sagged and should not be re-used. The tension of all springs should be pressure checked with a special fixture before deciding that they're suitable for use in a rebuilt engine (take the springs to an automotive machine shop for this check).

10.17 Measure the free length of each valve spring with a dial or vernier caliper

10.18 Check each valve spring for squareness

12.3 Gently tap the valve seals (arrow) into place with a deep socket and hammer - the intake seals are painted brown, while the exhaust seals are painted black (don't mix them up)

12.6 The small valve stem keepers are easier to position when coated with grease

18   Stand each spring on a flat surface and check it for squareness **(see illustration)**. If any of the springs are distorted or sagged, replace all of them with new parts.

19   Check the spring retainers and keepers for obvious wear and cracks. Any questionable parts should be replaced with new ones, as extensive damage will occur if they fail during engine operation.

20   Any damaged or excessively worn parts must be replaced with new ones.

21   If the inspection process indicates that the valve components are in generally poor condition and worn beyond the limits specified, which is usually the case in an engine that's being overhauled, reassemble the valves in the cylinder head and refer to Section 11 for valve servicing recommendations.

11   Valves - servicing

1   Because of the complex nature of the job and the special tools and equipment needed, servicing of the valves, the valve seats and the valve guides, commonly known as a valve job, should be done by a professional.

2   The home mechanic can remove and disassemble the head(s), do the initial cleaning and inspection, then reassemble and deliver them to a dealer service department or an automotive machine shop for the actual service work. Doing the inspection will enable you to see what condition the head(s) and valvetrain components are in and will ensure that you know what work and new parts are required when dealing with an automotive machine shop.

3   The dealer service department, or automotive machine shop, will remove the valves and springs, recondition or replace the valves and valve seats, recondition the valve guides, check and replace the valve springs, spring retainers and keepers (as necessary), replace the valve seals with new ones, reassemble the valve components and make sure the installed spring height is correct. The cylinder head gasket surface will also be resurfaced if it's warped.

4   After the valve job has been performed by a professional, the head(s) will be in like new condition. When the heads are returned, be sure to clean them again before installation on the engine to remove any metal particles and abrasive grit that may still be present from the valve service or head resurfacing operations. Use compressed air, if available, to blow out all the oil holes and passages.

12   Cylinder head - reassembly

Refer to illustrations 12.3 and 12.6

1   Regardless of whether or not the head was sent to an automotive machine shop for valve servicing, make sure it's clean before beginning reassembly. Note that there are several small core plugs (also called freeze plugs or expansion plugs) in the head. These should be replaced whenever the engine is overhauled or the cylinder head is reconditioned (see Section 15 for replacement procedure).

2   If the head was sent out for valve servicing, the valves and related components will already be in place. Begin the reassembly procedure with Step 8.

3   Install new seals on each of the valve guides. **Note:** *Intake and exhaust valves require different seals - DO NOT mix them up!* Gently tap each intake valve seal into place until it's seated on the guide **(see illustration)**. **Caution:** *Don't hammer on the valve seals once they're seated or you may damage them. Don't twist or cock the seals during installation or they won't seat properly on the valve stems.*

4   Beginning at one end of the head, lubricate and install the first valve. Apply moly-base grease or clean engine oil to the valve stem.

5   Drop the spring seat or shim(s) over the valve guide and set the valve spring and retainer in place.

6   Compress the springs with a valve spring compressor and carefully install the keepers in the upper groove, then slowly release the compressor and make sure the keepers seat properly. Apply a small dab of grease to each keeper to hold it in place if necessary **(see illustration)**.

7   Repeat the procedure for the remaining valves. Be sure to return the components to their original locations - don't mix them up!

8   Check the valve spring installed height with a dial or vernier caliper.

13   Pistons/connecting rods - removal

Refer to illustrations 13.1, 13.3, 13.4 and 13.6

Note: *Prior to removing the piston/connecting rod assemblies, remove the cylinder head(s), the oil pan and the oil pump pick-up tube by referring to the appropriate Sections in Chapter 2A.*

1   Use your fingernail to feel if a ridge has formed at the upper limit of ring travel (about 1/4-inch down from the top of each cylinder). If carbon deposits or cylinder wear have produced ridges, they must be completely removed with a special tool **(see illustration)**. Follow the manufacturer's instructions provided with the tool. Failure to remove the ridges before attempting to remove the piston/connecting rod assemblies may result in piston damage.

2   After the cylinder ridges have been removed, turn the engine upside-down so the crankshaft is facing up.

3   Before the connecting rods are removed, check the endplay with feeler gauges. Slide them between the first connecting rod and the crankshaft throw until the play is removed **(see illustration)**. The endplay is equal to the thickness of the feeler gauge(s). If the endplay exceeds the specified service limit, new connecting rods will be

13.1 A ridge reamer is required to remove the ridge from the top of each cylinder - do this before removing the pistons!

13.3 Check the connecting rod side clearance with a feeler gauge as shown here

13.4 The connecting rods and caps should be marked to indicate which cylinder they're installed in - if they aren't, mark them with a center punch to avoid confusion during reassembly - do not confuse the markings shown here as rod numbers; these are bearing size identifications

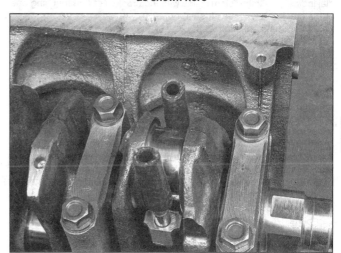

13.6 To prevent damage to the crankshaft journals and cylinder walls, slip sections of hose over the rod bolts before removing the pistons

2B

required. If new rods (or a new crankshaft) are installed, the endplay may fall under the service limit (if it does, the rods will have to be machined to restore it - consult an automotive machine shop for advice if necessary). Repeat the procedure for the remaining connecting rods.

4　　Check the connecting rods and caps for identification marks. If they aren't plainly marked, use a small center punch to make the appropriate number of indentations on each rod and cap (1, 2, 3, etc., depending on the engine type and cylinder they're associated with) **(see illustration)**.

5　　Loosen each of the connecting rod cap nuts 1/2-turn at a time until they can be removed by hand. Remove the number one connecting rod cap and bearing insert. Don't drop the bearing insert out of the cap. **Note:** *The 1.6L engines use conventional rod bolts (pressed into the rod) and nuts, while the 1.8L engine uses cap bolts that go through the rod cap and screw into the rod.*

6　　Slip a short length of plastic or rubber hose over each connecting rod cap bolt to protect the crankshaft journal and cylinder wall as the piston is removed **(see illustration)**.

7　　Remove the bearing insert and push the connecting rod/piston assembly out through the top of the engine. Use a wooden hammer handle to push on the upper bearing surface in the connecting rod. If resistance is felt, double-check to make sure that all of the ridge was

removed from the cylinder.

8　　Repeat the procedure for the remaining cylinders. **Note:** *Turn the crankshaft as needed to put the rod to be removed close to parallel with the cylinder bore, i.e. don't try to drive it out while at a large angle to the bore.*

9　　After removal, reassemble the connecting rod caps and bearing inserts in their respective connecting rods and install the cap nuts/bolts finger tight. Leaving the old bearing inserts in place until reassembly will help prevent the connecting rod bearing surfaces from being accidentally nicked or gouged.

10　Don't separate the pistons from the connecting rods (see Section 18 for additional information).

14　Crankshaft - removal

Refer to illustrations 14.1 and 14.3

Note: *The crankshaft can be removed only after the engine has been removed from the vehicle. It's assumed that the flywheel or driveplate, crankshaft sprocket, timing belt, oil pan, oil pick-up tube, oil pump and piston/connecting rod assemblies have already been removed. The rear main oil seal and retainer must be removed from the block before proceeding with crankshaft removal.*

1　　Before the crankshaft is removed, check the endplay. Mount a

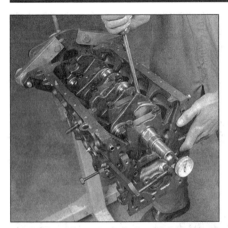

14.1 Checking crankshaft endplay with a dial indicator

14.3 Checking crankshaft endplay with a feeler gauge

15.1a A hammer and a large punch can be used to knock the core plugs sideways in their bores

dial indicator with the stem in line with the crankshaft and touching one of the crank throws **(see illustration)**.

2   Push the crankshaft all the way to the rear and zero the dial indicator. Next, pry the crankshaft to the front as far as possible and check the reading on the dial indicator. The distance that it moves is the endplay. If it's greater than specified, check the crankshaft thrust surfaces for wear. If no wear is evident, new thrust washers should correct the endplay.

3   If a dial indicator isn't available, feeler gauges can be used. Gently pry or push the crankshaft all the way to the front of the engine. Slip feeler gauges between the crankshaft and the front face of the number 3 (thrust) main bearing to determine the clearance **(see illustration)**.

4   Check the main bearing caps to see if they're marked to indicate their locations. They should be numbered consecutively from the front of the engine to the rear. If they aren't, mark them with number stamping dies or a center punch. Main bearing caps generally have a cast-in arrow, which points to the front of the engine. Loosen the main bearing cap bolts 1/4-turn at a time each, in the reverse order of the recommended tightening sequence **(see illustration 23.12)**, until they can be removed by hand.

5   Gently tap the caps with a soft-face hammer, then separate them from the engine block. If necessary, use the bolts as levers to remove the caps. Try not to drop the bearing inserts if they come out with the caps.

6   Carefully lift the crankshaft out of the engine. It may be a good idea to have an assistant available, since the crankshaft is quite heavy. With the bearing inserts in place in the engine block and main bearing caps or cap assembly, return the caps to their respective locations on the engine block and tighten the bolts finger tight.

15   Engine block - cleaning

Refer to illustrations 15.1a, 15.1b, 15.8 and 15.10
Caution: *The core plugs (also known as freeze or soft plugs) may be difficult or impossible to retrieve if they're driven completely into the block coolant passages.*

1   Using the blunt end of a punch, tap in on the outer edge of the core plug to turn the plug sideways in the bore. Then using pliers, pull the core plug from the engine block **(see illustrations)**.

2   Using a gasket scraper, remove all traces of gasket material from the engine block. Be very careful not to nick or gouge the gasket sealing surfaces.

3   Remove the main bearing caps or cap assembly and separate the bearing inserts from the caps and the engine block. Tag the bearings, indicating which cylinder they were removed from and whether they were in the cap or the block, then set them aside.

4   Remove all of the threaded oil gallery plugs from the block. The plugs are usually very tight - they may have to be drilled out and the

holes retapped. Use new plugs when the engine is reassembled.

5   If the engine is extremely dirty, it should be taken to an automotive machine shop to be steam cleaned or hot tanked.

6   After the block is returned, clean all oil holes and oil galleries one more time. Brushes specifically designed for this purpose are available at most auto parts stores. Flush the passages with warm water until the water runs clear, dry the block thoroughly and wipe all machined surfaces with a light, rust preventive oil. If you have access to compressed air, use it to speed the drying process and to blow out all the oil holes and galleries. **Warning:** *Wear eye protection when using compressed air!*

7   If the block isn't extremely dirty or sludged up, you can do an adequate cleaning job with hot soapy water and a stiff brush. Take plenty of time and do a thorough job. Regardless of the cleaning method used, be sure to clean all oil holes and galleries very thoroughly, dry the block completely and coat all machined surfaces with light oil.

8   The threaded holes in the block must be clean to ensure accurate torque readings during reassembly. Run the proper size tap into each of the holes to remove rust, corrosion, thread sealant or sludge and restore damaged threads **(see illustration)**. If possible, use compressed air to clear the holes of debris produced by this operation. Now is a good time to clean the threads on the head bolts and the main bearing cap bolts as well.

9   Reinstall the main bearing caps and tighten the bolts finger tight.

10   After coating the sealing surfaces of the new core plugs with Permatex no. 2 sealant, install them in the engine block **(see illustration)**. Make sure they're driven in straight and seated properly or leakage could result. Special tools are available for this purpose, but a large socket, with an outside diameter that will just slip into the core plug, a 1/2-inch drive extension and a hammer will work just as well.

11   Apply non-hardening sealant (such as Permatex no. 2 or Teflon pipe sealant) to the new oil gallery plugs and thread them into the holes in the block. Make sure they're tightened securely.

12   If the engine isn't going to be reassembled right away, cover it with a large plastic trash bag to keep it clean.

16   Engine block - inspection

Refer to illustrations 16.4a, 16.4b, 16.4c and 16.9

1   Before the block is inspected, it should be cleaned as described in Section 15.

2   Visually check the block for cracks, rust and corrosion. Look for stripped threads in the threaded holes. It's also a good idea to have the block checked for hidden cracks by an automotive machine shop that has the special equipment to do this type of work, especially if the vehicle had a history of overheating or using coolant. If defects are found, have the block repaired, if possible, or replaced.

15.1b Pull the core plugs from the block with pliers

15.8 All bolt holes in the block - particularly the main bearing cap and head bolt holes - should be cleaned and restored with a tap (be sure to remove debris from the holes after this is done)

15.10 A large socket on an extension can be used to drive the new core plugs into the bores

2B

16.4a Measure the diameter of each cylinder at a right angle to engine centerline (A), and parallel to engine centerline (B) - out-of-round is the difference between A and B; taper is the difference between A and B at the top of the cylinder and A and B at the bottom of the cylinder

16.4b The ability to "feel" when the telescoping gauge is at the correct point will be developed over time, so work slowly and repeat the check until you're satisfied that the bore measurement is accurate

3   Check the cylinder bores for scuffing and scoring.
4   Check the cylinders for taper and out-of-round conditions as follows **(see illustrations)**:
5   Measure the diameter of each cylinder at the top (just under the ridge area), center and bottom of the cylinder bore, parallel to the crankshaft axis.
6   Next, measure each cylinder's diameter at the same three locations perpendicular to the crankshaft axis.
7   The taper of each cylinder is the difference between the bore diameter at the top of the cylinder and the diameter at the bottom. The out-of-round specification of the cylinder bore is the difference between the parallel and perpendicular readings. Compare your results to this Chapter's Specifications.
8   If the cylinder walls are badly scuffed or scored, or if they're out-of-round or tapered beyond the limits given in this Chapter's Specifications, have the engine block rebored and honed at an automotive machine shop. If a rebore is done, oversize pistons and rings will be required.

16.4c The gauge is then measured with a micrometer to determine the bore size

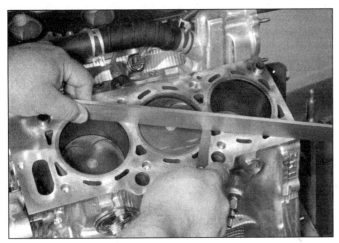

16.9 Check the block deck for distortion with a precision straightedge and feeler gauges

17.3a A "bottle brush" hone will produce better results if you have never done cylinder honing before

9   Using a precision straightedge and feeler gauge, check the block deck (the surface that mates with the cylinder head) for distortion **(see illustration)**. If it's distorted beyond the specified limit, it can be resurfaced by an automotive machine shop.

10   If the cylinders are in reasonably good condition and not worn to the outside of the limits, and if the piston-to-cylinder clearances can be maintained properly, then they don't have to be rebored. Honing is all that's necessary (refer to Section 17).

17   Cylinder honing

Refer to illustrations 17.3a and 17.3b

1   Prior to engine reassembly, the cylinder bores must be honed so the new piston rings will seat correctly and provide the best possible combustion chamber seal. **Note:** *If you don't have the tools or don't want to tackle the honing operation, most automotive machine shops will do it for a reasonable fee.*

2   Before honing the cylinders, install the main bearing caps or cap assembly (without bearing inserts) and tighten the bolts to the specified torque.

3   Two types of cylinder hones are commonly available - the flex hone or "bottle brush" type and the more traditional surfacing hone with spring-loaded stones. Both will do the job, but for the less-experienced mechanic the "bottle brush" hone will probably be easier to use. You'll

also need some kerosene or honing oil, rags and an electric drill motor. The drill motor should be operated at a steady, slow speed. Use a large 1/2-inch drill or a 3/8-inch variable-speed drill. Proceed as follows:

a) *Mount the hone in the drill motor, compress the stones and slip it into the first cylinder* **(see illustration)**. **Warning:** *Be sure to wear safety goggles or a face shield!*

b) *Lubricate the cylinder with plenty of honing oil, turn on the drill and move the hone up-and-down in the cylinder at a pace that will produce a fine crosshatch pattern on the cylinder walls. Ideally, the crosshatch lines should intersect at approximately a 60-degree angle* **(see illustration)**. *Be sure to use plenty of lubricant and don't take off any more material than is absolutely necessary to produce the desired finish.* **Note:** *Piston ring manufacturers may specify a smaller crosshatch angle than the traditional 60-degrees - read and follow any instructions included with the new rings.*

c) *Don't withdraw the hone from the cylinder while it's running. Instead, shut off the drill and continue moving the hone up-and-down in the cylinder until it comes to a complete stop, then compress the stones and withdraw the hone. If you're using a "bottle brush" type hone, stop the drill motor, then turn the chuck in the normal direction of rotation while withdrawing the hone from the cylinder.*

d) *Wipe the oil out of the cylinder and repeat the procedure for the remaining cylinders.*

4   After the honing job is complete, chamfer the top edges of the cylinder bores with a small file so the rings won't catch when the pistons are installed. Be very careful not to nick the cylinder walls with the end of the file.

5   The entire engine block must be washed again very thoroughly with warm, soapy water to remove all traces of the abrasive grit produced during the honing operation. **Note:** *The bores can be considered clean when a lint-free white cloth - dampened with clean engine oil - used to wipe them out doesn't pick up any more honing residue, which will show up as gray areas on the cloth. Be sure to run a brush through all oil holes and galleries and flush them with running water.*

6   After rinsing, dry the block and apply a coat of light rust preventive oil to all machined surfaces. Wrap the block in a plastic trash bag to keep it clean and set it aside until reassembly.

18   Pistons/connecting rods - inspection

Refer to illustrations 18.4a, 18.4b, 18.10 and 18.11

1   Before the inspection process can be carried out, the piston/connecting rod assemblies must be cleaned and the original piston rings removed from the pistons. **Note:** *Always use new piston rings when the engine is reassembled.*

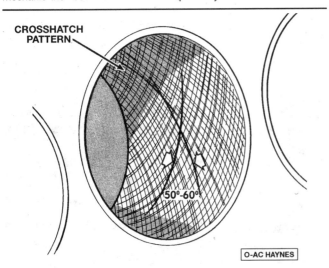

CROSSHATCH
PATTERN

50°-60°

O-AC HAYNES

17.3b The cylinder hone should leave a smooth, crosshatch pattern with the lines intersecting at approximately a 60-degree angle

18.4a The piston ring grooves can be cleaned with a special tool, as shown here . . .

18.4b . . . or a section of a broken ring

18.10 Check the ring groove clearance with a feeler gauge at several points around the groove

2   Using a piston ring installation tool, carefully remove the rings from the pistons. Be careful not to nick or gouge the pistons in the process.

3   Scrape all traces of carbon from the top of the piston. A hand-held wire brush or a piece of fine emery cloth can be used once the majority of the deposits have been scraped away. Do not, under any circumstances, use a wire brush mounted in a drill motor to remove deposits from the pistons. The piston material is soft and may be eroded away by the wire brush.

4   Use a piston ring groove-cleaning tool to remove carbon deposits from the ring grooves. If a tool isn't available, a piece broken off the old ring will do the job. Be very careful to remove only the carbon deposits - don't remove any metal and do not nick or scratch the sides of the ring grooves **(see Illustrations)**.

5   Once the deposits have been removed, clean the piston/rod assemblies with solvent and dry them with compressed air (if available). Make sure the oil return holes in the back sides of the ring grooves and the oil hole in the lower end of each rod are clear.

6   If the pistons and cylinder walls aren't damaged or worn excessively, and if the engine block is not rebored, new pistons won't be necessary. Normal piston wear appears as even vertical wear on the piston thrust surfaces and slight looseness of the top ring in its groove. New piston rings, however, should always be used when an engine is rebuilt.

7   Carefully inspect each piston for cracks around the skirt, at the pin bosses and at the ring lands.

8   Look for scoring and scuffing on the thrust faces of the skirt, holes in the piston crown and burned areas at the edge of the crown. If

the skirt is scored or scuffed, the engine may have been suffering from overheating and/or abnormal combustion, which caused excessively high operating temperatures. The cooling and lubrication systems should be checked thoroughly. A hole in the piston crown is an indication that abnormal combustion (preignition) was occurring. Burned areas at the edge of the piston crown are usually evidence of spark knock (detonation). If any of the above problems exist, the causes must be corrected or the damage will occur again. The causes may include intake air leaks, incorrect air/fuel mixture, incorrect ignition timing and EGR system malfunctions.

9   Corrosion of the piston, in the form of small pits, indicates that coolant is leaking into the combustion chamber and/or the crankcase. Again, the cause must be corrected or the problem may persist in the rebuilt engine.

10   Measure the piston ring groove clearance by laying a new piston ring in each ring groove and slipping a feeler gauge in beside it **(see illustration)**. Check the clearance at three or four locations around each groove. Be sure to use the correct ring for each groove - they are different. If the clearance is greater than that listed in this Chapter's Specifications, new pistons will have to be used.

11   Check the piston-to-bore clearance by measuring the bore (see Section 16) and the piston diameter. Make sure the pistons and bores are correctly matched. Measure the piston across the skirt, at a 90-degree angle to the piston pin **(see illustration)**. Subtract the piston diameter from the bore diameter to obtain the clearance. If it's greater than specified, the block will have to be rebored and new pistons and rings installed.

12   Check the piston-to-rod clearance by twisting the piston and rod in opposite directions. Any noticeable play indicates excessive wear, which must be corrected.

13   If the pistons must be removed from the connecting rods for any reason, the rods should be taken to an automotive machine shop, to be checked for bend and twist, since automotive machine shops have special equipment for this purpose.

14   Check the connecting rods for cracks and other damage. Temporarily remove the rod caps, lift out the old bearing inserts, wipe the rod and cap bearing surfaces clean and inspect them for nicks, gouges and scratches. After checking the rods, replace the old bearings, slip the caps into place and tighten the nuts finger tight. **Note:** *If the engine is being rebuilt because of a connecting rod knock, be sure to install new rods.*

18.11 Measure the piston diameter at a 90-degree angle to the piston pin, at the bottom of the piston pin area - a precision caliper may be used if a micrometer isn't available

19   Crankshaft - inspection

Refer to illustration 19.6

1   Clean the crankshaft with solvent and dry it with compressed air (if available).

2   Check the main and connecting rod bearing journals for uneven wear, scoring, pits and cracks.

2B

19.6 Measure the diameter of each crankshaft journal at several points to detect taper and out-of-round conditions

3   Remove all burrs from the crankshaft oil holes with a stone, file or scraper.

4   Clean the oil holes with a stiff brush and flush them with solvent.

5   Check the rest of the crankshaft for cracks and other damage. It should be magnafluxed to reveal hidden cracks - an automotive machine shop will handle the procedure.

6   Using a micrometer, measure the diameter of the main and connecting rod journals and compare the results to this Chapter's Specifications **(see illustration)**. By measuring the diameter at a number of points around each journal's circumference, you'll be able to determine whether or not the journal is out-of-round. Take the measurement at each end of the journal, near the crank throws, to determine if the journal is tapered. Crankshaft runout should be checked also, but large V-blocks and a dial indicator are needed to do it correctly. If you don't have the equipment, have a machine shop check the runout.

7   If the crankshaft journals are damaged, tapered, out-of-round or worn beyond the limits given in the Specifications, have the crankshaft reground by an automotive machine shop. Be sure to use the correct size bearing inserts if the crankshaft is reconditioned.

8   Check the oil seal journals at each end of the crankshaft for wear and damage. If the seal has worn a groove in the journal, or if it's nicked or scratched, the new seal may leak when the engine is reassembled. In some cases, an automotive machine shop may be able to repair the journal by pressing on a thin sleeve. If repair isn't feasible, a new or different crankshaft should be installed.

9   Refer to Section 20 and examine the main and rod bearing inserts.

20   Main and connecting rod bearings - inspection and selection

Inspection

Refer to illustration 20.1

1   Even though the main and connecting rod bearings should be replaced with new ones during the engine overhaul, the old bearings should be retained for close examination, as they may reveal valuable information about the condition of the engine **(see illustration)**.

2   Bearing failure occurs because of lack of lubrication, the presence of dirt or other foreign particles, overloading the engine and corrosion. Regardless of the cause of bearing failure, it must be corrected before the engine is reassembled to prevent it from happening again.

3   When examining the bearings, remove them from the engine block, the main bearing caps, the connecting rods and the rod caps and lay them out on a clean surface in the same general position as their location in the engine. This will enable you to match any bearing problems with the corresponding crankshaft journal.

4   Dirt and other foreign particles get into the engine in a variety of

20.1 When inspecting the main and connecting rod bearings, look for these problems

ways. It may be left in the engine during assembly, or it may pass through filters or the PCV system. It may get into the oil, and from there into the bearings. Metal chips from machining operations and normal engine wear are often present. Abrasives are sometimes left in engine components after reconditioning, especially when parts are not thoroughly cleaned using the proper cleaning methods. Whatever the source, these foreign objects often end up embedded in the soft bearing material and are easily recognized. Large particles will not embed in the bearing and will score or gouge the bearing and journal. The best prevention for this cause of bearing failure is to clean all parts thoroughly and keep everything spotlessly clean during engine assembly. Frequent and regular engine oil and filter changes are also recommended.

5   Lack of lubrication (or lubrication breakdown) has a number of interrelated causes. Excessive heat (which thins the oil), overloading (which squeezes the oil from the bearing face) and oil leakage or throw off (from excessive bearing clearances, worn oil pump or high engine speeds) all contribute to lubrication breakdown. Blocked oil passages, which usually are the result of misaligned oil holes in a bearing shell, will also oil starve a bearing and destroy it. When lack of lubrication is the cause of bearing failure, the bearing material is wiped or extruded from the steel backing of the bearing. Temperatures may increase to the point where the steel backing turns blue from overheating.

6   Driving habits can have a definite effect on bearing life. Low speed operation in too high a gear (lugging the engine) puts very high loads on bearings, which tends to squeeze out the oil film. These loads cause the bearings to flex, which produces fine cracks in the bearing face (fatigue failure). Eventually the bearing material will loosen in pieces and tear away from the steel backing. Short trip driving leads to corrosion of bearings because insufficient engine heat is produced to drive off the condensed water and corrosive gases. These products collect in the engine oil, forming acid and sludge. As the oil is carried to the engine bearings, the acid attacks and corrodes the bearing material.

7   Incorrect bearing installation during engine assembly will lead to bearing failure as well. Tight-fitting bearings leave insufficient bearing oil clearance and will result in oil starvation. Dirt or foreign particles trapped behind a bearing insert result in high spots on the bearing which lead to failure.

Cylinder Block

Mark
1, 2 or 3

Crankshaft

No. 1   No. 2   No. 3   No. 4   No. 5

Mark
0, 1 or 2

No. 1 No. 2 No. 3 No. 4 No. 5

Bearing

Mark
1, 2, 3, 4 or 5

P06617
EM7066
EM4293

20.10 If the number on the original main bearing is not clear, install a new bearing with a number that matches the number stamped into the block, there are five standard sizes - different journals may require different size bearings

Selection

Refer to illustration 20.10

8   If the original bearings are worn or damaged, or if the oil clearances are incorrect (see Section 23 or 25), the following procedures should be used to select the correct new bearings for engine reassembly. However, if the crankshaft has been reground, new undersize bearings must be installed - the following procedure should not be used if undersize bearings are required! The automotive machine shop that reconditions the crankshaft will provide or help you select the correct size bearings. Regardless of how the bearing sizes are determined, use the oil clearance, measured with Plastigage, as a guide to ensure the bearings are the right size.

22.3 When checking piston ring end gap, the ring must be square in the cylinder bore (this is done by pushing the ring down with the top of a piston as shown)

Main bearings

9   If you need to use a STANDARD size main bearing, install one that has the same number as the original bearing **(see illustration 20.10 for the bearing number locations)**. There are five sizes of main bearings.
10   If the number on the original main bearing has been obscured, locate the main journal grade numbers stamped into the oil pan mating surface on the engine block and the crankshaft counterweights **(see illustration)**.
11   Adding the block number to the crank number for a particular journal will give the recommended bearing size.

Connecting rod bearings

12   If you need to use a STANDARD size rod bearing, install one that has the same number as the number stamped into the connecting rod cap **(see illustration 13.4)**.

All bearings

13   Remember, the oil clearance is the final judge when selecting new bearing sizes. If you have any questions or are unsure which bearings to use, get help from a dealer parts or service department.

---

21   Engine overhaul - reassembly sequence

1   Before beginning engine reassembly, make sure you have all the necessary new parts, gaskets and seals as well as the following items on hand:

> *Common hand tools*
> *A 1/2-inch drive torque wrench*
> *Piston ring installation tool*
> *Piston ring compressor*
> *Short lengths of rubber or plastic hose*
>   *to fit over connecting rod bolts*
> *Plastigage*
> *Feeler gauges*
> *A fine-tooth file*
> *New engine oil*
> *Engine assembly lube or moly-base grease*
> *Gasket sealer*
> *Thread locking compound*

2   In order to save time and avoid problems, engine reassembly must be done in the following general order:

> *Piston rings (Part B)*
> *Crankshaft and main bearings (Part B)*
> *Piston/connecting rod assemblies (Part B)*
> *Rear main (crankshaft) oil seal (Part B)*
> *Cylinder head and lifters (Part A)*
> *Camshafts (Part A)*
> *Oil pump (Part A)*
> *Timing belt and sprockets (Part A)*
> *Timing belt covers (Part A)*
> *Oil pick-up (Part A)*
> *Oil pan (Part A)*
> *Intake and exhaust manifolds (Part A)*
> *Valve cover (Part A)*
> *Flywheel/driveplate (Part A)*

---

22   Piston rings - installation

Refer to illustrations 22.3, 22.4, 22.9a, 22.9b and 22.12

1   Before installing the new piston rings, the ring end gaps must be checked. It's assumed that the piston ring groove clearance has been checked and verified correct (see Section 18).
2   Lay out the piston/connecting rod assemblies and the new ring sets so the ring sets will be matched with the same piston and cylinder during the end gap measurement and engine assembly.
3   Insert the top (number one) ring into the first cylinder and square it up with the cylinder walls by pushing it in with the top of the piston **(see illustration)**. The ring should be near the bottom of the cylinder,

22.4 With the ring square in the cylinder, measure the end gap with a feeler gauge

22.9a Install the spacer/expander in the oil control ring groove

22.9b DO NOT use a piston ring installation tool when installing the oil ring side rails

at the lower limit of ring travel.

4   To measure the end gap, slip feeler gauges between the ends of the ring until a gauge equal to the gap width is found **(see illustration)**. The feeler gauge should slide between the ring ends with a slight amount of drag. Compare the measurement to that found in this Chapter's Specifications. If the gap is larger or smaller than specified, double-check to make sure you have the correct rings before proceeding.

5   If the gap is too small, replace the rings - DO NOT file the ends to increase the clearance.

6   Excess end gap isn't critical unless it's greater than the service limit listed in this Chapter's Specifications. Again, double-check to make sure you have the correct rings for your engine.

7   Repeat the procedure for each ring that will be installed in the first cylinder and for each ring in the remaining cylinders. Remember to keep rings, pistons and cylinders matched up.

8   Once the ring end gaps have been checked/corrected, the rings can be installed on the pistons.

9   The oil control ring (lowest one on the piston) is usually installed first. It's composed of three separate components. Slip the spacer/expander into the groove **(see illustration)**. If an anti-rotation tang is used, make sure it's inserted into the drilled hole in the ring groove. Next, install the lower side rail. Don't use a piston ring installation tool on the oil ring side rails, as they may be damaged. Instead, place one end of the side rail into the groove between the spacer/expander and the ring land, hold it firmly in place and slide a finger around the piston while pushing the rail into the groove **(see illustration)**. Next, install the upper side rail in the same manner.

10   After the three oil ring components have been installed, check to make sure that both the upper and lower side rails can be turned smoothly in the ring groove.

11   The number two (middle) ring is installed next. It's usually stamped with a mark which must face up, toward the top of the piston.

No. 1 Code Mark (1T or 1N)

No. 2 Code Mark (2T or 2N)

22.12 Install the compression rings with a ring expander - the mark must face up

Note: *Always follow the instructions printed on the ring package or box - different manufacturers may require different approaches. Do not mix up the top and middle rings, as they have different cross sections.*

12   Use a piston ring installation tool and make sure the ring's identification mark is facing the top of the piston, then slip the ring into the middle groove on the piston **(see illustration)**. Don't expand the ring any more than necessary to slide it over the piston.

13   Install the number one (top) ring in the same manner. Make sure the mark is facing up. Be careful not to confuse the number one and number two rings.

14   Repeat the procedure for the remaining pistons and rings.

23   Crankshaft - installation and main bearing oil clearance check

Refer to illustrations 23.10, 23.12, 23.14, 23.19a and 23.19b

1   Crankshaft installation is the first major step in engine reassembly. It's assumed at this point that the engine block and crankshaft have been cleaned, inspected and repaired or reconditioned.

2   Position the engine with the bottom facing up.

3   Remove the main bearing cap bolts and lift out the caps. Lay the caps out in the proper order.

4   If they're still in place, remove the old bearing inserts from the block and the main bearing caps. Wipe the main bearing surfaces of the block and caps with a clean, lint free cloth. They must be kept spotlessly clean!

Main bearing oil clearance check

5   Clean the back sides of the new main bearing inserts and lay the bearing half with the oil groove in each main bearing saddle in the block. Lay the other bearing half from each bearing set in the corresponding main bearing cap. Make sure the tab on each bearing insert fits into the recess in the block or cap. Also, the oil holes in the block must line up with the oil holes in the bearing insert. **Caution:** *Do not hammer the bearings into place and don't nick or gouge the bearing faces. No lubrication should be used at this time.*

6   The thrust bearings (washers) must be installed in the number three cap and saddle.

7   Clean the faces of the bearings in the block and the crankshaft main bearing journals with a clean, lint free cloth. Check or clean the oil holes in the crankshaft, as any dirt here can go only one way - straight through the new bearings.

8   Once you're certain the crankshaft is clean, carefully lay it in position in the main bearings.

9   Before the crankshaft can be permanently installed, the main bearing oil clearance must be checked.

10   Trim several pieces of the appropriate size Plastigage (they must be slightly shorter than the width of the main bearings) and place one

23.10 Lay the Plastigage strips (arrow) on the main bearing journals, parallel to the crankshaft centerline

23.12 Main bearing cap bolt tightening sequence

piece on each crankshaft main bearing journal, parallel with the journal axis **(see illustration)**.

11   Clean the faces of the bearings in the caps and install the caps in their respective positions (don't mix them up) with the arrows pointing toward the front of the engine. Don't disturb the Plastigage. Apply a light coat of oil to the bolt threads and the under- sides of the bolt heads, then install them.

12   Following the recommended sequence **(see illustration)**, tighten the main bearing cap bolts, in three steps, to the torque listed in this Chapter's Specifications. Don't rotate the crankshaft at any time during this operation!

13   Remove the bolts and carefully lift off the main bearing caps. Keep them in order. Don't disturb the Plastigage or rotate the crankshaft. If any of the main bearing caps are difficult to remove, tap them gently from side-to-side with a soft-face hammer to loosen them.

14   Compare the width of the crushed Plastigage on each journal to the scale printed on the Plastigage envelope to obtain the main bearing oil clearance **(see illustration)**. Check the Specifications to make sure it's correct.

15   If the clearance is not as specified, the bearing inserts may be the wrong size (which means different ones will be required - see Section 20). Before deciding that different inserts are needed, make sure that no dirt or oil was between the bearing inserts and the caps or block when the clearance was measured. If the Plastigage is noticeably wider

at one end than the other, the journal may be tapered (see Section 19).

16   Carefully scrape all traces of the Plastigage material off the main bearing journals and/or the bearing faces. Don't nick or scratch the bearing faces.

Final crankshaft installation

17   Carefully lift the crankshaft out of the engine. Clean the bearing faces in the block, then apply a thin, uniform layer of clean moly-base grease or engine assembly lube to each of the bearing surfaces. Coat the thrust washers as well.

18   Lubricate the crankshaft surfaces that contact the oil seals with moly-base grease, engine assembly lube or clean engine oil.

19   Make sure the crankshaft journals are clean, then lay the crankshaft back in place in the block. Clean the faces of the bearings in the caps, then apply lubricant to them. Install the caps in their respective positions with the arrows pointing toward the front of the engine. **Note:** *Be sure to install the thrust washers with the number 3 main journal.* The upper (block side) thrust washers can be rotated into position around the crank with the crank in the block, with the thrust washer grooves facing OUT. The tanged lower thrust washers should be placed on the caps with their grooves OUT and the tangs fitting into the cap slots **(see illustrations)**.

20   Apply a light coat of oil to the bolt threads and the undersides of the bolt heads, then install them. Tighten all main bearing cap bolts to the torque listed in this Chapter's Specifications, following the recommended sequence.

21   Rotate the crankshaft a number of times by hand to check for any

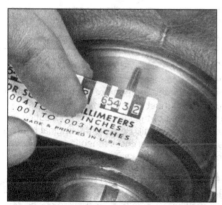

23.14 Compare the width of the crushed Plastigage to the scale on the envelope to determine the main bearing oil clearance (always take the measurement at the widest point of the Plastigage) - be sure to use the correct scale; standard and metric scales are included

23.19a Rotate the thrust washer into position with the oil grooves facing OUT

23.19b Install the thrust washer in the number three cap with the oil grooves facing OUT

2B

24.3 After removing the retainer from the block, support it on a couple of wood blocks and drive out the old seal with a punch or screwdriver and hammer

24.5 Drive the new seal into the retainer with a wood block or a section of pipe, if you have one large enough - make sure you don't cock the seal in the retainer bore

25.3 Align the oil hole in the bearing with the oil hole in the rod

Oil Hole

25.5 Stagger the ring end gaps around the piston, as shown, before installing the pistons

obvious binding.

22   Check the crankshaft endplay with a feeler gauge or a dial indicator as described in Section 14. The endplay should be correct if the crankshaft thrust faces aren't worn or damaged and new thrust washers have been installed.

23   Install a new rear main oil seal, then bolt the retainer to the block (see Section 24).

24   Rear main oil seal installation

Refer to illustrations 24.3 and 24.5

1   The crankshaft must be installed first and the main bearing caps bolted in place, then the new seal should be installed in the retainer and the retainer bolted to the block.

2   Check the seal contact surface on the crankshaft very carefully for scratches and nicks that could damage the new seal lip and cause oil leaks. If the crankshaft is damaged, the only alternative is a new or different crankshaft.

3   The old seal can be removed from the retainer by driving it out from the back side with a hammer and punch **(see illustration)**. Be sure to note how far it's recessed into the bore before removing it; the new seal will have to be recessed an equal amount. Be very careful not to scratch or otherwise damage the bore in the retainer or oil leaks could develop.

4   Make sure the retainer is clean, then apply a thin coat of engine oil to the outer edge of the new seal. The seal must be pressed squarely into the bore, so hammering it into place isn't recommended. If you don't have access to a press, sandwich the housing and seal between two smooth pieces of wood and press the seal into place with the jaws of a large vise. The pieces of wood must be thick enough to distribute the force evenly around the entire circumference of the seal. Work slowly and make sure the seal enters the bore squarely.

5   As a last resort, the seal can be tapped into the retainer with a

hammer. Use a block of wood to distribute the force evenly and make sure the seal is driven in squarely **(see illustration)**.

6   The seal lips must be lubricated with clean engine oil or moly-based grease before the seal/retainer is slipped over the crankshaft and bolted to the block, using a new gasket.

7   Tighten the bolts a little at a time to the torque listed in Chapter 2A Specifications.

25   Pistons/connecting rods - installation and rod bearing oil clearance check

Refer to illustrations 25.3, 25.5, 25.9, 25.11, 25.13, 25.15 and 25.17

1   Before installing the piston/connecting rod assemblies, the cylinder walls must be perfectly clean, the top edge of each cylinder must be chamfered, and the crankshaft must be in place.

2   Remove the cap from the end of the number one connecting rod (refer to the marks made during removal). Remove the original bearing inserts and wipe the bearing surfaces of the connecting rod and cap with a clean, lint-free cloth. They must be kept spotlessly clean.

Connecting rod bearing oil clearance check

3   Clean the back side of the new upper bearing insert, then lay it in place in the connecting rod. Make sure the tab on the bearing fits into the recess in the rod so the oil holes line up **(see illustration)**. Don't hammer the bearing insert into place and be very careful not to nick or gouge the bearing face. Don't lubricate the bearing at this time.

4   Clean the back side of the other bearing insert and install it in the rod cap. Again, make sure the tab on the bearing fits into the recess in the cap, and don't apply any lubricant. It's critically important that the mating surfaces of the bearing and connecting rod are perfectly clean

Front Mark (Cavity)

Front Mark (Protrusion)

25.9 Check to be sure both the mark on the piston and the mark on the connecting rod are aligned as shown

25.11 The piston can be driven (gently) into the cylinder bore with the end of a wooden or plastic hammer handle

25.13 Lay the Plastigage strips on each rod bearing journal, parallel to the crankshaft centerline

25.15 Install the connecting rod caps with the front mark (arrow) facing the timing belt end of the engine, and torque to Specifications - for the 90-degree second step, use an angle gauge as shown, or paint reference marks on the rod and the socket

25.17 Measure the width of the crushed Plastigage to determine the rod bearing oil clearance (be sure to use the correct scale - standard and metric scales are included)

2B

and oil free when they're assembled.

5   Position the piston ring gaps at staggered intervals around the piston **(see illustration)**.

6   Slip a section of plastic or rubber hose over each connecting rod cap bolt.

7   Lubricate the piston and rings with clean engine oil and attach a piston ring compressor to the piston. Leave the skirt protruding about 1/4-inch to guide the piston into the cylinder. The rings must be compressed until they're flush with the piston.

8   Rotate the crankshaft until the number one connecting rod journal is at BDC (bottom dead center) and apply a coat of engine oil to the cylinder wall.

9   With the dimple on top of the piston **(see illustration)** facing the front of the engine, gently insert the piston/connecting rod assembly into the number one cylinder bore and rest the bottom edge of the ring compressor on the engine block.

10   Tap the top edge of the ring compressor to make sure it's contacting the block around its entire circumference.

11   Gently tap on the top of the piston with the end of a wooden hammer handle **(see illustration)** while guiding the end of the connecting rod into place on the crankshaft journal. The piston rings may try to pop out of the ring compressor just before entering the cylinder bore, so keep some downward pressure on the ring compressor. Work slowly, and if any resistance is felt as the piston enters the cylinder, stop immediately. Find out what's hanging up and fix it before proceeding. **Caution:** *Do not, for any reason, force the piston into the*

cylinder - you might break a ring and/or the piston.

12   Once the piston/connecting rod assembly is installed, the connecting rod bearing oil clearance must be checked before the rod cap is permanently bolted in place.

13   Cut a piece of the appropriate size Plastigage slightly shorter than the width of the connecting rod bearing and lay it in place on the number one connecting rod journal, parallel with the journal axis **(see illustration)**.

14   Clean the connecting rod cap bearing face, remove the protective hoses from the connecting rod bolts and install the rod cap. Make sure the mating mark on the cap is on the same side as the mark on the connecting rod. Check the cap to make sure the front mark is facing the timing belt end of the engine.

15   Apply a light coat of oil to the undersides of the nuts, then install and tighten them to the torque listed in this Chapter's Specifications, working up to it in three steps. Use a thin-wall socket to avoid erroneous torque readings that can result if the socket is wedged between the rod cap and nut. If the socket tends to wedge itself between the nut and the cap, lift up on it slightly until it no longer contacts the cap. Do not rotate the crankshaft at any time during this operation. **Note:** *After reaching the specified torque, tighten each nut an additional 90-degrees (1/4-turn)* **(see illustration)**.

16   Remove the nuts and detach the rod cap, being very careful not to disturb the Plastigage.

17   Compare the width of the crushed Plastigage to the scale printed on the Plastigage envelope to obtain the oil clearance **(see illustration)**. Compare it to this Chapter's Specifications to make sure the clearance is correct.

18   If the clearance is not as specified, the bearing inserts may be the wrong size (which means different ones will be required). Before deciding that different inserts are needed, make sure that no dirt or oil was between the bearing inserts and the connecting rod or cap when the clearance was measured. Also, recheck the journal diameter. If the Plastigage was wider at one end than the other, the journal may be tapered (refer to Section 19).

Final connecting rod installation

19   Carefully scrape all traces of the Plastigage material off the rod journal and/or bearing face. Be very careful not to scratch the bearing, use your fingernail or the edge of a credit card to remove the Plastigage.
20   Make sure the bearing faces are perfectly clean, then apply a uniform layer of clean moly-base grease or engine assembly lube to both of them. You'll have to push the piston higher into the cylinder to expose the face of the bearing insert in the connecting rod, be sure to slip the protective hoses over the rod bolts first.
21   Slide the connecting rod back into place on the journal, remove the protective hoses from the rod cap bolts, install the rod cap and tighten the nuts to the torque listed in this Chapter's Specifications. Again, work up to the torque in three steps.
22   Repeat the entire procedure for the remaining pistons/connecting rods.
23   The important points to remember are:
 a) *Keep the back sides of the bearing inserts and the insides of the connecting rods and caps perfectly clean when assembling them.*
 b) *Make sure you have the correct piston/rod assembly for each cylinder.*
 c) *The dimple on the piston must face the front of the engine.*
 d) *Lubricate the cylinder walls with clean oil.*
 e) *Lubricate the bearing faces when installing the rod caps after the oil clearance has been checked.*

24   After all the piston/connecting rod assemblies have been properly installed, rotate the crankshaft a number of times by hand to check for any obvious binding.
25   As a final step, the connecting rod endplay must be checked. Refer to Section 13 for this procedure.
26   Compare the measured endplay to this Chapter's Specifications

to make sure it's correct. If it was correct before disassembly and the original crankshaft and rods were reinstalled, it should still be right. If new rods or a new crankshaft were installed, the endplay may be inadequate. If so, the rods will have to be removed and taken to an automotive machine shop for resizing.

26   Initial start-up and break-in after overhaul

Warning: *Have a fire extinguisher handy when starting the engine for the first time.*
1   Once the engine has been installed in the vehicle, double-check the engine oil and coolant levels.
2   With the spark plugs out of the engine and the ignition system and fuel pump disabled (see Section 4), crank the engine until oil pressure registers on the gauge or the light goes out.
3   Install the spark plugs, hook up the plug wires and restore the ignition system and fuel pump functions (see Section 4).
4   Start the engine. It may take a few moments for the fuel system to build up pressure, but the engine should start without a great deal of effort.
5   After the engine starts, it should be allowed to warm up to normal operating temperature. While the engine is warming up, make a thorough check for fuel, oil and coolant leaks.
6   Shut the engine off and recheck the engine oil and coolant levels.
7   Drive the vehicle to an area with minimum traffic, accelerate from 30 to 50 mph, then allow the vehicle to slow to 30 mph with the throttle closed. Repeat the procedure 10 or 12 times. This will load the piston rings and cause them to seat properly against the cylinder walls. Check again for oil and coolant leaks.
8   Drive the vehicle gently for the first 500 miles (no sustained high speeds) and keep a constant check on the oil level. It is not unusual for an engine to use oil during the break-in period.
9   At approximately 500 to 600 miles, change the oil and filter.
10   For the next few hundred miles, drive the vehicle normally. Do not pamper it or abuse it.
11   After 2000 miles, change the oil and filter again and consider the engine broken in.

Chapter 3
Cooling, heating and air conditioning systems

Contents

Specifications

General

Radiator cap pressure rating	10.7 to 14.9 psi
Thermostat rating	183 to 203 degrees F
Refrigerant type	
1993	R-12
1994 and later	R-134a
Refrigerant capacity	26.5 ounces

Torque specifications

Ft-lbs (unless otherwise indicated)

Thermostat housing bolts	82 in-lbs
Water pump-to-block bolts	132 in-lbs

1   General information

Engine cooling system

Refer to illustrations 1.1 and 1.6

All vehicles covered by this manual employ a pressurized engine cooling system with thermostatically-controlled coolant circulation **(see illustration)**. An impeller type water pump mounted on the front of the block pumps coolant through the engine. The coolant flows around each cylinder and toward the rear of the engine. Cast-in coolant passages direct coolant around the intake and exhaust ports, near the spark plug areas and in proximity to the exhaust valve guides.

A wax-pellet type thermostat is located in the thermostat housing at the transaxle end of the engine. During warm up, the closed thermostat prevents coolant from circulating through the radiator. When the engine reaches normal operating temperature, the thermostat opens and allows hot coolant to travel through the radiator, where it is cooled before returning to the engine.

The cooling system is sealed by a pressure-type radiator cap. This raises the boiling point of the coolant, and the higher boiling point of the coolant increases the cooling efficiency of the radiator. If the system pressure exceeds the cap pressure-relief value, the excess pressure in the system forces the spring-loaded valve inside the cap off its seat and allows the coolant to escape through the overflow tube into a coolant reservoir. When the system cools, the excess coolant is automatically drawn from the reservoir back into the radiator.

The coolant reservoir does double duty as both the point at which fresh coolant is added to the cooling system to maintain the proper fluid level and as a holding tank for overheated coolant.

This type of cooling system is known as a closed design because coolant that escapes past the pressure cap is saved and reused.

Heating system

The heating system consists of a blower fan and heater core located within the heater box under the right end of the dashboard, the inlet and outlet hoses connecting the heater core to the engine cooling system and the heater/air conditioning control head on the dashboard **(see illustration)**. Hot engine coolant is circulated through the heater core. When the heater mode is activated, a flap door opens to expose the heater box to the passenger compartment. A fan switch on the control head activates the blower motor, which forces air through the core, heating the air.

Air conditioning system

The air conditioning system consists of a condenser mounted in front of the radiator, an evaporator mounted adjacent to the heater core, a compressor mounted on the engine, a filter-drier which contains a high pressure relief valve and the plumbing connecting all of the above.

A blower fan forces the warmer air of the passenger compartment

1.1 Typical cooling system details

through the evaporator core (sort of a radiator-in-reverse), transferring the heat from the air to the refrigerant. The liquid refrigerant boils off into low pressure vapor, taking the heat with it when it leaves the evaporator. The compressor keeps refrigerant circulating through the system, pumping the warmed coolant through the condenser where it is cooled and then circulated back to the evaporator.

2   Antifreeze - general information

Refer to illustration 2.4

Warning: *Do not allow antifreeze to come in contact with your skin or painted surfaces of the vehicle. Rinse off spills immediately with plenty of water. Antifreeze is highly toxic if ingested. Never leave antifreeze lying around in an open container or in puddles on the floor; children and pets are attracted by it's sweet smell and may drink it. Check with local authorities about disposing of used antifreeze. Many communities have collection centers which will see that antifreeze is disposed of safely. Never dump used antifreeze on the ground or into drains.*
Note: *Non-toxic antifreeze is now manufactured and available at local auto parts stores, but even these types should be disposed of properly.*

The cooling system should be filled with a water/ethylene-glycol based antifreeze solution, which will prevent freezing down to at least -20 degrees F, or lower if local climate requires it. It also provides protection against corrosion and increases the coolant boiling point.

1.6 Underdash arrangement of the blower unit, evaporator unit and heater core

2.4 An inexpensive hydrometer can be used to test the condition of your coolant

The cooling system should be drained, flushed and refilled every 30,000 miles or every two years (see Chapter 1). The use of antifreeze solutions for periods of longer than two years is likely to cause damage and encourage the formation of rust and scale in the system. If your tap water is "hard", i.e. contains a lot of dissolved minerals, use distilled water with the antifreeze.

Before adding antifreeze to the system, check all hose connections, because antifreeze tends to search out and leak through very minute openings. Engines do not normally consume coolant. Therefore, if the level goes down, find the cause and correct it.

The exact mixture of antifreeze-to-water you should use depends on the relative weather conditions. The mixture should contain at least 50 percent antifreeze, but should never contain more than 70 percent antifreeze. Consult the mixture ratio chart on the antifreeze container before adding coolant. Hydrometers are available at most auto parts stores to test the ratio of antifreeze to water **(see illustration)**. Use antifreeze which meets the vehicle manufacturer's specifications.

3   Thermostat - check and replacement

Warning: *Do not attempt to remove the radiator cap, coolant or thermostat until the engine has cooled completely.*

Check

1   Before assuming the thermostat is responsible for a cooling system problem, check the coolant level (Chapter 1), drivebelt tension (Chapter 1) and temperature gauge (or light) operation.
2   If the engine takes a long time to warm up (as indicated by the temperature gauge or heater operation), the thermostat is probably stuck open. Replace the thermostat with a new one.
3   If the engine runs hot, use your hand to check the temperature of the lower radiator hose. If the hose is not hot, but the engine is, the thermostat is probably stuck in the closed position, preventing the coolant inside the engine from traveling through the radiator. Replace the thermostat. **Caution:** *Do not drive the vehicle without a thermostat. The computer may stay in open loop and emissions and fuel economy will suffer.*
4   If the lower radiator hose is hot, it means that the coolant is flowing and the thermostat is open. Consult the Troubleshooting Section at the front of this manual for further diagnosis.

Replacement

Refer to illustrations 3.7, 3.9 and 3.10

5   Disconnect the negative cable from the battery. **Caution:** *If the stereo in your vehicle is equipped with an anti-theft system, make sure you have the correct activation code before disconnecting the battery.*
6   Drain the coolant from the radiator (see Chapter 1).
7   Disconnect the Engine Coolant Temperature (ECT) switch connector from the water inlet located just under the distributor at the left end of the cylinder head **(see illustration)**.
8   Detach the housing from the engine. Be prepared for some coolant to spill as the gasket seal is broken. The radiator hose can be left attached to the housing, unless the housing itself is to be replaced.
9   Remove the thermostat, noting the direction in which it was installed in the housing, and thoroughly clean the sealing surfaces **(see illustration)**.
10   Fit a new gasket onto the thermostat **(see illustration)**. Make sure it is evenly fitted all the way around.
11   Install the thermostat and housing, positioning the jiggle pin at the highest point.
12   Tighten the housing fasteners to the torque listed in this Chapter's Specifications and reinstall the remaining components in the reverse order of removal.
13   Refill the cooling system, run the engine and check for leaks and proper operation.

4   Engine cooling fan and relay - check and replacement

Warning: *To avoid possible injury, keep clear of the fan blades, as they may start turning at any time!*

Check

Refer to illustrations 4.2 and 4.3

1   If the radiator fan won't shut off when the engine is cool, disconnect the wiring connector from the Engine Coolant Temperature (ECT) switch **(see illustration 3.7)**. With the key ON, the fan should now

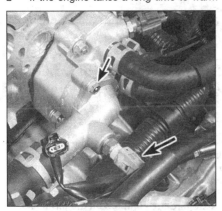

3.7 Disconnect the ECT connector (arrow) and remove the two nuts (arrow indicates the upper nut) retaining the thermostat cover to the water inlet

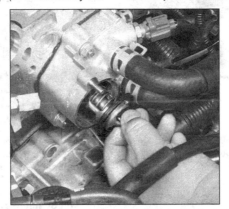

3.9 The thermostat is installed with the spring end towards the cylinder head

3.10 The thermostat gasket, which is actually a grooved sealing ring, fits around the edge of the thermostat

4.2 The ECT (arrow) for the electric fan control is mounted in the thermostat housing - test for continuity with one lead on the terminal and one on the ECT body

4.3 Disconnect the fan wiring connector (arrow) and connect jumper wires directly to the positive and negative terminals of the battery - this view is from below on the driver's side

operate. If not, check the fan relay, wiring between the ECT and the relay, and the fan motor itself.

2   The ECT can be tested for continuity with an ohmmeter. Disconnect the wiring connector and attach one lead of the ohmmeter to the prong on the ECT, and the other lead to the body of the ECT **(see illustration)**. When the engine is cold (below 180-degrees F) there should be continuity. When the engine is warm (above 199-degrees F), there should be NO continuity.

3   To test an inoperative fan motor (one that doesn't come on when the engine gets hot or when the air conditioner is on), first check the fuses and/or fusible links (see Chapter 12). Then disconnect the electrical connector at the motor and use fused jumper wires to connect the fan directly to the battery **(see illustration)**. If the fan still does not work, replace the fan motor. **Warning:** *Do not allow the test clips to contact each other or any metallic part of the vehicle.*

4   If the motor tested OK in the previous test but is still inoperative, then the fault lies in the relays, fuse, or wiring. The fan relay and main engine relay can be tested as described below.

Relay check

Refer to illustrations 4.5, 4.6 and 4.7

5   Locate the main relay box, located in the engine compartment, on the driver's side (see Chapter 12). Air-conditioned models have extra relays in a separate box next to the battery **(see illustration)**.

6   Remove the cooling fan relay number 1 and, using an ohmmeter, test for continuity as shown **(see illustration)**. Both Nippondenso and Bosch-made relays are used, and the terminals are numbered differently. Be sure to test either relay as shown in the illustration.

7   If the fan relays check OK, remove the main engine relay and test it as shown **(see illustration)**. There should be continuity between terminals 3 and 5, and between 2 and 4. There should be NO continuity between terminals 1 and 2. With battery voltage applied across terminals 3 and 5, there should be continuity between 1 and 2, and NO continuity between 2 and 4. If both relays test OK, we recommend you take the vehicle to a dealer or other qualified repair facility for further diagnosis, due to the complexity and variety of the circuits involved.

4.5 Main relay box - main engine relay, AC relay and fan relay locations:

A   *Air conditioning relay*
B   *No. 3 cooling fan relay*
C   *No. 2 cooling fan relay*
D   *No. 1 cooling fan relay*
E   *Main engine relay*
F   *Fan circuit breaker*

4.6 Test the cooling fan relay number 1 (Nippondenso) for continuity - with no voltage applied, there should be continuity between 1 and 2, and 3 and 4 - with voltage applied across 1 and 2, there should be NO continuity between 3 and 4 - on Bosch relays, disregard the numbers on the terminals, test it just like this Nippondenso relay

4.7 **Main engine relay terminal guide**

Replacement

Refer to illustrations 4.9a, 4.9b, 4.11, 4.12 and 4.13

8   Disconnect the negative battery cable. **Caution:** *If the stereo in your vehicle is equipped with an anti-theft system, make sure you have the correct activation code before disconnecting the battery.*

9   Disconnect the wiring connector at the fan motor. **Note:** *Models equipped with air-conditioned have two cooling fans. The one on the front side of the radiator is cooling fan no. 2, which provides additional cooling when the air conditioning is on. This fan and its relay can be tested and removed/replaced with the same procedures as the engine cooling fan no. 1* **(see illustrations).**

10   Drain enough coolant (see Chapter 1) to disconnect the upper radiator hose at the radiator, then disconnect the coolant overflow hose from the top of the radiator.

11   Unbolt the fan shroud from the radiator and lift the fan/shroud assembly from the vehicle **(see illustration).**

12   Hold the fan blades and remove the fan retaining nut (and spacer, if equipped) **(see illustration). Note:** *On air-conditioned models, the number 2 (condenser) cooling fan blade is retained by a clip, not a nut.*

13   Unbolt the fan motor from the shroud **(see illustration).**

14   Installation is the reverse of removal.

5   Radiator and coolant reservoir - removal and installation

Warning: *Do not start this procedure until the engine is completely cool.*

Radiator

Refer to illustrations 5.6, 5.7 and 5.8

1   Disconnect the negative battery cable. **Caution:** *If the stereo in your vehicle is equipped with an anti-theft system, make sure you have the correct activation code before disconnecting the battery.*

2   Drain the coolant into a container (see Chapter 1).

3   Remove both the upper and lower radiator hoses.

4   Disconnect the reservoir hose from the radiator filler neck.

5   Remove the cooling fan (see Section 4).

6   If equipped with an automatic transaxle, disconnect the cooler

4.9a **The air conditioning fan in front of the radiator is mounted on the passenger side with a plastic pin (arrow) - the right arrow indicates the wiring connector**

4.9b **The left side of the air conditioning fan is mounted with a bolt at the hood latch support (arrow) and one lower bolt accessible through the hole in the bumper cover**

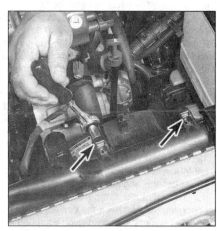

4.11 **Remove the two lower fan shroud bolts from below, then the two top fasteners (arrows) and lift out the cooling fan and shroud assembly**

3

4.12 **Remove the fan from the motor**

4.13 **Remove the motor from the shroud**

5.6 Remove the automatic transaxle cooler lines and the lower radiator hose (arrows)

5.7 Remove the upper hold-down clamps from each end of the radiator

lines from the radiator **(see illustration)**. Place a drip pan to catch the fluid and cap the fittings.

7   Remove the two upper radiator mounting brackets **(see illustration)**. **Note:** *The bottom of the radiator is retained by grommeted projections that fit into holes in the body.*

8   Lift out the radiator **(see illustration)**. Be aware of dripping fluids and the sharp fins.

9   With the radiator removed, it can be inspected for leaks, damage and internal blockage. If in need of repairs, have a professional radiator shop or dealer service department perform the work as special techniques are required.

10   Bugs and dirt can be cleaned from the radiator with compressed air and a soft brush. Don't bend the cooling fins as this is done. **Warning:** *Wear eye protection when using compressed air.*

11   Installation is the reverse of the removal procedure. Be sure the rubber mounts are in place on the bottom of the radiator.

12   After installation, fill the cooling system with the proper mixture of antifreeze and water. Refer to Chapter 1 if necessary.

13   Start the engine and check for leaks. Allow the engine to reach normal operating temperature, indicated by both radiator hoses becoming hot. Recheck the coolant level and add more if required.

14   On automatic transmission equipped models, check and add fluid as needed.

Coolant reservoir

Refer to illustration 5.15

15   On most models, the coolant reservoir simply pulls up and out of the bracket next to the battery **(see illustration)**.

16   Pour the coolant into a container. Wash out and inspect the reservoir for cracks and chafing. Replace it if damaged.

17   Installation is the reverse of removal.

6   Water pump - check

1   A failure in the water pump can cause serious engine damage due to overheating.

2   With the engine running and warmed to normal operating temperature, squeeze the upper radiator hose. If the water pump is working properly, a pressure surge should be felt as the hose is released. **Warning:** *Keep hands away from fan blades!*

3   Water pumps are equipped with weep or vent holes **(see illustration 7.7)**. If a failure occurs in the pump seal, coolant will leak from this hole. In most cases it will be necessary to use a flashlight to find the hole on the water pump by looking through the space behind the pulley just below the water pump shaft.

4   If the water pump shaft bearings fail there may be a howling sound at the front of the engine while it is running. Bearing wear can be

5.8 Remove the radiator carefully, and do not lose the rubber mounts - they must be in place on the bottom projections when the radiator is reinstalled

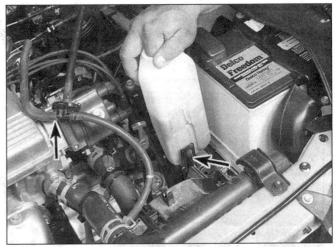

5.15 Pull the coolant reservoir hose assembly (left arrow), then pull the reservoir bottle out of its bracket (right arrow)

felt if the water pump pulley is rocked up and down. Do not mistake drivebelt slippage, which causes a squealing sound, for water pump failure. Spray automotive drivebelt dressing on the belts to eliminate the belt as a possible cause of the noise.

7.4 Use a screwdriver to pry the wiring clip out of the dipstick tube bracket, then remove the one bolt retaining the dipstick tube to the engine and pull the tube out

7.5 Disconnect the water temperature sender (arrow) from the water neck

7.6a From above, remove the two nuts (smaller arrows) retaining the water neck to the cylinder head, then remove the top bolt (larger arrow) from the water pump

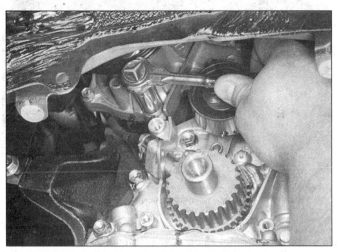

7.6b From below, remove the two remaining water pump assembly-to-block bolts - do not remove the bolts retaining the pump halves together until the assembly is removed from the block

7.7 Remove the water pump assembly, then disassemble the pump and replace the gaskets - The three small arrows indicate the water pump-to-block bolts, while the two larger arrows indicate the weep holes

3

7 Water pump - removal and installation

Refer to illustrations 7.4, 7.5, 7.6a, 7.6b and 7.7
Warning: *Do not start this procedure until the engine is completely cool.*

1   Disconnect the negative battery cable and drain the cooling system (see Chapter 1). **Caution:** *If the stereo in your vehicle is equipped with an anti-theft system, make sure you have the correct activation code before disconnecting the battery.*

2   Refer to Chapter 1 and remove the power steering belt, alternator/water pump belt and air conditioning belt. Then remove the upper power steering mounting bracket.

3   Refer to Chapter 2A and remove the upper timing belt covers.

4   Remove the oil dipstick. Remove the bolt retaining the dipstick tube to the engine and pull the dipstick tube from the oil pump housing **(see illustration)**.

5   Behind the water pump, remove the two nuts retaining the right-side water neck to the cylinder head, and unplug the water temperature gauge sender connector from the sender **(see illustration)**.

6   Remove the three bolts retaining the water pump to the engine block and remove the water pump and water neck assembly. The pulley can remain on the water pump during removal **(see illustrations)**.

7   Disassemble the water pump and replace the gaskets.

Thoroughly clean all sealing surfaces, removing the O-ring and cleaning the groove **(see illustration)**. Assemble the water pump assembly.

8   Using a new O-ring, install the pump assembly to the block. Use a new gasket on the water neck. **Note:** *If the pump has been replaced after many miles of usage, it's a good idea to also replace the hose connecting the water pump to the water neck.*

9   Install the remaining parts in the reverse order of removal. When reinstalling the dipstick tube, use a new O-ring where it pushes into the oil pump.

10   Refill the cooling system (see Chapter 1), run the engine and check for leaks and proper operation.

8 Coolant temperature sending unit - check and replacement

Warning: *Do not start this procedure until the engine is completely cool.*

Check

1   If the coolant temperature gauge is inoperative, check the fuses first (see Chapter 12).

2   If the temperature gauge indicates excessive temperature after running awhile, see the Troubleshooting Section in the front of the manual.

9.4 With the connector disconnected from the blower motor, apply fused power and ground to the motor terminals (arrow) - replace the blower if it doesn't operate

9.6 Blower motor resistor location (arrow) - the resistor is retained by two screws

9.9 Remove the three screws and lower the blower motor from the housing

3   If the temperature gauge indicates Hot as soon as the engine is started cold, disconnect the wire at the coolant temperature sender **(see illustration 7.5)**. If the gauge reading drops, replace the sending unit. If the reading remains high, the wire to the gauge may be shorted to ground or the gauge is faulty.

4   If the coolant temperature gauge fails to show any indication after the engine has been warmed up, (approximately 10 minutes) and the fuses checked out OK, shut off the engine. Disconnect the wire at the sending unit and, using a jumper wire, connect the wire to a clean ground on the engine. Briefly turn on the ignition without starting the engine. If the gauge now indicates Hot, replace the sending unit.

5   If the gauge fails to respond, the circuit may be open or the gauge may be faulty - see Chapter 12 for additional information.

Replacement

6   Drain the coolant (see Chapter 1).

7   Disconnect the wiring connector from the sending unit.

8   Using a deep socket or a wrench, remove the sending unit.

9   Install the new unit and tighten it securely. Do not use thread sealer as it may electrically insulate the sending unit.

10   Reconnect the wiring connector, refill the cooling system and check for coolant leakage and proper gauge function.

9   Blower unit - check, removal and installation

Refer to illustrations 9.4, 9.6 and 9.9

1   The blower unit is located in the passenger compartment above the right front footwell. If the blower doesn't work, check the fuse and all connections in the circuit for looseness and corrosion. Make sure the battery is fully charged.

2   Remove the glove compartment liner, the glove compartment door and the right lower dash panel (see Chapter 11).

3   If the blower motor does not operate, disconnect the electrical connector at the blower motor, turn the ignition key On (engine not running) and check for battery voltage on the black wire terminal with the blower speed switch ON. If battery voltage is not present, there is a problem in the ignition feed circuit.

4   If battery voltage is present, reconnect the terminal to the blower motor and backprobe the black/white wire with a jumper wire connected to ground. If the motor still does not operate, the motor is probably faulty. Apply fused power and ground connections to the blower motor terminals, if the motor does not operate, replace the motor **(see illustration)**.

5   If the motor is good, but doesn't operate at any speed, the heater/air conditioning control switch is probably faulty. Remove the control assembly (see Section 11) and check for continuity through the switch in each position.

6   If the blower motor operates at High speed, but not at one or more of the lower speeds, check the blower motor resistor, located under the instrument panel on the passenger side **(see illustration)**.

7   Disconnect the electrical connector from the blower motor resistor. Remove the screws and withdraw the resistor from the housing.

8   Using a continuity tester on the blower motor resistor, there should be continuity between all terminals. If not, replace the resistor.

9   If the blower motor must be replaced, remove the bracket retaining the wiring connector to the blower, then remove the three mounting screws and lower the blower assembly from the housing **(see illustration)**. The fan can be removed and reused on the new blower motor.

10   Installation is the reverse of removal. Check for proper operation.

10   Heater core - removal and installation

Refer to illustrations 10.3, 10.7, 10.8, 10.9, 10.10a, 10.10b, 10.10c, 10.11, 10.12a and 10.12b

Warning: *These models are equipped with airbags. The airbag is armed and can deploy (inflate) anytime the battery is connected. To prevent accidental deployment (and possible injury), turn the ignition key to LOCK and disconnect the negative battery cable whenever working near airbag components. After the battery is disconnected, wait at least two minutes before beginning work (the system has a back-up capacitor that must fully discharge). For more information see Chapter 12.*

Note 1: *The following procedure details removing the heater core assembly by itself, but it is much easier to remove the heater core housing if the evaporator (cooling) assembly is removed first, although this necessitates having the refrigerant discharged and recovered*

10.3 Disconnect the heater hoses at the
firewall (arrow)

10.7 Remove the right dashboard-to-floor
brace - besides the mounting bolts
(arrows), you must also unbolt several
ground wires from the brace before
removing it

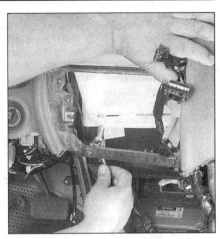

10.8 Remove the center ventilation duct

10.9 Pull up and out on this duct/door assembly (arrow) then pull
it down and out to allow more working room around
the heater unit

before work begins. See Section 16 for evaporator removal, and do not
discharge the refrigerant without reading the Warning in Section 12.

Note 2: *The factory recommends removal of the entire instrument
panel and dropping the steering column to remove the heater core.
This involves disconnecting numerous electrical connectors and there
is the potential for breakage of delicate plastic tabs on various components. This is a difficult job for the average home mechanic. It is
possible to remove the heater core assembly without removing the
dash, and is the procedure outlined below.*

1   Disconnect the negative cable from the battery. **Caution:** *If the*

*stereo in your vehicle is equipped with an anti-theft system, make sure
you have the correct activation code before disconnecting the battery.*

2   Drain the cooling system (see Chapter 1).

3   Working in the engine compartment, disconnect the heater hoses
at the firewall **(see illustration)**. Push the rubber seal around the hoses
toward the inside of the vehicle, releasing it from the sheetmetal.

4   Refer to Chapters 11 and 12 and remove the center console,
glove compartment, glove compartment liner, ashtray, radio and center dash bezels.

5   Refer to Section 11 of this Chapter to remove the heater/air conditioning controls.

6   Refer to Chapter 6 and remove the ECM without disconnecting
the connectors. Set the ECM aside to allow room under the heater
core housing.

7   There are two gold-colored metal braces from the dashboard to
the floor. The left one should be unbolted from the floor, but it need not
be entirely removed from the vehicle. The right brace should be
unbolted and removed **(see illustration)**. **Caution:** *There are Phillips
screws retaining the brace to the backside of the dash plastic. Use the
right size Phillips bit and be careful. Seat your screwdriver squarely into
the slots while removing them. They are in tight and the heads could
strip.*

8   Unbolt and remove the center ventilation duct **(see illustration)**.

9   Remove the heater duct/control door that is directly above and in
front of the heater unit **(see illustration)**.

10   Loosen the nuts on the studs that retain the left side of the evaporator housing (see Section 16). There are three studs retaining the
heater unit to the firewall. Remove the nuts from these studs **(see
illustrations)**.

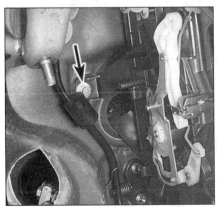

10.10a Remove the nut from the stud near
the upper arm of the accelerator
pedal (arrow)

10.10b Remove the stud/nut located at
the lower right corner of the heater
core housing (arrow)

10.10c Remove the last nut from the stud
at the upper right corner (arrow) of the
heater core housing

3

11   Pull the heater unit out from behind the dash **(see illustration)**. Keep plenty of towels or rags on the carpeting to catch any coolant that may drip. **Caution:** *Work slowly and carefully to avoid breaking any plastic components during removal. The assembly must be pulled out (toward the rear of the vehicle) far enough for the plastic tabs to clear the firewall studs and then moved to the left to clear the lip of the evaporator housing before pulling the unit down and out.*
12   Once the heater unit is removed from the vehicle, remove the clamps retaining the heater core tubes to the housing. Slide the heater core out of the housing **(see illustrations)**.
13   Installation is the reverse order of removal. **Note:** *The nuts used on the firewall studs for both the heater core housing and the evaporator housing are designed for one-time use on the assembly line. After removing them, purchase new metric nuts and lockwashers to reinstall the housing to the studs.*
14   Refill the cooling system, reconnect the battery and run the engine. Check for leaks and proper system operation.

11   Heater and air conditioning control assembly -check, removal and installation

Refer to illustrations 11.4 and 11.5
Warning: *These models are equipped with airbags. The airbag is armed and can deploy (inflate) anytime the battery is connected. To prevent accidental deployment (and possible injury), turn the ignition key to LOCK and disconnect the negative battery cable whenever working near airbag components. After the battery is disconnected, wait at least two minutes before beginning work (the system has a back-up capacitor that must fully discharge). For more information see Chapter 12.*

10.11 After the housing tabs clear the firewall studs and the housing is clear of the lip on the evaporator housing, pull the heater unit down and out to the right

Removal and installation

1   Disconnect the negative cable from the battery. **Caution:** *If the stereo in your vehicle is equipped with an anti-theft system, make sure you have the correct activation code before disconnecting the battery.*
2   Remove the center cluster trim panels (see Chapter 11).
3   Pull off the control knobs.
4   Remove the mounting screws located on the front of the control assembly **(see illustration)**.
5   Pull the control out slightly. Twist the flags on the control cable

10.12a Remove the two screws and clamps (arrows) . . .

10.12b . . . then slide the heater core out of the housing

11.4 Remove these screws to release the control panel

11.5 Twist the plastic flag (arrow) on each cable to release it from the control unit, then lift the cable end eye off the control lever pin

11.9 To adjust the air inlet damper cable, move the arm away from the firewall, attach the cable end and tighten the clamp

11.10 To adjust the air mix control cable, push the lever away from the cable clamp and tighten the clamp

11.11 Adjust the mode damper control cable with the lever is pulled toward the cable clamp, then tighten the clamp

mounts and remove the cables from the control **(see illustration)**. Disconnect the electrical connectors.

6   Installation is the reverse of the removal procedure.

7   Run the engine and check for proper functioning of the heater (and air conditioning, if equipped).

Cable adjustment

Refer to illustrations 11.9, 11.10 and 11.11

8   With the cables attached at the control end and the control assembly installed in the dash, adjust the cables at their ends. The controls should be set to: RECIRC, COOL, and DEF.

9   To adjust the air inlet damper control cable set the damper lever to RECIRC, install the cable and clamp it in place **(see illustration)**.

10   To adjust the air mix control cable, set the air mix damper to COOL, install the cable and lock the clamp while applying slight pressure on the outer cable **(see illustration)**.

11   To adjust the mode damper control cable, set the mode damper to the DEF mode, hook the cable end on and tighten the clamp **(see illustration)**.

11.12 With the air conditioning switch On, there should be continuity between terminals 5 and 6; and 1 and 3

11.13 The blower speed selector switch should exhibit continuity as follows:

Low - between 3 and 7
M1 - between 3, 7 and 8
M2 - between 3, 6 and 7
HI - between 3, 5 and 7

Electrical checks

12   Check the air conditioning switch continuity. When the switch is pushed in (ON), there should be continuity between 5 and 6, and 1 and 3 **(see illustration)**.

13   Test the blower speed control switch for continuity **(see illustration)**. If the switch fails any of the tests, replace the control assembly.

12   Air conditioning and heating system - check and maintenance

Air conditioning system

Refer to illustration 12.1

Warning: *The air conditioning system is under high pressure. Do not loosen any hose fittings or remove any components until the system has been discharged. Air conditioning refrigerant should be properly discharged into an EPA-approved recovery/recycling unit by a dealer service department or an automotive air conditioning repair facility. Always wear eye protection when disconnecting air conditioning system fittings.*

1   The following maintenance checks should be performed on a regular basis to ensure that the air conditioner continues to operate at peak efficiency **(see illustration)**:

a) *Inspect the condition of the compressor drivebelt. If it is worn or deteriorated, replace it (see Chapter 1).*

b) *Check the drivebelt tension and, if necessary, adjust it (see Chapter 1).*

3

12.1 Basic components of the air conditioning system

Cooling Unit
● Expansion Valve
● Evaporator
● Blower Resistor
● Thermistor

Heater Unit
● Heater Radiator

Blower Unit
● Blower Motor

Relays

Receiver

Condenser Fan
● Condenser Fan Motor

Condenser

Compressor
● Magnetic Clutch
● Refrigerant Temperature Switch

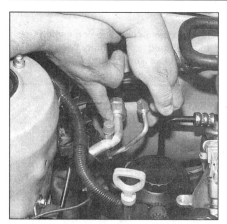

12.9 With the system operating, the evaporator outlet line (large tubing) should feel slightly warmer than the inlet line (small tubing)

12.10 Check the temperature of the output air in the center register with a thermometer - it should be 35-40 degrees below the ambient air temperature

12.11 The sight glass is located on top of the receiver/drier (arrow)

c) *Inspect the system hoses. Look for cracks, bubbles, hardening and deterioration. Inspect the hoses and all fittings for oil bubbles or seepage. If there is any evidence of wear, damage or leakage, replace the hose(s).*

d) *Inspect the condenser fins for leaves, bugs and any other foreign material that may have embedded itself in the fins. Use a "fin comb" or compressed air to remove debris from the condenser.*

e) *Make sure the system has the correct refrigerant charge.*

2   It's a good idea to operate the system for about ten minutes at least once a month. This is particularly important during the winter months because long term non-use can cause hardening, and subsequent failure, of the seals.

3   Leaks in the air conditioning system are best spotted when the system is brought up to operating temperature and pressure, by running the engine with the air conditioning ON for five minutes. Shut the engine off and inspect the air conditioning hoses and connections. Traces of oil usually indicate refrigerant leaks.

4   Because of the complexity of the air conditioning system and the special equipment required to effectively work on it, accurate troubleshooting of the system should be left to a professional technician.

5   If the air conditioning system doesn't operate at all, check the fuse panel and the air conditioning relay, located in the fuse/relay box in the engine compartment. Refer to Sections 4, 9 and 11 for electrical checks of heating/air conditioning system components.

6   The most common cause of poor cooling is simply a low system refrigerant charge. If a noticeable drop in cool air output occurs, the following quick check will help you determine if the refrigerant level is low. For more complete information on the air conditioning system, refer to the *Haynes Automotive Heating and Air Conditioning Manual.*

Checking the refrigerant charge

Refer to illustrations 12.9, 12.10 and 12.11

7   Warm the engine up to normal operating temperature.

8   Place the air conditioning temperature selector at the coldest setting and put the blower at the highest setting. Open the doors (to make sure the air conditioning system doesn't cycle off as soon as it cools the passenger compartment).

9   With the compressor engaged - the clutch will make an audible click and the center of the clutch will rotate. After the system reaches operating temperature, feel the two pipes connected to the evaporator at the firewall **(see illustration)**.

10   The pipe leading from the condenser outlet to the evaporator (small tubing) should be cold, and the evaporator outlet line (the larger tubing that leads back to the compressor) should be slightly colder (3 to 10 degrees F). If the evaporator outlet is considerably warmer than the inlet, the system needs a charge. Insert a thermometer in the center air distribution duct while operating the air conditioning system **(see**

illustration) - the temperature of the output air should be 35 to 40 degrees F below the ambient air temperature (down to approximately 40 degrees F). If the ambient (outside) air temperature is very high, say 110 degrees F, the duct air temperature may be as high as 60 degrees F, but generally the air conditioning is 35 to 40 degrees F cooler than the ambient air. If the air isn't as cold as it used to be, the system probably needs a charge. Further inspection or testing of the system is beyond the scope of the home mechanic and should be left to a professional.

11   Inspect the sight glass If the refrigerant looks foamy when running, it's low **(see illustration)**. When ambient temperatures are very hot, bubbles may show in the sight glass even with the proper amount of refrigerant. With the proper amount of refrigerant, when the air conditioning is turned off, the sight glass should show refrigerant that foams, then clears.

Adding refrigerant

Refer to illustrations 12.12 and 12.15

Caution: *Refrigerant has changed from the use of R-12, through 1993 models, to the "environmentally friendly" R-134a used in 1994 and later models. The two refrigerants are NOT compatible. Even after purging and evacuating an R-12 system, there is enough residual oil and refrigerant in the hoses and components that simply filling the system with R-134a cannot be done. Special fittings and manifold gauge sets are used on the different refrigerant types so that an accidental hook-up of the two systems cannot be made. When replacing entire components, additional refrigerant oil should be added equal to the amount that is removed with the component being replaced. Refrigerant oils, just like refrigerant R-12 vs. R-134a, are not compatible. Be sure to read the can before adding any oil to the system, to make sure it is compatible with the type of system being repaired.*

Note: *Because of Federal regulations by the Environmental Protection Agency, R-12 refrigerant is not available for home-mechanic use, however, cans of R-134 refrigerant are commonly available in auto parts stores. Models with R-12 systems will have to be serviced at a dealership or air conditioning shop.*

12   Buy an automotive charging kit at an auto parts store. A charging kit includes a 14-ounce can of R-134a refrigerant, a tap valve and a short section of hose that can be attached between the tap valve and the system low side service valve **(see illustration)**. Because one can of refrigerant may not be sufficient to bring the system charge up to the proper level, it's a good idea to buy a couple of additional cans. Try to find at least one can that contains red refrigerant dye. If the system is leaking, the red dye will leak out with the refrigerant and help you pinpoint the location of the leak.

13   Connect the charging kit by following the manufacturer's instructions.

12.12 A basic charging kit is available at most auto parts stores - it must say R-134a and so must the cans of refrigerant you buy

12.15 Add R-134a refrigerant to the low-side port only - the procedure will go faster if you wrap the can with a warm, wet towel to prevent icing

14   Back off the valve handle on the charging kit and screw the kit onto the refrigerant can, making sure first that the O-ring or rubber seal inside the threaded portion of the kit is in place. **Warning:** *Wear protective eyewear when dealing with pressurized refrigerant cans.*

15   Remove the dust cap from the low-side charging port and attach the quick-connect fitting on the kit hose **(see illustration)**. **Warning:** *DO NOT hook the charging kit hose to the system high side! The fittings on the charging kit are designed to fit only on the low side of the system.*

16   Warm the engine to normal operating temperature and turn on the air conditioner. Keep the charging kit hose away from the fan and other moving parts.

17   Turn the valve handle on the kit until the stem pierces the can, then back the handle out to release the refrigerant. You should be able to hear the rush of gas. Add refrigerant to the low side of the system until both the outlet and the evaporator inlet pipe feel about the same temperature. Allow stabilization time between each addition. **Warning:** *Never add more than two cans of refrigerant to the system. The can may tend to frost up, slowing the procedure. Wrap a shop towel wet with hot water around the bottom of the can to keep it from frosting.*

12.25 The drain hose from the heater/air conditioning unit (arrow) should be kept clear to allow drainage of condensation - shown here from underneath, the hose is on the right side, below the power steering pump

18   If you have an accurate thermometer, you can place it in the center air conditioning duct inside the vehicle to monitor the air temperature. A charged system that is working properly, should output air down to approximately 40 degrees F.

19   When the can is empty, turn the valve handle to the closed position and release the connection from the low-side port. Replace the dust cap.

20   Remove the charging kit from the can and store the kit for future use with the piercing valve in the UP position, to prevent inadvertently piercing the can on the next use.

Heating systems

Refer to illustration 12.25

21   If the air coming out of the heater vents isn't hot, the problem could stem from any of the following causes:

a) *The thermostat is stuck open, preventing the engine coolant from warming up enough to carry heat to the heater core. Replace the thermostat (see Section 3).*

b) *A heater hose is blocked, preventing the flow of coolant through the heater core. Feel both heater hoses at the firewall. They should be hot. If one of them is cold, there is an obstruction in one of the hoses or in the heater core, or the heater control valve is shut. Detach the hoses and back flush the heater core with a water hose. If the heater core is clear but circulation is impeded, remove the two hoses and flush them out with a water hose.*

c) *If flushing fails to remove the blockage from the heater core, the core must be replaced. (see Section 10).*

22   If the blower motor speed does not correspond to the setting selected on the blower switch, the problem could be a bad fuse, circuit, switch, blower motor resistor or motor (see Sections 9 and 11).

23   If there isn't any air coming out of the vents:

a) *Turn the ignition ON and activate the fan control. Place your ear at the heating/air conditioning register (vent) and listen. Most motors are audible. Can you hear the motor running?*

b) *If you can't (and have already verified that the blower switch and the blower motor resistor are good), the blower motor itself is probably bad (see Section 9).*

24   If the carpet under the heater core is damp, or if antifreeze vapor or steam is coming through the vents, the heater core is leaking. Remove it (see Section 10) and install a new unit (most radiator shops will not repair a leaking heater core).

25   Inspect the drain hose from the heater/air conditioning assembly at the right side of the firewall, make sure it is not clogged **(see illustration)**.

13.3 After the system has been discharged, unbolt the two refrigerant lines from the top of the receiver/drier and cap them - there is one bolt and one screw to remove (arrows)

14.4 Disconnect the wiring harness connector (large arrow) at the compressor, then unbolt the flanges (two smaller arrows) and detach the refrigerant lines from the compressor

13   Air conditioning receiver/drier - removal and installation

Refer to illustration 13.3

Warning: *The air conditioning system is under high pressure. Do not loosen any hose fittings or remove any components until the system has been discharged. Air conditioning refrigerant should be properly discharged into an EPA-approved recovery/recycling unit by a dealer service department or an automotive air conditioning repair facility. Always wear eye protection when disconnecting air conditioning system fittings.*

1   Have the refrigerant discharged and recovered by an air conditioning technician.

2   Refer to Chapter 11 and remove the grille.

3   Disconnect the refrigerant lines **(see illustration)** from the receiver/drier and cap the open fittings to prevent entry of moisture.

4   Loosen the pinch bolt and slip the receiver/drier out of the bracket.

5   Installation is the reverse of removal.

6   Have the system evacuated, charged and leak tested by the shop that discharged it. If the receiver was replaced, have them add new refrigeration oil to the compressor, about 0.7 ounces for R-12 systems, or 0.34 ounces for R-134a systems. Use only the refrigerant oil compatible with the refrigerant of your system (R-12 vs. R-134a).

14.5 Remove the compressor mounting bolts (arrows indicate the two bottom bolts, two more are near the top of the compressor) and remove the compressor

15.3 Disconnect the refrigerant line on the right side by unbolting this flange (arrow)

15.4 Remove the condenser mounting bolts - there is one bolt at each end (right side shown)

16.1 Evaporator unit installation details

Cooling Unit

Air Duct

Glove Box Assembly

Front Door Scuff Plate

14 Air conditioning compressor - removal and installation

Refer to illustrations 15.4 and 15.5
Warning: *The air conditioning system is under high pressure. Do not loosen any hose fittings or remove any components until the system has been discharged. Air conditioning refrigerant should be properly discharged into an EPA-approved recovery/recycling unit by a dealer service department or an automotive air conditioning repair facility. Always wear eye protection when disconnecting air conditioning system fittings.*
1   Have the refrigerant discharged by an automotive air conditioning technician.
2   Disconnect the negative cable from the battery. **Caution:** *If the stereo in your vehicle is equipped with an anti-theft system, make sure you have the correct activation code before disconnecting the battery.*
3   Remove the drivebelt from the compressor (see Chapter 1).
4   Detach the wiring connector and disconnect the refrigerant lines **(see illustration)**.
5   Unbolt the compressor and lift it from the vehicle **(see illustration)**.
6   If a new or rebuilt compressor is being installed, follow the directions supplied with the compressor regarding the proper level of oil prior to installation.
7   Installation is the reverse of removal. Replace any O-rings with new ones specifically made for the type of refrigerant in your system and lubricate them with refrigerant oil, also designed specifically for your system (R-12 vs. R-134a).
8   Have the system evacuated, recharged and leak tested by the shop that discharged it.

15 Air conditioning condenser - removal and installation

Refer to illustrations 15.3 and 15.4
Warning: *The air conditioning system is under high pressure. Do not loosen any hose fittings or remove any components until the system*

has been discharged. Air conditioning refrigerant should be properly discharged into an EPA-approved recovery/recycling unit by a dealer service department or an automotive air conditioning repair facility. Always wear eye protection when disconnecting air conditioning system fittings.
1   Have the refrigerant discharged by an air conditioning technician.
2   Remove the radiator as described in Section 5.
3   Remove the grille and right headlight assembly for access (see Chapter 11). Disconnect the condenser inlet and outlet fittings **(see illustration)**. Cap the open fittings immediately to keep moisture and contamination out of the system. **Note:** *The left-side fitting is connected to the receiver/drier (see Section 13).*
4   Remove the two condenser mounting bolts, pull the condenser back and lift it out **(see illustration)**.
5   Install the condenser, brackets and bolts, making sure the rubber cushions fit on the mounting points properly.
6   Reconnect the refrigerant lines, using new O-rings where needed. If a new condenser has been installed, add approximately 1.4 to 1.7 ounces of new refrigerant oil of the correct type (R-12 vs. R-134a).
7   Reinstall the remaining parts in the reverse order of removal.
8   Have the system evacuated, charged and leak tested by the shop that discharged it.

16 Air conditioning evaporator and expansion valve - removal and installation

Refer to illustrations 16.1, 16.2, 16.4 and 16.6
Warning: *The air conditioning system is under high pressure. Do not loosen any hose fittings or remove any components until the system has been discharged. Air conditioning refrigerant should be properly discharged into an EPA-approved recovery/recycling unit by a dealer service department or an automotive air conditioning repair facility. Always wear eye protection when disconnecting air conditioning system fittings.*
1   Remove the glove compartment assembly **(see illustration)**.

2   Disconnect the air conditioning lines at the firewall, use a back-up wrench so as not to damage the fittings **(see illustration)**. Cap the open fittings after disassembly to prevent the entry of air or dirt.

3   Remove two nuts and three screws retaining the evaporator unit to the firewall and pull the unit out of the vehicle **(see illustration 16.1)**.

4   With the evaporator unit on the bench, remove the screws and clips and separate the top and bottom halves of the case and pull out the evaporator **(see illustration)**.

5   Pull the thermistor sensor probe from the evaporator core and unbolt the expansion valve and the two short refrigerant lines **(see illustration 16.4)**.

6   The evaporator core can be cleaned with a "fin comb" and blown off with compressed air **(see illustration)**. **Warning:** *Be sure to wear eye protection when using compressed air.*

7   If the evaporator core is replaced with a new unit, add 1.4 ounces of new refrigerant oil of the correct type (R-12 vs. R-134a) to the system.

8   The remainder of the installation is the reverse of the removal process. Be sure to use new O-rings, and new gaskets on the expansion valve.

9   Have the system evacuated, charged and leak tested by the shop that discharged it.

16.2 Use a back-up wrench when disconnecting the air conditioning lines at the firewall

16.4 Separate the two halves of the evaporator housing and remove the core

A/C Amplifier and Harness

Blower Resistor

Thermistor

Lower Case

Upper Case

Evaporator

Liquid and Suction Tube

Drain Hose

Expansion Valve

16.6 The fins of the core can be cleaned with a fin comb - use the side of the tool with the correct fins-per-inch spacing for your core

Chapter 4
Fuel and exhaust systems

Contents

Specifications

Fuel system

Fuel pressure
  Ignition ON, engine not running .... 38 to 44 psi
  Engine idling
    Vacuum sensing hose detached .... 38 to 44 psi
    Vacuum sensing hose attached .... 31 to 37 psi
  Fuel system hold pressure .... 21 psi
Fuel injector resistance .... 13.4 to 14.2 ohms
Idle Air Control (IAC) valve resistance .... 19 to 23 ohms
Air conditioning idle-up valve solenoid resistance .... 30 to 34 ohms

Idle Speed
Automatic transmission .... 750 rpm
Manual transmission .... 700 rpm

Torque specification
Ft-lbs
Throttle body mounting bolts 14
Fuel rail mounting bolts 14

2.3 To depressurize the fuel system, unplug the electrical connector from the circuit opening relay, start the engine and allow it to stall

3.2 Bridge terminals FP and +B on the test connector using a jumper wire or paper clip

1   General information

The fuel system consists of a fuel tank, an electric fuel pump (located in the fuel tank), an EFI/fuel pump relay, fuel injectors, a fuel pressure regulator, an air cleaner assembly and a throttle body unit. All models covered by this manual are equipped with the Multi Point Fuel Injection (MPFI) system.

Multi Point Fuel Injection (MPFI) system

Multi point fuel injection uses timed impulses to sequentially inject the fuel directly into the intake port of each cylinder. The injectors are controlled by the Electronic Control Module (ECM). The ECM monitors various engine parameters and delivers the exact amount of fuel, in the correct sequence, into the intake ports. The throttle body serves only to control the amount of air passing into the system. Because each cylinder is equipped with an injector mounted immediately adjacent to the intake valve, much better control of the fuel/air mixture ratio is possible.

Fuel pump and lines

Fuel is circulated from the fuel tank to the fuel injection system, and back to the fuel tank, through a pair of metal lines running along the underside of the vehicle. An electric fuel pump is attached to the fuel sending unit inside the fuel tank. A vapor return system routes all vapors and hot fuel back to the fuel tank through a separate return line.

The fuel pump will operate as long as the engine is cranking or running and the ECM is receiving ignition reference pulses from the electronic ignition system (see Chapter 5). If there are no reference pulses, the fuel pump will shut off after 2 or 3 seconds.

Exhaust system

The exhaust system includes an exhaust manifold fitted with an exhaust oxygen sensor, a catalytic converter, an exhaust pipe, and a muffler.

The catalytic converter is an emission control device added to the exhaust system to reduce pollutants. A single-bed converter is used in combination with a three-way (reduction) catalyst. Refer to Chapter 6 for more information regarding the catalytic converter.

2   Fuel pressure relief

Refer to illustration 2.3

Warning: *Gasoline is extremely flammable, so take extra precautions when you work on any part of the fuel system. Don't smoke or allow open flames or bare light bulbs near the work area, and don't work in a garage where a natural gas-type appliance (such as a water heater or a clothes dryer) with a pilot light is present. Since gasoline is carcinogenic, wear latex gloves when there's a possibility of being exposed to fuel, and, if you spill any fuel on your skin, rinse it off immediately with soap and water. Mop up any spills immediately and do not store fuel-soaked rags where they could ignite. The fuel system is under constant pressure, so, if any fuel lines are to be disconnected, the fuel pressure in the system must be relieved first. When you perform any kind of work on the fuel system, wear safety glasses and have a Class B type fire extinguisher on hand.*

1   Before servicing any fuel system component, you must relieve the fuel pressure to minimize the risk of fire or personal injury.

2   Remove the fuel filler cap - this will relieve any pressure built up in the tank.

3   Remove the radio (see Chapter 12) and cup holder for access to the circuit opening relay. Unplug the electrical connector from the relay **(see illustration)**.

4   Start the engine and wait for the engine to stall, then turn the ignition key to Off.

5   The fuel system is now depressurized. **Note:** *Place a rag around the fuel line before removing any hose clamp or fitting to prevent any residual fuel from spilling onto the engine.*

6   Before working on the fuel system, disconnect the cable from the negative terminal of the battery. **Caution:** *If the stereo in your vehicle is equipped with an anti-theft system, make sure you have the correct activation code before disconnecting the battery.*

3   Fuel pump/fuel pressure - check

Warning: *Gasoline is extremely flammable, so take extra precautions when you work on any part of the fuel system. Don't smoke or allow open flames or bare light bulbs near the work area, and don't work in a garage where a natural gas-type appliance (such as a water heater or a clothes dryer) with a pilot light is present. Since gasoline is carcinogenic, wear latex gloves when there's a possibility of being exposed to fuel, and, if you spill any fuel on your skin, rinse it off immediately with soap and water. Mop up any spills immediately and do not store fuel-soaked rags where they could ignite. The fuel system is under constant pressure, so, if any fuel lines are to be disconnected, the fuel pressure in the system must be relieved first. When you perform any kind of work on the fuel system, wear safety glasses and have a Class B type fire extinguisher on hand.*

Fuel pump operation check

Refer to illustrations 3.2, 3.6a and 3.6b

1   Turn ON the ignition switch (but do not start the engine).

2   On 1993 and 1994 models and 1995 models with the 1.6L engine, bridge terminals +B and FP of the test connector with a jumper wire **(see illustration)**. **Note:** *On 1995 1.8L engines and all 1996 and later models (OBD II), it is not possible to power the fuel pump using the test connector. On these models, start the engine to obtain fuel pressure readings.*

3.6a Typical electrical schematic of the fuel pump circuit

3.6b Check for battery voltage directly at the fuel pump electrical connector on the top of the fuel tank

3   The fuel pump is now activated. Listen for fuel pump noises from the fuel tank (under the rear seat) and verify that there is pressure in the hose from the fuel filter.

4   Remove the jumper wire. Close the cap on the test connector.

5   Turn the ignition switch OFF.

6   If the fuel pump did not operate, inspect the following electrical components: the EFI 15-amp fuse and the ignition switch 30-amp fuse (AM2) **(see illustration)** and/or the EFI main relay and the circuit opening relay, (see Steps 33 through 38), the fuel pump **(see illustration)**; and the wiring and electrical connectors (see the wiring diagrams at the end of the book).

Fuel pressure check

Refer to illustrations 3.7, 3.11a and 3.11b

7   A fuel pressure gauge, capable of measuring a minimum of 50-psi, equipped with a banjo fitting on the end of the hose (Toyota special service tool no. SST 09268-45012) is required for the following procedure. There are a couple of alternatives if you are unable to

3.7 Cut the head off the bolt (12 mm diameter/1.25 thread pitch) and drill a hole directly through the bolt, lengthwise. Grind the end to accept the pressure gauge hose and drill another hole to allow system pressure to flow. It is important that this hole is drilled in the correct location. The easiest method is to use the banjo bolt that was removed from the fuel filter and place it directly next to the tool for the correct alignment of this passage for fuel flow

obtain the special Toyota fuel pressure gauge set:

a) *Obtain a 12 mm banjo fitting that will adapt to your fuel pressure gauge hose with a hose clamp.*

b) *If you can't find the correct size banjo fitting, obtain a 12 mm bolt with 1.25 mm thread pitch, cut the head off and drill a hole through the center and one through the side, perpendicular to the lengthwise hole. Add a locknut with the same thread pitch and seal the threads with teflon tape **(see illustration)**.*

8   Remove the fuel tank cap to relieve any pressure that has built up in the tank.

9   Verify that the battery voltage is 12 volts or more (see Chapter 5).

10   Relieve the fuel pressure (see Section 2).

11   There are two methods possible for testing the fuel pressure:

a) *If you have the special banjo fitting (Toyota tool number SST 09268-45012) required to attach the fuel pressure gauge, remove*

3.11a If the factory tools are available, install the fuel pressure gauge onto the end of the fuel rail

3.11b If you are using the homemade tool, install the fuel pressure gauge to the top of the fuel filter (located in the engine compartment)

the fuel rail bolt at the end of the fuel rail and install the special tool into the fuel rail **(see illustration)**.

b) If you have constructed the drilled-out bolt and locknut tool, detach one side of the fuel filter **(see illustration)** and install the fuel pressure gauge at this point.

12   To attach the fuel pressure gauge:

a) If you are using the factory setup, use the special banjo fitting on the fuel rail to attach the fuel pressure gauge to the fuel rail. Be sure to use crush washers on both sides of the banjo fitting.

b) If you are using a drilled-out 12 mm bolt, working in the engine compartment, attach the bolt to the fuel filter, tighten the locknut and attach the fuel pressure gauge hose with a hose clamp.

13   Wipe off any gasoline that has leaked out of the fuel rail (or filter).

14   Place the transmission in Neutral (manual) or Park (automatic) and apply the parking brake.

15   On 1993 and 1994 models and 1995 models with the 1.6L engine, bridge terminals +B and FP of the test connector **(see illustration 3.2)**. **Note:** *On 1995 1.8L engines and all 1996 and later models (OBD II), it is not possible to power the fuel pump using the test connector. On these models, start the engine to obtain fuel pressure readings.*

16   Turn the ignition to ON (engine not running). Measure the fuel pressure and compare it to the fuel pressure listed in this Chapter's Specifications.

a) If the pressure is high, check for a restricted fuel return line. If the line is clear, replace the pressure regulator.

b) If the pressure is low, pinch the fuel return line. If the pressure goes up, replace the fuel pressure regulator. If the pressure does not increase, check the fuel feed line, the fuel pump and the fuel filter.

17   Remove the jumper wire from the service electrical connector or fuel pump connector.

18   Start the engine.

a) Measure the fuel pressure at idle and compare your reading to the fuel pressure listed in this Chapter's Specifications.

b) If the pressure is not as specified, check the vacuum sensing hose and fuel pressure regulator (see Steps 20 through 24).

19   Stop the engine and verify that the fuel pressure remains at 21 psi or more for five minutes after the engine is turned off. If the pressure bleeds down, the fuel pressure regulator, the fuel pump or a fuel injector may be leaking.

Fuel pressure regulator check

Refer to illustrations 3.20 and 3.21

20   Disconnect and plug the vacuum hose from the fuel pressure regulator and connect a hand-held vacuum pump to the regulator. Start the engine and read the fuel pressure gauge without vacuum applied to the fuel pressure regulator. Apply vacuum to the regulator and check the fuel pressure again **(see illustration)**. The fuel pressure should decrease as vacuum increases. Compare your readings with the values listed in this Chapter's Specifications.

21   Reconnect the vacuum hose to the regulator and check the fuel pressure at idle, comparing your reading with the value listed in this Chapter's Specifications. Disconnect the hose and watch the gauge -

3.20 First check the fuel pressure without vacuum applied to the fuel pressure regulator and then with vacuum applied - fuel pressure should DECREASE as vacuum INCREASES

3.21 Connect a vacuum gauge to the vacuum line leading to the fuel pressure regulator and check the vacuum source

3.30a Location of the fuel system relays, sensors and actuators

3.30b Locate and remove the EFI relay and check for battery voltage to the relay with the ignition key ON

3.31 Remove the circuit opening relay and check for battery voltage

the pressure should jump up to the maximum specified pressure as soon as the hose is disconnected. If the pressure at idle was too high (with the hose disconnected), connect a vacuum gauge to the hose and check for vacuum (see illustration). If there is no reading on the gauge, check the air intake plenum and intake manifold for a vacuum leak.

22   If the fuel pressure is LOW, pinch the fuel return line shut and watch the gauge. If the pressure doesn't rise, the fuel pump is defective or there is a restriction in the fuel feed line. If the pressure rises sharply, replace the fuel pressure regulator (see Section 13).

23   If the indicated fuel pressure is too high, relieve the fuel pressure (see Section 2), disconnect the fuel return line and blow through it to check for blockage. If there is no blockage, replace the fuel pressure regulator (see Section 13).

24   If the fuel pressure does not fluctuate as described in Step 21, replace the fuel pressure regulator (see Section 13).

25   Carefully remove the fuel pressure gauge. Be sure to cover the fit-

ting with a rag before loosening it.

26   Using new sealing washers, reattach the pipe banjo fitting to the fuel rail.

27   Wipe up any spilled gasoline.

28   Start the engine and check for leaks.

EFI main relay and circuit opening relay checks

Voltage checks

Refer to illustrations 3.30a, 3.30b and 3.31

29   There are two relays involved in the fuel pump circuit. First, test for battery voltage to the EFI main relay and then the circuit opening relay.

30   Remove the EFI main relay from the electrical connector and with the ignition key ON (engine not running), check for battery voltage (see illustrations).

31   If battery voltage is present, insert the relay back into the connector and check for battery voltage at the circuit opening relay (see

3.33 EFI main relay checks on Nippondenso style relay

3.34 Apply battery voltage to terminals 1 and 2 and check for continuity between terminals 3 and 5

3.35 EFI main relay checks on Bosch style relay

3.36 Apply battery voltage to terminals 85 and 86 and confirm that continuity exists across terminals 87 and 30

3.37 Circuit opening relay checks

accompanying illustration and illustration 2.3). This will require removal of the radio (see Chapter 12).

32   If battery voltage is present at the relay connectors, check the relays.

EFI main relay (Nippondenso type)

Refer to illustrations 3.33 and 3.34

33   Using an ohmmeter, check for continuity across terminals 1 and 2 **(see illustration)**. Check that there is no continuity across terminals 3 and 5.

34   Apply battery voltage across terminals 1 and 2 **(see illustration)**. Using an ohmmeter, check for continuity across terminals 3 and 5. Continuity should exist. If the test results are incorrect, replace the relay.

EFI main relay (Bosch type)

Refer to illustrations 3.35 and 3.36

35   Using an ohmmeter, check for continuity across terminals 86 and 85 **(see illustration)**. Check that there is no continuity across terminals 87 and 30.

36   Apply battery voltage across terminals 86 and 85 **(see illustration)**. Using an ohmmeter, check for continuity across terminals 87 and 30. Continuity should exist. If the test results are incorrect, replace the relay.

Circuit opening relay

Refer to illustrations 3.37 and 3.38

37   Using an ohmmeter, check for continuity across terminals ST and E1 **(see illustration)**. Also, check for continuity across +B and FC. Check that there is no continuity across terminals +B and FP.

38   Apply battery voltage across terminals ST and E1 **(see illustration)**. Using an ohmmeter, check for continuity across terminals +B and FP. Continuity should exist. If the test results are incorrect, replace the relay.

3.38 Apply battery voltage to ST and E1 and check for continuity across terminals FP and +B

4   Fuel pump - removal and installation

Refer to illustrations 4.4, 4.5, 4.6, 4.7, 4.8, 4.13 and 4.14

Warning: *Gasoline is extremely flammable, so take extra precautions when you work on any part of the fuel system. Don't smoke or allow open flames or bare light bulbs near the work area, and don't work in a garage where a natural gas-type appliance (such as a water heater or a clothes dryer) with a pilot light is present. Since gasoline is carcinogenic, wear latex gloves when there's a possibility of being exposed to fuel, and, if you spill any fuel on your skin, rinse it off immediately with soap and water. Mop up any spills immediately and do not store fuel-soaked rags where they could ignite. The fuel system is under constant pressure, so, if any fuel lines are to be disconnected, the fuel pressure in the system must be relieved first. When you perform any kind of work on the fuel system, wear safety glasses and have a Class B type fire extinguisher on hand.*

4.4 Remove the fuel pump/fuel level sending unit access cover screws (arrows) and lift the cover off

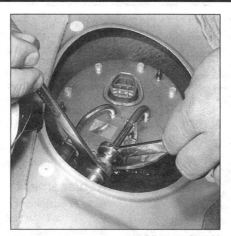

4.5 Use a flare-nut wrench and a back-up wrench to remove the fuel feed line; remove the clamp and hose from the fuel return line fitting

4.6 Remove the fuel pump/sending unit assembly mounting bolts (arrows)

1   Remove the fuel tank cap.

2   Disconnect the cable from the negative terminal of the battery. **Caution:** *If the stereo in your vehicle is equipped with an anti-theft system, make sure you have the correct activation code before disconnecting the battery.*

3   Remove the rear seat from inside the passenger compartment (see Chapter 11).

4   Remove the fuel pump/sending unit access cover **(see illustration)**.

5   Disconnect the electrical connector. Disconnect the fuel lines **(see illustration)**.

6   Remove the fuel pump/sending unit retaining bolts **(see illustration)**.

7   Carefully withdraw the fuel pump/fuel level sending unit assembly from the fuel tank **(see illustration)**.

8   Pry the lower end of the fuel pump loose from the bracket **(see illustration)**.

9   Remove the rubber cushion from the lower end of the fuel pump.

10   Remove the clip securing the inlet screen to the pump.

11   Remove the screen and inspect it for contamination. If it is dirty, replace it.

12   If you are only replacing the fuel pump inlet screen, install the new screen, the clip and the rubber cushion, push the lower end of the pump back into the bracket and install the pump/sending unit assembly in the fuel tank.

13   If you are replacing the fuel pump, remove the hose clamp at the

4.7 Lift the fuel pump/sending unit assembly from the fuel tank at an angle so as not to damage the inlet screen or float arm

upper end of the pump and disconnect the pump from the hose **(see illustration)**.

14   Disconnect the wires from the pump terminals and remove the pump **(see illustration)**.

15   Installation is the reverse of removal.

4.8 Separate the fuel pump from the frame by gently prying outward

4.13 Remove the clamp from the fuel pump outlet hose

4.14 Remove the electrical connector from the fuel pump

5.4 Position the probes of the ohmmeter onto terminals 1 and 2 and observe the fuel level sending unit resistance

5   Fuel level sending unit - check and replacement

Warning: *Gasoline is extremely flammable, so take extra precautions when you work on any part of the fuel system. Don't smoke or allow open flames or bare light bulbs near the work area, and don't work in a garage where a natural gas-type appliance (such as a water heater or a clothes dryer) with a pilot light is present. Since gasoline is carcinogenic, wear latex gloves when there's a possibility of being exposed to fuel, and, if you spill any fuel on your skin, rinse it off immediately with soap and water. Mop up any spills immediately and do not store fuel-soaked rags where they could ignite. The fuel system is under constant pressure, so, if any fuel lines are to be disconnected, the fuel pressure in the system must be relieved first. When you perform any kind of work on the fuel system, wear safety glasses and have a Class B type fire extinguisher on hand.*

Check

Refer to illustrations 5.4 and 5.8

1   Before performing any tests on the fuel level sending unit, completely fill the tank with fuel.

2   Remove the rear seat and the fuel pump/sending unit access cover **(see illustration 4.4)**.

3   Disconnect the fuel level sending unit electrical connector located on top of the fuel tank.

4   Position the ohmmeter probes on the electrical connector terminals (terminals pink (+) and black (-) check for resistance **(see illustration)**. Use the 200-ohm scale on the ohmmeter.

5   With the fuel tank completely full, the resistance should be about

4.0 ohms.

6   Reconnect the electrical connector and drive the vehicle until the tank is nearly empty (or siphon the fuel into an approved fuel container using a siphoning kit - not your mouth.

7   Check the resistance. The resistance of the sending unit should now be about 110 ohms.

8   If the readings are incorrect, replace the sending unit. **Note:** *The test can also be performed with the fuel level sending unit removed from the fuel tank. Using an ohmmeter, check the resistance of the sending unit with the float arm completely down (tank empty) and with the arm up (tank full)* **(see illustration)**. *The resistance should change steadily from 110 ohms to approximately 2.0 to 4.0 ohms.*

Replacement

Refer to illustrations 5.11 and 5.12

9   Remove the fuel pump/fuel level sending unit assembly from the fuel tank (see Section 4).

10   Carefully angle the sending unit out of the opening without damaging the fuel level float located at the bottom of the assembly **(see illustration 4.7)**.

11   Disconnect the electrical connectors from the sending unit **(see illustration)**.

12   Remove the screw from the side of the sending unit bracket and separate the sending unit from the assembly **(see illustration)**.

13   Installation is the reverse of removal.

6   Fuel lines and fittings - inspection and replacement

Warning: *Gasoline is extremely flammable, so take extra precautions when you work on any part of the fuel system. Don't smoke or allow open flames or bare light bulbs near the work area, and don't work in a garage where a natural gas-type appliance (such as a water heater or a clothes dryer) with a pilot light is present. Since gasoline is carcinogenic, wear latex gloves when there's a possibility of being exposed to fuel, and, if you spill any fuel on your skin, rinse it off immediately with soap and water. Mop up any spills immediately and do not store fuel-soaked rags where they could ignite. The fuel system is under constant pressure, so, if any fuel lines are to be disconnected, the fuel pressure in the system must be relieved first. When you perform any kind of work on the fuel system, wear safety glasses and have a Class B type fire extinguisher on hand.*

Inspection

1   Once in a while, you will have to raise the vehicle to service or replace some component (an exhaust pipe hanger, for example). Whenever you work under the vehicle, always inspect fuel lines and all fittings and connections for damage or deterioration.

5.8 An accurate check of the sending unit can be made by removing it from the fuel tank and observing the resistance with the float down (empty) and then up (full)

5.11 Remove the electrical connector from the fuel level sending unit

5.12 Remove the screws that retain the fuel level sending unit

2   Check all hoses and pipes for cracks, kinks, deformation or obstructions.

3   Make sure all hoses and pipe clips attach their associated hoses or pipes securely to the underside of the vehicle.

4   Verify all hose clamps attaching rubber hoses to metal fuel lines or pipes are snug enough to assure a tight fit between the hoses and pipes.

Replacement

Refer to illustration 6.6

5   If you must replace any damaged sections, use original equipment replacement hoses or pipes constructed from exactly the same material as the section you are replacing. Do not install substitutes constructed from inferior or inappropriate material or you could cause a fuel leak or a fire.

6   Always, before detaching or disassembling any part of the fuel line system, note the routing of all hoses and pipes and the orientation of all clamps and clips to assure that replacement sections are installed in exactly the same manner. When attaching hoses to metal lines, overlap them as shown **(see illustration)**.

7   Before detaching any part of the fuel system, be sure to relieve the fuel line and tank pressure by removing the fuel tank cap and disconnecting the battery. Cover the fitting being disconnected with a rag to absorb any fuel that may spray out.

6.6 When attaching a section of rubber hose to a metal fuel line, be sure to overlap the hose as shown, secure it to the line with a new hose clamp of the proper type

7   Fuel tank - removal and installation

Refer to illustrations 7.6, 7.9a, 7.9b and 7.10

Warning: *Gasoline is extremely flammable, so take extra precautions when you work on any part of the fuel system. Don't smoke or allow open flames or bare light bulbs near the work area, and don't work in a garage where a natural gas-type appliance (such as a water heater or a*

4

7.6 Typical fuel tank and related components

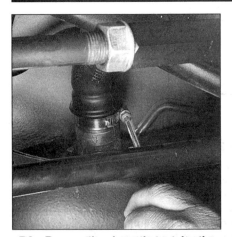

7.9a Remove the clamp that retains the fuel filler hose

7.9b Loosen the clamp and detach the fuel vapor line from the fuel tank

7.10 Remove the tank strap bolts (arrows) from the body

clothes dryer) with a pilot light is present. Since gasoline is carcinogenic, wear latex gloves when there's a possibility of being exposed to fuel, and, if you spill any fuel on your skin, rinse it off immediately with soap and water. Mop up any spills immediately and do not store fuel-soaked rags where they could ignite. The fuel system is under constant pressure, so, if any fuel lines are to be disconnected, the fuel pressure in the system must be relieved first. When you perform any kind of work on the fuel system, wear safety glasses and have a Class B type fire extinguisher on hand.

1   This procedure is much easier to perform if the fuel tank is empty. Some models may have a drain plug for this purpose. If for some reason the drain plug can't be removed, postpone the job until the tank is empty or siphon the fuel into an approved container using a siphoning kit (available at most auto parts stores). **Warning:** *Do not start the siphoning action by mouth!*

2   Remove the fuel filler cap to relieve fuel tank pressure. Relieve the fuel system pressure (see Section 2)

3   Detach the cable from the negative terminal of the battery. **Caution:** *If the stereo in your vehicle is equipped with an anti-theft system, make sure you have the correct activation code before disconnecting the battery.*

4   If the tank is full or nearly full, drain the fuel into an approved container.

5   Raise the vehicle and place it securely on jackstands.

6   Familiarize yourself with the layout of the fuel tank assembly before proceeding **(see illustration)**.

7   Remove the center exhaust pipe and the heat insulator from the vehicle (see Section 14).

8   Support the fuel tank with a floor jack. Place a sturdy plank between the jack head and the fuel tank to protect the tank.

9   Disconnect the fuel lines, the vapor return line and the fuel filler hose **(see illustrations)**. **Note:** *Be sure to plug the hoses to prevent leakage and contamination of the fuel system.*

10   Remove the bolts from the fuel tank retaining straps **(see illustration)**.

11   Lower the tank enough to disconnect the electrical connector and ground strap from the fuel pump/fuel gauge sending unit, if you have not already done so.

12   Remove the tank from the vehicle.

13   Installation is the reverse of removal.

8   Fuel tank cleaning and repair - general information

1   Any repairs to the fuel tank or filler neck should be carried out by a professional who has experience in this critical and potentially dangerous work. Even after cleaning and flushing of the fuel system, explosive fumes can remain and ignite during repair of the tank.

2   If the fuel tank is removed from the vehicle, it should not be

9.3 Remove the bolts (arrows) that retain the air cleaner housing to the engine compartment

placed in an area where sparks or open flames could ignite the fumes coming out of the tank. Be especially careful inside garages where a natural gas-type appliance is located, because the pilot light could cause an explosion.

9   Air cleaner assembly - removal and installation

Refer to illustration 9.3

1   Detach the clips and remove the air filter and the filter element (see Chapter 1).

2   Disconnect the air intake hose from the assembly.

3   Remove the three bolts and remove the air cleaner assembly from the engine compartment **(see illustration)**.

4   Installation is the reverse of removal.

10   Accelerator cable - removal, installation and adjustment

Refer to illustrations 10.2, 10.3 and 10.4

Removal

1   Detach the cable from the negative terminal of the battery. **Caution:** *If the stereo in your vehicle is equipped with an anti-theft system, make sure you have the correct activation code before disconnecting the battery.*

10.2 Loosen the locknuts on the accelerator cable

10.3 Rotate the throttle lever and remove the cable end from the slot

10.4 Separate the cable from the accelerator pedal assembly and slide the cable end out of the slot (arrow) in the housing

2   Loosen the locknut on the threaded portion of the throttle cable at the throttle body **(see illustration)**.
3   Rotate the throttle lever and slip the throttle cable end out of the slot in the lever **(see illustration)**.
4   Detach the throttle cable from the accelerator pedal **(see illustration)**. Remove the two bolts securing the cable retainer to the firewall.
5   From inside the vehicle, pull the cable through the firewall.

Installation and adjustment

6   Installation is the reverse of removal. Make sure the cable casing grommet seats properly in the firewall.
7   To adjust the cable, fully depress the accelerator pedal and check that the throttle is fully opened.

8   If not fully opened, loosen the locknuts, depress accelerator pedal and adjust the cable until the throttle is fully open.
9   Tighten the locknuts and recheck the adjustment. Make sure the throttle closes fully when the pedal is released.

11 Electronic Fuel Injection (EFI) system - general information

Refer to illustrations 11.1a and 11.1b

1   These models are equipped with an Electronic Fuel Injection (EFI) system. The EFI system is composed of three basic subsystems: fuel

4

11.1a Schematic of the Electronic Fuel Injection (EFI) system for all models except California

11.1b Schematic of the Electronic Fuel Injection (EFI) system for California models

---

system, air induction system and electronic control system **(see illustrations)**.

Fuel system

2   An electric fuel pump located inside the fuel tank supplies fuel under constant pressure to the fuel rail, which distributes fuel evenly to all injectors. From the fuel rail, fuel is injected into the intake ports, just above the intake valves, by fuel injectors. The amount of fuel supplied by the injectors is precisely controlled by an Electronic Control Module (ECM). A pressure regulator controls system pressure in relation to intake manifold vacuum. A fuel filter between the fuel pump and the fuel rail filters fuel to protect the components of the system.

Air induction system

3   The air induction system consists of an air filter housing, the throttle body and the duct connecting the two. An Intake Air Temperature (IAT) sensor monitors the temperature of the incoming air. This information helps the ECM determine the amount of fuel to be injected by the injectors. The throttle plate inside the throttle body is controlled by the driver. As the throttle plate opens, the speed of the incoming air increases, which lowers the temperature of the air. The IAT sends this information to the ECM and the ECM signals the injectors to increase the amount of fuel delivered to the intake ports.

Electronic control system

4   The Computer Control System controls the EFI and other systems

by means of an Electronic Control Module (ECM), which employs a microcomputer. The ECM receives signals from a number of information sensors which monitor such variables as intake air temperature, throttle angle, coolant temperature, engine rpm, vehicle speed and exhaust oxygen content. These signals help the ECM determine the injection duration necessary for the optimum air/fuel ratio. Some of these sensors and their corresponding ECM-controlled relays are not contained within EFI components, but are located throughout the engine compartment. For further information regarding the ECM and its relationship to the engine electrical and ignition system, see Chapter 6.

---

12   Electronic Fuel Injection (EFI) system - check

Refer to illustrations 12.6, 12.7, 12.8 and 12.9

1   Check the ground wire connections for tightness. Check all wiring and electrical connectors that are related to the system. Loose electrical connectors and poor grounds can cause many problems that resemble more serious malfunctions.
2   Check to see that the battery is fully charged, as the control unit and sensors depend on an accurate supply voltage in order to properly meter the fuel.
3   Check the air filter element - a dirty or partially blocked filter will severely impede performance and economy (see Chapter 1).
4   If a blown fuse is found, replace it and see if it blows again. If it

12.6 With the engine off, use aerosol carburetor cleaner (make sure it is safe for use with catalytic converters and oxygen sensors), a toothbrush and a rag to clean the throttle body - open the throttle plate so you can clean behind it

12.7 Use a stethoscope or a screwdriver to determine if the injectors are working properly - they should make a steady clicking sound that rises and falls with engine speed changes

does, search for a grounded wire in the harness related to the system.

5   Check the air intake duct from the air cleaner housing to the intake manifold for leaks, which will result in an excessively lean mixture. Also check the condition of the vacuum hoses connected to the intake manifold.

6   Remove the air intake duct from the throttle body and check for carbon and residue build-up. If it's dirty, clean it with aerosol carburetor cleaner (make sure the can says it's safe for use with oxygen sensors and catalytic converters) and a toothbrush **(see illustration)**.

7   With the engine running, place a stethoscope against each injector, one at a time, and listen for a clicking sound, indicating operation **(see illustration)**. If you don't have an automotive stethoscope you can use a long screwdriver; just place the tip of the screwdriver against the injector body and press your ear against the handle.

8   If there is a problem with an injector, purchase a special injector test light ("noid" light) and install it into the injector electrical connector **(see illustration)**. Start the engine and make sure that each injector connector flashes the noid light. This will test for the proper voltage signal to the injector.

9   With the engine OFF and the fuel injector electrical connectors disconnected, measure the resistance of each injector **(see illustration)**. Each injector should measure about 13.4 to 14.2 ohms. If not, the injector is probably faulty.

10   The remainder of the system checks should be left to a dealer

service department or other qualified repair shop, as there is a chance that the control unit may be damaged if not performed properly.

---

13   Electronic Fuel Injection (EFI) system - component check and replacement

Warning: *Gasoline is extremely flammable, so take extra precautions when you work on any part of the fuel system. Don't smoke or allow open flames or bare light bulbs near the work area, and don't work in a garage where a natural gas-type appliance (such as a water heater or a clothes dryer) with a pilot light is present. Since gasoline is carcinogenic, wear latex gloves when there's a possibility of being exposed to fuel, and, if you spill any fuel on your skin, rinse it off immediately with soap and water. Mop up any spills immediately and do not store fuel-soaked rags where they could ignite. The fuel system is under constant pressure, so, if any fuel lines are to be disconnected, the fuel pressure in the system must be relieved first. When you perform any kind of work on the fuel system, wear safety glasses and have a Class B type fire extinguisher on hand.*

Caution: *If the stereo in your vehicle is equipped with an anti-theft system, make sure you have the correct activation code before disconnecting the battery.*

4

12.8 Install the "noid" light into the fuel injector electrical connector and check to see that it blinks with the engine running

12.9 Using an ohmmeter, measure the resistance across the terminals of the injector

Port name	At idle	Other than idle
P	No vacuum	Vacuum
E	No vacuum	Vacuum
R	No vacuum	Vacuum

13.2a Throttle body vacuum port guide and table

13.2b Connect a vacuum gauge to the vacuum line

Throttle body

Refer to illustrations 13.2a, 13.2b, 13.10 and 13.11

Check

1   Verify that the throttle linkage operates smoothly.
2   Start the engine, detach each vacuum hose and, using a vacuum gauge, check the vacuum at each port on the throttle body with the engine at idle and above idle, then compare your observations with the vacuum table **(see illustrations)**.

Replacement

Warning: *Wait until the engine is completely cool before beginning this procedure.*

3   Detach the cable from the negative terminal of the battery (see the **Caution** at the beginning of this Section).
4   Loosen the hose clamps and remove the air intake duct.
5   Detach the accelerator cable from the throttle lever (see Section 10).
6   Detach the throttle cable bracket and set it aside (it's not necessary to detach the throttle cable from the bracket).
7   If your vehicle is equipped with an automatic transmission, detach the throttle valve (TV) cable from the throttle linkage (see Chapter 7B), detach the TV cable brackets from the engine and set the cable and brackets aside.
8   Clearly label, then detach, all vacuum and coolant hoses from the throttle body. Plug the coolant hoses to prevent coolant loss.
9   Disconnect the electrical connector from the throttle position sensor (TPS).
10   Remove the four throttle body mounting bolts **(see illustration)**.
11   Detach the throttle body and gasket **(see illustration)** from the intake manifold.
12   Using a soft brush and carburetor cleaner, thoroughly clean the throttle body casting, then blow out all passages with compressed air. **Caution:** *Do not clean the throttle position sensor with anything. Just wipe it off carefully with a clean, soft cloth.*
13   Installation of the throttle body is the reverse of removal.
14   Be sure to tighten the throttle body mounting bolts to the torque listed in this Chapter's Specifications.

Throttle position sensor (TPS)

Refer to illustrations 13.16, 13.17 and 13.20

Check

15   Disconnect the electrical connector from the throttle position sensor (TPS). On California models, apply vacuum to the throttle positioner.

13.10 A typical throttle body is retained by four bolts/nuts (arrows)

16   Insert a feeler gauge of the specified thickness between the throttle stop screw and the stop lever **(see illustration)**.
17   Using an ohmmeter, measure the resistance between the indicated terminal pairs **(see illustration)**.
18   If the resistance is not as specified, insert a 0.90 mm (0.035 in.) feeler gauge between the throttle stop screw and lever, and connect the ohmmeter to terminals IDL and E2. Loosen the TPS mounting screws and slowly rotate the sensor clockwise until the ohmmeter reads infinity.
19   Tighten the mounting screws, and using the proper feeler gauge, recheck the continuity between the specified terminals.

Replacement

20   If adjustment doesn't bring the sensor within specifications, disconnect it, remove the screws and replace it with a new one **(see illustration)**, then adjust it as described in Step 18.

Fuel pressure regulator

Check

21   Refer to the fuel pump/fuel pressure check procedure (see Section 3).

Replacement

Refer to illustrations 13.26 and 13.27

22   Relieve the fuel pressure (see Section 2) and detach the cable

13.11 Typical throttle body assembly and
related components

13.16 To check the throttle position sensor (TPS), insert a feeler
gauge of the specified thickness between the throttle stop screw
and the stop lever, then measure the resistance between the
proper terminals

Clearance between lever and stop screw	Between terminals	Resistance
0 mm (0 in.)	VTA − E2	0.2 − 6.0 kΩ
0.40 mm (0.016 in.)	IDL − E2	2.3 kΩ or less
0.90 mm (0.035 in.)	IDL − E2	Infinity
Throttle valve fully open	VTA − E2	3.3 − 10.0 kΩ
−	VC − E2	4.0 − 8.5 kΩ

13.17 Use the terminal guide and the continuity table to
check the TPS

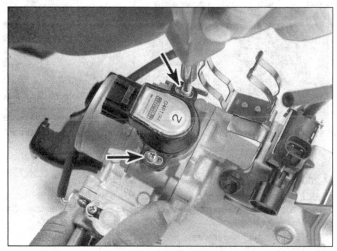

13.20 Remove the two set screws (arrows) to change the TPS

from the negative terminal of the battery (see the **Caution** at the beginning of this Section).
23   Detach the vacuum sensing hose from the regulator.
24   Place a metal container or shop towel under the fuel return hose.
25   Slide the clamp down the hose and remove the fuel return hose
from the regulator.

13.26 To remove the fuel pressure regulator from the fuel rail, detach the fuel return hose, remove the two regulator bolts (arrows) and separate the regulator from the fuel rail (fuel rail removed for clarity)

13.27 If the fuel pressure regulator is cocked during installation, it will not seal properly

13.29 Install the lead from the tachometer into the IG (-) terminal of the test connector located in the corner of the engine compartment

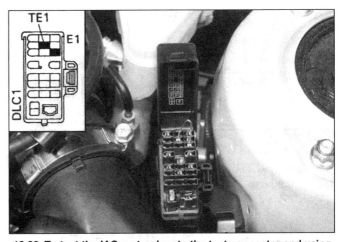

13.30 To test the IAC motor, locate the test connector and using a jumper wire or paper clip, bridge terminals TE1 and E1

13.34 Using an ohmmeter, check the resistance between +B and RSC or RSO

26 Remove the pressure regulator mounting bolts **(see illustration)** and detach the pressure regulator from the fuel rail.

27 Use a new O-ring and make sure that the pressure regulator is installed properly on the fuel rail **(see illustration)**.

28 The remainder of installation is the reverse of removal.

Idle air control (IAC) valve

Note: *The minimum idle speed is pre-set at the factory and should not require adjustment under normal operating conditions; however if the throttle body has been replaced or you suspect the minimum idle speed has been tampered with (for example, if the idle speed screw was removed from the throttle body) have the vehicle checked by a dealer service department or a qualified automotive repair shop.*

Check

Refer to illustrations 13.29, 13.30 and 13.34

29 Apply the parking brake, shift the transaxle to Neutral (manual) or Park (automatic) and block the drive wheels. Install the lead of a tachometer to the IG (–) terminal on the test connector **(see illustration)**. Start the engine and allow it to reach normal operating temperature. Check the idle speed and compare it to the idle speed listed in this Chapter's Specifications.

30 Using a jumper wire, bridge terminals TE1 and E1 of the test connector **(see illustration)**.

31 The engine speed should increase to approximately 1,000 to

1,200 rpm for five seconds then return to normal idle speed.

  a) *If the engine speed changes as described, the IAC valve is okay.*
  b) *If the engine speed does not change as described, measure the IAC valve resistance.*

32 Remove the jumper wire.

33 Disconnect the IAC valve electrical connector.

34 Measure the resistance between the middle terminal and each of

13.37 Remove the mounting screws that retain the IAC valve to the throttle body

13.45 Number each injector electrical connector before disconnecting them from the fuel rail

13.48 Remove the bolts (arrow) that retain the fuel rail to the intake manifold

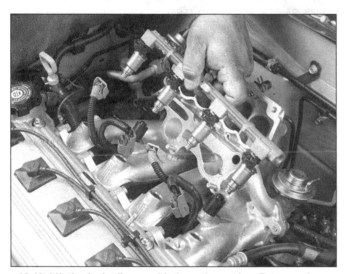

13.49 Lift the fuel rail assembly from the engine. Beware of any fuel that may spill out of the fuel pressure regulator or fuel rail while you are lifting it out

13.51a Remove the O-ring from the injector

4

the other two outer terminals **(see illustration)**. Compare your results to the IAC valve resistance in this Chapter's Specifications.

 a) *If the resistance is as specified, the IAC valve is okay (but there may be a problem with the wiring or the ECM).*
 b) *If the resistance is not as specified, replace the IAC valve.*

35   Connect the IAC valve electrical connector.

Replacement

Refer to illustration 13.37

36   Remove the throttle body (see Steps 3 through 11). **Note:** *The IAC valve and assembly are difficult to reach, therefore it is recommended to remove the throttle body so that the new IAC valve assembly can be installed properly.*

37   Remove the mounting screws and detach the IAC valve and gasket **(see illustration)**.

38   If the IAC assembly was replaced, be sure to install the Temperature Vacuum Valve (TVV) from the original assembly into the new unit (if equipped).

39   Installation of the IAC valve is the reverse of removal. Be sure to use a new gasket when installing the IAC valve.

Fuel rail and fuel injectors

Check

40   Refer to the fuel injection system checking procedure (see Section 12).

Replacement

Refer to illustrations 13.45, 13.48, 13.49, 13.51a, 13.51b and 13.51c

41   Relieve the fuel pressure (see Section 2).

42   Detach the cable from the negative terminal of the battery (see the **Caution** at the beginning of this Section).

43   Remove the PCV hose from the cylinder head and intake manifold.

44   Remove the air intake plenum (see Steps 65 through 74).

45   Carefully mark each injector connector with a felt pen or paint **(see illustration)**. Disconnect the fuel injector electrical connectors and set the injector wire harness aside.

46   Detach the vacuum sensing hose from the fuel pressure regulator.

47   Disconnect the fuel lines from the fuel pressure regulator and the fuel rail.

48   Remove the fuel rail mounting bolts **(see illustration)**.

49   Remove the fuel rail with the fuel injectors attached **(see illustration)**.

50   Remove the fuel injector(s) from the fuel rail and set them aside in a clearly labeled storage container.

51   If you intend to re-use the same injectors, replace the grommets and O-rings **(see illustrations)**.

13.51b Remove the grommet from the top of the injector

52   Installation of the fuel injectors is the reverse of removal.

53   Tighten the fuel rail mounting bolts to the torque listed in this Chapter's Specifications.

Air conditioning idle-up valve

Check

Refer to illustrations 13.58, 13.59 and 13.60

54   Apply the parking brake, shift the transaxle to Neutral (manual) or

13.51c Remove the O-rings from the bores in the intake manifold

Park (automatic) and block the drive wheels. Install the lead of a tachometer to the IG (–) terminal on the test connector **(see illustration 13.29)**. Start the engine and allow it to reach normal operating temperature and idle speed, then turn the air conditioning system ON.

55   Using a jumper wire, bridge terminals TE1 and E1 of the check electrical connector.

56   Verify that the engine speed increases to approximately 1,000 to 1,200 rpm for approximately three seconds after engaging the test terminals, then returns to normal. After 15 seconds check the idle speed again, it should be approximately 100 rpm greater than normal.

a) *If the engine speed changes as described, the air conditioning idle-up valve is okay.*

b) *If the rpm increases more than 100 rpm, adjust the rpm range by turning the adjustment screw accordingly.*

c) *If the engine speed does not change or if it decreases, measure the air conditioning idle-up valve resistance.*

57   Remove the jumper wire.

58   Disconnect the air conditioning idle-up valve electrical connector **(see illustration)**.

59   Measure the resistance between the terminals **(see illustration)**. It should be between 30 and 34 ohms.

a) *If the resistance is as specified, the air conditioning idle-up valve is okay (but there may be a problem with the wiring or the ECM).*

b) *If the resistance is not as specified, replace the valve (see below).*

60   Apply battery voltage across the terminals and check that air flows from port E to port F **(see illustration)** . **Note:** *Port E is the top port and port F is the bottom port.* Remove battery voltage and observe that air does not flow from port E through port F.

61   If the test results are incorrect, replace the air conditioning idle-up valve.

13.58 Schematic of the air conditioning idle-up system

13.59 Check for continuity on the air conditioning idle-up solenoid

13.60 With battery voltage applied to the solenoid, air should flow through port E and out port F

13.73 Remove the bolts (arrows) that retain the air intake plenum to the intake manifold

Replacement

62   Remove the mounting screws and detach the idle-up valve and gasket.

63   Installation of the idle-up valve is the reverse of removal.

64   Be sure to use a new gasket when installing the idle-up valve.

Air intake plenum

Removal

Refer to illustration 13.73

Warning: *Wait until the engine is completely cool before beginning this procedure.*

65   Detach the cable from the negative terminal of the battery (see the **Caution** at the beginning of this Section).

66   Disconnect the electrical connectors at the IAC valve, throttle position sensor (TPS) and EGR/EVAP canister control solenoid.

67   Detach the accelerator cable (see Section 10) and transmission linkage (see Chapter 7) from the throttle body assembly.

68   Remove the accelerator cable from the intake manifold (see Section 10).

69   Clearly label, then detach, the vacuum lines from air intake plenum, the EGR valve and the fuel pressure regulator.

70   Detach the PCV system by disconnecting the hose from the fitting on the air intake plenum.

71   Remove the plenum bracket and bolt (if equipped).

72   Detach the coolant hoses from the throttle body and plug them.

73   Remove the air intake plenum retaining bolts **(see illustration)** and the lower (side) retaining bolts.

74   Remove the air intake plenum and throttle body as an assembly from the lower intake manifold.

Installation

75   Be sure to clean and inspect the mounting surface of the lower intake manifold (see Chapter 2A) and the air intake plenum before positioning the new gasket onto the lower intake mounting face. Install the air intake plenum and throttle body assembly onto the intake manifold. Ensure the gasket remains in place. Install the upper intake manifold retaining bolts and tighten the bolts to the torque listed in this Chapter's Specifications. Installation is otherwise the reverse of removal.

14   Exhaust system servicing - general information

Refer to illustration 14.1

Warning: *Inspection and repair of exhaust system components should*

14.1 Exploded view of a typical exhaust system

4

be done only after the system components have cooled completely.

1   The exhaust system consists of the exhaust manifold, catalytic converter, the muffler, the tailpipe and all connecting pipes, brackets, hangers and clamps. The exhaust system is attached to the body with mounting brackets and rubber hangers **(see illustration)**. If any of these parts are damaged or deteriorated, excessive noise and vibration will be transmitted to the body.

2   Conducting regular inspections of the exhaust system will keep it safe and quiet. Look for any damaged or bent parts, open seams, holes, loose connections, excessive corrosion or other defects which could allow exhaust fumes to enter the vehicle. Deteriorated exhaust system components should not be repaired - they should be replaced with new parts.

3   If the exhaust system components are extremely corroded or rusted together, they will probably have to be cut from the exhaust system. The convenient way to accomplish this is to have a muffler repair shop remove the corroded sections with a cutting torch. If, however, you want to save money by doing it yourself and you don't have an oxy/acetylene welding outfit with a cutting torch, simply cut off the old components with a hack-saw. If you have compressed air, special pneumatic cutting chisels can also be used. If you do decide to tackle the job at home, be sure to wear eye protection to protect your eyes from metal chips and work gloves to protect your hands.

4   Here are some simple guidelines to apply when repairing the exhaust system:

a) *Work from the back to the front when removing exhaust system components.*

b) *Apply penetrating oil to the exhaust system component fasteners to make them easier to remove.*

c) *Use new gaskets, hangers and clamps when installing exhaust system components.*

d) *Apply anti-seize compound to the threads of all exhaust system fasteners during reassembly.*

e) *Be sure to allow sufficient clearance between newly installed parts and all points on the underbody to avoid overheating the floor pan and possibly damaging the interior carpet and insulation. Pay particularly close attention to the catalytic converter and its heat shield.* **Warning:** *The catalytic converter operates at very high temperatures and takes a long time to cool. Wait until it's completely cool before attempting to remove the converter. Failure to do so could result in serious burns.*

Chapter 5
Engine electrical systems

Contents

Specifications

Ignition timing (all models)
With test terminals TE1 and E1 grounded	10-degrees BTDC
Without test terminals TE1 and E1 grounded	5 to 15-degrees BTDC

Ignition coil resistance (cold)
Distributors with internal igniters	
Primary resistance	1.11 to 1.75 ohms
Secondary resistance	9.0 to 15.7K ohms
Distributors with external igniters	
Primary resistance	0.36 to 0.55 ohms
Secondary resistance	9.0 to 15.4K ohms

Distributor
Air gap	0.008 to 0.016 inch
Pick-up coil resistance (Toyota)	
Distributors with internal igniters	
Cold (below 103-degrees F)	
G+ to G- terminals	185 to 275 ohms
NE+ to NE- terminals	370 to 550 ohms
Hot (above 104-degrees F)	
G+ to G- terminals	240 to 325 ohms
NE+ to NE- terminals	475 to 650 ohms
Distributors with external igniters	
Cold (below 103-degrees F)	
G+ to G- terminals	185 to 275 ohms
NE+ to NE- terminals	1,630 to 2,740 ohms
Hot (above 104-degrees F)	
G+ to G- terminals	240 to 325 ohms
NE+ to NE- terminals	2,065 to 3,225 ohms
Pick-up coil resistance (Geo)	
1993 and 1994 models	
Cold (below 103-degrees F)	
Between terminals 3 and 6	185 to 275 ohms
Between terminals 2 and 5	370 to 550 ohms
Hot (above 104-degrees F)	
Between terminals 3 and 6	240 to 325 ohms
Between terminals 2 and 5	475 to 650 ohms

5

Distributor (continued)

1995 and later models

    Cold (below 103-degrees F)

        Between terminals 3 and 6 (VIN 6) or

            terminals 1 and 2 (VIN 8) .... 185 to 275 ohms

        Between terminals 2 and 5 .... 370 to 550 ohms

    Hot (above 104-degrees F)

        Between terminals 3 and 6 (VIN 6)

            or terminals 1 and 2 (VIN 8) .... 240 to 325 ohms

        Between terminals 2 and 5 .... 475 to 650 ohms

Charging system

Charging voltage .... 13.9 to 15.1 volts

Standard amperage

    All lights and accessories turned off .... Less than 10 amps

    Headlights (hi-beam) and heater blower motor turned on .... 30 amps or more

Alternator brush length

    Standard 13/32-inch

    Minimum 1/16-inch

1   General information

The engine electrical systems include all ignition, charging and starting components. Because of their engine related functions, these components are discussed separately from chassis electrical devices such as the lights, the instruments, etc. (which are included in Chapter 12).

Always observe the following precautions when working on the electrical systems:

a) *Be extremely careful when servicing engine electrical components. They are easily damaged if checked, connected or handled improperly.*

b) *Never leave the ignition switch on for long periods of time (10 minutes maximum) with the engine off.*

c) *Don't disconnect the battery cables while the engine is running.*

d) *Maintain correct polarity when connecting a battery cable from another vehicle during jump starting.*

e) *Always disconnect the negative cable first and hook it up last or the battery may be shorted by the tool being used to loosen the cable clamps.*

It's also a good idea to review the safety-related information regarding the engine electrical systems located in the *Safety first* section near the front of this manual before beginning any operation included in this Chapter.

2   Battery - emergency jump starting

Refer to the *Booster battery (jump) starting* procedure at the front of this manual.

3   Battery - removal and installation

Refer to illustration 3.1

1   Starting with the negative battery cable **(see illustration)**, disconnect both cables from the battery terminals. **Caution:** *If the stereo in your vehicle is equipped with an anti-theft system, make sure you have the correct activation code before disconnecting the battery.*

2   Remove the battery hold-down clamp.

3   Lift out the battery. Be careful, it's heavy.

4   While the battery is out, inspect the carrier (tray) for corrosion.

5   If you are replacing the battery, make sure that you get one that's identical, with the same dimensions, amperage rating, cold cranking rating, etc. as the original.

6   Installation is the reverse of removal.

4   Battery cables - check and replacement

Caution: *If the stereo in your vehicle is equipped with an anti-theft system, make sure you have the correct activation code before disconnecting the battery.*

1   Periodically inspect the entire length of each battery cable for damage, cracked or burned insulation and corrosion. Poor battery cable connections can cause starting problems and decreased engine performance.

2   Check the cable-to-terminal connections at the ends of the cables for cracks, loose wire strands and corrosion. The presence of white, fluffy deposits under the insulation at the cable terminal connection is a sign that the cable is corroded and should be replaced. Check the terminals for distortion, missing mounting bolts and corrosion.

3   When removing the cables, always disconnect the negative cable first and hook it up last or the battery may be shorted by the tool used to loosen the cable clamps. Even if only the positive cable is being replaced, be sure to disconnect the negative cable from the battery first (see Chapter 1 for further information regarding battery cable removal).

4   Disconnect the old cables from the battery, then trace each of them to their opposite ends and detach them from the starter solenoid and ground terminals. Note the routing of each cable to ensure correct installation.

5   If you are replacing either or both of the old cables, take them with you when buying new cables. It is vitally important that you replace the cables with identical parts. Cables have characteristics that make them easy to identify: positive cables are usually red, larger in cross-section and have a larger diameter battery post clamp; ground cables are usually black, smaller in cross-section and have a slightly smaller diameter clamp for the negative post.

6   Clean the threads of the solenoid or ground connection with a wire brush to remove rust and corrosion. Apply a light coat of battery terminal corrosion inhibitor, or petroleum jelly, to the threads to prevent future corrosion.

7   Attach the cable to the solenoid or ground connection and tighten the mounting nut/bolt securely.

8   Before connecting a new cable to the battery, make sure that it reaches the battery post without having to be stretched.

9   Connect the positive cable first, followed by the negative cable.

5   Ignition system - general information and precautions

Refer to illustrations 5.3a and 5.3b

1   There are two types of ignition systems equipped on the models

covered by this manual - the external igniter system or the internal igniter system. On the latter ignition system, the igniter is located within the distributor housing. On both systems the ignition coil is mounted inside the distributor.

2   The electronic ignition system includes the ignition switch, the battery, the igniter, the pick-up coil, the ignition coil, the primary (low voltage) and secondary (high voltage) wiring circuits, the distributor and the spark plugs. The ignition system is controlled by the Electronic Control Module (ECM). Using data provided by information sensors which monitor various engine functions (such as rpm, intake air volume, engine temperature, etc.), the ECM ensures a perfectly timed spark under all conditions. This system is known as Electronic Spark Advance (ESA).

3   The breakerless ignition systems are divided into two groups; external igniter distributors and internal igniter distributors **(see illustrations)**. When diagnosing these units, be sure to make all the necessary ignition system checks before replacing any components, as they are expensive and usually non-returnable.

3.1 To remove the battery, detach the negative battery cable first, then the positive cable, remove the hold-down strap nut and bolt (arrows) and remove the hold-down strap

5.3a Exploded view of an external igniter distributor

5.3b Exploded view of an internal igniter distributor

6.1 To use a calibrated ignition tester (available at most auto parts stores), remove an ignition wire from a cylinder, connect the spark plug boot to the tester and clip the tester to a good ground - if there is enough voltage to fire the plug, sparks will be clearly visible between the electrode tip and the tester body as the engine is turned over

4   When working on the ignition system, take the following precautions:

   a) *Do not keep the ignition switch on for more than 10 seconds if the engine will not start.*
   b) *Always connect a tachometer in accordance with the manufacturer's instructions. Some tachometers may be incompatible with this ignition system. Consult a dealer service department before buying a tachometer for use with this vehicle.*
   c) *Never allow the ignition coil terminals to touch ground. Grounding the coil could result in damage to the igniter and/or the ignition coil.*
   d) *Do not disconnect the battery when the engine is running.*
   e) *Make sure the igniter is properly grounded.*

6   Ignition system - check

Refer to illustrations 6.1, 6.7 and 6.9

Warning: *Because of the high voltage generated by the ignition system, extreme care should be taken whenever an operation is performed involving ignition components. This not only includes the igniter, coil, distributor and spark plug wires, but related components such as plug connectors, tachometer and other test equipment also.*

1   If the engine turns over but won't start, disconnect the spark plug wire from any spark plug and attach it to a calibrated tester (available at most auto parts stores) **(see illustration)**. Connect the clip on the tester to a bolt or metal bracket on the engine. If you're unable to obtain a calibrated ignition tester, remove the wire from one of the spark plugs and using an insulated tool, pull back the boot and hold the end of the wire about 1/4-inch from a good ground.

2   Crank the engine and watch the end of the tester or spark plug wire to see if a bright blue, well-defined sparks occur.

3   If sparks occur, sufficient voltage is reaching the plug to fire it (repeat the check at the remaining plug wires to verify that the distributor cap and rotor are OK). However, the plugs themselves may be fouled, so remove and check them as described in Chapter 1.

4   If no sparks or intermittent sparks occur, remove the distributor cap and check the cap and rotor as described in Chapter 1. If moisture is present, dry out the cap and rotor, then reinstall the cap and repeat the spark test.

6.7 Check for battery voltage to the positive side (+) of the ignition coil

5   If there's still no spark, detach the coil secondary wire from the distributor cap and hook it up to the tester (reattach the plug wire to the spark plug), then repeat the spark check. Again, if you don't have a tester, hold the end of the wire about 1/4-inch from a good ground.

6   If sparks now occur, the distributor cap, rotor or plug wire(s) may be defective.

7   If no sparks occur, check the primary wire connections at the coil to make sure they're clean and tight. Check for voltage to the coil on the primary circuit from the ignition switch **(see illustration)**. Check the ignition coil (see Section 7) and the distributor pick-up coil (see Section 11). Make any necessary repairs, then repeat the check again.

8   If there's still no spark, the coil-to-cap wire may be bad (check the resistance with an ohmmeter and compare it to the spark plug wire resistance Specifications found in Chapter 1). If a known good wire doesn't make any difference in the test results, the igniter may be defective.

9   Check for battery voltage to the igniter **(see illustration)** with the ignition key ON, engine not running. If voltage is available and there is still no spark, replace the igniter (see Section 10).

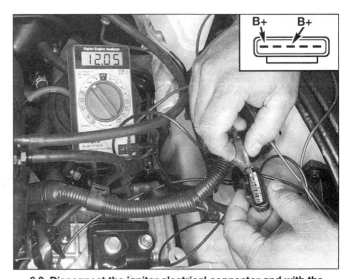

6.9 Disconnect the igniter electrical connector and with the ignition key ON (engine not running), check for battery voltage to the igniter (external igniter shown - on models with an internal igniter, check for voltage on the brown wire to the igniter)

7.2 Carefully pry the plastic shield at the locking tab to release it from the ignition coil

7 Ignition coil - check and replacement

Caution: *If the stereo in your vehicle is equipped with an anti-theft system, make sure you have the correct activation code before disconnecting the battery.*

Check

Refer to illustrations 7.2, 7.4a and 7.4b

1   Detach the cable from the negative terminal of the battery (see the **Caution** above).

2   Remove the plastic shield from the coil **(see illustration)**.

3   Remove the mounting bolts from the coil electrical connectors and install the ohmmeter probes.

4   Using an ohmmeter:

  a) *Measure the resistance between the positive and negative terminals of the coil* **(see illustration)**. *Compare your reading with the specified coil primary resistance listed in this Chapter's Specifications.*

  b) *Measure the resistance between the positive terminal and the high tension terminal* **(see illustration)**. *Compare your reading with the specified coil secondary resistance listed in this Chapter's Specifications.*

5   If either of the above tests yield resistance values outside the specified amount, replace the coil.

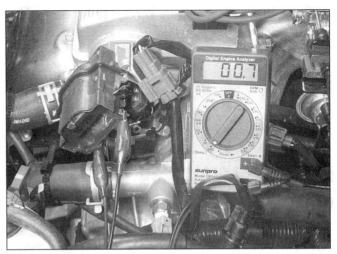

7.4a To check the primary resistance of the coil, measure the resistance between the positive and the negative terminals

Replacement

Refer to illustration 7.9

6   Detach the cable from the negative terminal of the battery (see the **Caution** above).

7   Remove the heat shield from the coil.

8   Label and disconnect the wires from the coil terminals.

9   Remove the coil mounting screws **(see illustration)**.

10   Installation is the reverse of removal.

8 Distributor - removal and installation

Removal

Refer to illustrations 8.5 and 8.7

1   Detach the cable from the negative battery terminal. **Caution:** *If the stereo in your vehicle is equipped with an anti-theft system, make sure you have the correct activation code before disconnecting the battery.*

2   Disconnect the electrical connectors from the distributor.

3   Look for a raised "1" on the distributor cap. This marks the location for the number one cylinder spark plug wire terminal. If the cap does not have a mark for the number one terminal, locate the number one spark plug and trace the wire back to the terminal on the cap.

5

7.4b To check the secondary resistance of the coil, measure the resistance between the positive terminal and the high tension terminal

7.9 Remove the retaining screws (arrows) and lift the coil from the distributor housing

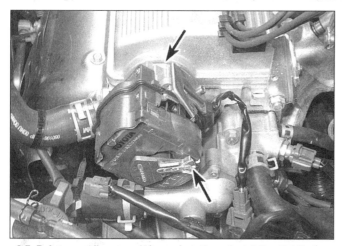

8.5 Paint or scribe a mark (arrow) on the edge of the distributor housing immediately below the rotor tip to ensure that the rotor is pointing in the same direction when the distributor is reinstalled. Also, paint or scribe another mark across the cylinder head and the distributor body (arrow) to ensure that the distributor is aligned correctly when it is reinstalled

4   Remove the distributor cap (see Chapter 1) and turn the engine over until the rotor is pointing toward the number one spark plug terminal (see locating TDC procedure in Chapter 2A).

5   Make a mark on the edge of the distributor base directly below the rotor tip and in line with it. Also, mark the distributor base and the engine block to ensure that the distributor is installed correctly **(see illustration)**.

6   If equipped with collar bolts, loosen but do not remove the two bolts in the distributor collar. This will give the distributor shaft clearance.

7   Remove the distributor hold-down bolt **(see illustration)**, then pull the distributor straight out to remove it. **Caution:** *DO NOT turn the crankshaft while the distributor is out of the engine, or the alignment marks will be useless.*

Installation

Refer to illustrations 8.8 and 8.9

Note: *If the crankshaft has been moved while the distributor is out, locate Top Dead Center (TDC) for the number one piston (see Chapter 2A) and position the distributor and the rotor accordingly.*

8   Install a new O-ring onto the distributor housing **(see illustration)**.

9   Align the cut-out portion of the coupling with the groove in the housing **(see illustration)**.

10   Insert the distributor into the engine in exactly the same relationship to the block that it was in when removed.

11   If the distributor does not seat completely, recheck the alignment marks between the distributor base and the block to verify that the distributor is in the same position it was in before removal. Also check the

8.8 Install a new O-ring in to the groove in the distributor housing

8.7 Remove the hold-down bolt from the distributor body and pull the distributor straight out

rotor to see if it's aligned with the mark you made on the edge of the distributor base.

12   Loosely install the distributor hold-down bolt(s).

13   Installation is the reverse of removal.

14   Check the ignition timing (see Section 9) and tighten the distributor hold-down bolt securely.

---

9   Ignition timing - check and adjustment

Refer to illustrations 9.1, 9.2, 9.3 and 9.5

Note: *The following ignition timing procedure applies to most models covered by this manual. However, if the procedure specified on the VECI label of your vehicle differs from this one, use the procedure found on the VECI label.*

1   Connect a tachometer according to the manufacturer's specifications **(see illustration)**.

2   Locate the diagnostic connector and insert a jumper wire between terminals E1 and TE1 **(see illustration)**.

3   With the ignition switch off, connect a timing light according to the manufacturer's specifications **(see illustration)**. Most timing lights are powered by the battery. Also, an inductive style pick-up is installed onto the number one cylinder spark plug wire.

4   Locate the timing marks on the front cover and the crankshaft pulley.

5   Start the engine and allow it to warm up to normal operating temperature (upper radiator hose hot). Verify that the engine idle is correct (750 rpm with an automatic transaxle and 700 rpm with a manual transaxle). Aim the timing light at the timing scale on the front cover **(see illustration)**. The mark on the crankshaft pulley should line up

8.9 If you have set the engine at TDC compression for number one cylinder, align the cut-out portion of the coupling with the groove in the distributor housing

9.1 Connect the tachometer lead to the IG terminal of the test connector

9.2 Attach a jumper wire between terminals E1 and TE1 of the test connector

with the 10-degree mark on the scale. If necessary, loosen the distributor hold-down bolt and slowly rotate the distributor until the timing marks align. Tighten the hold-down bolt and recheck the timing.

6   Remove the jumper wire from the diagnostic connector and confirm that the ignition timing advances to 12 to 22-degrees BTDC.

7   Turn the engine off and remove the tachometer and the timing light.

10   Igniter - replacement

Refer to illustration 10.3

1   Detach the cable from the negative terminal of the battery. **Caution:** *If the stereo in your vehicle is equipped with an anti-theft system, make sure you have the correct activation code before disconnecting the battery.*

Externally mounted igniter

2   Disconnect the electrical connector from the igniter.

3   Remove the screws from the bracket assembly and pull the igniter/bracket assembly out of the engine compartment **(see illustration)**.

4   Installation is the reverse of removal.

Internally mounted igniter

5   Remove the ignition coil from the distributor (see Section 7).

6   Disconnect the electrical connector from the igniter.

7   Remove the screws from the igniter assembly and pull the igniter/bracket assembly out of the engine compartment **(see illustration 5.3b)**.

8   Installation is the reverse of removal.

9.3 Tools needed to check and adjust the ignition timing

1   *Vacuum plugs* - *Vacuum hoses will, in most cases, have to be disconnected and plugged. Molded plugs in various shapes and sizes are available for this*

2   *Inductive pick-up timing light* - *Flashes a bright, concentrated beam of light when the number one spark plug fires. Connect the leads according to the instructions supplied with the light*

3   *Distributor wrench* - *On some models, the hold-down bolt for the distributor is difficult to reach and turn with conventional wrenches or sockets. A special wrench like this must be used*

9.5 Point the timing light at the timing marks with the engine at idle

10.3 Remove the igniter screws (arrows) and lift the igniter from the engine compartment

5

11   Pick-up coil - check and replacement

Pick-up coil check

Refer to illustrations 11.1

1   Disconnect the electrical connector at the distributor and using an ohmmeter, measure the resistance between the pick-up coil terminals **(see illustration)**.
2   Compare the measurements to those listed in this Chapter's Specifications. If the resistance is not as specified, replace the pick-up coil.

Air gap check

Refer to illustrations 11.5

3   Detach the cable from the negative terminal of the battery. **Caution:** *If the stereo in your vehicle is equipped with an anti-theft system, make sure you have the correct activation code before disconnecting the battery.*
4   Remove the distributor from the engine (see Section 8).
5   Using a brass feeler gauge, measure the gap between the signal rotor and the pick-up coil projection **(see illustration)**. Compare your measurement to the air gap listed in this Chapter's Specifications. If the air gap is not as specified, replace the distributor, as the air gap is not adjustable. Excessive air gap is usually a sign of wear in the distributor shaft bushing.

Replacement

Refer to illustrations 11.9, 11.10 and 11.11

6   Detach the cable from the negative terminal of the battery. **Caution:** *If the stereo in your vehicle is equipped with an anti-theft system, make sure you have the correct activation code before disconnecting the battery.*
7   Remove the distributor from the engine (see Section 8).
8   Remove the coil from the distributor (see Section 7).
9   Remove the set screws that retain the pick-up coil to the distributor **(see illustration)**.
10   Remove the pick-up coil from the distributor **(see illustration)**.
11   Remove the condenser from the distributor **(see illustration)** and replace it.
12   Installation is the reverse of removal.

12   Charging system - general information and precautions

Refer to illustrations 12.1 and 12.4

The charging system includes the alternator, an internal voltage regulator, a charge indicator, the battery, a fusible link and the wiring between all the components **(see illustration)**. The charging system supplies electrical power for the ignition system, the lights, the radio, etc. The alternator is driven by a drivebelt at the front of the engine.
These models are equipped with either a Nippondenso or a Delco alternator.

11.1 Check the resistance between the terminals on the pick-up coil indicated in this Chapter's Specifications.

11.5 Measure the air gap between the signal rotor and the pick-up coil projection - if the gap is not within specification, replace the distributor

The purpose of the voltage regulator is to limit the alternator's voltage to a preset value. This prevents power surges, circuit overloads, etc., during peak voltage output.
The fusible link is a short length of insulated wire integral with the engine compartment wiring harness **(see illustration)**. The link is several wire gauges smaller in diameter than the circuit it protects. See

11.9 Remove the pick-up coil set screws (arrows)

11.10 Lift the pick-up coil from the distributor

11.11 Remove the ignition condenser from the distributor

12.1 Nippondenso alternator charging system schematic

Chapter 12 for additional information regarding fusible links.

The charging system doesn't ordinarily require periodic maintenance. However, the drivebelt, battery and wires and connections should be inspected at the intervals outlined in Chapter 1.

The dashboard warning light should come on when the ignition key is turned to Start, then should go off immediately. If it remains on, there is a malfunction in the charging system. Some vehicles are also equipped with a voltage gauge. If the voltage gauge indicates abnormally high or low voltage, check the charging system (see Section 13).

Be very careful when making electrical circuit connections to a vehicle equipped with an alternator and note the following:

a) *When reconnecting wires to the alternator from the battery, be sure to note the polarity.*

b) *Before using arc welding equipment to repair any part of the vehicle, disconnect the wires from the alternator and the battery terminals.*

c) *Never start the engine with a battery charger connected.*

d) *Always disconnect both battery leads before using a battery charger.*

e) *The alternator is driven by an engine drivebelt which could cause serious injury if your hand, hair or clothes become entangled in it with the engine running.*

f) *Because the alternator is connected directly to the battery, it could arc or cause a fire if overloaded or shorted out.*

g) *Wrap a plastic bag over the alternator and secure it with rubber bands before steam cleaning the engine.*

5

12.4 Typical charging system fuses and fusible link

Terminal F

13.7 If the alternator is putting out less than standard voltage, ground terminal F, start the engine and check the voltage at the battery - if the reading is greater than standard voltage, replace the regulator; if the reading is less than standard, check the alternator or have it checked by a dealer service department or other qualified repair shop

13 Charging system - check

Refer to illustrations 13.7 and 13.8

1   If a malfunction occurs in the charging circuit, don't automatically assume that the alternator is causing the problem. First check the following items:

a) *Check the drivebelt tension and its condition. Replace it if worn or deteriorated.*

b) *Make sure the alternator mounting and adjustment bolts are tight.*

c) *Inspect the alternator wiring harness and the electrical connectors at the alternator and voltage regulator. They must be in good condition and tight.*

d) *Check the fusible link located at the positive battery cable or the large main fuses in the engine compartment. If it's burned, determine the cause, repair the circuit and replace the link or fuse (the vehicle won't start and/or the accessories won't work if the fusible link or fuse blows).*

e) *Check all the fuses that are in series with the charging system circuit (see illustration 12.4). The location of these fuses and fusible links may vary from year and model but the designations are the same; main fusible link 3.0W, Alt H fuse (100 amp), AM1 (40 amp), AM2 (30 amp), IG (10 amp), Gauge 10A, and ALT-S (7.5 amp).*

f) *Start the engine and check the alternator for abnormal noises (a shrieking or squealing sound indicates a bad bushing).*

g) *Check the specific gravity of the battery electrolyte. If it's low, charge the battery (doesn't apply to maintenance free batteries).*

h) *Make sure that the battery is fully charged (one bad cell in a battery can cause overcharging by the alternator).*

i) *Disconnect the battery cables (negative first, then positive). **Caution:** If the stereo in your vehicle is equipped with an anti-theft system, make sure you have the correct activation code before disconnecting the battery. Inspect the battery posts and the cable clamps for corrosion. Clean them thoroughly if necessary (see Section 4 and Chapter 1). Reconnect the positive cable, then the negative cable.*

2   Using a voltmeter, check the battery voltage with the engine off. It should be approximately 12 volts.

3   Start the engine and check the battery voltage again. It should now be approximately 13.5 to 15.1 volts.

4   Turn on the headlights. The voltage should drop and then come back up, if the charging system is working properly.

5   If the voltage reading is greater than the specified charging voltage, replace the voltage regulator (see Section 15).

6   If the voltmeter reading is less than standard voltage, check the regulator and alternator as follows.

7   Remove the rear cover from the alternator. Ground terminal F **(see illustration)**, start the engine, check the voltage at the battery and

13.8 Hook up an ammeter as shown to check alternator output

compare your reading to the standard voltage.

a) *If the voltmeter reading is greater than standard voltage, replace the regulator.*

b) *If the voltmeter reading is less than standard voltage, check the alternator (or have it checked by a dealer service department if you do not have an ammeter).*

8   If you have an ammeter, hook it up to the charging system as shown **(see illustration)**. If you don't have an ammeter, you can also use an inductive-type current indicator. This device is inexpensive, readily available at auto parts stores and accurate enough to perform simple amperage checks like the following test.

9   With the engine running at 2,000 rpm, check the reading on the ammeter with all accessories and lights off, then again with the high-beam headlights on and the heater blower switch turned to the HI position. Compare your readings to the standard amperage listed in this Chapter's Specifications.

10   If the ammeter reading is less than standard amperage, repair or replace the alternator.

14 Alternator - removal and installation

Refer to illustrations 14.2 and 14.3

1   Detach the cable from the negative terminal of the battery. **Caution:** *If the stereo in your vehicle is equipped with an anti-theft system, make sure you have the correct activation code before disconnecting the battery.*

2   Detach the electrical connectors from the alternator **(see illustration)**.

3   Loosen the alternator adjustment, pivot and lock bolts **(see illustration)** and detach the drivebelt.

4   Remove the adjustment and lock bolts from the alternator adjustment bracket.

5   Separate the alternator and bracket from the engine.

14.2 Disconnect the electrical connections from the alternator

14.3 Alternator installation details

Pivot Bolt

Adjusting Bolt

Lock Bolt

Alternator Wire

Drive Belt

Alternator Connector

Alternator

6   If you are replacing the alternator, take the old alternator with you when purchasing a replacement unit. Make sure that the new/rebuilt unit is identical to the old alternator. Look at the terminals - they should be the same in number, size and locations as the terminals on the old alternator. Finally, look at the identification markings - they will be stamped in the housing or printed on a tag or plaque affixed to the housing. Make sure that these numbers are the same on both alternators.

7   Many new/rebuilt alternators do not have a pulley installed, so you may have to switch the pulley from the old unit to the new/rebuilt one. When buying an alternator, find out the shop's policy regarding installation of pulleys - some shops will perform this service free of charge.

8   Installation is the reverse of removal.

9   After the alternator is installed, adjust the drivebelt tension (see Chapter 1).

10   Check the charging voltage to verify proper operation of the alternator (see Section 13).

15 Alternator components - check and replacement

Note: *This procedure is for Nippondenso alternators only. If your vehicle is equipped with a Delco alternator, exchange the alternator for a new or rebuilt unit in the event of failure.*

Nippondenso alternators

Disassembly

Refer to illustrations 15.2a, 15.2b, 15.2c, 15.2d, 15.3, 15.4a, 15.4b, 15.5 and 15.7

1   Remove the alternator (see Section 14) and place it on a clean workbench.

2   Remove the rear cover nuts, the nut and terminal insulator and the rear cover **(see illustrations)**.

3   Remove the five voltage regulator and brush holder mounting

Drive End Frame (Stator)

Retainer

Bearing Cover

Rear Bearing

Bearing Cover

Pulley

Rotor

Front Bearing

Brush

Spring

IC Regulator

Cord Clip

Rear End Cover

Brush Holder Cover

Rectifier End Frame

Rectifier Holder

Brush Holder

Rubber Insulator

Terminal Insulator

15.2a Exploded view of a typical USA model alternator assembly

15.2b   Exploded view of a typical Canadian model alternator assembly

15.2c   Remove the three nuts from the rear cover

15.2d   Take the nut, washer and insulator off terminal B and remove the alternator end cover

15.3   Once the rear cover is removed, remove the five screws (arrows) that retain the voltage regulator and the brush holder

15.4a   Remove the brush holder

15.4b   Remove the regulator

15.5   Measure the exposed length of the brushes and compare your measurements to the specified minimum length to determine if they should be replaced

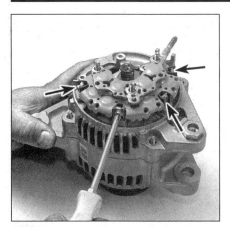

15.7 Remove the mounting screws (arrows) that retain the rectifier assembly

15.12a Continuity should exist between the rotor slip rings

15.12b Check the continuity between the rotor and the slip rings. There should be NO continuity

screws **(see illustration)**.

4   Remove the brush holder and the regulator from the rear end frame **(see illustrations)**. If you are only replacing the regulator, proceed to Step 8, install the new unit, reassemble the alternator and install it on the engine (see Section 14). If you are going to replace the brushes, proceed with the next Step.

5   Measure the exposed length of each brush **(see illustration)** and compare it to the minimum length listed in this Chapter's Specifications. If the length of either brush is less than the specified minimum, replace the brushes and brush holder assembly. **Note:** *On some models, it may be necessary to solder the new brushes in place.*

6   Make sure that each brush moves smoothly in the brush holder.

7   Remove the rectifier assembly **(see illustration)**. Remove the four rubber insulators and the seal plate.

8   Scribe or paint marks on the front and rear end frame housings of the alternator to facilitate reassembly.

9   Remove the nut retaining the pulley to the rotor shaft and remove the pulley.

10   Remove the four nuts retaining the front and rear end frames together, then separate the rear end frame assembly from the front end frame **(see illustrations 15.2a and 15.2b)**.

11   Remove the thrust washer and remove the rotor from the front end frame.

Component checks

Refer to illustrations 15.12a, 15.12b, 15.13, 15.14a, 15.14b, 15.14c and 15.14d

12   Check for an open between the two slip rings **(see illustration)**.

There should be 2 to 4 ohms resistance between the slip rings. Check for grounds between each slip ring and the rotor **(see illustration)**. There should be no continuity (infinite resistance) between the rotor and either slip ring. If the rotor fails either test, or if the slip rings are excessively worn, the rotor is defective.

13   Check for opens between each end terminal of the stator windings **(see illustration)**. If either reading is high (infinite resistance), the stator is defective. Check for a grounded stator winding between each stator terminal and the frame. If there's continuity between any stator winding and the frame the stator is defective.

14   Check the positive and negative rectifiers.

a) *First start the checks on the positive diode assembly by touching the positive probe of the ohmmeter onto the diode terminal and the negative probe onto one of the other designated diode terminals* **(see illustration)**. *Then reverse the probes and check again* **(see illustration)**. *The diode should have continuity with the ohmmeter one way and no continuity when the probes are reversed* **(see illustration)**. *Check each of the terminals in this manner. If any of the diodes fail the test, the diode assembly is defective.*

b) *Now, check the negative diode assembly by touching the negative probe of the ohmmeter onto the NEGATIVE TERMINALS* **(see illustration)** *and the other probe onto each rectifier terminal. Reverse the polarity (reverse probes) and check to make sure there is no continuity in one position and continuity in the other position. Check each of the terminals in this manner. If any of the diodes fail the test, the diode assembly is defective.*

5

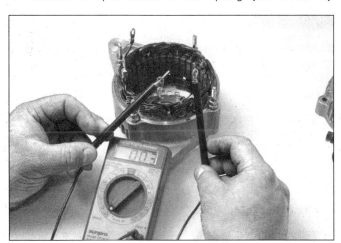

15.13 Check for continuity between the stator windings

+ Positive Probe

- Negative Probe

15.14a Position the positive probe of the ohmmeter onto the diode assembly positive post and the negative probe to ground. Continuity should exist

USA

CANADA

15.14b   First, check the positive rectifier diodes

Reassembly

Refer to illustration 15.16

15   Install the components in the reverse order of removal, noting the following:

16   Install the brush holder by depressing each brush with a small screwdriver to clear the shaft **(see illustration)**.

17   Install the voltage regulator and brush holder screws into the rear frame.

18   Install the rear cover and tighten the three nuts securely.

19   Install the terminal insulator and tighten it with the nut.

20   Install the alternator (see Section 14).

16   Starting system - general information and precautions

Refer to illustration 16.2

The sole function of the starting system is to turn over the engine quickly enough to allow it to start.

The starting system consists of the battery, the starter motor, the starter solenoid and the electrical circuit connecting the components. The solenoid is mounted directly on the starter motor **(see illustration)**.

The solenoid/starter motor assembly is installed on the upper part of the engine, next to the transaxle bellhousing.

When the ignition key is turned to the START position, the starter solenoid is actuated through the starter control circuit. The starter solenoid then connects the battery to the starter. The battery supplies the electrical energy to the starter motor, which does the actual work of cranking the engine.

The starter motor on a vehicle equipped with a manual transaxle can be operated only when the clutch pedal is depressed; the starter on a vehicle equipped with an automatic transaxle can be operated only when the transaxle selector lever is in Park or Neutral.

Always observe the following precautions when working on the starting system:

a) *Excessive cranking of the starter motor can overheat it and cause serious damage. Never operate the starter motor for more than 15 seconds at a time without pausing to allow it to cool for at least two minutes.*

15.14c   **Switch the polarity of the ohmmeter probes and confirm that now there is NO continuity within the diodes. Check each diode (four total) individually**

b) *The starter is connected directly to the battery and could arc or cause a fire if mishandled, overloaded or short circuited.*

c) *Always detach the cable from the negative terminal of the battery before working on the starting system.* **Caution:** *If the stereo in your vehicle is equipped with an anti-theft system, make sure you have the correct activation code before disconnecting the battery.*

17   Starter motor - testing in vehicle

Refer to illustration 17.5

Note: *Before diagnosing starter problems, make sure the battery is fully charged.*

1   If the starter motor does not turn at all when the switch is operated, make sure that the shift lever is in Neutral or Park (automatic transaxle) or that the clutch pedal is depressed (manual transaxle).

USA

CANADA

15.14d   **Now, check each diode on the negative rectifier diode assembly**

15.16 To facilitate installation of the brush holder, depress each brush with a small screwdriver to clear the shaft

2   Make sure that the battery is charged and that all cables, both at the battery and starter solenoid terminals, are clean and secure.

3   If the starter motor spins but the engine is not cranking, the overrunning clutch in the starter motor is slipping and the starter motor must be replaced.

4   If, when the switch is actuated, the starter motor does not operate at all but the solenoid clicks, then the problem lies with either the battery, the main solenoid contacts or the starter motor itself (or the engine is seized).

5   If the solenoid plunger cannot be heard when the switch is actuated, the battery is bad, the fusible link is burned (the circuit is open), the starter relay **(see illustration)** is defective or the starter solenoid itself is defective. **Note:** *Follow the relay testing procedure in Chapter 4, Section 3 to diagnose a defective relay.*

6   To check the solenoid, connect a jumper lead between the battery (+) and the ignition switch terminal (the small terminal) on the

16.2 Exploded view of a typical starter/solenoid assembly

End Cover

O-Ring

O-Ring

Field Frame

O-Ring

Armature

Front Bearing

Rear Bearing

Brush Holder

Through Bolt

Bearing

Idler Gear

Starter Housing

Magnetic Switch Assembly

Spring

Steel Ball

Clutch Assembly

5

Starter

Starter Relay

PNP Switch (A/T)

MAIN FL (3.0W)

Clutch Start Switch (M/T)

ALT H-Fuse (100A)

AM1 H-Fuse (40A)

17.5 Location of the starter relay

A/T   M/T

Air Cleaner Hose and Cap

IAT Connector

Wire Clamp

Starter

Starter Connector

Starter Wire

18.5 Starter motor/solenoid mounting details

solenoid. If the starter motor now operates, the solenoid is OK and the problem is in the ignition switch, Neutral start switch or in the wiring.

7   If the starter motor still does not operate, remove the starter/solenoid assembly for disassembly, testing and repair.

8   If the starter motor cranks the engine at an abnormally slow speed, first make sure that the battery is charged and that all terminal connections are tight. If the engine is partially seized, or has the wrong viscosity oil in it, it will crank slowly.

9   Run the engine until normal operating temperature is reached, then disconnect the coil wire from the distributor cap and ground it on the engine.

10   Connect a voltmeter positive lead to the battery positive post and connect the negative lead to the negative post.

11   Crank the engine and take the voltmeter readings as soon as a steady figure is indicated. Do not allow the starter motor to turn for more than 15 seconds at a time. A reading of nine volts or more, with the starter motor turning at normal cranking speed, is normal. If the reading is nine volts or more but the cranking speed is slow, the motor is faulty. If the reading is less than nine volts and the cranking speed is slow, the solenoid contacts are probably burned, the starter motor is bad, the battery is discharged or there is a bad connection.

18   Starter motor - removal and installation

Refer to illustration 18.5

Note: *The starter/solenoid assembly cannot be repaired using separate components. In the event of failure, exchange the starter/solenoid assembly for a new or rebuilt complete unit.*

1   Detach the cable from the negative terminal of the battery. **Caution:** *If the stereo in your vehicle is equipped with an anti-theft system, make sure you have the correct activation code before disconnecting the battery.*

2   Remove the battery from the engine compartment.

3   Disconnect and remove the cruise control assembly from the engine compartment (see Chapter 12).

4   Detach the electrical connectors from the starter/solenoid assembly.

5   Remove the starter motor mounting bolts **(see illustration)**.

6   Remove the bracket from the upper section of the starter/solenoid assembly. **Note:** *It is necessary to loosen one or two of the bracket bolts to allow the starter/solenoid assembly to partially drop down to gain access to the remaining bracket assembly bolts and hardware.*

7   Installation is the reverse of removal.

Chapter 6
Emissions and engine control systems

Contents

Specifications

EGR temperature sensor resistance

112-degrees F	69 to 89 K-ohms
212-degrees F	11 to 15 K-ohms
302-degrees F	2 to 4 K-ohms

1 General information

Refer to illustrations 1.1a, 1.1b, 1.4a, 1.4b, 1.4c, 1.6a and 1.6b

To minimize pollution of the atmosphere from incompletely burned and evaporating gases and to maintain good driveability and fuel economy, a number of emission control systems are used on these vehicles **(see illustrations)**. They include the:

Positive Crankcase Ventilation (PCV) system
Evaporative Emission Control (EVAP) system
Exhaust Gas Recirculation (EGR) system
Three-way catalytic converter (TWC) system
Electronic Fuel Injection (EFI) system

The Sections in this Chapter include general descriptions, checking procedures within the scope of the home mechanic and component replacement procedures (when possible) for each of the systems listed above.

Before assuming an emissions control system is malfunctioning, check the fuel and ignition systems carefully (see Chapters 4 and 5). The diagnosis of some emission control devices requires specialized tools, equipment and training. If checking and servicing become too difficult or if a procedure is beyond the scope of your skills, consult your dealer service department or other repair shop.

This doesn't mean, however, that emission control systems are particularly difficult to maintain and repair. You can quickly and easily perform many checks and do most of the regular maintenance at home with common tune-up and hand tools. **Note:** *The most frequent cause of emissions problems is simply a loose or broken electrical connector or vacuum hose, so always check the electrical connectors and vacuum hoses first* **(see illustrations)**.

Pay close attention to any special precautions outlined in this Chapter. It should be noted that the illustrations of the various systems may not exactly match the system installed on your vehicle because of

6

1.1a Emission and engine control components on the 1.8L engine

1	Crankshaft Position sensor	5	EGR valve	8	Air intake resonator
2	MAP sensor	6	Throttle Position Sensor	9	IAC valve
3	EGR vacuum switching valve	7	Test terminal	10	Oxygen sensor
4	EGR vacuum modulator				

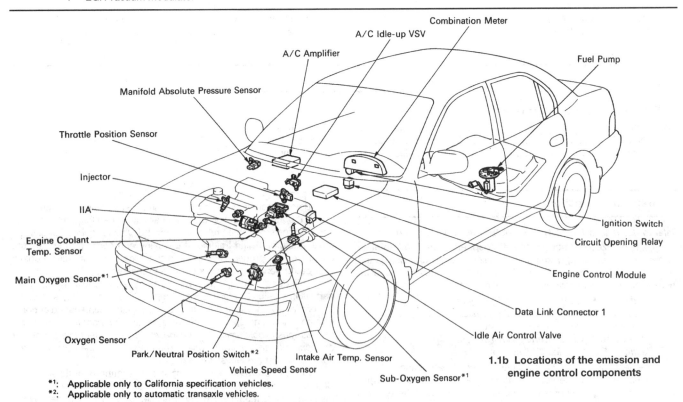

1.1b Locations of the emission and engine control components

*1: Applicable only to California specification vehicles.
*2: Applicable only to automatic transaxle vehicles.

1.4a Vacuum hose routing diagram for 1993 through 1995 models - all except California models and 1995 1.8L engines

1.4b Vacuum hose routing diagram for 1993 through 1995 California models - except 1995 1.8L engines

6

1.4c Vacuum hose routing diagram for 1995 1.8L engines and all 1996 and later models

1.6a The Vehicle Emissions Control Information (VECI) label contains such essential information as the types of emission control systems installed on the engine, the idle speed and ignition timing specifications

1.6b The VECI label also contains the vacuum hose routing diagram

changes made by the manufacturer during production or from year-to-year.

The Vehicle Emissions Control Information (VECI) label and a vacuum hose diagram are located on the hood **(see illustrations)**. These contain important emissions specifications and setting procedures, and a vacuum hose schematic with emissions components identified. When servicing the engine or emissions systems, the VECI label in your particular vehicle should always be checked for up-to-date information.

2   Electronic control system - general information and ECM removal and installation

General information

1   The fuel injection system is controlled by means of a microcomputer known as the Electronic Control Module (ECM).
2   The ECM receives signals from various sensors which monitor changing engine operating conditions such as intake air volume, intake air temperature, coolant temperature, engine rpm, acceleration/deceleration, exhaust oxygen content, etc. These signals are utilized by the ECM to determine the correct fuel injection duration.
3   The system is analogous to the central nervous system in the human body: The sensors (nerve endings) constantly relay signals to the ECM (brain), which processes the data and, if necessary, sends out a command to change the operating parameters of the engine (body).
4   Here's a specific example of how one portion of this system operates: An oxygen sensor, located in the exhaust manifold, constantly monitors the oxygen content of the exhaust gas. If the percentage of oxygen in the exhaust gas is incorrect, an electrical signal is sent to the ECM. The ECM takes this information, processes it and then sends a command to the fuel injection system telling it to change the air/fuel mixture. This happens in a fraction of a second and it goes on continuously when the engine is running. The end result is an air/fuel mixture ratio which is constantly maintained at a predetermined ratio, regardless of driving conditions.
5   In the event of a sensor malfunction, a backup circuit will take over to provide driveability until the problem is identified and fixed.

Precautions

6   Follow these steps:
a) *Always disconnect the power by either turning off the ignition switch or disconnecting the battery terminals before unplugging any electrical connectors.* **Warning:** *These models are equipped with airbags. The airbag is armed and can deploy (inflate) anytime the battery is connected. To prevent accidental deployment (and possible injury), turn the ignition key to LOCK and disconnect the negative battery cable whenever working near airbag components. After the battery is disconnected, wait at least two minutes before beginning work. This system has a back-up capacitor that must fully discharge. For more information, see Chapter 12.* **Caution:** *If the stereo in your vehicle is equipped with an anti-theft system, make sure you have the correct activation code before disconnecting the battery.*
b) *When installing a battery, be particularly careful to avoid reversing the positive and negative battery cables.*
c) *Do not subject EFI components, emissions-related components or the ECM to severe impact during removal or installation.*
d) *Do not be careless during troubleshooting. Even slight terminal contact can invalidate a testing procedure and damage one of the numerous transistor circuits.*
e) *Never attempt to work on the ECM or open the ECM cover. The ECM is protected by a government-mandated extended warranty that will be nullified if you tamper with or damage the ECM.*
f) *If you are inspecting electronic control system components during rainy weather, make sure that water does not enter any part. When washing the engine compartment, do not spray these parts or their electrical connectors with water.*

2.10 The ECM is located behind the center console - CAREFULLY disconnect the electrical connectors (arrows)

ECM removal and installation

Refer to illustration 2.10

7   Disconnect the negative cable from the battery (see Chapter 5). **Caution:** *If the stereo in your vehicle is equipped with an anti-theft system, make sure you have the correct activation code before disconnecting the battery.*
8   Remove the lower finish panel on the passenger side under the glove compartment (see Chapter 11).
9   Remove the center console from the passenger compartment (see Chapter 11).
10   Disconnect the electrical connectors from the ECM **(see illustration)**. Each connector has a locking tab which must be disengaged before the connector is unplugged.
11   Remove the bolts from the ECM brackets.
12   Lift the ECM from the vehicle.
13   Installation is the reverse of removal.

3   On Board Diagnosis (OBD) system - description and trouble code access

Note: *This procedure does not include the diagnostic codes or the code extracting procedure for 1996 and later models equipped with the OBD II system. These models require a special SCAN tool to read out the various levels of coded information. Have the 1996 and later models diagnosed by a dealer service department or other qualified repair shop in the event of computer failure.*

General information

The ECM contains a built-in self-diagnosis system which detects and identifies malfunctions occurring in the network. When the ECM detects a problem, three things happen: the CHECK ENGINE light comes on, the trouble is identified and a diagnostic code is recorded and stored. The ECM stores the failure code assigned to the specific problem area until the diagnosis system is canceled by removing the EFI fuse with the ignition switch off.

The CHECK ENGINE warning light, which is located on the instrument panel, comes on when the ignition switch is turned to ON and the engine is not running. When the engine is started, the warning light should go out. If the light remains on, the self-diagnosis system has detected a malfunction.

Obtaining diagnostic code output

Refer to illustration 3.3

1   To obtain an output of diagnostic codes, verify first that the battery voltage is above 11 volts, the throttle is fully closed, the transaxle is in Neutral, the accessory switches are off and the engine is at normal operating temperature.

6

3.3 To access the self diagnosis system, locate the test connector in the engine compartment and using a jumper wire or paper clip, bridge terminals TE1 and E1

3.7 Typical location of the 15A EFI fuse

2   Turn the ignition switch to ON (engine not running). Do not start the engine.

3   Use a jumper wire to bridge terminals TE1 and E1 of the test connector **(see illustration)**. **Note:** *The self-diagnosis system can be accessed by using either test terminal number 1 (engine compartment) or test terminal number 2 (under driver's dash).*

4   Read the diagnosis code as indicated by the number of flashes of the "CHECK ENGINE" light on the dash. Normal system operation is indicated by Code No. 1 (no malfunctions) for all models. The "CHECK ENGINE" light displays a Code No. 1 by blinking once every 0.25 seconds. Each code will be displayed by first blinking the first digit of the code, then pause, and blink the second digit of the code. For example; Code 24 (IAT sensor) will flash two times, pause, and then flash four times. Each flash will be the exact same length but the distinction will be the pause that separates the digits of the code. Only code 1 (normal operation) will flash continuously without a pause.

5   If there are any malfunctions in the system, their corresponding trouble codes are stored in computer memory and the light will blink the requisite number of times for the indicated trouble codes. If there's more than one trouble code in the memory, they'll be displayed in numerical order (from lowest to highest) with a pause between each one. After the code with the largest number of flashes has been displayed, there will be another pause and then the sequence will begin all over again. **Note:** *The diagnostic trouble codes 25, 26, 27 and 71 use a special diagnostic capability called "two-trip detection logic".*

With this system, when a malfunction is first detected, it is temporarily stored into the ECM on the first trip. The engine must be turned off and the vehicle taken on another trip to allow the malfunction to be stored permanently in the ECM. This will distinguish a true problem from a false alarm on vehicles with these particular codes entered into the ECM. Normally the self-diagnosis system will detect the malfunctions, but in the event the home mechanic wants to double-check the diagnosis by canceling the codes and rechecking, then it will be necessary to go on two test drives to confirm any malfunctions with these particular codes.

6   To ensure correct interpretation of the flashing "CHECK ENGINE" light, watch carefully for the interval between the end of one code and the beginning of the next; otherwise, you will become confused by the apparent number of flashes and misinterpret the display (the length of this interval varies with the model year).

Canceling a diagnostic code

Refer to illustration 3.7

7   After the malfunctioning component has been repaired/replaced, the trouble codes stored in computer memory must be canceled. To accomplish this, simply remove the 15A EFI fuse **(see illustration)** for at least 10 seconds with the ignition switch off.

8   A stored code can also be canceled by removing the cable from the negative battery terminal, but other memory systems (such as the clock and radio presets) will also be canceled. **Caution:** *If the stereo in your vehicle is equipped with an anti-theft system, make sure you have the correct activation code before disconnecting the battery.*

9   If the diagnosis code is not canceled, it will be stored by the ECM and appear with any new codes in the event of future trouble.

10   Should it become necessary to work on engine components requiring removal of the battery terminal, always check to see if a diagnostic code has been recorded before disconnecting the battery.

Diagnostic Trouble Codes

Code	Circuit or system	Diagnosis	Trouble area
Code 1	Normal	The CHECK ENGINE light flashes on and off rapidly when no codes are identified	
Code 12	RPM signal	No rpm signal to the ECM within several seconds after the engine is cranked	Distributor or circuit Crankshaft position sensor or circuit ECM or circuit
Code 13	RPM signal	No rpm signal to the ECM with engine speed above 1,500 rpm	Distributor or circuit Crankshaft position sensor or circuit ECM or circuit
Code 14	Ignition signal	No ignition signal to the ECM	Igniter or circuit Ignition coil Ignition switch or circuit ECM

Code	Circuit or system	Diagnosis	Trouble area
Code 16	ECM control signal	Problem between the engine controls and transaxle controls inside the ECM	ECM
Code 21	Main oxygen sensor	Problem in the main oxygen sensor circuit	Main oxygen sensor or circuit ECM
Code 22	Coolant temperature	Open or short in the coolant temperature sensor circuit	Coolant temperature sensor or circuit ECM
Code 24	Intake air temperature sensor	Open or short in the intake air temperature sensor circuit	Intake air temperature sensor or circuit ECM
Code 25	Oxygen sensor or circuit	An excessively lean air/fuel ratio has been indicated by the oxygen sensor circuit	Injector or circuit Oxygen sensor or circuit ECM Fuel pressure regulator Coolant temperature sensor or circuit Intake air temperature sensor or circuit Vacuum or exhaust leak Contaminated fuel Ignition system
Code 26	Oxygen sensor or circuit	An overly rich air/fuel ratio has been indicated by the oxygen sensor circuit	Injector or injector circuit Coolant temperature sensor or circuit Oxygen sensor or circuit Intake air temperature sensor or circuit Fuel pressure regulator EVAP system EGR system MAP sensor or circuit ECM Air intake system
Code 27	Sub-oxygen sensor	Open or shorted circuit in the sub-oxygen sensor circuit	Sub-oxygen sensor or circuit ECM
Code 31	MAP sensor	Open or short in MAP sensor circuit	MAP sensor or circuit ECM
Code 41	Throttle position sensor	Open or short in the throttle position sensor circuit	Throttle position sensor or circuit ECM
Code 42	Vehicle speed sensor	No speed signal for 8 seconds when the engine speed is between 3,000 and 5,000 rpm and the transaxle is in gear	Vehicle speed sensor or circuit ECM Speedometer Instrument panel printed circuit
Code 43	Starter signal	No starter signal to the ECM until engine speed reaches 800 rpm with the vehicle not moving	Starter signal circuit Ignition switch ECM
Code 51	Switch condition signal	No throttle position signal, gear selector signal or air conditioning signal to the ECM	Air conditioning switch or circuit Air conditioning amplifier Neutral Start switch Throttle Position sensor ECM
Code 52	Knock sensor signal	Open or short circuit in knock sensor circuit	Knock sensor or circuit ECM
Code 71	EGR system	EGR temperature signal is too low	EGR system (EGR valve, hoses, etc.) EGR temperature sensor or circuit EGR vacuum switching valve ECM

6

4.1 Compare the indicated resistance values specified on this graph - note that as the temperature increases (as the engine warms up) the resistance decreases

4.2 To check the coolant temperature sensor, use an ohmmeter to measure the resistance between the two sensor terminals

4.3 Use a voltmeter and probe the coolant temperature sensor connector for reference voltage with the ignition key ON (engine not running). It should be approximately 5.0 volts

4   Information sensors

Note 1: *Most of the components described in this Section are protected by a Federally mandated extended warranty. See your dealer for the details regarding your vehicle.*

Note 2: *Refer to Chapters 4 and 5 for additional information on the location and the diagnostic procedures for the sensors that are not directly covered in this Section.*

Coolant temperature sensor

General description

Refer to illustration 4.1

1   The coolant temperature sensor is a thermistor (a resistor which varies the value of its voltage output in accordance with temperature changes). As the sensor temperature DECREASES, the resistance values will INCREASE. As the sensor temperature INCREASES, the resistance values will DECREASE **(see illustration)**. A failure in this sensor circuit should set a Code 22. This code indicates a failure in the coolant temperature sensor circuit, so in most cases the appropriate solution to the problem will be either repair of a connector or wire, or replacement of the sensor.

Check

Refer to illustrations 4.2 and 4.3

2   To check the sensor, disconnect the electrical connector and measure the resistance across the sensor terminals **(see illustration)**. With the engine completely cold (68-degrees F) the resistance should be 2,000 to 3,000 ohms. Next, start the engine and warm it up until it reaches operating temperature (180-degrees F) - the resistance should be 200 to 400 ohms. **Note:** *If necessary, remove the sensor and perform the tests in a pan of heated water to simulate the conditions. Compare the resistance values with the accompanying graph.*

3   If the resistance values of the coolant temperature sensor are correct, check the circuit for the proper signal voltage. Turn the ignition key ON (engine not running) and check for reference voltage **(see illustration)**. It should be approximately 5 volts.

Replacement

4   To remove the sensor, depress the locking tabs, unplug the electrical connector, then carefully unscrew the sensor. **Caution:** *Handle the coolant sensor with care. Damage to this sensor will affect the*

operation of the entire fuel injection system.

5   Before installing the new sensor, wrap the threads with Teflon sealing tape to prevent leakage and thread corrosion.

6   Installation is the reverse of removal.

Oxygen sensor

General description

7   These models are equipped with either a single oxygen sensor system or a dual-stage oxygen sensor system. On dual-stage systems, the main oxygen sensor is mounted ahead of the front catalytic converter and monitors the exhaust gases exiting the engine. The sub oxygen sensor monitors the exhaust gases after they have passed through the front catalytic converter. Each oxygen sensor monitors the oxygen content of the exhaust gas stream. The oxygen content in the exhaust reacts with the oxygen sensor to produce a voltage output which varies from 0.1-volt (high oxygen, lean mixture) to 0.9-volts (low oxygen, rich mixture). The ECM constantly monitors this variable voltage output to determine the ratio of oxygen to fuel in the mixture. The ECM alters the air/fuel mixture ratio by controlling the pulse width (open time) of the fuel injectors. A mixture ratio of 14.7 parts air to 1 part fuel is the ideal mixture ratio for minimizing exhaust emissions, thus allowing the catalytic converter to operate at maximum efficiency. It is this ratio of 14.7 to 1 which the ECM and the oxygen sensor attempt to maintain at all times.

8   The oxygen sensor produces no voltage when it is below its normal operating temperature of about 600-degrees F. During this initial period before warm-up, the ECM operates in open loop mode.

9   If the engine reaches normal operating temperature and/or has been running for two or more minutes, and if the main oxygen sensor is producing a steady signal voltage below 0.70-volts at 1,500 or more rpm, the ECM will set a Code 21. Code 27 will indicate a problem with the sub oxygen sensor.

10   When there is a problem with the oxygen sensor or its circuit, the ECM operates in the open loop mode - that is, it controls fuel delivery in accordance with a programmed default value instead of feedback information from the oxygen sensor.

11   The proper operation of the oxygen sensor depends on four conditions:

a)   *Electrical* - *The low voltages generated by the sensor depend upon good, clean connections which should be checked whenever a malfunction of the sensor is suspected or indicated.*

b)   ***Outside air supply*** - *The sensor is designed to allow air circula-*

tion to the internal portion of the sensor. Whenever the sensor is removed and installed or replaced, make sure the air passages are not restricted.

c) **Proper operating temperature** - The ECM will not react to the sensor signal until the sensor reaches approximately 600-degrees F. This factor must be taken into consideration when evaluating the performance of the sensor.

d) **Unleaded fuel** - The use of unleaded fuel is essential for proper operation of the sensor. Make sure the fuel you are using is of this type.

12   In addition to observing the above conditions, special care must be taken whenever the sensor is serviced.

a) The oxygen sensor has a permanently attached pigtail and electrical connector which should not be removed from the sensor. Damage to or removal of the pigtail or electrical connector can adversely affect operation of the sensor.

b) Grease, dirt and other contaminants should be kept away from the electrical connector and the louvered end of the sensor.

c) Do not use cleaning solvents of any kind on the oxygen sensor.

d) Do not drop or roughly handle the sensor.

e) The silicone boot must be installed in the correct position to prevent the boot from being melted and to allow the sensor to operate properly.

Check

Refer to illustrations 4.13, 4.15, 4.16, 4.17, 4.18 and 4.19

13   To check the oxygen sensor use a digital voltmeter to monitor the millivolt signal from the oxygen sensor during actual operating conditions. Locate the oxygen sensor electrical connector and backprobe the black wire on the harness side of the oxygen sensor connector **(see illustration)**. To properly backprobe the connector insert a long straight pin (a T-pin is preferred) alongside the wire until the pin contacts the metal wire terminal inside the connector. Connect the positive

4.13 Insert a pin into the backside of the oxygen sensor connector on the correct terminal and check for a millivolt output signal generated by the sensor

probe of a voltmeter onto the pin and the negative probe to ground.

14   Start the engine and monitor the voltage signal (millivolts) of the main oxygen sensor as the engine warms-up. The oxygen sensor will produce a steady voltage signal at first (open loop) of approximately 0.1 to 0.2 volts with the engine cold. After a period of approximately two minutes, the engine will reach operating temperature and the oxygen sensor voltage will fluctuate between 0.1 to 0.9 volts (closed loop). If the oxygen sensor fails to operate as described, replace it.

15   To check the sub-oxygen sensor, locate the electrical connector **(see illustration)** and check it in the same manner as the main oxygen sensor.

6

Heated Oxygen Sensor Connector for Wiring Side

Heated Oxygen Sensor Connector for Sensor Side

4.15 It will be necessary to remove the front passenger seat to gain access to the sub-oxygen sensor electrical connector

Heated Oxygen Sensor

4.16 To test the oxygen sensor heater, disconnect the harness connector and check the resistance across terminals HT and +B of the oxygen sensor connector. It should be between 11 to 17 ohms

4.17 Check for the voltage to the heater on the black/red wire (+) and the blue/black wire (-). It should be approximately 12 volts (battery voltage)

16   Also check the sub-oxygen sensor heater (if equipped) as follows: Disconnect the oxygen sensor electrical connector and connect an ohmmeter between the +B and HT terminals on the oxygen sensor side of the connector **(see illustration)**. It should measure approximately 11.0 to 17.0 ohms. **Note:** *Not all models are equipped with a heated oxygen sensor. Models with heated oxygen sensors will be equipped with a four-wire electrical connector.*

17   Check for proper supply voltage to the oxygen sensor heater. With the ignition key ON (engine not running), check for battery voltage at the black/red wire (positive [+]) and the blue/black wire (negative [-]) on the harness side of the connector **(see illustration)**.

18   On 1993 and 1994 models, it's also possible to check the oxygen sensor in another manner. With the engine completely warmed up and the oxygen sensor connected, connect a voltmeter to the test connector VF1 (positive probe +) and E1 (negative probe -) **(see illustration)**. **Note:** *Use only an analog type voltmeter because it will be necessary to watch the needle fluctuations.*

19   Run the engine at 2,500 rpm for approximately two minutes and then jump terminals TE1 and E1 of the test connector **(see illustration)**. Check the number of times the needle fluctuates in 10 seconds. It should fluctuate eight times or more. If it does not, warm the engine up again and repeat the test.

20   If the voltmeter still does not fluctuate eight times or more, remove the jumper wire from terminals TE1 and E1 of the test connector. Maintain engine speed at 2,500 rpm and measure the voltage

between terminals VF1 and E1. If the voltage reading is more than 0 volts, then replace the oxygen sensor with a new part. If the voltage reading is 0 volts, access the self diagnostic codes (see Section 3) and check for any malfunctions.

21   If codes 21, 25 or 26 are obtained, then remove the PCV hose from the valve cover (see Section 8) and measure the voltage between VF1 and E1. If the voltage is 0 volts, replace the oxygen sensor. If the voltage reading is more than 0 volts, repair the over-rich running condition.

22   If codes other than 21, 25 or 26 are obtained, repair the particular sensor or circuit.

Replacement

Refer to illustration 4.26

Note: *Because it is installed in the exhaust manifold or pipe, which contracts when cool, the oxygen sensor may be very difficult to loosen when the engine is cold. Rather than risk damage to the sensor (assuming you are planning to reuse it in another manifold or pipe), start and run the engine for a minute or two, then shut it off. Be careful not to burn yourself during the following procedure.*

23   Disconnect the cable from the negative terminal of the battery. **Caution:** *If the stereo in your vehicle is equipped with an anti-theft system, make sure you have the correct activation code before discon-*

4.18 Connect the probes of the voltmeter to terminals VF1 (+) and E1 (-), raise the engine speed to 2,500 rpm and jump terminals TE1 and E1 with a jumper wire or paper clip

4.19 With terminals TE1 and E1 of the test connector jumpered observe the number of needle sweeps in a 10-second time period

4.26 Slotted sockets are available for easing oxygen sensor removal

4.33 Check for reference voltage on the MAP sensor connector yellow wire terminal. It should be approximately 5.0 volts

4.35 Install a vacuum pump to the MAP sensor and check for signal voltage on the light green/red (+) wire and brown wire (-) without vacuum applied. It should be approximately 3.0 to 4.0 volts

necting the battery.

24   Raise the vehicle and place it securely on jackstands.

25   Carefully disconnect the electrical connector from the sensor pigtail lead.

26   Remove the oxygen sensor from the exhaust system **(see illustration). Caution:** *Excessive force may damage the threads.* **Note:** *Some oxygen sensors are threaded directly into the exhaust manifold while others are mounted in the exhaust manifold or pipe with two bolts. Refer to illustrations 1.4a, 1.4b and 1.4c for the location of the oxygen sensors.*

27   Anti-seize compound must be used on the threads of the sensor to facilitate future removal. The threads of new sensors will already be coated with this compound, but if an old sensor is removed and reinstalled, recoat the threads.

28   Install the sensor and tighten it securely.

29   Reconnect the electrical connector of the pigtail lead to the main engine wiring harness.

30   Lower the vehicle and reconnect the cable to the negative terminal of the battery.

Throttle Position Sensor (TPS)

General description

31   The Throttle Position Sensor (TPS) is located on the end of the throttle shaft on the throttle body (see Chapter 4). By monitoring the output voltage from the TPS, the ECM can alter fuel delivery based on throttle valve angle (driver demand). A broken or loose TPS can cause intermittent bursts of fuel from the injector and an unstable idle because the ECM thinks the throttle is moving. All the checks and replacement procedures are covered in Chapter 4.

MAP sensor

General Information

32   The MAP sensor monitors the intake manifold pressure changes resulting from changes in engine load and speed and converts the information into a voltage output. The ECM uses the MAP sensor to control fuel delivery and ignition timing. The ECM will receive information as a voltage signal. This signal can be detected using a voltmeter. Under ideal conditions, the voltage will vary from 4.0 volts with the engine off (no vacuum) to 0.5 volts with the engine idling (25 in-Hg vacuum).

Check

Refer to illustrations 4.33, 4.35 and 4.36

33   Turn the ignition On (do not start the engine). Disconnect the electrical connector and check the reference voltage from the MAP sensor

on the yellow wire terminal. It should be approximately 5.0 volts **(see illustration)**.

34   Remove the vacuum hose from the MAP sensor and install a hand-held vacuum pump.

35   Reconnect the electrical connector to the MAP sensor. Back-probe the MAP sensor harness connector using straight pins on the light green/red wire (+) positive and brown wire (-) negative **(see illustration)**. Without vacuum, the sensor voltage should be approximately 3.0 to 4.0 volts.

36   Use the hand-held vacuum pump and apply 25 in-Hg of vacuum to the MAP sensor and observe the voltage readings. The voltmeter should read approximately 0.5 to 1.5 volts **(see illustration)**.

37   If the test results are incorrect, replace the MAP sensor.

Intake Air Temperature (IAT) sensor

General description

Refer to illustrations 4.38, 4.39, 4.40, 4.42 and 4.43

38   The intake air temperature sensor is located inside the air cleaner housing. This sensor is a resistor which changes value according to the temperature of the air entering the engine. Low temperatures produce a high resistance value (for example, at 68-degrees F the resistance is 2,000 to 3,000 ohms) while high temperatures produce low

6

4.36 Now apply vacuum to the MAP sensor an observe that the voltage decreases to approximately 0.5 to 1.5 volts

4.38 The air intake temperature sensor resistance will DECREASE when the temperature of the air INCREASES

4.39 Location of the IAT sensor

4.40 Check the IAT sensor reference voltage on the yellow/black (+) wire

resistance values (at 176-degrees F the resistance is 200 to 400 ohms **(see illustration)**. The ECM supplies approximately 5-volts (reference voltage) to the air temperature sensor. The IAT sensor alters the voltage according to the temperature of the incoming air. The signal voltage sent back to the ECM will be high when the air temperature is cold and low when the air temperature is warm. Any problems with the air temperature sensor will usually set a code 24.

Check

39   To check the air temperature sensor, disconnect the two prong electrical connector **(see illustration)**. Turn the ignition key ON, but do not start the engine.

40   Measure the voltage (reference voltage) on the yellow/black wire terminal. The VOM should read approximately 5-volts **(see illustration)**.

41   If the reference voltage is not correct, have the ECM diagnosed by a dealer service department or other repair shop.

42   Measure the resistance across the air temperature sensor terminals **(see illustration)**. The resistance should be HIGH when the air temperature is LOW. Next, start the engine and let it idle. Wait awhile and let the engine reach operating temperature. Turn the ignition OFF, disconnect the air temperature sensor and measure the resistance across the terminals. The resistance should be LOW when the air temperature is HIGH. If the sensor does not exhibit this change in resistance, replace it.

EGR temperature sensor (California models)

General Description

43   The EGR temperature sensor is mounted near the EGR valve. This sensor detects the temperature of the exhaust as it moves through the

4.42 Checking the IAT sensor resistance

4.44 Disconnect the EGR gas temperature sensor connector and check the resistance of the sensor

4.50 The knock sensor (arrow) is located under the intake manifold

EGR valve. The information is sent to the ECM and in turn the EGR on/off time is regulated precisely and more efficiently. Any malfunction with the EGR temperature sensor will set a code 71.

Check

Refer to illustration 4.44

44   Disconnect the harness connector for the EGR temperature sensor **(see illustration)** and measure the resistance of the sensor at various temperatures. Refer to the Specifications listed in this Chapter for a list of the temperatures and the resistance values.

Replacement

45   Disconnect the harness connector for the EGR temperature sensor and using an open-end wrench, remove the sensor from the intake manifold.

46   Installation is the reverse of removal.

Vehicle speed sensor

General description

47   The Vehicle Speed Sensor (VSS) is located on the output section of the transaxle (see Chapter 7B). The sensor is electronically controlled and sends a pulsing voltage signal to the ECM, which the ECM converts to miles per hour.

48   Any problems with the VSS and its circuit will set a code 42. Have the vehicle speed sensor, circuit and the ECM diagnosed by a dealership service department or other qualified repair shop.

4.51 Check that NO continuity exists on the sensor terminal to the body of the sensor

Knock sensor

General Description

49   Irregular octane levels in modern gasoline can cause detonation in an engine. Detonation is sometimes referred to as "spark knock". The knock sensor sends a voltage signal to the ECM when no spark knock is occurring and the ECM provides normal advance. When the knock sensor detects abnormal vibration (spark knock), it turns off the circuit to the ECM, and distributor timing is retarded until the knock is eliminated. Any problems with the knock sensor or sensor circuit will set a code 52.

Check

Refer to illustrations 4.50 and 4.51

50   The knock sensor is located on the firewall side of the engine block, under the intake manifold **(see illustration)**. It will be necessary to remove the air intake plenum (see Chapter 4) and the intake manifold (see Chapter 2A) to gain access to the knock sensor.

51   Using an ohmmeter, check that there is no continuity between the terminal on the knock sensor and the body **(see illustration)**.

52   If continuity exists, replace the sensor.

Crankshaft Position Sensor (1995 1.8L engine and all 1996 and later models)

Refer to illustration 4.53 and 4.54

General Description

53   The crankshaft position sensor is located in the timing belt cover near the crankshaft pulley **(see illustration)**. The crankshaft position sensor relays a signal to the ECM to indicate the exact position (angle) of the crankshaft.

Check

54   Using an ohmmeter, measure the resistance of the crankshaft

4.53 Location of the crankshaft sensor near the timing belt cover

4.54 Check the resistance of the crankshaft sensor on the electrical connector

5.10 Apply air pressure into the charcoal canister purge control valve A (inlet) and confirm that the valve allows the air to pass into the charcoal canister

ECT	TVV	Throttle Position	Canister Check Valve			Check Valve in Cap	Evaporated Fuel (HC)
			(1)	(2)	(3)		
Below 35°C (95°F)	CLOSED	—	—	—	—	—	HC from tank is absorbed into the canister.
Above 54°C (129°F)	OPEN	Below port P	CLOSED	—	—	—	HC from tank is absorbed into the canister.
		Above port P	OPEN	—	—	—	HC from canister is led into air intake chamber.
High pressure in tank	—	—	—	OPEN	CLOSED	CLOSED	HC from tank is absorbed into the canister.
High vacuum in tank	—	—	—	CLOSED	OPEN	OPEN	Air is led into the fuel tank.

5.2 Typical EVAP system and operation chart

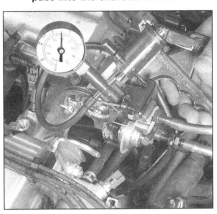

5.11 Apply air pressure to the port A on the TVV (top port) and confirm that air does not pass through the valve when the temperature is below 95-degrees F

position sensor **(see illustration)**. It should be between 1,630 to 3,225 ohms depending on the temperature; the warmer the temperature of the sensor, the higher the resistance value. If the resistance is not within the specified range, replace the sensor with a new part.
55   To replace the sensor, remove the front pulley (see Chapter 2A), disconnect the electrical connector and remove the bolts from the crankshaft position sensor.
56   Installation is the reverse of removal.

---

5   Evaporative Emission Control (EVAP) system

General description

Refer to illustration 5.2
1   This system is designed to trap and store fuel that evaporates from the fuel tank, throttle body and intake manifold that would normally enter the atmosphere in the form of hydrocarbon (HC) emissions.
2   The Evaporative Emission Control (EVAP) system consists of a charcoal-filled canister, the lines connecting the canister to the fuel tank, the Temperature Vacuum Valve (TVV) and a check valve **(see illustration)**.
3   Fuel vapors are transferred from the fuel tank and throttle body to a canister where they're stored when the engine isn't running. When the engine is running, the fuel vapors are purged from the canister by intake airflow and consumed in the normal combustion process.
4   The charcoal canister is equipped with a check valve that incor-

porates three check balls. Depending upon the running conditions and the pressure in the fuel tank, the check balls open and close the passageways to the TVV (consequently the throttle body) and fuel tank.

Check

Refer to illustrations 5.10 and 5.11
5   Poor idle, stalling and poor driveability can be caused by an inoperative check valve, a damaged canister, split or cracked hoses or hoses connected to the wrong fittings. Check the fuel filler cap for a damaged or deformed gasket (see Chapter 1).
6   Evidence of fuel loss or fuel odor can be caused by liquid fuel leaking from fuel lines, a cracked or damaged canister, an inoperative check valve, disconnected, misrouted, kinked, deteriorated or damaged vapor or control hoses.
7   Inspect each hose attached to the canister for kinks, leaks and cracks along its entire length. Repair or replace as necessary.
8   Look for fuel leaking from the bottom of the canister. If fuel is leaking, replace the canister and check the hoses and hose routing.
9   Inspect the canister. If it's cracked or damaged, replace it.
10   Check for a clogged filter or a stuck check valve. Using low pressure compressed air, blow into the canister tank pipe **(see illustration)**. Air should flow freely from the other pipes. If a problem is found, replace the canister.
11   Check the operation of the TVV. With the engine completely cold, use a hand-held pump and direct air into port A **(see illustration)**. Air should not pass through the TVV. Now warm the engine to operating temperature (above 129-degrees F) and observe that air passes through the TVV. Replace the valve if the test results are incorrect.

To reduce NOx emissions, part of the exhaust gases are recirculated through the EGR valve to the intake manifold to lower the maximum combustion temperature.

ECT	RPM	VSV	Throttle Position	Pressure in the EGR Valve Pressure Chamber		EGR Vacuum Modulator	EGR Valve	Exhaust Gas
Below 47°C (117°F)	–	****	–		–	–	CLOSED	Not recirculated
Above 53°C (127°F)	Below 4,000 rpm	*** ON	OFF	–		–	CLOSED	Not recirculated
			Below port E	–		–	CLOSED	Not recirculated
			Between port E and port R	(1) LOW	* Pressure constantly alternating between low and high	OPENS passage to atmosphere	CLOSED	Not recirculated
				(2) HIGH		CLOSES passage to atmosphere	OPEN	Recirculated
			Above port R	(3) HIGH	**	CLOSES passage to atmosphere	OPEN	Recirculated (increase)
	Above 4,400 rpm	(4) OFF	–	–		–	CLOSED	Not recirculated

Remarks: * Pressure increase ──── Modulator closes ───── EGR valve opens ──── Pressure drops
                         EGR valve closes ◄──── Modulator opens

** When the throttle valve is positioned above port R, the EGR vacuum modulator will close the atmosphere passage and open the EGR valve to increase the exhaust gas, even if the exhaust pressure is insufficiently low.

*** VSV switched ON when product of engine speed multiplied by vacuum sensor valve exceeds a specified valve.

**** If terminals TE1 and E1 of data link connector 1 are connected, the VSV switches ON.

6.1 Typical EGR system and operation chart

6.4 Apply vacuum to the EGR valve and confirm that the valve opens and allows exhaust gases to circulate. Once it is activated, the EGR valve should hold steady (no loss in vacuum)

6.7a To remove the EGR vacuum modulator filters for cleaning, remove the cap . . .

6.7b . . . then pull out the two filters and blow them out with compressed air - be sure the coarse side of the outer filter faces the atmosphere (out) when reinstalling the filters

Charcoal canister replacement

12   Clearly label, then detach the vacuum hoses from the canister.
13   Remove the mounting clamp bolts, lower the canister with the bracket, disconnect the hoses from the check valve and remove it from the vehicle.
14   Installation is the reverse of removal.

---

6   Exhaust Gas Recirculation (EGR) system

General description

Refer to illustration 6.1
1   To reduce oxides of nitrogen emissions, some of the exhaust gases are recirculated through the EGR valve to the intake manifold to lower combustion temperatures **(see illustration)**.
2   The EGR system consists of the EGR valve, the EGR modulator, vacuum switching valve (VSV), the Electronic Control Module (ECM) and the EGR gas temperature sensor.

Check

EGR valve

Refer to illustration 6.4
3   Start the engine and allow it to idle.
4   Detach the vacuum hose from the EGR valve and attach a hand-held vacuum pump in its place **(see illustration)**.
5   Apply vacuum to the EGR valve. Vacuum should remain steady

and the engine should run poorly.
   a) *If the vacuum doesn't remain steady and the engine doesn't run poorly, replace the EGR valve and recheck it.*
   b) *If the vacuum remains steady but the engine doesn't run poorly, remove the EGR valve and check the valve and the intake manifold for blockage. Clean or replace parts as necessary and recheck.*

EGR vacuum modulator filter

Refer to illustrations 6.7a and 6.7b
6   Remove the vacuum modulator.
7   Remove the cover and check the filters **(see illustrations)**.
8   Clean or replace the filters, reinstall the cover and the modulator.

EGR system

Refer to illustrations 6.9 and 6.11
9   Disconnect the hose from the EGR valve and install a three-way union and vacuum gauge between the EGR valve and the vacuum modulator **(see illustration)**.
10   Start the engine and connect terminals TE1 and E1 on the test terminal **(see illustration 3.3)**.
   a) *With the coolant temperature below 117-degrees F (cold), verify that the vacuum gauge indicates zero (no vacuum) at 2,500 rpm.*
   b) *With the engine barely warm, verify that the vacuum gauge indicates low vacuum at 2,500 rpm.*

6.9 Install a vacuum gauge between the vacuum modulator and the EGR valve using a three way adapter

6.11 Check the resistance on the EGR VSV using an ohmmeter. It should be between 37 and 44 ohms

6.18 Remove the nuts that retain the EGR valve assembly to the engine

c) *With the engine fully warmed up, raise the rpm to 2,500 and confirm the vacuum gauge indicates low vacuum.*
11 Check the operation of the VSV.
a) *The VSV is located on the intake manifold.*
b) *Check the resistance of the VSV. It should be between 37 and 44 ohms* **(see illustration)**.
c) *If the tests are incorrect, replace the VSV with a new part.*

Component replacement

EGR valve
Refer to illustration 6.18
12 Disconnect the cable from the negative terminal on the battery.
13 Remove the air cleaner housing (see Chapter 4).
14 Disconnect the accelerator cable from the throttle body (see Chapter 4).
15 Remove the throttle body from the air intake plenum (see Chapter 4).
16 Remove the EGR vacuum modulator (see Steps 20 and 21).
17 Remove the EGR pipe.
18 Remove the EGR mounting bolts **(see illustration)** and separate the EGR valve from the engine compartment.
19 Installation is the reverse of removal.

EGR vacuum modulator
20 Label and disconnect the vacuum hoses and remove the EGR vacuum modulator from it's bracket.
21 Installation is the reverse of removal.

7 Positive Crankcase Ventilation (PCV) system

General information
Refer to illustration 7.1
1 The Positive Crankcase Ventilation (PCV) system reduces hydrocarbon emissions by scavenging crankcase vapors. It does this by circulating fresh air from the air cleaner through the crankcase, where it mixes with blow-by gases and is then rerouted through a PCV valve to the intake manifold **(see illustration)**.
2 The main components of the PCV system are the PCV valve, a fresh air intake and the vacuum hoses connecting these components to the engine.
3 To maintain idle quality, the PCV valve restricts the flow when the intake manifold vacuum is high. If abnormal operating conditions (such as piston ring problems) arise, the system is designed to allow excessive amounts of blow-by gases to flow back through the crankcase

7.1 Diagram of the PCV system

vent tube into the air cleaner to be consumed by normal combustion.
4 This system directs the blow-by into the throttle body which, over time, can cause an oily residue build up in the area near the throttle plate. Consequently, it's a good idea to periodically clean this residue from the throttle body. Refer to Chapter 4 for this cleaning procedure.

Check
5 To check the valve, first pull it out of the grommet in the valve cover and shake the valve. It should rattle, indicating that it's not clogged with deposits. If the valve does not rattle, replace it with a new one.
6 Start the engine and allow it to idle, then place your finger over the valve opening. If vacuum is felt, the PCV valve is working properly. If no vacuum is felt, the PCV valve may be bad or the hose may be plugged. Also, check for vacuum leaks at the valve, filler cap and all the hoses.

Replacement
7 Pull straight up on the valve to remove it. Check the rubber grommet for cracks and distortion. If it's damaged, replace it.
8 If the valve is clogged, the hose is also probably plugged. Remove the hose and clean it with solvent.
9 After cleaning the hose, inspect it for damage, wear and deterioration. Make sure it fits snugly on the fittings.
10 If necessary, install a new PCV valve.
11 Install the clean PCV hose. Make sure that the PCV valve and hose are secure.

8 Catalytic converter

Refer to illustrations 8.2, 8.4 and 8.5
Note: *Because of a federally mandated extended warranty which covers emissions-related components such as the catalytic converter, check with a dealer service department before replacing the converter at your own expense.*

General description
1 To reduce hydrocarbon, carbon monoxide and oxides of nitrogen emissions, all vehicles are equipped with a three-way catalyst system which oxidizes and reduces these chemicals, converting them into

6

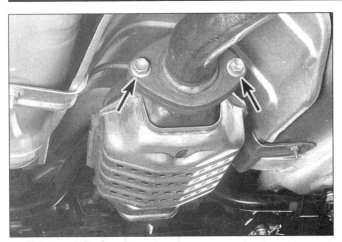

8.2 Be sure to spray penetrating lubricant onto the catalytic converter mounting bolts before attempting to unscrew them

harmless nitrogen, carbon dioxide and water.

2   The catalytic converter is mounted in the exhaust system much like a muffler **(see illustration)**.

Check

3   Periodically inspect the catalytic converter-to-exhaust pipe mating flanges and bolts. Make sure that there are no loose bolts and no leaks between the flanges.

4   Look for dents in or damage to the catalytic converter protector **(see illustration)**. If any part of the protector is damaged or dented enough to touch the converter, repair or replace it.

5   Inspect the heat insulator for damage. Make sure that there is adequate clearance between the heat insulator and the catalytic converter **(see illustration)**.

8.4 Periodically inspect the shield for dents and other damage - if a dent is deep enough to touch the surface of the converter, replace the shield

Heat Insulator

8.5 Periodically inspect the heat insulator to make sure there's adequate clearance between it and the converter

Replacement

6   To replace the catalytic converter, refer to Chapter 4.

Chapter 7 Part A
Manual transaxle

Contents

7A

Specifications

Torque specifications

Ft-lbs (unless otherwise indicated)

Back-up light switch	30
Upper transaxle-to-engine bolts **(see illustration 5.32)**	
Bolts A	47
Bolt B	34
Stiffener plate bolts	17
Lower transaxle-to-engine bolts	17

1   General information

The vehicles covered by this manual are equipped with a 5-speed manual transaxle or a 3- or 4-speed automatic transaxle. Information on the manual transaxle is included in this Part of Chapter 7. Service procedures for the automatic transaxle are contained in Chapter 7, Part B.

The manual transaxle is a compact, two-piece, lightweight aluminum alloy housing containing both the transmission and differential assemblies. A C50 transaxle is used with the 1.6L engine; a C52 unit is used with the 1.8L engine. Both units are virtually identical except for different first-gear ratios.

Because of the complexity, unavailability of replacement parts and special tools necessary, internal repair procedures for the manual transaxle are beyond the scope of this manual. For readers who wish to tackle a transaxle rebuild, exploded views and a brief *Manual transaxle overhaul - general information* Section are provided. The bulk of information in this Chapter is devoted to removal and installation procedures.

2.1 To disconnect the shift cables from the transaxle linkage, remove these two clips and washers (arrows)

2.2 To detach the shift cable assembly from the cable bracket, remove these two retainers (arrows) with a pair of pliers

2.5 To disconnect the shift cables from the shift lever, remove these clips and washers (arrow)

2   Shift cables - removal and installation

Refer to illustrations 2.1, 2.2 and 2.5

1   In the engine compartment, remove the retaining clips and washers and disconnect the shift cables from the selecting bellcrank **(see illustration)**.

2   Remove the cable retainers from the cable bracket **(see illustration)**.

3   Inside the vehicle, remove the floor console (see Chapter 11).

4   Remove the cable retainers from the shift lever base **(see illustration 3.3a or 3.3b)**.

5   Remove the retaining clips and washers from the cable ends **(see illustration)** and disconnect the cables from the shift lever assembly.

6   Trace the cable assembly to the firewall and remove the weatherproofing grommet. Pull the cable assembly through the firewall.

7   Installation is the reverse of removal.

3   Shift lever - removal and installation

Refer to illustrations 3.3a and 3.3b

1   Remove the center console (see Chapter 11).

2   Remove the shift cable retainers and disconnect both cables from the shift lever (see Section 2).

Shift Cable Grommet Retainer No. 2
No. 2 Grommet
No. 1 Grommet
Shift Cable Grommet Retainer No. 1

Shift Control Cable

Select Control Cable

Console Box Mounting Bracket

Shift Lever Assembly (Type A)

Console Box Mounting Bracket

Shift Lever Assembly (Type B)

3.3a Shift control cables and shift lever assembly details (1993 through 1995 models)

3.3b Shift control cables and shift lever assembly details (1996 and later models)

3   Remove the retaining bolts from the shift lever base **(see illustrations)** and detach the shift lever from the vehicle. **Note:** *If you're replacing the shift lever assembly, it could be either of the two units shown in each illustration. Take the shift lever assembly with you when purchasing a replacement unit to ensure that you get the right unit for your vehicle.*
4   Installation is the reverse of removal.

4   Back-up light switch - check and replacement

Check

1   The back-up light switch is located on top of the transaxle.
2   Turn the ignition key to the On position and move the shift lever to the Reverse position. The switch should close the back-up light circuit and turn on the back-up lights.
3   If it doesn't, check the back-up light fuse (see Chapter 12).
4   If the fuse is okay, verify that there's voltage available on the battery side of the switch (with the ignition turned to On).
5   If there's no voltage on the battery side of the switch, check the wire between the fuse and the switch; if there is voltage, put the shift lever in reverse and see if there's voltage on the ground side of the switch.
6   If there's no voltage on the ground side of the switch, replace the switch (see below); if there is voltage, note whether one or both back-up lights are out.
7   If only one bulb is out, replace it; if they're both out, the bulbs could be the problem, but it's more likely that the wire between the switch and the bulbs has an open somewhere.

Replacement

Refer to illustration 4.8

8   Disconnect the electrical connector from the back-up light switch **(see illustration).**
9   Unscrew and remove the old switch.
10   To test the new switch before installation, simply check continuity across the switch terminals: with the plunger depressed, there should be continuity; with the plunger free, there should be no continuity.
11   Screw in the new switch and tighten it securely.
12   Connect the electrical connector.
13   Check the switch to ensure that the circuit is working properly.

4.8 Unplug the electrical connector from the back-up light switch (arrow)

7A

5   Manual transaxle - removal and installation

Removal

Refer to illustrations 5.11a, 5.11b, 5.18, 5.19, 5.20, 5.22, 5.23 and 5.24

1   Disconnect the negative cable from the battery. **Caution:** *If the stereo in your vehicle is equipped with an anti-theft system, make sure you have the correct activation code before disconnecting the battery.*
2   Remove the air cleaner assembly (see Chapter 4).
3   Remove the coolant reservoir (see Chapter 3).
4   Remove the clutch release cylinder and the clutch hydraulic line (see Chapter 8).
5   Unplug the electrical connectors from the back-up light switch (see Section 4) and the speed sensor (see Chapter 6).
6   Locate the ground cable on top of the transaxle. Remove the cable retaining bolt and detach the ground cable from the transaxle.
7   Disconnect the shift cables from the transaxle (see Section 2).
8   Detach any wire harness clamps from the engine and/or transaxle and set the harnesses aside.
9   Remove the upper starter mounting bolt (see Chapter 5).
10   Remove the two upper and the single front transaxle-to-engine mounting bolts. Note the location of any ground connectors or brack-

5.11a Remove the left engine mount stay

5.11b Remove the left engine mount
retaining bolt

5.18 Disconnect the front engine mount

5.19 Remove the rear engine mount

5.20 Remove the center support member

5.22 On 1.6L models, remove the
stiffener plate

ets, so that they may be installed in their original location.

11   Remove the left engine mount stay and the left engine mount retaining bolt **(see illustrations)**.

12   Support the engine. This can be done from above by using an engine hoist, or by placing a jack (with a wood block as an insulator) under the engine oil pan. The engine must be supported at all times while the transaxle is out of the vehicle.

13   Loosen the wheel lug nuts. Raise the vehicle and support it securely on jackstands. Remove the wheels.

14   Remove the splash shields (see Chapter 2).

15   Drain the transaxle fluid (see Chapter 1).

16   Remove the driveaxles (see Chapter 8).

17   Remove the front exhaust pipe (see Chapter 4).

18   Disconnect the front engine mount **(see illustration)**.

19   Remove the rear engine mount **(see illustration)**.

20   Remove the center support member **(see illustration)**.

21   Remove the starter motor (see Chapter 5).

22   On 1.6L models, remove the stiffener plate **(see illustration)**.

23   On 1.8L models, remove the engine rear end plate **(see illustration)**.

24   Remove the left engine mount **(see illustration)**.

25   Support the transaxle with a jack (preferably a special jack made for this purpose). If you're using a floor jack, be sure to place a wood block between the lifting pad and the transaxle to protect the cast aluminum housing. Safety chains will help steady the transaxle on the jack.

26   Remove the rest of the bolts securing the transaxle to the engine.

27   Make a final check that all wires and hoses have been disconnected from the transaxle.

28   Lower the left (driver's) end of the engine, then roll the transaxle and jack toward the side of the vehicle. Once the input shaft is clear of the splines in the clutch hub, lower the transaxle and remove it from under the vehicle. Try to keep the transaxle as level as possible. **Caution:** *Do not depress the clutch pedal while the transaxle is removed from the vehicle.*

29   The clutch components can now be inspected (see Chapter 8). In

5.23 On 1.8L models, remove the engine
rear end plate

5.24 Remove the left engine mount

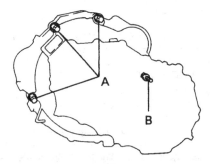

5.32 Tighten bolts A and B to the torque
listed in this Chapter's Specifications

most cases, new clutch components should be routinely installed whenever the transaxle is removed.

Installation

Refer to illustration 5.32

30   If removed, install the clutch components (see Chapter 8).

31   With the transaxle secured to the jack as on removal, raise it into position and then carefully slide it forward, engaging the input shaft with the splines in the clutch hub. Do not use excessive force to install the transaxle - if the input shaft does not slide into place, readjust the angle of the transaxle so it is level and/or turn the input shaft so the splines engage properly with the clutch.

32   Install the transaxle-to-engine bolts **(see illustration)**. Tighten the bolts to the torque listed in this Chapter's Specifications.

33   Install the transaxle mount nuts and bolts. Tighten all nuts and bolts securely.

34   Install any suspension components which were detached or removed. Tighten all nuts and bolts to the torque listed in the Chapter 10 Specifications.

35   Remove the jacks supporting the transaxle and the engine.

36   Install the various items removed previously. Refer to Chapter 4 for information regarding the exhaust pipe, Chapter 5 for the starter motor and Chapter 8 for the driveaxles.

37   Make sure that the wiring harness connectors for the back-up light switch and the speed sensor, and any other electrical devices, are plugged in. And make sure that all harness clamps are reattached to the engine and/or transaxle.

38   If the transaxle was drained, fill it with the specified lubricant to the proper level (see Chapter 1).

39   Lower the vehicle.

40   Connect the shift cables (see Section 3).

41   Connect the negative battery cable. Road test the vehicle to check for proper transaxle operation and check for leakage.

6   Manual transaxle overhaul - general information

Refer to illustrations 6.4a, 6.4b and 6.4c

1   Overhauling a manual transaxle is a difficult job for the do-it-your-selfer. It involves the disassembly and reassembly of many small parts. Numerous clearances must be precisely measured and, if necessary, changed with select-fit spacers and snap-rings. As a result, if transaxle problems arise, it can be removed and installed by a competent do-it-yourselfer, but overhaul should be left to a transmission repair shop. Rebuilt transaxles may be available - check with your dealer parts department and auto parts stores. At any rate, the time and money involved in an overhaul is almost sure to exceed the cost of a rebuilt unit.

2   Nevertheless, it's not impossible for an inexperienced mechanic to rebuild a transaxle if the special tools are available and the job is done in a deliberate step-by-step manner so nothing is overlooked.

3   The tools necessary for an overhaul include internal and external snap-ring pliers, a bearing puller, a slide hammer, a set of pin punches, a dial indicator and possibly a hydraulic press. In addition, a large, sturdy workbench and a vise or transaxle stand will be required.

4   During disassembly of the transaxle, make careful notes of how each piece comes off, where it fits in relation to other pieces and what holds it in place. Exploded views are included **(see illustrations)** to show where the parts go - but actually noting how they are installed when you remove the parts will make it much easier to get the transaxle back together.

5   Before taking the transaxle apart for repair, it will help if you have some idea what area of the transaxle is malfunctioning. Certain problems can be closely tied to specific areas in the transaxle, which can make component examination and replacement easier. Refer to the *Troubleshooting* section at the front of this manual for information regarding possible sources of trouble.

7A

6.4a An exploded view of the manual transaxle assembly (1 of 3)

Clutch Release Bearing
Clutch Release Fork Assembly
Clutch Release Fork Boot
Vehicle Speed Sensor
Vehicle Speed Sensor Driven Gear
Control Lever Housing Support Bracket
Oil Seal
Transaxle Case
Transaxle Case Receiver
Clutch Release Bearing Retainer
Plate Washer
Magnet
Differential Side Bearing Outer Race
Oil Seal
Input Shaft Front Bearing
Differential Case Assembly
Output Shaft Cover
Output Shaft Front Bearing

No. 1 Shift Fork

Reverse Shift Fork

Screw Plug

Spring Seat

Spring

Snap Ring

Ball

No. 1 Shift Fork Shaft

Reverse Shift Arm Bracket

No. 3 Shift Fork Shaft

No. 3 Shift Fork

Reverse Idler Gear

Thrust Washer

Idler Gear Shaft

Shift Head

Output Shaft Assembly

No. 2 Shift Fork

Input Shaft Assembly

No. 2 Shift Fork Shaft

5th Driven Gear

Snap Ring

Rear Bearing Retainer

Snap Ring

**6.4b An exploded view of the manual
transaxle assembly (2 of 3)**

Spacer

Needle Roller Bearing

5th Gear

Synchronizer Ring

No. 3 Hub Sleeve

Key Spring

Snap Ring

No. 3
Clutch Hub

Reverse Restrict Pin

Slotted Spring Pin

No. 2
Oil Receiver Pipe

Screw Plug

Lock Ball Assembly

Screw Plug

Outer Race

Plate Washer

Shift and Select
Lever Assembly

No. 1 Oil Receiver Pipe

**6.4c An exploded view of
the manual transaxle
assembly (3 of 3)**

Selecting Bellcrank

Oil Seal

Plug

Transmission Case
Cover

Transmission
Case

Plug

Chapter 7 Part B
Automatic transaxle

Contents

Specifications

Shift lock system

Shift lock solenoid resistance	
1993 and 1994	
A131L	30 to 35 ohms
A245E	21 to 27 ohms
1995 and later	21 to 27 ohms
Key interlock solenoid resistance	12.5 to 16.5 ohms

Torque specifications

	Ft-lbs (unless otherwise indicated)
Neutral start switch	48 in-lbs
Torque converter-to-driveplate bolts	
A131L	156 in-lbs
A245E	18
Transaxle-to-engine bolts	
A131L	47
A245E	
Upper bolts	47
Lower bolts **(see illustration 9.27)**	
1993 and 1994	
Bolt A	47
Bolt B	18
Bolt C	17
Bolt D	47
1995 and later	
Bolt A	17
Bolt B	18
Bolt C	34
Bolt D	47
Valve body bolts	84 in-lbs
Manual valve retaining bolts (A131L)	84 in-lbs
Wire retainer bolt (A245E)	56 in-lbs
Detent spring bolt(s)	84 in-lbs

7B

1 General information

All vehicles covered in this manual are equipped with either a 5-speed manual transaxle or a 3- or 4-speed automatic transaxle. All information on the automatic transaxle is included in this Part of Chapter 7. Information for the manual transaxle can be found in Part A of this Chapter.

The A131L is a three-speed automatic transaxle. Its shift points are controlled by the governor and the throttle valve. The A245E is an electronically controlled four-speed automatic transaxle with fourth gear being an overdrive gear. Shifts are attained by the use of shift solenoids, which are controlled by the Powertrain Control Module. Both transaxles utilize a lock-up torque converter.

Because of the complexity of the automatic transaxles and the specialized equipment necessary to perform most service operations, this Chapter contains only those procedures related to general diagnosis, routine maintenance, adjustment and removal and installation.

If the transaxle requires major repair work, it should be left to a dealer service department or an automotive or transmission repair shop. You can, however, remove and install the transaxle yourself and save the expense, even if the repair work is done by a transmission shop.

2 Diagnosis - general

Note: *Automatic transaxle malfunctions may be caused by five general conditions: poor engine performance, improper adjustments, hydraulic malfunctions, mechanical malfunctions or malfunctions in the computer or its signal network. Diagnosis of these problems should always begin with a check of the easily repaired items: fluid level and condition (see Chapter 1), shift linkage adjustment and throttle linkage adjustment. Next, perform a road test to determine if the problem has been corrected or if more diagnosis is necessary. If the problem persists after the preliminary tests and corrections are completed, additional diagnosis should be done by a dealer service department or transmission repair shop. Refer to the Troubleshooting section at the front of this manual for information on symptoms of transaxle problems.*

Preliminary checks

1 Drive the vehicle to warm the transaxle to normal operating temperature.

2 Check the fluid level as described in Chapter 1:

  a) *If the fluid level is unusually low, add enough fluid to bring the level within the designated area of the dipstick, then check for external leaks (see below).*

  b) *If the fluid level is abnormally high, drain off the excess, then check the drained fluid for contamination by coolant. The presence of engine coolant in the automatic transmission fluid indicates that a failure has occurred in the internal radiator walls that separate the coolant from the transmission fluid (see Chapter 3).*

  c) *If the fluid is foaming, drain it and refill the transaxle, then check for coolant in the fluid, or a high fluid level.*

3 Check the engine idle speed. **Note:** *If the engine is malfunctioning, do not proceed with the preliminary checks until it has been repaired and runs normally.*

4 Check the throttle valve cable for freedom of movement. Adjust it if necessary (see Section 4). **Note:** *The throttle cable may function properly when the engine is shut off and cold, but it may malfunction once the engine is hot. Check it cold and at normal engine operating temperature.*

5 Inspect the shift cable (see Section 5). Make sure that it's properly adjusted and that the cable operates smoothly.

Fluid leak diagnosis

6 Most fluid leaks are easy to locate visually. Repair usually consists of replacing a seal or gasket. If a leak is difficult to find, the following procedure may help.

7 Identify the fluid. Make sure it's transmission fluid and not engine oil or brake fluid (automatic transmission fluid is a deep red color).

8 Try to pinpoint the source of the leak. Drive the vehicle several miles, then park it over a large sheet of cardboard. After a minute or two, you should be able to locate the leak by determining the source of the fluid dripping onto the cardboard.

9 Make a careful visual inspection of the suspected component and the area immediately around it. Pay particular attention to gasket mating surfaces. A mirror is often helpful for finding leaks in areas that are hard to see.

10 If the leak still cannot be found, clean the suspected area thoroughly with a degreaser or solvent, then dry it.

11 Drive the vehicle for several miles at normal operating temperature and varying speeds. After driving the vehicle, visually inspect the suspected component again.

12 Once the leak has been located, the cause must be determined before it can be properly repaired. If a gasket is replaced but the sealing flange is bent, the new gasket will not stop the leak. The bent flange must be straightened.

13 Before attempting to repair a leak, check to make sure that the following conditions are corrected or they may cause another leak. **Note:** *Some of the following conditions cannot be fixed without highly specialized tools and expertise. Such problems must be referred to a transmission shop or a dealer service department.*

Gasket leaks

14 Check the pan periodically. Make sure the bolts are tight, no bolts are missing, the gasket is in good condition and the pan is flat (dents in the pan may indicate damage to the valve body inside).

15 If the pan gasket is leaking, the fluid level or the fluid pressure may be too high, the vent may be plugged, the pan bolts may be too tight, the pan sealing flange may be warped, the sealing surface of the transaxle housing may be damaged, the gasket may be damaged or the transaxle casting may be cracked or porous. If sealant instead of gasket material has been used to form a seal between the pan and the transaxle housing, it may be the wrong sealant.

Seal leaks

16 If a transaxle seal is leaking, the fluid level or pressure may be too high, the vent may be plugged, the seal bore may be damaged, the seal itself may be damaged or improperly installed, the surface of the shaft protruding through the seal may be damaged or a loose bearing may be causing excessive shaft movement.

17 Make sure the dipstick tube seal is in good condition and the tube is properly seated. Periodically check the area around the speedometer gear or sensor for leakage. If transmission fluid is evident, check the O-ring for damage.

Case leaks

18 If the case itself appears to be leaking, the casting is porous and will have to be repaired or replaced.

19 Make sure the oil cooler hose fittings are tight and in good condition.

Fluid comes out vent pipe or fill tube

20 If this condition occurs, the transaxle is overfilled, there is coolant in the fluid, the case is porous, the dipstick is incorrect, the vent is plugged or the drain-back holes are plugged.

3 Oil seal replacement

1 Oil leaks frequently occur due to wear of the driveaxle oil seals and/or the speedometer drive gear oil seal and O-rings. Replacement of these seals is relatively easy, since the repairs can usually be performed without removing the transaxle from the vehicle.

Driveaxle oil seals

Refer to illustrations 3.4 and 3.6

2 The driveaxle oil seals are located on the sides of the transaxle,

3.4 Carefully pry out the driveaxle oil seal with a seal removal tool or a large screwdriver; make sure you don't damage the seal bore or the new seal may leak

3.6 Use a seal installer, a large socket or a piece of pipe to install the new seal

3.9 Unplug the speed sensor electrical connector (arrow), remove the bolt (arrow) and pull the speed sensor unit straight out of the transaxle

where the inner ends of the driveaxles are splined into the differential side gears. If you suspect that a driveaxle oil seal is leaking, raise the vehicle and support it securely on jackstands. If the seal is leaking, you'll see lubricant on the side of the transaxle, below the seal.

3   Remove the driveaxle (see Chapter 8).

4   Using a screwdriver or pry bar, carefully pry the oil seal out of the transaxle bore **(see illustration)**.

5   If the oil seal cannot be removed with a screwdriver or pry bar, a special oil seal removal tool (available at auto parts stores) will be required.

6   Using a seal installer, a large section of pipe or a large deep socket as a drift, install the new oil seal. Drive it into the bore squarely and make sure it's completely seated **(see illustration)**. On A131L transaxles, a fully-seated seal should be flush with the surface of the transaxle housing; on A245E units, a fully-seated left seal should be recessed about 13/64-inch, a right seal about 1/8-inch.

7   Lubricate the lip of the new seal with multi-purpose grease, then install the driveaxle (see Chapter 8). Be careful not to damage the lip of the new seal.

Speed sensor O-ring

Refer to illustrations 3.9 and 3.10

8   The speed sensor is located on the transaxle housing. Look for lubricant around the sensor housing to determine if the O-ring is leaking.

9   Unplug the electrical connector and unbolt the vehicle speed sensor from the transaxle **(see illustration)**.

10   Using a scribe or a small screwdriver, remove the O-ring from the sensor **(see illustration)** and install a new O-ring. Lubricate the new O-ring with automatic transmission fluid to protect it during installation of the sensor.

11   Installation is the reverse of removal.

4   Throttle valve (TV) cable - check, adjustment and replacement

Check

Refer to illustrations 4.3a and 4.3b

1   Remove the duct between the air cleaner and the throttle body (see Chapter 5).

2   Have an assistant press the accelerator pedal all the way to the floor and hold it while you measure the distance between the end of the boot and the stopper on the cable.

3   If the measurement taken is as shown **(see illustrations)**, the cable is properly adjusted. If it's out-of range, adjust it as follows.

Adjustment

4   Have your assistant continue to hold the pedal down while you loosen the adjusting nuts and adjust the cable housing so that the distance between the end of the boot and the stopper on the cable is within the range shown.

5   Tighten the adjusting nuts securely, recheck the clearance and

7B

3.10 Remove the oil seal O-ring from the speed sensor with a small screwdriver; make sure you don't scratch the surface of the sensor or gouge the O-ring groove

Adjusting Nut

Rubber Boot

1/32 to 3/64 inch

Cable Stopper

Outer Cable

4.3a Throttle cable adjustment details (A131L)

1/32 to 3/64 inch

4.3b Throttle cable adjustment details (A245E)

4.11a On A131L models, remove the two bolts that attach the apply tube bracket, remove the bracket . . .

4.11b . . . and carefully pry out both ends of all four oil tubes - make sure you don't bend or kink the tubes

4.13 Remove the manual detent spring

4.14a On A131L models, remove the manual valve . . .

4.14b . . . remove all 14 valve body retaining bolts and remove the valve body

4.14c On A245E models, remove the wire retainer . . .

make sure the throttle valve opens all the way when the throttle is depressed.

Replacement

Refer to illustrations 4.11a, 4.11b, 4.13, 4.14a, 4.14b, 4.14c, 4.14d and 4.15

6   Loosen the cable locknut and detach the cable from the bracket at the throttle body.
7   Disconnect the cable from the throttle linkage.
8   Detach the cable from the bracket on the transaxle.
9   Follow the cable down to the front of the transaxle, where it enters the transaxle housing right behind the neutral start switch. Remove the cable hold-down bolt.

10   Remove the pan, drain the transaxle fluid and remove the filter (see Chapter 1).
11   On A131L models, remove the oil tubes **(see illustrations)**.
12   On A245E models, unplug the electrical connectors for the solenoids.
13   Remove the manual detent spring **(see illustration)**.
14   Remove the manual valve (A131L) and valve body **(see illustrations)**.
15   Disconnect the throttle valve cable from the cam on top of the valve body **(see illustration)**.
16   Installation is the reverse of removal. Be sure to tighten the valve body, manual valve, wire retainer and detent spring bolts to the torque listed in this Chapter's Specifications. Refer to Chapter 1 for the torque

4.14d . . . remove all 17 valve body retaining bolts and remove the valve body

4.15 Disengage the plug on the lower end of the throttle valve cable from the cam on top of the valve body

5.1a To disconnect the shift cable from the manual shift lever at the transaxle, remove this nut

5.1b To detach the shift cable from the bracket on the front of the transaxle, pry off this clip

5.3a Before attempting to remove the shift lever handle, remove this lock . . .

5.3b . . . then carefully extract the two white overdrive leads from the blue electrical connector at the back of the shift lever base

5.3c Remove the four shift lever base bolts, tip the base on its side and remove the overdrive leads; note how they're routed forward, then back - they must be routed exactly the same way when installing the shift lever handle and overdrive switch

specifications for the pan bolts and the type and quantity of transaxle fluid required to refill the transaxle.

5   Shift cable - removal, installation and adjustment

Removal and installation

Refer to illustrations 5.1a, 5.1b, 5.3a, 5.3b, 5.3c, 5.3d, 5.4a, 5.4b, 5.5a, 5.5b and 5.6

1   Disconnect the shift cable from the manual shift lever at the transaxle and detach it from the bracket on the front of the transaxle **(see illustrations)**.

2   Remove the center console (see Chapter 11).

3   **Caution:** *Do not attempt to remove the shift lever handle until the overdrive switch leads have been disconnected from the blue connector at the rear of the shift lever base, or you will break the leads to the switch.* On A245E models, removing the shift lever handle is tricky because the leads for the overdrive switch are routed down through the handle, under the shift lever base and back to the blue connector at the rear of the base. And there is no connector between the switch in the handle and the blue connector. The two white leads are an integral part of the overdrive switch. If you try to pull them from the switch, you will have to buy a new switch. Fortunately, it's not absolutely necessary to remove the shift lever handle, *unless* you need to replace the handle itself, the gear-position indicator panel or the shift lever base. If necessary, unbolt the shift lever base (four bolts), follow the two white leads back to the blue connector at the rear of the shift lever base,

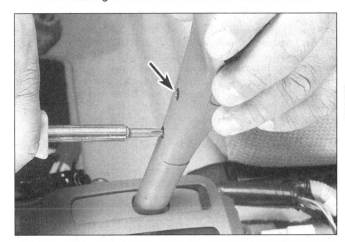

5.3d To remove the shift lever handle, remove these two screws and pull the handle straight up, being extremely careful not to damage the two white leads for the overdrive switch

carefully extract both leads from the connector, remove the shift lever handle retaining screws and remove the handle **(see illustrations)**. Note how the overdrive switch leads are routed forward, then back, underneath the shift lever base, and make sure you route them the same way during installation.

7B

5.4a To detach the gear position indicator panel from the shift lever base, remove these four screws (arrows) . . .

5.4b . . . then detach the shift indicator panel light and remove the panel

5.5a To disconnect the shift cable from the shift lever, pull out the retaining clip . . .

5.5b . . . and pry the cable from the pin on the shift lever

5.6 To detach the shift cable from the shift lever base, pry off this clip

4   Remove the gear-position indicator panel retaining screws, lift up the gear-position indicator panel and disconnect the light bulb **(see illustrations)**. If you removed the shift lever handle, remove the gear-position indicator panel; if you didn't remove the shift lever handle, tie the gear-position indicator panel to the shift lever handle so that you have room to work.

5   Remove the retaining clip and disconnect the shift cable from the shift lever **(see illustrations)**.

6   Remove the retaining clip from the front edge of the shift lever base **(see illustration)**.

7   Pull the cable through the grommet in the firewall.

8   Installation is the reverse of removal.

9   When you're done, adjust the shift cable.

Adjustment

10   Loosen the nut on the manual shift lever at the transaxle **(see illustration 5.1)**.

11   Push the lever toward the right side of the vehicle until it stops, then return it two notches to the Neutral position.

12   Move the shift lever inside the vehicle to the Neutral position.

13   While holding the lever with a slight pressure toward the Reverse position, tighten the nut securely.

14   Check the operation of the transaxle in each shift lever position (try to start the engine in each gear - the starter should operate in the Park and Neutral positions only).

6   Neutral start switch - check, adjustment and replacement

Adjustment

Refer to illustration 6.4

1   If the engine will start with the shift lever in any position other than Park or Neutral, adjust the neutral start switch.

2   Apply the park brake and block the rear wheels. Raise the front of the vehicle and place it securely on jackstands. Shift the transaxle into Neutral.

3   Unplug the electrical connector from the switch and loosen the switch retaining bolts.

4   Touch the ohmmeter leads to the switch terminals inside the electrical connector and rotate the switch until there is continuity between the terminals, indicating that it's now in the Neutral position **(see illustration)**. Tighten the bolts securely.

Replacement

Refer to illustration 6.11

5   Disconnect the negative cable from the battery. **Caution:** *If the stereo in your vehicle is equipped with an anti-theft system, make sure you have the correct activation code before disconnecting the battery.*

6   Shift the transaxle into Neutral.

6.4 With the transaxle in Neutral, check continuity with an ohmmeter as shown: loosen the switch retaining bolts, touch the leads of the ohmmeter to the switch terminals inside the electrical connector and rotate the switch until the meter indicates continuity and tighten the bolts

7   Remove the nut and lift off the shift lever.
8   Unplug the electrical connector.
9   Remove the retaining bolts and lift the switch off the shift shaft.
10   To install, line up the flats on the shift shaft with the flats in the switch and push the switch onto the shaft.
11   Rotate the switch until the neutral basic line aligns with the groove (see illustration). Tighten the bolts securely and connect the electrical connector.

6.11 Rotate the switch until the neutral basic line aligns with the groove and tighten the bolts

12   Install the shift lever, connect the negative battery cable and verify the engine will not start with the shift lever in any position other than Park or Neutral, if necessary follow the adjustment procedure above.

7   Shift lock system - description, check and component replacement

Description

Refer to illustrations 7.1a and 7.1b

1   The shift lock system (see illustrations) prevents the shift lever from being shifted out of Park or Neutral until the brake pedal is applied.

7.1a Shift lock system components

7B

7.1b Shift lock system electrical schematic

7.4 Terminal guide, key interlock solenoid

7.10 Terminal guide, shift lock solenoid

O———O: Continuity

Terminal Shift Position	P	P₁	P₂
P position (Release button is pushed)	O	O	
P position (Release button is pushed)	O	O	
	O		O
R,N,D,2,L position	O		O

7.13 Terminal guide and continuity table, shift lock control switch

Key interlock solenoid

Refer to illustration 7.4

2   Remove the steering column covers (see Chapter 11).
3   Unplug the electrical connector for the key interlock solenoid.
4   Using an ohmmeter, measure the resistance between the indicated terminals **(see illustration)**, and compare your measurements with the resistance listed in this Chapter's Specifications.
5   Apply battery voltage between the same two terminals. Verify that the solenoid makes an audible "click" when energized.
6   If the key interlock solenoid fails either of these tests, replace it.
7   Install the steering column covers.

Shift lock solenoid

Refer to illustration 7.10

8   Remove the floor console (see Chapter 11).
9   Unplug the shift lock solenoid connector.
10   Using an ohmmeter, measure the resistance between the indicated terminals **(see illustration)**, and compare your measurement with the resistance listed in this Chapter's Specifications.
11   Apply battery voltage to the same two terminals and verify that there's an audible "click" from the solenoid.
12   If the shift lock solenoid fails either of these tests, replace it.

Shift lock control switch

Refer to illustration 7.13

13   Verify that there's continuity between the indicated terminals in

A   B

IG   ACC   SLS ⊖   SLS ⊕

STP   E   KLS ⊕   P₂   P   P₁

Control Computer

7.15 Terminal guide and voltage table, shift lock control computer

Connector	Terminal	Measuring condition		Voltage (V)
A	ACC − E		Ignition switch ACC position	10 − 14
	IG − E		ignition switch ON position	10 − 14
	STP − E		Depress brake pedal	10 − 14
	KLS − E	①	Ignition switch ACC position and P position	0
		②	Ignition switch ACC position and except P position	8 − 14
		③	(Approx-after one second)	6 − 9
B	SLS ⊕ − SLS ⊖	①	Ignition switch ON position and P position	0
		②	Depress brake pedal	8.5 − 13.5
		③	(Approx-after 20 seconds)	5.5 − 9.5
		④	Except P position	0
	P₁ − P	①	Ignition switch ON, P position and depress brake pedal	0
		②	Except P position	9 − 13.5
	P₂ − P₁	③	Ignition switch ACC position and P position	9 − 13.5
		④	Except P position	0

each shift lever position (see illustration).

14   If the shift lock control switch fails any of these tests, replace it.

Shift lock control computer

Refer to illustration 7.15

15   Using a voltmeter, measure the voltage at the indicated terminals (see illustration) and compare your measurements with the voltage values specified in the accompanying illustration. Note: *Do NOT unplug the computer connector; instead, "backprobe" the connector (probe through the back of the wiring harness connector with a small T-head needle).*

16   If the shift lock control computer fails any of the tests, replace it.

17   Install the floor console (see Chapter 11).

8   Transaxle mount - check and replacement

Refer to illustration 8.1

1   Insert a large screwdriver or prybar between the transaxle mount and the body and try to pry it away from the body (see illustration).

2   The transaxle mount should not move excessively. If it does, replace the mount.

3   To replace a mount, support the transaxle with a jack, remove the nuts and bolts and remove the mount. It may be necessary to raise the transaxle slightly to provide enough clearance to remove the mount.

4   Installation is the reverse of removal.

7B

8.1 To check any of the three transaxle mounts, insert a large screwdriver or prybar between the mount and the body as shown, and try to lever the mount from side to side or up and down - there should be a little movement, but it should be firm; if the mount moves too easily or looks cracked and torn, replace it (upper left transaxle mount shown)

9.4 Remove these bolts (arrows) from the upper side of the left transaxle mount (there are two more bolts, but they're underneath, on the front side)

9.5 Remove this bolt (arrow) and detach the ground cable from the top of the transaxle

9   Automatic transaxle - removal and installation

Removal

Refer to illustrations 9.4, 9.5, 9.6, 9.14a, 9.14b, 9.14c, 9.16, 9.19a, 9.19b, 9.20 and 9.21

1   Detach the cable from the negative battery terminal. **Caution:** *If the stereo in your vehicle is equipped with an anti-theft system, make sure you have the correct activation code before disconnecting the battery.*

2   If you're planning to reuse the same transaxle, simply remove the cable retaining clip from the bracket and disconnect the throttle valve cable from the linkage on the throttle body; if you're planning to replace the transaxle, disconnect the throttle valve cable from the valve body (in either case, see Section 4).

3   Remove the air cleaner housing (see Chapter 4).

4   Remove the upper bolts from the left transaxle mount **(see illustration)**. (There are two more bolts, but you won't be able to reach them until the vehicle is raised.)

5   Detach the ground cable **(see illustration)** from the transaxle. Unplug the electrical connectors for the speed sensor (see Section 3), neutral start switch (see Section 6) and solenoid (A245E only), next to the neutral start switch on the front left corner of the transaxle. Detach any wiring harness clamps from the transaxle and set the wiring harnesses aside.

6   Remove the upper transaxle-to-engine bolts **(see illustration)**. Remove the upper transaxle-to-starter motor bolt (see Chapter 5).

7   Raise the vehicle and support it securely on jackstands.

8   Remove the engine under covers.

9   Disconnect the shift cable from the transaxle (see Section 5).

10   Remove the exhaust pipe section between the exhaust manifold and the catalytic converter (see Chapter 4).

11   Drain the transaxle fluid and on three-speed models, the differential fluid (see Chapter 1).

12   Remove the driveaxles (see Chapter 8). **Note:** *It's not absolutely necessary to completely remove the driveaxles; you can detach the inner CV joints and suspend them out of the way. However, you'll have more room to work if you remove the driveaxles. And this is an good time to inspect the CV joint boots for tears and deterioration and, if necessary, repack them with new CV joint grease* (see Chapter 8).

13   Support the engine using a hoist from above, or a jack and a wood block under the oil pan to spread the load.

14   Remove the bolts and nuts that attach the center support brace and suspension member to the vehicle **(see illustrations)**.

15   Detach the starter motor leads, remove the lower starter-to-transaxle bolt and remove the starter (see Chapter 5).

16   Detach the oil cooler line retaining clamps from the transaxle, then disconnect the two line fittings from the transaxle **(see illustration)**.

17   To detach the dipstick tube from the transaxle, remove the single bracket bolt from the front of the bellhousing, then pull straight up

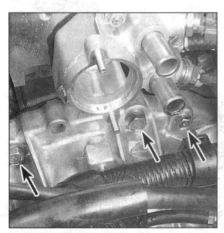

9.6 Remove the two upper transaxle-to-engine bolts (arrows); the bolt on the right (arrow) is the upper starter bolt

9.14a Remove the four front support brace bolts (arrows) . . .

9.14b . . . the three rear support brace nuts (arrows) . . .

9.14c ... and the five bolts (arrows) from each suspension member (left suspension member shown, right member identical)

9.16 Unbolt the oil cooler line clamps (arrows) from the transaxle, unscrew the line fittings (arrows) and disconnect the lines from the transaxle

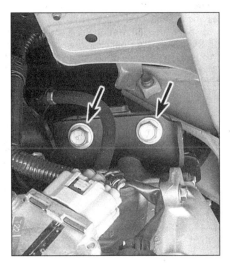

9.19a Remove these two bolts (arrows) from the underside of the left transaxle mount

9.19b Remove the nut and through bolt (arrows) from the front and rear mounts (front mount shown, rear mount similar)

9.20 Mark the relationship of the torque converter to the driveplate to ensure proper dynamic balance when it's reattached, then remove all six torque converter bolts (bolt showing in access window) by rotating the crankshaft to bring each bolt to the bottom, where you can get at it

on the tube.

18 Support the transaxle with a jack - preferably a special jack made for this purpose. Safety chains will help steady the transaxle on the jack.

19 Remove the remaining two bolts from the underside of the transaxle mount (see illustration). Remove the bolts from the front and rear mounts (see illustration) so that the engine can be tilted slightly to the left to allow easier removal and installation of the transaxle.

20 Remove the torque converter inspection cover. Mark the relationship of the torque converter to the driveplate so they can be installed in the same position (see illustration). Remove the six torque converter mounting bolts. Turn the crankshaft for access to each one in turn.

21 Remove the lower engine-to-transaxle bolts: the three lowest bolts are shown in illustration 9.20, and there's another bolt on the backside of the engine, right below the lower starter bolt. Remove the lower transaxle-to-engine bolt, on the front side of the transaxle (see illustration).

22 Move the transaxle to the side to disengage it from the engine block dowel pins and make sure the torque converter is detached from the driveplate. Secure the torque converter to the transaxle so that it will not fall out during removal. Lower the transaxle from the vehicle.

7B

9.21 Remove this front lower transaxle-to-engine bolt (arrow)

Installation

Refer to illustration 9.27

23 Make sure that the torque converter is securely engaged in the transaxle prior to installation.

24 With the transaxle secured to the jack, raise it into position. Be sure to keep it level so the torque converter does not slide forward. Connect the cooler lines.

25 Move the transaxle carefully into place until the dowel pins are engaged and the torque converter is engaged.

26 Rotate the torque converter to align the bolt holes with the holes in the driveplate. The match marks on the torque converter and driveplate, made during step 20, must align.

27 Install the lower transaxle-to-engine bolts **(see illustration)** and tighten them to the torque listed in this Chapter's Specifications.

28 Install the torque converter-to-driveplate bolts. Tighten them to the torque listed in this Chapter's Specifications. Install the torque converter cover.

29 Install the support brace and suspension member. Tighten the bolts and nuts securely.

30 Remove the jacks supporting the transaxle and the engine.

31 Install the starter motor (see Chapter 5). (It's easier to install the upper bolt after the vehicle has been lowered.)

32 Install the dipstick tube into the transaxle and attach the dipstick bracket to the transaxle.

33 Connect the oil cooler line fittings and the line retaining clamps to the transaxle.

34 Install and/or connect the driveaxles to the transaxle (see Chapter 8).

35 Install and adjust the neutral start switch (see Section 6).

36 Connect and adjust the shift cable (see Section 5) and the throttle valve cable (see Section 4).

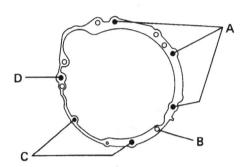

9.27 A245E transaxle-to-engine bolt torque guide - refer to the torque listed in this Chapter's Specifications for each bolt

37 Plug in the electrical connectors for the solenoid (A245E), neutral start switch and vehicle speed sensor. Make sure that the wiring harnesses are routed properly and clamped to the transaxle housing.

38 Install the exhaust pipe between the exhaust manifold and the catalytic converter (see Chapter 5).

39 Remove the jackstands and lower the vehicle.

40 Install the upper transaxle bolts **(see illustration 9.27)** and tighten them to the torque listed in this Chapter's Specifications. Install the upper starter motor bolt, if you haven't already done so, and tighten it to the torque listed in this Chapter's Specifications.

41 Fill the transaxle with the proper type and amount of fluid (see Chapter 1). Run the vehicle and check for fluid leaks.

Chapter 8
Clutch and driveaxles

Contents

Specifications

Clutch

Fluid type	See Chapter 1
Pedal freeplay..	See Chapter 1
Driveaxle standard length	
Saginaw type	
Left driveaxle...	21-17/64 inches
Right driveaxle	33-3/4 inches
Toyota type	
Left driveaxle...	20-51/64 inches +/- 13/64-inch
Right driveaxle	33-11/64 inches +/- 13/64-inch

Torque specifications

	Ft-lbs (unless otherwise indicated)
Clutch master cylinder mounting nuts..	108 in-lbs
Clutch pressure plate-to-flywheel bolts...	168 in-lbs
Clutch release cylinder mounting bolts	108 in-lbs
Driveaxle/hub nut...	159
Wheel lug nuts	See Chapter 1

8

Release Bearing with Hub

Release Fork

Flywheel

Clutch Disc

Clutch Cover

Boot

2.1 Typical clutch assembly details

1   General information

The information in this Chapter deals with the components from the rear of the engine to the front wheels, except for the transaxle, which is dealt with in Chapters 7A and 7B. For the purposes of this Chapter, these components are grouped into two categories: clutch and driveaxles. Separate Sections within this Chapter offer general descriptions and checking procedures for both groups.

Since nearly all the procedures covered in this Chapter involve working under the vehicle, make sure it's securely supported on sturdy jackstands or a hoist where the vehicle can be easily raised and lowered.

2   Clutch - description and check

Refer to illustration 2.1

1   All vehicles with a manual transaxle use a single dry plate, diaphragm spring type clutch **(see illustration)**. The clutch disc has a splined hub which allows it to slide along the splines of the transaxle input shaft. The clutch and pressure plate are held in contact by spring pressure exerted by the diaphragm in the pressure plate.

2   The clutch release system is operated by hydraulic pressure. The hydraulic release system consists of the clutch pedal, a master cylinder and fluid reservoir, the hydraulic line, a slave cylinder which actuates the clutch release lever and the clutch release (or throw-out) bearing.

3   When pressure is applied to the clutch pedal to release the clutch, hydraulic pressure is exerted against the outer end of the clutch release lever. As the lever pivots, the shaft fingers push against the release bearing. The bearing pushes against the fingers of the diaphragm spring of the pressure plate assembly, which in turn releases the clutch plate.

4   Terminology can be a problem regarding the clutch components because common names have in some cases changed from that used by the manufacturer. For example, the driven plate is also called the clutch plate or disc, the pressure plate assembly is sometimes referred to as the clutch cover, the clutch release bearing is sometimes called a throw-out bearing, and the release cylinder is sometimes called the operating or slave cylinder.

5   Other than replacing components that have obvious damage, some preliminary checks should be performed to diagnose a clutch system failure.

a) *The first check should be of the fluid level in the clutch master cylinder (see Chapter 1). If the fluid level is low, add fluid as necessary and inspect the hydraulic clutch system for leaks. If the master cylinder reservoir has run dry, bleed the system (see Section 7) and retest the clutch operation.*

b) *To check "clutch spin down time," run the engine at normal idle speed with the transaxle in Neutral (clutch pedal up - engaged). Disengage the clutch (pedal down), wait several seconds and shift the transaxle into Reverse. No grinding noise should be heard. A grinding noise would most likely indicate a problem in the pressure plate or the clutch disc.*

c) *To check for complete clutch release, run the engine (with the parking brake applied to prevent movement) and hold the clutch pedal approximately 1/2-inch from the floor. Shift the transaxle between 1st gear and Reverse several times. If the shift is not smooth, component failure is indicated. Check the release cylinder pushrod travel. With the clutch pedal depressed completely the release cylinder pushrod should extend substantially. If it doesn't, check the fluid level in the clutch master cylinder.*

d) *Visually inspect the clutch pedal bushing at the top of the clutch pedal to make sure there is no sticking or excessive wear.*

e) *Under the vehicle, check that the clutch release lever is solidly mounted on the ball stud.*

3   Clutch components - removal, inspection and installation

Warning: *Dust produced by clutch wear and deposited on clutch components may contain asbestos, which is hazardous to your health. DO NOT blow it out with compressed air and DO NOT inhale it. DO NOT use gasoline or petroleum based solvents to remove the dust. Brake system cleaner should be used to flush the dust into a drain pan. After the clutch components are wiped clean with a rag, dispose of the contaminated rags and cleaner in a labeled, covered container.*

Removal

Refer to illustration 3.6

1   Access to the clutch components is normally accomplished by removing the transaxle, leaving the engine in the vehicle. If, of course, the engine is being removed for major overhaul, then the opportunity

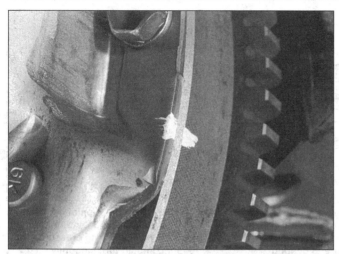

3.6   Mark the relationship of the pressure plate to the flywheel (in case you're going to reuse the same pressure plate)

3.10   Examine the clutch disc for evidence of excessive wear, such as smeared friction material, chewed-up rivets, worn hub splines and distorted damper cushions or springs

should always be taken to check the clutch for wear and replace worn components as necessary. However, the relatively low cost of the clutch components compared to the time and labor involved in gaining access to them warrants their replacement any time the engine or transaxle is removed, unless they are new or in near-perfect condition. The following procedures assume that the engine will stay in place.

2   Remove the release cylinder (see Section 6). Hang it out of the way with a piece of wire - it isn't necessary to disconnect the hose.

3   Remove the transaxle from the vehicle (see Chapter 7A). Support the engine while the transaxle is out. Preferably, an engine hoist should be used to support it from above. However, if a jack is used underneath the engine, make sure a piece of wood is used between the jack and oil pan to spread the load. **Caution:** *The pick-up for the oil pump is very close to the bottom of the oil pan. If the pan is bent or distorted in any way, engine oil starvation could occur.*

4   The release fork and release bearing can remain attached to the transaxle for the time being.

5   To support the clutch disc during removal, install a clutch alignment tool through the clutch disc hub.

6   Carefully inspect the flywheel and pressure plate for indexing marks. The marks are usually an X, an O or a white letter. If they cannot be found, scribe marks yourself so the pressure plate and the flywheel will be in the same alignment during installation **(see illustration)**.

7   Slowly loosen the pressure plate-to-flywheel bolts. Work in a diagonal pattern and loosen each bolt a little at a time until all spring pressure is relieved. Then hold the pressure plate securely and completely remove the bolts, followed by the pressure plate and clutch disc.

Inspection

Refer to illustrations 3.10, 3.12a and 3.12b

8   Ordinarily, when a problem occurs in the clutch, it can be attributed to wear of the clutch driven plate assembly (clutch disc). However, all components should be inspected at this time.

9   Inspect the flywheel for cracks, heat checking, score marks and other damage. If the imperfections are slight, a machine shop can resurface it to make it flat and smooth. Refer to Chapter 2 for the flywheel removal procedure.

10   Inspect the lining on the clutch disc. There should be at least 1/16-inch of lining above the rivet heads. Check for loose rivets, distortion, cracks, broken springs and other obvious damage **(see illustration)**. As mentioned above, ordinarily the clutch disc is replaced as a matter of course, so if in doubt about the condition, replace it with a new one.

11   The release bearing should be replaced along with the clutch disc (see Section 4).

12   Check the machined surface and the diaphragm spring fingers of the pressure plate **(see illustrations)**. If the surface is grooved or

3.12a   Replace the pressure plate if any of these conditions are noted

3.12b   Examine the pressure plate friction surface for score marks, cracks and evidence of overheating (blue spots)

otherwise damaged, replace the pressure plate assembly. Also check for obvious damage, distortion, cracking, etc. Light glazing can be removed with emery cloth or sandpaper. If a new pressure plate is indicated, new or factory rebuilt units are available.

8

3.14 Center the clutch disc in the pressure plate with a clutch alignment tool

4.3 Reach behind the release lever and disengage the lever from the ball stud by pulling on the retention spring, then remove the lever and bearing

4.4 To check the operation of the bearing, hold it by the outer race and rotate the inner race while applying pressure - the bearing should turn smoothly - if it doesn't, replace it

Installation

Refer to illustration 3.14

13   Before installation, carefully wipe the flywheel and pressure plate machined surfaces clean. It's important that no oil or grease is on these surfaces or the lining of the clutch disc. Handle these parts only with clean hands.

14   Position the clutch disc and pressure plate with the clutch held in place with an alignment tool **(see illustration)**. Make sure it's installed properly (most replacement clutch plates will be marked "flywheel side" or something similar - if not marked, install the clutch disc with the damper springs or cushion toward the transaxle).

15   Tighten the pressure plate-to-flywheel bolts only finger tight, working around the pressure plate.

16   Center the clutch disc by ensuring the alignment tool is through the splined hub and into the recess in the crankshaft. Wiggle the tool up, down or side-to-side as needed to bottom the tool. Tighten the pressure plate-to-flywheel bolts a little at a time, working in a criss-cross pattern to prevent distortion of the cover. After all of the bolts are snug, tighten them to the torque listed in this Chapter's Specifications. Remove the alignment tool.

17   Using high-temperature grease, lubricate the inner groove of the release bearing (see Section 4). Also place grease on the release lever contact areas and the transaxle input shaft bearing retainer.

18   Install the clutch release bearing (see Section 4).

19   Install the transaxle, release cylinder and all components removed previously, tightening all fasteners to the proper torque specifications.

4   Clutch release bearing and lever - removal, inspection and installation

Warning: *Dust produced by clutch wear and deposited on clutch components may contain asbestos, which is hazardous to your health. DO NOT blow it out with compressed air and DO NOT inhale it. DO NOT use gasoline or petroleum-based solvents to remove the dust. Brake system cleaner should be used to flush it into a drain pan. After the clutch components are wiped clean with a rag, dispose of the contaminated rags and cleaner in a labeled, covered container.*

Removal

Refer to illustration 4.3

1   Disconnect the negative cable from the battery. **Caution:** *If the stereo in your vehicle is equipped with an anti-theft system, make sure you have the correct activation code before disconnecting the battery.*

2   Remove the transaxle (see Chapter 7).

3   Remove the clutch release lever from the ball stud, then remove the bearing from the lever **(see illustration)**.

4.5 Apply a light coat of high-temperature grease to the transaxle bearing retainer and also fill the release bearing groove

4.6 Apply high temperature grease to the release lever in the areas indicated

Inspection

Refer to illustration 4.4

4   Hold the bearing by the outer race and rotate the inner race while applying pressure **(see illustration)**. If the bearing doesn't turn smoothly or if it's noisy, replace the bearing/hub assembly with a new one. Wipe the bearing with a clean rag and inspect it for damage, wear and cracks. Don't immerse the bearing in solvent - it's sealed for life and to do so would ruin it. Also check the release lever for cracks and bends.

Installation

Refer to illustrations 4.5 and 4.6

5   Fill the inner groove of the release bearing with high-temperature grease. Also apply a light coat of the same grease to the transaxle input shaft splines and the front bearing retainer **(see illustration)**.

6   Lubricate the release lever ball socket, lever ends and release cylinder pushrod socket with high-temperature grease **(see illustration)**.

7   Attach the release bearing to the release lever.

8   Slide the release bearing onto the transaxle input shaft front bear-

5.2 To release the clutch pushrod from the clutch pedal, remove this clip (arrow) and the clevis pin

5.5 Typical clutch master cylinder details

ing retainer while passing the end of the release lever through the opening in the clutch housing. Push the clutch release lever onto the ball stud until it's firmly seated.

9   Apply a light coat of high-temperature grease to the face of the release bearing where it contacts the pressure plate diaphragm fingers.

10   The remainder of installation is the reverse of the removal procedure.

5   Clutch master cylinder - removal, overhaul and installation

Note: *Before beginning this procedure, contact local parts stores and dealer service departments concerning the purchase of a rebuild kit or a new master cylinder. Availability and cost of the necessary parts may dictate whether the cylinder is rebuilt or replaced with a new one. If you decide to rebuild the cylinder, inspect the bore as described in Step 11 before purchasing parts.*

Removal

Refer to illustration 5.2

1   Disconnect the negative cable from the battery. **Caution:** *If the stereo in your vehicle is equipped with an anti-theft system, make sure you have the correct activation code before disconnecting the battery.*

2   Under the dashboard, disconnect the pushrod from the top of the clutch pedal. It's held in place with a clevis pin. To remove the clevis pin, remove the clip **(see illustration)**.

3   Disconnect the hydraulic line at the clutch master cylinder. If

available, use a flare-nut wrench on the fitting, to protect the fitting from being rounded off. Have rags handy as some fluid will be lost as the line is removed. **Caution:** *Don't allow brake fluid to come into contact with paint, as it will damage the finish.*

4   From under the dash, remove the nuts which attach the master cylinder to the firewall. Remove the master cylinder, again being careful not to spill any of the fluid.

Overhaul

Refer to illustrations 5.5, 5.6 and 5.8

5   Remove the reservoir cap and drain all fluid from the master cylinder. Drive out the spring pin **(see illustration)** with a hammer and punch, then carefully pry off the reservoir.

6   If you're working on a 1995 or earlier Corolla, use a small screwdriver and bend out the staked part of the piston stop plate until it's flush with the surface of the stop plate **(see illustration)**. Remove the stop plate, gasket and pushrod from the cylinder.

7   If you're working on a Geo Prizm or a 1996 or later Corolla, remove the dust boot, depress the pushrod and remove the snap-ring with a pair of snap-ring pliers. Pull out the pushrod and washer.

8   Tap the master cylinder on a block of wood to eject the piston assembly from inside the bore **(see illustration)**. **Note:** *If the rebuild kit supplies a complete piston assembly, ignore the Steps which don't apply.*

5.6 If you're working on a 1995 or earlier Corolla, use a small screwdriver to bend the staked part of the piston stop plate out until it's flush with the surface of the stop plate, then remove the stop plate, gasket and pushrod from the cylinder bore

5.8 Invert the cylinder and tap it against a block of wood to eject the piston

8

6.3 Use a flare-nut wrench when disconnecting the hydraulic line fitting (left arrow) to prevent rounding off the corners of the tubing nut, then remove the two mounting bolts (right arrows)

9　Separate the spring from the piston.

10　Carefully remove the seal from the piston.

11　Inspect the bore of the master cylinder for deep scratches, score marks and ridges. The surface must be smooth to the touch. If the bore isn't perfectly smooth, the master cylinder must be replaced with a new or factory rebuilt unit.

12　If the cylinder will be rebuilt, use the new parts contained in the rebuild kit and follow any specific instructions which may have accompanied the rebuild kit. Wash all parts to be re-used with brake cleaner, denatured alcohol or clean brake fluid. DO NOT use petroleum-based solvents.

13　Attach the seal to the piston. The seal lips must face away from the pushrod end of the piston.

14　Assemble the spring on the other end of the piston.

15　Lubricate the bore of the cylinder and the seals with plenty of fresh brake fluid.

16　Carefully guide the piston assembly into the bore, being careful not to damage the seals. Make sure the spring end is installed first, with the pushrod end of the piston closest to the opening.

17　If you're working on a 1995 or earlier Corolla, position the pushrod and a new gasket in the bore, compress the spring and install a new stop plate. If you're working on a Geo Prizm or a 1996 or later Corolla, install the pushrod and washer, depress the pushrod and install a new snap-ring, making sure it seats completely in its groove. Install a new dust boot.

18　Install the fluid reservoir with a new grommet. Drive in the spring pin with a small hammer and punch. Make sure the pin protrudes about 1/8-inch, or less, on each side of the reservoir bracket.

Installation

19　Position the master cylinder on the firewall, installing the mounting nuts finger-tight.

20　Connect the hydraulic line to the master cylinder, moving the cylinder slightly as necessary to thread the fitting properly into the bore. Don't cross-thread the fitting as it's installed.

21　Tighten the mounting nuts and the hydraulic line fitting securely.

22　Connect the pushrod to the clutch pedal.

23　Fill the clutch master cylinder reservoir with brake fluid conforming to DOT 3 specifications and bleed the clutch system (see Section 7).

24　Check the clutch pedal height and freeplay (see Chapter 1).

6　Clutch release cylinder - removal, overhaul and installation

---

Note: *Before beginning this procedure, contact local parts stores and dealer service departments concerning the purchase of a rebuild kit or a new release cylinder. Availability and cost of the necessary parts may dictate whether the cylinder is rebuilt or replaced with a new one. If it's decided to rebuild the cylinder, inspect the bore as described in Step 8 before purchasing parts.*

Removal

Refer to illustration 6.3

1　Disconnect the negative cable from the battery. **Caution:** *If the stereo in your vehicle is equipped with an anti-theft system, make sure you have the correct activation code before disconnecting the battery.*

2　Raise the vehicle and support it securely on jackstands.

3　Disconnect the hydraulic line at the release cylinder. If available, use a flare-nut wrench on the fitting, which will prevent the fitting from being rounded off **(see illustration)**. Have a small can and rags handy, as some fluid will be spilled as the line is removed.

4　Remove the release cylinder mounting bolts.

5　Remove the release cylinder.

Overhaul

Refer to illustration 6.6

6　Remove the pushrod and the boot **(see illustration)**.

7　Tap the cylinder on a block of wood to eject the piston and seal. Remove the spring from inside the cylinder.

8　Carefully inspect the bore of the cylinder. Check for deep

6.6 Typical clutch release cylinder details

Release Cylinder

Spring

Piston

Push Rod

Boot

8.4 The clutch start switch is located under the dash on a bracket in front of the clutch pedal

Clutch Start Switch

8 ± 0.5 mm
(0.31 ± 0.020 in.)

8.5 Using an ohmmeter, check the continuity of the clutch start switch - there should be continuity when the switch is On (pedal depressed) and no continuity when it's Off (pedal released)

scratches, score marks and ridges. The bore must be smooth to the touch. If any imperfections are found, the release cylinder must be replaced with a new one.
9   Using the new parts in the rebuild kit, assemble the components using plenty of fresh brake fluid for lubrication. Note the installed direction of the spring and the seal.

Installation

10   Install the release cylinder on the clutch housing. Make sure the pushrod is seated in the release fork pocket.
11   Connect the hydraulic line to the release cylinder. Tighten the connection.
12   Fill the clutch master cylinder with brake fluid (conforming to DOT 3 specifications).
13   Bleed the system (see Section 7).
14   Lower the vehicle and connect the negative battery cable.

---

7   Clutch hydraulic system - bleeding

1   The hydraulic system should be bled of all air whenever any part of the system has been removed or if the fluid level has been allowed to fall so low that air has been drawn into the master cylinder. The procedure is similar to bleeding a brake system.
2   Fill the master cylinder with new brake fluid conforming to DOT 3 specifications. **Caution:** *Do not re-use any of the fluid coming from the system during the bleeding operation or use fluid which has been inside an open container for an extended period of time.*
3   Raise the vehicle and place it securely on jackstands to gain access to the release cylinder, which is located on the left side of the clutch housing.
4   Locate the bleeder valve on the clutch release cylinder (right above the fitting for the hydraulic fluid line). Remove the dust cap which fits over the bleeder valve and push a length of plastic hose over the valve. Place the other end of the hose into a clear container with about two inches of brake fluid in it. The hose end must be submerged in the fluid.
5   Have an assistant depress the clutch pedal and hold it. Open the bleeder valve on the release cylinder, allowing fluid to flow through the hose. Close the bleeder valve when fluid stops flowing from the hose. Once closed, have your assistant release the pedal.
6   Continue this process until all air is evacuated from the system, indicated by a full, solid stream of fluid being ejected from the bleeder valve each time and no air bubbles in the hose or container. Keep a close watch on the fluid level inside the clutch master cylinder reservoir; if the level drops too low, air will be sucked back into the system and the process will have to be started all over again.
7   Install the dust cap and lower the vehicle. Check carefully for proper operation before placing the vehicle in normal service.

---

8   Clutch start switch - check and replacement

Check

Refer to illustrations 8.4 and 8.5
1   Check the clutch pedal height and freeplay and the pushrod freeplay (see Chapter 1).
2   Verify that the engine will not start when the clutch pedal is released. Verify that the engine will start when the clutch pedal is depressed all the way.
3   If the clutch start switch doesn't perform as described, adjust and, if necessary, replace it.
4   Locate the switch **(see illustration)** and unplug the electrical connector.
5   Verify that there is continuity between the clutch start switch terminals when the switch is On (pedal depressed) **(see illustration)**.
6   Verify that no continuity exists between the switch terminals when the switch is Off (pedal released).
7   If the switch fails either of the tests, replace it.

Replacement

8   Remove the nut nearest the plunger end of the switch and unscrew the switch. Unplug the electrical connector.
9   Installation is the reverse of removal. The switch is self-adjusting, so there's no need for adjustment.
10   Verify again that the engine doesn't start when the clutch pedal is released, and does start when the pedal is depressed.

---

9   Driveaxles - general information and inspection

1   Power is transmitted from the transaxle to the wheels through a pair of driveaxles. The inner end of each driveaxle is splined into the differential side gears. The outer ends of the driveaxles are splined to the axle hubs and locked in place by a large nut.
2   The inner ends of the driveaxles are equipped with sliding constant velocity joints, which are capable of both angular and axial motion. Each inner joint assembly consists of a tripod bearing and a joint housing (outer race) in which the joint is free to slide in and out as the driveaxle moves up and down with the wheel. The joints can be disassembled and cleaned in the event of a boot failure (see Section 11), but if any parts are damaged, the joints must be replaced as a unit. When buying parts for a driveaxle, or a complete replacement driveaxle assembly, make sure you get the right components: some 1993 through 1995 models use Saginaw driveaxles, others use Toyota units; all 1996 models use Saginaw units. Both driveaxles are similar in design, but the parts are not necessarily interchangeable. Unless an authorized Toyota dealer parts department says otherwise, make sure you obtain Saginaw parts for Saginaw units, and Toyota parts for Toyota units.
3   The outer CV joints are the "Rzeppa" type, which consists of ball bearings running between an inner race and an outer cage, is capable of angular but not axial movement. The outer joints should be cleaned, inspected and repacked, but they cannot be disassembled. If an outer joint on a Toyota driveaxle is damaged, it must be replaced along with the axleshaft (the outer joint and axleshaft are sold as a single component). The outer joint on Saginaw driveaxles can be removed from the shaft and replaced separately.

8

10.4a Remove the cotter pin . . .

10.4b . . . and the nut lock

10.5 Use a large prybar to immobilize the hub while loosening the driveaxle hub nut

4   The boots should be inspected periodically for damage and leaking lubricant. Torn CV joint boots must be replaced immediately or the joints can be damaged. Boot replacement involves removal of the driveaxle (see Section 10). **Note:** *Some auto parts stores carry "split" type replacement boots, which can be installed without removing the driveaxle from the vehicle. This is a convenient alternative; however, the driveaxle should be removed and the CV joint disassembled and cleaned to ensure the joint is free from contaminants such as moisture and dirt which will accelerate CV joint wear.* The most common symptom of worn or damaged CV joints, besides lubricant leaks, is a clicking noise in turns, a clunk when accelerating after coasting and vibration at highway speeds. To check for wear in the CV joints and driveaxle shafts, grasp each axle (one at a time) and rotate it in both directions while holding the CV joint housings, feeling for play indicating worn splines or sloppy CV joints. Also check the driveaxle shafts for cracks, dents and distortion.

10   Driveaxle - removal and installation

Removal

Refer to illustrations 10.4a, 10.4b, 10.5, 10.6, 10.9 and 10.10

1   Disconnect the cable from the negative terminal of the battery. **Caution:** *If the stereo in your vehicle is equipped with an anti-theft system, make sure you have the correct activation code before disconnecting the battery.*

2   Set the parking brake.

3   Loosen the front wheel lug nuts, raise the vehicle and support it securely on jackstands. Remove the wheel.

4   Remove the cotter pin and the bearing nut lock from the driveaxle hub nut **(see illustrations)**.

5   Remove the driveaxle hub nut and washer. To prevent the hub from turning, wedge a prybar between two of the wheel studs and allow the prybar to rest against the ground or the floorpan of the vehicle **(see illustration)**.

6   To loosen the driveaxle from the hub splines, tap the end of the driveaxle with a soft-faced hammer or a hammer and a brass punch **(see illustration)**. **Note:** *Don't attempt to push the end of the driveaxle through the hub yet. Applying force to the end of the driveaxle, beyond just breaking it loose from the hub, can damage the driveaxle or transaxle.* If the driveaxle is stuck in the hub splines and won't move, it may be necessary to remove the brake disc (see Chapter 9) and push it from the hub with a two-jaw puller after Step 8 is performed.

7   Remove the engine splash shields (see Chapter 1). Place a drain pan underneath the transaxle to catch the lubricant that will spill out when the driveaxles are removed.

8   Remove the nuts and bolt securing the balljoint to the control arm, then pry the control arm down to separate the components (see Chapter 10)

9   Pull out on the steering knuckle and detach the driveaxle from the hub **(see illustration)**. Don't let the driveaxle hang by the inner CV joint after the outer end has been detached from the steering knuckle, as the inner joint could become damaged. Support the outer end of the driveaxle with a piece of wire, if necessary.

10   Carefully pry the inner CV joint out of the transaxle **(see illustration)**.

11   Refer to Chapter 7 for the driveaxle oil seal replacement procedure.

10.6 Using a brass punch, strike the end of the driveaxle sharply with a hammer; when it breaks free, it will move noticeably

10.9 Pull the steering knuckle out and slide the end of the driveaxle out of the hub

10.10 To separate the inner end of the driveaxle from the transaxle, pry on the CV joint housing like this with a large screwdriver or prybar - you may need to give the prybar a sharp rap with a brass hammer

11.3 Lift the tabs on all the boot clamps with a screwdriver, then open the clamps

11.4a Remove the boot from the inner CV joint and slide the joint housing from the tripod

Installation

12 Installation is the reverse of the removal procedure, but with the following additional points:

a) *Push the driveaxle sharply in to seat the retaining ring on the inner CV joint in the groove in the differential side gear.*

b) *Tighten the driveaxle hub nut to the torque listed in this Chapter's Specifications, then install the nut lock and a new cotter pin.*

c) *Install the wheel and lug nuts, lower the vehicle and tighten the lug nuts to the torque listed in the Chapter 1 Specifications.*

d) *Check the transaxle or differential lubricant and add, if necessary, to bring it to the proper level (see Chapter 1).*

11 Driveaxle boot replacement and CV joint inspection

Note: *If the CV joints must be overhauled (usually due to torn boots), explore all options before beginning the job. Complete rebuilt driveaxles are available on an exchange basis, which eliminates much time and work. Whichever route you choose to take, check on the cost and availability of parts before disassembling the vehicle.*

1 Remove the driveaxle (see Section 10).

Disassembly

Refer to illustrations 11.3, 11.4a, 11.4b, 11.6 and 11.7

2 Mount the driveaxle in a vise with wood lined jaws (to prevent damage to the axleshaft). Check the CV joint for excessive play in the radial direction, which indicates worn parts. Check for smooth operation throughout the full range of motion for each CV joint. If a boot is torn, disassemble the joint, clean the components and inspect for damage due to loss of lubrication and possible contamination by foreign matter.

3 Using a small screwdriver, pry the retaining tabs on the clamps up to loosen them and slide them off **(see illustration)**.

4 Using a screwdriver, carefully pry up on the edge of the outer boot and push it away from the CV joint. Old and worn boots can be cut off. Pull the inner CV joint boot back from the housing and slide the housing from the tripod **(see illustration)**. **Note:** *If you are only replacing the outer boot on a Saginaw driveaxle, it isn't necessary to remove the inner joint. Mark the relationship of the outer joint to the shaft, then expand the snap-ring and slide the joint from the shaft* **(see illustration)**. *Use a new snap-ring upon installation.*

5 Mark the tripod and axleshaft to ensure that they are reassembled properly.

6 Remove the tripod joint snap-ring with a pair of snap-ring pliers **(see illustration)**.

7 Use a hammer and a brass punch to drive the tripod joint from the driveaxle **(see illustration)**.

8 If you haven't already cut them off, remove both boots. If you're working on a right-side Toyota-type driveaxle, you'll also have to cut off the clamp for the dynamic damper and slide the damper off.

Check

9 Thoroughly clean all components, including the outer CV joint assembly, with solvent until the old CV joint grease is completely

8

11.4b On Saginaw driveaxles the outer joint can be removed from the shaft by expanding the snap-ring

11.6 Remove the snap-ring with a pair of snap-ring pliers

11.7 Drive the tripod joint from the driveaxle with a brass punch and hammer; be careful not to damage the bearing surfaces or the splines on the shaft

11.10a Wrap the splined area of the axleshaft with tape to prevent damage to the boots when removing or installing them

11.10b Install the tripod with the recessed portion of the splines facing the axleshaft

11.10c Place grease at the bottom of the CV joint housing

removed. Inspect the bearing surfaces of the inner tripods and housings for cracks, pitting, scoring and other signs of wear. It's very difficult to inspect the bearing surfaces of the inner and outer races of the outer CV joint, but you can at least check the surfaces of the ball bearings themselves. If they're in good shape, the races probably are too; if they're not, neither are the races. If the inner CV joint is worn, you can buy a new inner CV joint and install it on the old axleshaft; if the outer CV joint on a Toyota driveaxle is worn, you'll have to purchase a new outer CV joint *and* axleshaft (they're sold preassembled). The outer joint on Saginaw driveaxles can be replaced separately.

Reassembly

Refer to illustrations 11.10a, 11.10b, 11.10c, 11.10d, 11.11, 11.12a, 11.12b and 11.12c

10   Wrap the splines on the end the axleshaft with electrical tape to protect the boots from the sharp edges of the splines **(see illustration)**. Slide the clamps and boot(s) onto the axleshaft, then place the tripod on the shaft. **Note:** *If you're working on a right side Toyota-type driveaxle, be sure to install the dynamic damper and a new clamp before installing the inner boot.* Apply grease to the tripod assembly and inside the housing. Insert the tripod into the housing and pack the remainder of the grease around the tripod. **(see illustrations)**.

11   Slide the boot into place, making sure both ends seat in their grooves. Adjust the length of the driveaxle to the dimension listed in this Chapter's Specifications **(see illustration)**.

12   Equalize the pressure in the boot, then tighten and secure the boot clamps **(see illustrations)**.

11.10d Install the boot and clamps onto the axleshaft, then insert the tripod into the housing, followed by the rest of the grease

11.11 The driveaxle standard length should be set to the dimension listed in this Chapter's Specifications before the boot clamps are tightened

11.12a Equalize the pressure inside the boot by inserting a small, dull screwdriver between the boot and the outer race

11.12b To install the new clamps, bend the tang down . . .

11.12c . . . then tap the tabs over to hold it in place

Chapter 9 Brakes

Contents

Specifications

General

Brake fluid type	See Chapter 1
Brake pedal height	5-21/32 to 6-1/2 inches
Brake pedal freeplay	3/64 to 1/4 inch
Brake pedal reserve distance	At least 2-3/4 inches
Brake light switch-to-pedal clearance	1/64 to 3/32 inch
Power brake booster pushrod-to-master cylinder piston clearance	0.0 inch

Disc brakes

Minimum brake pad thickness	See Chapter 1
Disc thickness	
Standard	0.866 inch
Minimum*	0.787 inch
Disc runout limit	0.002 inch

Drum brakes

Drum inside diameter*	
Standard	7.874 inches
Maximum*	7.913 inches

*Note: *If different specifications are cast into the disc or drum, they supersede information printed here.*

Parking brake

Parking brake lever travel	4 to 7 clicks

Torque specifications

	Ft-lbs (unless otherwise indicated)
Brake hose-to-caliper banjo bolts	22
Caliper mounting bolts	25
Caliper torque plate bolts	65
Master cylinder-to-brake booster nuts	108 in-lbs
Power brake booster mounting nuts	108 in-lbs
Wheel cylinder mounting bolts	88 in-lbs
Wheel lug nuts	See Chapter 1

9

2.1 Anti-Lock Brake System (ABS) component locations

1   General information

The vehicles covered by this manual are equipped with hydraulically operated front and rear brake systems. The front brakes are disc type and the rear brakes are drum type. Both the front and rear brakes are self adjusting. The disc brakes automatically compensate for pad wear, while the drum brakes incorporate an adjustment mechanism which is activated as the parking brake is applied.

Hydraulic system

The hydraulic system consists of two separate circuits. The master cylinder has separate reservoirs for the two circuits, and, in the event of a leak or failure in one hydraulic circuit, the other circuit will remain operative. A dual proportioning valve on the firewall provides brake balance between the front and rear brakes.

Power brake booster

The power brake booster, utilizing engine manifold vacuum and atmospheric pressure to provide assistance to the hydraulically operated brakes, is mounted on the firewall in the engine compartment.

Parking brake

The parking brake operates the rear brakes only, through cable actuation. It's activated by a lever mounted in the center console.

Service

After completing any operation involving disassembly of any part of the brake system, always test drive the vehicle to check for proper braking performance before resuming normal driving. When testing the brakes, perform the tests on a clean, dry, flat surface. Conditions other than these can lead to inaccurate test results.

Test the brakes at various speeds with both light and heavy pedal pressure. The vehicle should stop evenly without pulling to one side or the other. Avoid locking the brakes, because this slides the tires and diminishes braking efficiency and control of the vehicle.

Tires, vehicle load and wheel alignment are factors which also affect braking performance.

2   Anti-lock Brake System (ABS) - general information

Refer to illustration 2.1

1   The anti-lock brake system (ABS) **(see illustration)** is designed to maintain vehicle steerability, directional stability and optimum deceleration under severe braking conditions and on most road surfaces. It does so by monitoring the rotational speed of each wheel and controlling the brake line pressure to each wheel during braking. This prevents the wheel from locking up.

Components

Actuator assembly

2   The actuator assembly consists of an electric hydraulic pump and four solenoid valves. The electric pump provides hydraulic pressure to charge the reservoirs in the actuator, which supplies pressure to the braking system. The pump and reservoirs are housed in the actuator assembly. The solenoid valves modulate brake line pressure during ABS operation. The body contains four valves - one for each wheel.

Speed sensors

Refer to illustrations 2.4 and 2.5

3   The speed sensors, which are located at each wheel, generate small electrical pulsations when the toothed sensor rotors are turning, sending a variable voltage signal to the ABS electronic control unit (ECU) indicating wheel rotational speed.

4   The front speed sensors **(see illustration)** are mounted on the front backing plates in close relationship to the toothed sensor rotors, which are integral with the outer constant velocity (CV) joints.

5   The rear wheel sensors are bolted to the brake backing plates or axle carriers **(see illustration)**. The sensor rotors are integral with the rear brake drum assemblies.

ABS computer

6   The ABS electronic control unit (ECU), which is mounted under the dashboard, is the "brain" of the ABS system. The function of the ECU is to accept and process information received from the wheel speed sensors to control the hydraulic line pressure, avoiding wheel

2.4 ABS front wheel speed sensor and
sensor rotor

2.5 ABS rear wheel speed sensor and
sensor rotor

3.5 Before removing the caliper, be sure to depress the piston
into the bottom of its bore in the caliper with a large C-clamp to
make room for the new pads

lock up. The ECU also constantly monitors the system, even under
normal driving conditions, to find faults within the system.

7   If a problem develops within the system, an "ABS" light will glow
on the dashboard. A diagnostic code will also be stored in the ECU,
which, when retrieved by a service technician, will indicate the problem
area or component.

Diagnosis and repair

8   If a dashboard warning light comes on and stays on while the
vehicle is in operation, the ABS system requires attention. Although a
special electronic ABS diagnostic tester, or Tech II scan tool, is neces-

sary to properly diagnose the system, the home mechanic can perform
a few preliminary checks before taking the vehicle to a dealer service
department or other repair shop which is equipped with a tester.
   a) *Check the brake fluid level in the reservoir.*
   b) *Check that all electrical connectors are securely connected.*
   c) *Check the fuses.*
9   If the above preliminary checks do not rectify the problem, the
vehicle should be diagnosed and repaired by a dealer service department or other repair shop.

3   Disc brake pads - replacement

Refer to illustrations 3.5 and 3.6a through 3.6u
Warning: *Disc brake pads must be replaced on both front wheels at
the same time - never replace the pads on only one wheel. Also, the
dust created by the brake system may contain asbestos, which is
harmful to your health. Never blow it out with compressed air and don't
inhale any of it. An approved filtering mask should be worn when working on the brakes. Do not, under any circumstances, use petroleum-
based solvents to clean brake parts. Use brake system cleaner only!*
1   Remove the cap from the brake fluid reservoir.
2   Loosen the wheel lug nuts, raise the front of the vehicle and support it securely on jackstands. Block the wheels at the opposite end.
3   Remove the wheels. Work on one brake assembly at a time, using
the assembled brake for reference if necessary.
4   Inspect the brake disc carefully as outlined in Section 5. If
machining is necessary, follow the information in that Section to
remove the disc, at which time the pads can be removed as well.
5   Push the piston back into its bore to provide room for the new
brake pads. A C-clamp can be used to accomplish this **(see illustra-**

9

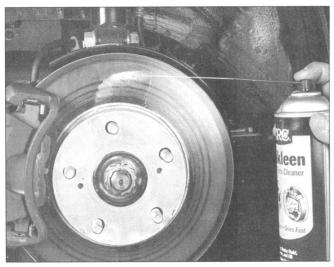

3.6a   Always wash the brakes with brake cleaner before disassembling anything

3.6b   To remove the caliper, remove the bolts indicated by the upper and lower arrows (the middle arrow points to the brake hose banjo bolt, which shouldn't be unscrewed unless the caliper is being removed for overhaul)

3.6c   Remove the caliper . . .

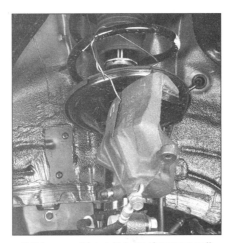

3.6d   . . . and hang it from the strut coil spring with a piece of coat hanger or wire; do not allow the caliper to hang by the brake hose

3.6e   Remove the upper anti-squeal spring . . .

3.6f   . . . and the lower anti-squeal spring

3.6g   Remove the outer shim . . .

3.6h   . . . and the inner shim from the outer brake pad

3.6i Remove the outer brake pad

3.6j Remove the outer shim . . .

3.6k . . . and the inner shim from the inner brake pad

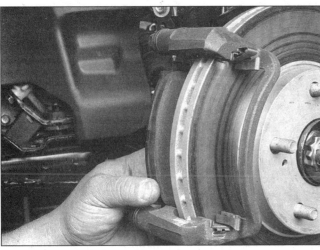

3.6l Remove the inner brake pad

3.6m Remove the four pad support plates; inspect the plates for damage and replace as necessary (good plates should "snap" into place in the torque plate; if they're weak or distorted, replace them)

tion). As the piston is depressed to the bottom of the caliper bore, the fluid in the master cylinder will rise. Make sure that it doesn't overflow. If necessary, siphon off some of the fluid.

6   Follow the accompanying photos (illustrations 3.6a through 3.6u), for the actual pad replacement procedure. Be sure to stay in

order and read the caption under each illustration.

7   When reinstalling the caliper, be sure to tighten the mounting bolts to the torque listed in this Chapter's Specifications. After the job has been completed, firmly depress the brake pedal a few times to

3.6n Pry the wear indicator off the old inner brake pad and transfer it to the new inner pad (if tho wear indicator is worn or bent, replace it)

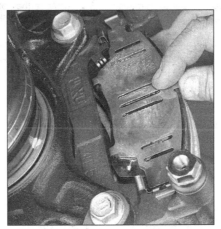

3.6o Install the pad support plates, the new inner brake pads and the shims; make sure the ears on the pad are properly engaged with the pad support plates as shown

3.6p Install the pad support plates, the outer pad and the shims

9

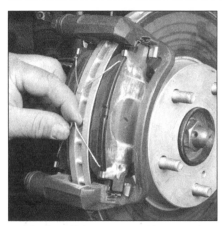

3.6q Install the upper and lower anti-squeal springs; make sure both springs are properly engaged with the pads as shown

3.6r Pull out the upper and lower sliding pins and clean them off (if either rubber boot is damaged, remove it by prying the flange of the metal bushing that retains the boot) . . .

3.6s . . . apply a coat of high-temperature grease to the pins before installing them

3.6t Install the caliper and tighten the caliper bolts to the torque listed in this Chapter's Specifications

3.6u If you have difficulty installing the caliper over the new pads, use a C-clamp to bottom the piston in its bore, then try again - it should now slip over the pads

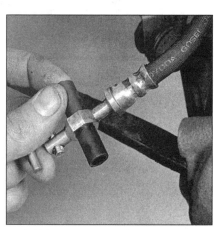

4.2 Using a piece of rubber hose of the appropriate size, plug the brake line; this will prevent brake fluid from leaking out and dirt and moisture from contaminating the fluid in the hose

bring the pads into contact with the disc. Check the level of the brake fluid, adding some if necessary. Check the operation of the brakes carefully before placing the vehicle into normal service.

---

4   Disc brake caliper - removal, overhaul and installation

Warning: *Dust created by the brake system may contain asbestos, which is harmful to your health. Never blow it out with compressed air and don't inhale any of it. An approved filtering mask should be worn when working on the brakes. Do not, under any circumstances, use petroleum-based solvents to clean brake parts. Use brake system cleaner.*
Note: *If an overhaul is indicated (usually because of fluid leakage), explore all options before beginning the job. New and factory rebuilt calipers are available on an exchange basis, which makes this job quite easy. If it's decided to rebuild the calipers, make sure a rebuild kit is available before proceeding. Always rebuild the calipers in pairs - never rebuild just one of them.*

Removal
Refer to illustration 4.2
1   Loosen the front wheel lug nuts, raise the front of the vehicle and

place it securely on jackstands. Remove the wheel.
2   Remove the bolt and disconnect the brake hose from the caliper **(see illustration 3.6b)**. Plug the brake hose to keep contaminants out of the brake system and to prevent losing any more brake fluid than is necessary **(see illustration)**.
3   Refer to Section 3 for the caliper removal procedure (it's part of the brake pad replacement procedure).

Overhaul
Refer to illustrations 4.4a, 4.4b, 4.5, 4.7 and 4.8
4   To overhaul the caliper, remove the boot set ring and the boot **(see illustrations)**. Before you remove the piston, place a wood block or some rags between the piston and caliper to prevent damage as it is removed.
5   To remove the piston from the caliper, apply compressed air to the brake fluid hose connection on the caliper body **(see illustration)**. Use only enough pressure to ease the piston out of its bore. **Warning:** *Be careful not to place your fingers between the piston and the caliper, as the piston may come out with some force.*
6   Inspect the mating surfaces of the piston and caliper bore wall. If there is any scoring, rust, pitting or bright areas, replace the complete caliper unit with a new one.
7   If these components are in good condition, remove the piston

4.4a An exploded view of a typical brake caliper assembly

4.4b Using a screwdriver, remove the cylinder boot set ring

4.5 With the caliper padded to catch the piston, use compressed air to force the piston out of its bore - make sure your hands or fingers are not between the piston and caliper

9

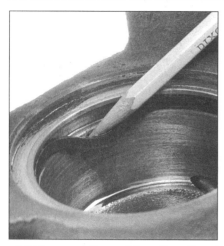

4.7 To remove the seal from the caliper bore, use a plastic or wooden tool, such as a pencil

4.8 Push out each sliding bushing through the boot, pull it free, then remove the dust boots

5.2 To remove the torque plate, remove these two bolts (arrows); the pad support plates might fall off while the torque plate is removed, so it's a good idea to note how they're installed before removing the torque plate

seal from the caliper bore using a wooden or plastic tool **(see illustration)**. Metal tools may damage the cylinder bore.

8   Push the sliding bushings out of the caliper ears **(see illustration)** and remove the dust boots from both ends.

9   Wash all the components with brake system cleaner.

10   To reassemble the caliper, you should already have the correct rebuild kit for your vehicle.

11   Submerge the new piston seal and the piston in brake fluid and install them into the caliper bore. Do not force the piston into the bore, but make sure it is squarely in place, then apply firm (but not excessive) pressure to install it.

12   Install the new piston dust boot and set ring.

13   Lubricate the sliding bushings with silicone-based grease (supplied in the kit) and push them into the caliper ears. Install the dust boots.

Installation

14   Install the caliper by reversing the removal procedure. Remember to replace the copper sealing washers (gaskets) at the brake hose-to-caliper connection (new washers normally come with the rebuild kit).

15   Bleed the brake circuit according to the procedure in Section 10.

Make sure there are no leaks from the hose connections. Test the brakes carefully before returning the vehicle to normal service.

---

5   Brake disc - inspection, removal and installation

Inspection

Refer to illustrations 5.2, 5.3, 5.4a, 5.4b, 5.5a and 5.5b

1   Loosen the wheel lug nuts, raise the vehicle and support it securely on jackstands. Remove the wheel and install two lug nuts to hold the disc in place.

2   Remove the brake caliper as outlined in Section 4. It isn't necessary to disconnect the brake hose. After removing the caliper bolts, suspend the caliper out of the way with a piece of wire **(see illustration 3.6d)**. Remove the two torque plate-to-steering knuckle bolts **(see illustration)** and detach the torque plate.

3   Visually inspect the disc surface for score marks and other damage. Light scratches and shallow grooves are normal after use and may not always be detrimental to brake operation, but deep scoring - over 0.039-inch (1.0 mm) - requires disc removal and refinishing by an

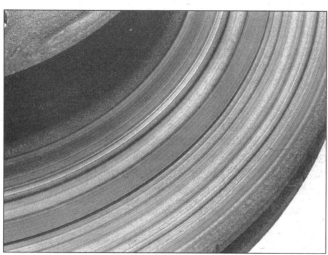

5.3 The brake pads on this vehicle were obviously neglected, as they wore down to the rivets and cut deep grooves into the disc - wear this severe means the disc must be replaced

5.4a To check disc runout, mount a dial indicator as shown and rotate the disc

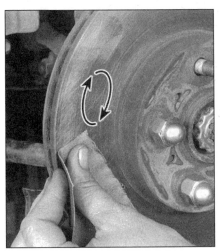

5.4b Using a swirling motion, remove the glaze from the disc surface with sandpaper or emery cloth

5.5a The minimum wear dimension is cast into the back side of the disc

5.5b Use a micrometer to measure disc thickness

automotive machine shop. Be sure to check both sides of the disc **(see illustration)**. If pulsating has been noticed during application of the brakes, suspect disc runout.

4   To check disc runout, place a dial indicator at a point about 1/2-inch from the outer edge of the disc **(see illustration)**. Set the indicator to zero and turn the disc. The indicator reading should not exceed the specified allowable runout limit. If it does, the disc should be refinished by an automotive machine shop. **Note:** *The discs should be resurfaced regardless of the dial indicator reading, as this will impart a smooth finish and ensure a perfectly flat surface, eliminating any brake pedal pulsation or other undesirable symptoms related to questionable discs. At the very least, if you elect not to have the discs resurfaced, remove the glaze from the surface with emery cloth or sandpaper, using a swirling motion* **(see illustration)**.

5   It's absolutely critical that the disc not be machined to a thickness under the specified minimum thickness. The minimum wear (or discard) thickness is cast into the inside of the disc **(see illustration)**. The disc thickness can be checked with a micrometer **(see illustration)**.

Removal

6   Remove the lug nuts which were installed to hold the disc in place and remove the disc from the hub.

Installation

7   Place the disc in position over the threaded studs.
8   Install the torque plate and caliper assembly over the disc and position it on the steering knuckle. Tighten the torque plate bolts to the torque listed in this Chapter's Specifications.
9   Install the wheel, then lower the vehicle to the ground. Tighten the lug nuts to the torque listed in the Chapter 1 Specifications. Depress the brake pedal a few times to bring the brake pads into contact with the disc. Bleeding won't be necessary unless the brake hose was disconnected from the caliper. Check the operation of the brakes carefully before driving the vehicle.

6   Drum brake shoes - replacement

Refer to illustrations 6.4a through 6.4ff and 6.5
Warning: *Drum brake shoes must be replaced on both wheels at the same time - never replace the shoes on only one wheel. Also, the dust created by the brake system may contain asbestos, which is harmful to your health. Never blow it out with compressed air and don't inhale any of it. An approved filtering mask should be worn when working on the brakes. Do not, under any circumstances, use petroleum-based sol-*

vents to clean brake parts. Use brake system cleaner only!
Caution: *Whenever the brake shoes are replaced, the return and hold-down springs should also be replaced. Due to the continuous heating/cooling cycle the springs are subjected to, they lose tension over a period of time and may allow the shoes to drag on the drum and wear at a much faster rate than normal.*

1   Loosen the wheel lug nuts, raise the rear of the vehicle and support it securely on jackstands. Block the front wheels to keep the vehicle from rolling.
2   Release the parking brake.
3   Remove the wheel. **Note:** *All four rear brake shoes must be replaced at the same time, but to avoid mixing up parts, work on only one brake assembly at a time.*
4   Follow the accompanying illustrations for the brake shoe replacement procedure **(see illustrations 6.4a through 6.4ff)**. Be sure to stay in order and read the caption under each illustration. **Note:** *If the brake drum cannot be easily pulled off the axle and shoe assembly, make sure the parking brake is completely released. If the drum still cannot be pulled off, the brake shoes will have to be retracted. This is done by first removing the plug from the backing plate. With the plug removed, push the lever off the adjuster star wheel with a narrow screwdriver while turning the adjuster wheel with another screwdriver, moving the*

6.4a Mark the relationship of the drum to the hub, so the drum will retain its dynamic balance after reassembly

9

shoes away from the drum **(see illustration 6.4b)**. *The drum should now come off.*

5   Before reinstalling the drum, it should be checked for cracks, score marks, deep scratches and hard spots, which will appear as small discolored areas. If the hard spots cannot be removed with fine emery cloth or if any of the other conditions listed above exist, the drum must be taken to an automotive machine shop to have it resurfaced. **Note:** *Professionals recommend resurfacing the drums each time a brake job is done. Resurfacing will eliminate the possibility of out-of-round drums. If the drums are worn so much that they can't be resurfaced without exceeding the maximum allowable diameter (stamped into the drum), then new ones will be required* **(see illustration)**. *At the very least, if you elect not to have the drums resurfaced, remove the glaze from the surface with emery cloth using a swirling motion.*

6   Install the brake drum on the axle flange.

6.4b If the brake drum is hanging up on the shoes because of excessive wear, insert two screwdrivers through the hole in the backing plate, push the adjuster lever away from the star wheel and turn the star wheel to retract the brake shoes

6.4c An exploded view of the drum brake assembly

Bleeder Plug   Piston   Boot   Cup   Spring   C-Washer   Shoe Lever   Parking Brake Shoe Lever   C-Washer   Adjusting Lever Spring   Rear Shoe   Pin   Plug   Front Shoe   Adjuster   Cup   Shoe Hold-Down Spring   Cup   Anchor Spring

6.4d Before removing anything, place a drain pan under the brake assembly, clean the brake assembly with brake cleaner and allow it to dry; DO NOT USE COMPRESSED AIR TO BLOW OFF BRAKE DUST! (hub removed for clarity)

6.4e Unhook the return spring from its hole in the front shoe . . .

6.4f . . . then pull the other end out of the hole in the rear shoe and remove the adjuster and spring

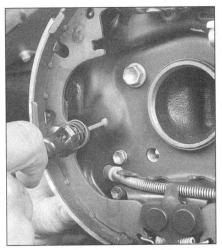

6.4g Using a hold-down spring tool, remove the hold-down spring by pushing in and rotating it 1/4-turn . . .

6.4h . . . remove the outer cup, the spring and the inner cup . . .

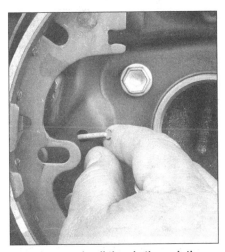

6.4i . . . and pull the pin through the backing plate

6.4j Remove the front shoe and unhook the anchor spring from the rear shoe

6.4k Remove the rear shoe hold-down spring, cups and pin

6.4l Flip the rear shoe over, force the spring back from the parking brake lever as shown . . .

6.4m . . . and disengage the parking brake cable from the parking brake lever

9

6.4n Take the rear shoe to a clean work bench and unhook the adjusting lever spring from the shoe

6.4o Pry off the C-washer (don't lose the shim underneath) . . .

6.4p . . . and remove the parking brake lever and the adjusting lever from the old rear shoe

6.4q Attach the parking brake lever and adjusting lever to the new rear shoe and secure them with a new C-washer (don't forget the shim)

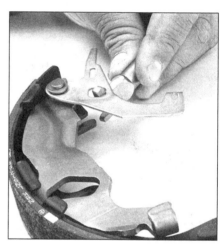

6.4r Engage the rear part of the adjuster with the shoe lever as shown . . .

6.4s . . . rotate the shoe lever back against the rear shoe . . .

6.4t . . . hook the short end of the adjusting lever spring into the shoe lever . . .

6.4u . . . and hook the long end of the spring into the hole in the rear shoe

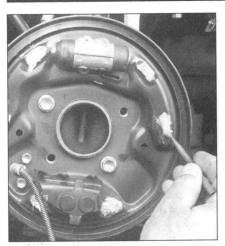

6.4v Apply high-temperature grease to the friction points of the backing plate

6.4w Insert the pin for the rear shoe hold-down spring through the hole in the backing plate

6.4x Attach the parking brake cable to the parking brake lever

6.4y Bring the rear shoe into position, insert the hold-down pin through the shoe, install the inner cup on the pin . . .

6.4z . . . install the hold-down spring and outer cup . . .

6.4aa . . . compress the spring with a brake spring tool, give the outer cup a 1/4-turn twist and lock it down

6.4bb Place the adjuster assembly in position and insert it into the rear part of the adjuster that you installed on the rear shoe on the bench

6.4cc Attach the anchor spring to the rear shoe . . .

9

6.4dd . . . attach it to the front shoe . . .

6.4ee . . . place the front shoe in position and hook both ends of the return spring into their respective holes in the front and rear shoes

6.4ff Install the front shoe hold-down pin, spring and inner and outer cups and lock the hold-down assembly into place with a brake spring tool

7   Mount the wheel and install the lug nuts. Using a screwdriver inserted through the adjusting hole in the backing plate **(see illustration 6.4b)**, turn the adjuster star wheel until the brake shoes drag on the drum as the drum is rotated, then back off the star wheel until the shoes don't drag. Lower the vehicle and tighten the lug nuts to the torque listed in the Chapter 1 Specifications.

8   Make a number of forward and reverse stops and operate the parking brake to adjust the brakes until satisfactory pedal action is obtained.

9   Check the operation of the brakes carefully before driving the vehicle.

7   Wheel cylinder - removal, overhaul and installation

Note: *If an overhaul is indicated (usually because of fluid leaks or sticky operation), explore all options before beginning the job. New wheel cylinders are available, which makes this job quite easy. If it's decided to rebuild the wheel cylinder, make sure a rebuild kit is available before proceeding. Never overhaul only one wheel cylinder - always rebuild both of them at the same time.*

Removal

Refer to illustration 7.4

1   Raise the rear of the vehicle and support it securely on jackstands. Block the front wheels to keep the vehicle from rolling.

2   Remove the brake shoe assembly (see Section 6).

3   Remove all dirt and foreign material from around the wheel cylinder.

4   Disconnect the brake line **(see illustration)** with a flare-nut wrench, if available. Don't pull the brake line away from the wheel cylinder.

5   Remove the wheel cylinder mounting bolts.

6   Detach the wheel cylinder from the brake backing plate and place it on a clean workbench. Immediately plug the brake line to prevent fluid loss and contamination.

Overhaul

7   Remove the bleeder screw, cups, pistons, boots and spring assembly from the wheel cylinder body **(see illustration 6.4c)**.

8   Clean the wheel cylinder with brake fluid, denatured alcohol or brake system cleaner. **Warning:** *Do not, under any circumstances, use petroleum-based solvents to clean brake parts!*

9   Use filtered, unlubricated compressed air to dry the wheel cylinder and blow out the passages.

10   Check the bore for corrosion and score marks. Crocus cloth can be used to remove light corrosion and stains, but the cylinder must be replaced with a new one if the defects cannot be removed easily, or if the bore is scored.

11   Lubricate the new cups with brake fluid.

12   Assemble the brake cylinder components. Make sure the cup lips face in.

6.5 The maximum drum diameter is cast into the drum

7.4 Disconnect the brake line fitting (1), then remove the two wheel cylinder bolts (2)

8.2 Unplug the electrical connector for the fluid level warning switch (arrow points to the left master cylinder mounting nut)

Installation

13   Place the wheel cylinder in position and install the bolts finger tight. Connect the brake line to the cylinder, being careful not to cross-thread the fitting. Tighten the wheel cylinder bolts to the torque listed in this Chapter's Specifications.
14   Tighten the brake line securely and install the brake shoe assembly (see Section 6).
15   Bleed the brakes (see Section 10).
16   Check the operation of the brakes carefully before driving the vehicle.

8   Master cylinder - removal, overhaul and installation

Note: *Before deciding to overhaul the master cylinder, check on the availability and cost of a new or factory rebuilt unit and also the availability of a rebuild kit. If you decide to rebuild the cylinder, inspect the bore as described in Step 12 before purchasing parts.*

Removal

Refer to illustrations 8.2, 8.4 and 8.6

1   Remove the air cleaner assembly (see Chapter 4).
2   Unplug the electrical connector for the fluid level warning switch **(see illustration)**.
3   Remove as much fluid as possible from the reservoir with a syringe.
4   Place rags under the fittings and prepare caps or plastic bags to cover the ends of the lines once they're disconnected. **Caution:** *Brake fluid will damage paint. Cover all body parts and be careful not to spill fluid during this procedure. Loosen the fittings at the ends of the brake*

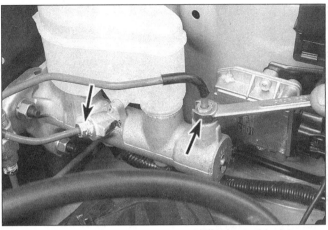

8.4 Loosen the brake line fittings (arrows) with a flare-nut wrench

lines where they enter the master cylinder **(see illustration)**. *To prevent rounding off the flats, use a flare-nut wrench, which wraps around the fitting hex.*
5   Pull the brake lines away from the master cylinder and plug the ends to prevent contamination.
6   Remove the three nuts attaching the master cylinder to the power booster **(see illustration)**. Pull the master cylinder off the studs to remove it. Again, be careful not to spill the fluid as this is done. Remove and discard the old gasket between the master cylinder and the power brake booster.

8.6 Master cylinder mounting details

9

8.8a The brake fluid reservoir is retained by a screw

8.8b After the reservoir has been removed, pull the grommets from the master cylinder body; if they're hard, cracked or damaged, or have been leaking, replace them

8.9 Using a Phillips screwdriver, depress the pistons, then remove the stopper bolt; be sure to replace the sealing washer for the stopper bolt

8.10 Depress the pistons again and remove the snap-ring with a pair of snap-ring pliers

Overhaul

Refer to illustrations 8.8a, 8.8b, 8.9, 8.10, 8.11a, 8.11b and 8.11c

7   Before attempting the overhaul of the master cylinder, obtain the proper rebuild kit, which will contain the necessary replacement parts and also any instructions which may be specific to your model.

8   Remove the reservoir retaining screw, pull off the reservoir and remove the grommets **(see illustrations)**.

9   Place the cylinder in a vise and use a punch or Phillips screwdriver to depress the pistons until they bottom against the other end of the master cylinder. Hold the pistons in this position and remove the stopper bolt from the master cylinder **(see illustration)**.

10   Carefully remove the snap-ring at the end of the master cylinder **(see illustration)**.

11   The internal components can now be removed from the bore **(see illustrations)**. Make a note of the proper order of the components so they can be returned to their original locations. **Note:** *The two springs are different, so pay particular attention to their installed order.*

12   Carefully inspect the bore of the master cylinder. Any deep score marks or other damage will mean a new master cylinder is required. DO NOT attempt to hone the bore.

13   Replace all parts included in the rebuild kit, following any instructions in the kit. Clean all re-used parts with brake system cleaner. **Warning:** *Do not use any petroleum-based solvents. During reassembly, lubricate all parts liberally with clean brake fluid.*

14   Push the assembled components into the bore, bottoming them against the end of the master cylinder, then install the stopper bolt.

15   Install the new snap-ring, making sure it's seated properly in the groove.

16   Install the reservoir grommets, reservoir and screw.

17   Before installing the master cylinder, it should be bench bled. Since you'll have to apply pressure to the master cylinder piston and, at the same time, control flow from the brake line outlets, the master cylinder should be mounted in a vise, with the jaws of the vise clamping on the mounting flange.

18   Insert threaded plugs into the brake line outlet holes and snug them down so no air will leak past them, but not so tight that they can't be easily loosened.

19   Fill the reservoir with brake fluid of the recommended type (see Chapter 1).

20   Remove one plug and push the piston assembly into the bore to expel the air from the master cylinder. A large Phillips screwdriver can be used to push on the piston assembly.

21   To prevent air from being drawn back into the master cylinder, the plug must be replaced and snugged down before releasing the pressure on the piston.

22   Repeat the procedure until only brake fluid is expelled from the brake line outlet hole. When only brake fluid is expelled, repeat the procedure at the other outlet hole and plug. Be sure to keep the master cylinder reservoir filled with brake fluid to prevent the introduction of air into the system.

23   Since high pressure isn't involved in the bench bleeding procedure, an alternative to the removal and replacement of the plugs with each stroke of the piston assembly is available. Before pushing in on the piston assembly, remove the plug as described in Step 20. Before

8.11a An exploded view of the master cylinder assembly

8.11b After the snap-ring has been removed, the primary (No. 1) piston assembly can be removed

8.11c Remove the cylinder from the vise and tap it against a block of wood until the secondary (No. 2) piston is exposed. Pull the piston assembly STRAIGHT OUT - if it becomes even slightly cocked, the bore may be damaged

9

8.27 Have an assistant depress the brake pedal and hold it down, then loosen the fitting nut, allowing the air and fluid to escape; repeat this procedure on both fittings until the fluid is clear of air bubbles

9.3 Unscrew the brake line threaded fitting with a flare-nut wrench to protect the fitting corners from being rounded off

9.4 Pull off the U-clip with a pair of pliers

releasing the piston, however, instead of replacing the plug, simply put your finger tightly over the hole to keep air from being drawn back into the master cylinder. Wait several seconds for brake fluid to be drawn from the reservoir into the bore, then depress the piston again, removing your finger as brake fluid is expelled. Be sure to put your finger back over the hole each time before releasing the piston, and when the bleeding procedure is complete for that outlet, replace the plug and tighten it before going on to the other port.

Installation

Refer to illustration 8.27

24   Install the master cylinder over the studs on the power brake booster and tighten the nuts only finger-tight at this time. Don't forget to use a new gasket.

25   Thread the brake line fittings into the master cylinder. Since the master cylinder is still a bit loose, it can be moved slightly so the fittings thread in easily. Don't strip the threads as the fittings are tightened.

26   Tighten the mounting nuts to the torque listed in this Chapter's Specifications. Tighten the brake line fittings securely.

27   Fill the master cylinder reservoir with fluid, then bleed the master cylinder and the brake system (see Section 10). To bleed the master cylinder on the vehicle, have an assistant depress the brake pedal and hold it down. Loosen the fitting to allow air and fluid to escape **(see illustration)**. Tighten the fitting, then allow your assistant to return the pedal to its rest position. Repeat this procedure on both fittings until the fluid is free of air bubbles. Check the operation of the brake system carefully before driving the vehicle.

9   Brake hoses and lines - inspection and replacement

Inspection

1   About every six months, with the vehicle raised and supported securely on jackstands, the rubber hoses which connect the steel brake lines with the front and rear brake assemblies should be inspected for cracks, chafing of the outer cover, leaks, blisters and other damage. These are important and vulnerable parts of the brake system and inspection should be complete. A light and mirror will be helpful for a thorough check. If a hose exhibits any of the above conditions, replace it with a new one.

Replacement

Front brake hose

Refer to illustrations 9.3 and 9.4

2   Loosen the wheel lug nuts, raise the vehicle and support it

securely on jackstands. Remove the wheel.

3   At the frame bracket, unscrew the brake line fitting from the hose **(see illustration)**. Use a flare-nut wrench to prevent rounding off the corners. If the bracket begins to bend, hold the hose fitting with an open-end wrench.

4   Remove the U-clip from the female fitting at the bracket with a pair of pliers **(see illustration)**, then pass the hose through the bracket.

5   At the caliper end of the hose, remove the banjo fitting bolt, then separate the hose from the caliper. Note that there are two copper sealing washers on either side of the fitting - they should be replaced with new ones during installation.

6   Remove the U-clip from the strut bracket, then feed the hose through the bracket.

7   To install the hose, pass the caliper fitting end through the strut bracket, then connect the fitting to the caliper with the banjo bolt and copper washers. Make sure the locating lug on the fitting is engaged with the hole in the caliper, then tighten the bolt to the torque listed in this Chapter's Specifications.

8   Push the metal support into the strut bracket and install the U-clip. Make sure the hose isn't twisted between the caliper and the strut bracket.

9   Route the hose into the frame bracket, again making sure it isn't twisted, then connect the brake line fitting, starting the threads by hand. Install the U-clip, then tighten the fitting securely.

10   Bleed the caliper (see Section 10).

11   Install the wheel and lug nuts, lower the vehicle and tighten the lug nuts to the torque listed in the Chapter 1 Specifications.

Rear brake hose

12   The rear brake hose serves as the flexible connection between two rigid metal lines, one on the body and the other on the axle. Both ends of the hose are attached to these metal lines with threaded fittings and U-clips. Refer to Steps 2, 3 and 4 above. Be sure to bleed the wheel cylinder when you're done (see Section 10).

Metal brake lines

13   When replacing brake lines, be sure to use the correct parts. Don't use copper tubing for any brake system components. Purchase steel brake lines from a dealer or auto parts store.

14   Prefabricated brake line, with the tube ends already flared and fittings installed, is available at auto parts stores and dealer parts departments. These lines are also bent to the proper shapes.

15   When installing the new line, make sure it's securely supported in the brackets and has plenty of clearance between moving or hot components.

16   After installation, check the master cylinder fluid level and add fluid as necessary. Bleed the brake system (see Section 10) and test the brakes carefully before driving the vehicle in traffic.

10.8 When bleeding the brakes, a hose is connected to the bleed screw at the caliper or wheel cylinder and then submerged in brake fluid - air will be seen as bubbles in the tube and container (all air must be expelled before moving to the next wheel)

10 Brake hydraulic system - bleeding

Refer to illustration 10.8

Warning 1: *If you are working on a Geo Prizm model, this procedure might not completely purge the air from the hydraulic system. The manufacturer specifies that a Tech 1 scan tool be used to "rehome" the pistons (which brings them to their uppermost positions) within the modulator before bleeding the system. The normal state of the pistons is in the uppermost position, but if there is a malfunction in the system they may not have returned to this position, in which case it won't be possible to successfully bleed the brakes. If the BRAKE, ABS or ABS ACTIVE lights on the dash are illuminated after bleeding the brakes and will not go out, or if the brake pedal feels spongy or unusually hard, DO NOT drive the vehicle. Instead, have it towed to a dealer service department or other repair shop equipped with a Tech 1 tool.*

Warning 2: *Wear eye protection when bleeding the brake system. If the fluid comes in contact with your eyes, immediately rinse them with water and seek medical attention.*

Note: *Bleeding the hydraulic system is necessary to remove any air that manages to find its way into the system when it's been opened during removal and installation of a hose, line, caliper or master cylinder.*

1   You'll probably have to bleed the system at all four brakes if air has entered it due to low fluid level, or if the brake lines have been disconnected at the master cylinder.

2   If a brake line was disconnected only at a wheel, then only that caliper or wheel cylinder must be bled.

3   If a brake line is disconnected at a fitting located between the master cylinder and any of the brakes, that part of the system served by the disconnected line must be bled.

4   Remove any residual vacuum from the brake power booster by applying the brake several times with the engine off.

5   Remove the master cylinder reservoir cover and fill the reservoir with brake fluid. Reinstall the cover. **Note:** *Check the fluid level often during the bleeding operation and add fluid as necessary to prevent the fluid level from falling low enough to allow air bubbles into the master cylinder.*

6   Have an assistant on hand, as well as a supply of new brake fluid, a clear plastic container partially filled with clean brake fluid, a length of 3/16-inch plastic, rubber or vinyl tubing to fit over the bleeder valve and a wrench to open and close the bleeder valve.

7   Beginning at the right rear wheel, loosen the bleeder valve slightly, then tighten it to a point where it's snug but can still be loosened quickly and easily.

8   Place one end of the tubing over the bleeder valve and submerge the other end in brake fluid in the container **(see illustration)**.

9   Have the assistant pump the brakes slowly a few times to get pressure in the system, then hold the pedal down firmly.

10   While the pedal is held down, open the bleeder valve just enough to allow a flow of fluid to leave the valve. Watch for air bubbles to exit the submerged end of the tube. When the fluid flow slows after a couple of seconds, close the valve and have your assistant release the pedal.

11   Repeat Steps 9 and 10 until no more air is seen leaving the tube, then tighten the bleeder valve and proceed to the left front wheel, the left rear wheel and the right front wheel, in that order, and perform the same procedure. Be sure to check the fluid in the master cylinder reservoir frequently.

12   Never use old brake fluid. It contains moisture which will deteriorate the brake system components.

13   Refill the master cylinder with fluid at the end of the operation.

14   Check the operation of the brakes. The pedal should feel solid when depressed, with no sponginess. If necessary, repeat the entire process. **Warning:** *Do not operate the vehicle if you're in doubt about the effectiveness of the brake system.*

11 Power brake booster - check, removal and installation

Operating check

1   Depress the brake pedal several times with the engine off and make sure there's no change in the pedal reserve distance.

2   Depress the pedal and start the engine. If the pedal goes down slightly, operation is normal.

Airtightness check

3   Start the engine and turn it off after one or two minutes. Depress the brake pedal slowly several times. If the pedal depresses less each time, the booster is airtight.

4   Depress the brake pedal while the engine is running, then stop the engine with the pedal depressed. If there's no change in the pedal reserve travel after holding the pedal for 30 seconds, the booster is airtight.

Removal

Refer to illustrations 11.6, 11.10a and 11.10b

5   Power brake booster units shouldn't be disassembled. They require special tools not normally found in most automotive repair stations or shops. Because of its critical relationship to brake performance, the booster should be replaced with a new or rebuilt one.

6   Disconnect the hose leading from the engine to the booster **(see illustration)**. Be careful not to damage the hose when removing it from

11.6 Detach this hose (arrow) from the power brake booster; make sure you don't puncture or tear the hose during removal

9

11.10a To disconnect the power brake booster pushrod from the brake pedal, remove the retaining clip and clevis pin (center arrow); to detach the booster from the firewall, remove the four mounting nuts (arrows, upper right nut not visible in this photo)

11.10b Power brake booster installation details

the booster fitting.

7   Remove the brake master cylinder (see Section 8).

8   Remove the steering column lower finish panel (see Chapter 11).

9   Remove the pedal return spring.

10   Locate the pushrod clevis connecting the booster to the brake pedal **(see illustrations)**. Remove the clevis pin retaining clip with pliers and pull out the pin.

11   Remove the four nuts and washers holding the brake booster to the firewall **(see illustration 11.10)**; you may need a light to see them.

12   Slide the booster straight out from the firewall until the studs clear the holes.

Installation

Refer to illustrations 11.14a and 11.14b

13   Installation is basically the reverse of removal **(see illustration)**. Tighten the booster mounting nuts to the torque listed in this Chapter's Specifications. Be sure to use a new clevis retaining clip if the old clip is loose.

14   If the power booster unit is being replaced, the clearance between the master cylinder piston and the pushrod in the vacuum booster must be measured and, if necessary, adjusted. Using a depth micrometer or vernier calipers, measure the distance from the seat (recessed area) in the master cylinder to the master cylinder mounting flange. Next, measure the distance from the end of the vacuum booster pushrod to the mounting face of the booster (including gasket)

where the master cylinder mounting flange seats. The measurements should be the same **(see illustration)**. If not, turn the adjusting screw on the end of the power booster pushrod until the clearance is within the specified limit **(see illustration)**.

15   After the final installation of the master cylinder and brake hoses and lines, the brake pedal height and freeplay must be adjusted and the system must be bled. See the appropriate Sections of this Chapter for the procedures.

12   Parking brake - adjustment

Refer to illustration 12.3

1   The parking brake lever, when properly adjusted, should travel four to seven clicks, when a moderate pulling force is applied. If it travels less than the specified minimum number of clicks, there's a chance the parking brake might not be releasing completely and might be dragging on the drum. If the lever can be pulled up more than the specified maximum number of clicks, the parking brake may not hold adequately on an incline, allowing the car to roll.

2   To gain access to the parking brake cable adjuster, remove the center console (see Chapter 11).

3   Loosen the locknut (the upper nut) while holding the adjusting nut (lower nut) with a wrench **(see illustration)**. Turn the adjusting nut until the desired travel is attained. Tighten the locknut.

4   Install the center console.

11.14a There should be no clearance between the booster pushrod and the master cylinder pushrod, but no interference either; if there is interference between the two, the brakes may drag; if there is clearance, there will be excessive brake pedal travel

Clearance
0.0 inch

11.14b To adjust the length of the booster pushrod, hold the serrated portion of the rod with a pair of pliers and turn the adjusting screw in or out, as necessary, to achieve the desired setting

12.3 Loosen the locknut, then turn the adjusting nut until the desired handle travel is obtained

13.4 Unscrew the bolts (arrows) from the backing plate and pass the cable through

13.5 Remove this nut (arrow) and detach this cable bracket from the frame near the forward end of the strut rod

13.6 Remove this bolt (arrow) and detach this cable bracket from the floor pan

13   Parking brake cables - replacement

Equalizer-to-parking brake cable

Refer to illustrations 13.4, 13.5, 13.6 and 13.8

1   Loosen the rear wheel lug nuts, raise the rear of the vehicle and support it securely on jackstands. Block the front wheels. Remove the wheel.

2   Make sure the parking brake is completely released, then remove the brake drum.

3   Remove the brake shoes and disconnect the cable from the parking brake lever (see Section 6).

4   Remove the two cable retaining bolts from the backing plate **(see illustration)** and pull the cable through the backing plate.

5   Unbolt the cable clamp near the forward end of the strut rod **(see illustration)**.

6   Unbolt the cable clamp from the floor pan, just to the left of the center tunnel **(see illustration)**.

7   Remove the exhaust pipe and catalytic converter heat shields (see Chapter 6).

8   Unclamp the cable from the rear retaining bracket, pull the nylon bushing out of the front bracket and disconnect the cable from the equalizer **(see illustration)**.

9   Installation is the reverse of removal. Apply a light coat of grease to the portion of the cable end that engages with the equalizer.

10   Adjust the parking brake when you're done (see Section 12).

Equalizer-to-brake lever cable

11   Remove the center console (see Chapter 11).

12   With the lever in the down (off) position, remove the locknut and the adjusting nut (see Section 12) and detach the cable from the lever.

13   Raise the rear of the vehicle and place it securely on jackstands.

14   Remove the exhaust pipe and catalytic converter heat shields (see Chapter 4).

15   Turn the cable end 90-degrees and disconnect it from the equalizer **(see illustration 13.8)**.

16   Pry out the rubber grommet from the floorpan and pull the cable through the hole in the pan.

17   Installation is the reverse of removal. Apply a light coat of grease to the portion of the cable end that engages with the equalizer. And coat the sealing edge of the rubber grommet with silicone to ensure that it remains watertight.

18   Adjust the parking brake lever when you're done (see Section 12).

14   Brake pedal - check and adjustment

Pedal height

Refer to illustrations 14.1 and 14.10

1   Measure the pedal height **(see illustration)** and compare your

13.8 Remove the clamp retaining bolt (right arrows), pry the nylon bushing out of the bracket (center arrows) and disengage the forward end of the cable from the equalizer (left arrows)

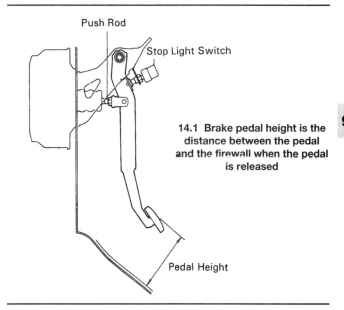

Push Rod

Stop Light Switch

14.1 Brake pedal height is the distance between the pedal and the firewall when the pedal is released

Pedal Height

9

14.10 Clearance "A" is the distance between the brake light switch and the pedal arm

measurement to the pedal height listed in this Chapter's Specifications. If the pedal height is incorrect, adjust it as follows:

2   Remove the steering column lower finish panel and air duct.

3   Unplug the electrical connector from the brake light switch.

4   Loosen the brake light switch locknut and remove the brake light switch.

5   Loosen the pushrod locknut.

6   Adjust the pedal height by turning the pedal pushrod.

7   Tighten the pushrod locknut.

8   Install the brake light switch and turn it until it lightly contacts the pedal stopper.

9   Back off the brake light switch one turn.

10   Measure the distance (clearance "A") between the brake light switch and the pedal **(see illustration)** and compare your measurement to the clearance listed in this Chapter's Specifications. If the clearance is not as specified, repeat the previous two steps and try again.

11   Tighten the brake light switch locknut.

12   Plug in the brake light switch electrical connector.

13   Verify that brake lights come on when the brake pedal is depressed, and go off when the brake pedal is released.

14   Check the pedal freeplay (see below).

Pedal freeplay

Refer to illustrations 14.16

15   Stop the engine, if it's running, and depress the brake pedal several times until there's no more vacuum left in the booster.

16   Push in the pedal until you feel some resistance, then measure the distance between the release pedal and this point at which you can feel resistance **(see illustration)**. Compare your measurement with the pedal freeplay listed in this Chapter's Specifications. If the pedal freeplay is incorrect, adjust it as follows:

17   Check the brake light switch clearance. If the brake light switch clearance is okay, troubleshoot the brake system.

Pedal reserve

18   Start the engine, depress the brake pedal a few times, then press down hard and hold it.

19   Pedal reserve travel is measured from the floor to the top of the pedal while it's being depressed. Compare your measurement to the pedal reserve listed in this Chapter's Specifications.

20   If the pedal reserve is less than specified, check the adjustment of the rear brake shoes and/or the power brake booster pushrod-to-master cylinder piston clearance. If the brake pedal feels spongy, bleed the brake system (see Section 10).

Pedal Freeplay
1 — 6 mm

14.16 Brake pedal freeplay is the distance between the pedal when it's released and the point at which some resistance is first felt when the pedal is depressed

15 Brake light switch - check and replacement

Check

1   The brake light switch is located on a bracket at the top of the brake pedal **(see illustration 14.1)**. The switch activates the brake lights at the rear of the vehicle when the pedal is depressed.

2   To check the brake light switch, simply note whether the brake lights come on when the pedal is depressed and go off when the pedal is released. If they don't, adjust the switch as described in Section 14 (adjusting the switch is part of brake pedal adjustment).

3   If the lights still don't come on, either the switch is not getting voltage, the switch itself is defective, or the circuit between the switch and the lights is defective. There is always the remote possibility that all of the brake light bulbs are burned out, but this is not very likely.

4   Use a voltmeter or test light to verify that there's voltage present at one side of the switch connector. If no voltage is present, troubleshoot the circuit from the switch to the fuse box. If there is voltage present, check for voltage on the other terminal when the brake pedal is depressed. If no voltage is present, replace the switch. If there is voltage present, troubleshoot the circuit from the switch to the brake lights (see the *Wiring diagrams* at the end of Chapter 12).

Replacement

5   Disconnect the negative battery cable from the battery.

6   Unplug the electrical connector for the brake light switch.

7   Loosen the locknut **(see illustration 14.10)** and unscrew the switch from the pedal bracket.

8   Installation is the reverse of removal.

9   Adjust the brake pedal and brake light switch (see Section 14).

Chapter 10
Suspension and steering systems

Contents

Specifications

Torque specifications

Ft-lbs (unless otherwise indicated)

Front suspension

Balljoints
Balljoint-to-control arm bolt/nuts	105
Balljoint-to-steering knuckle nut	87

Control arm
Front pivot bolt	161
Rear pivot stud nut (1993 through 1995)	101
Rear pivot bolt (1996 and later)	129

Front stabilizer bar

Bracket
Rear bolt	37
Front bolt	108
Nut	168 in-lbs
Link nuts	33

Front struts
Strut-to-steering knuckle bolts/nuts	203
Strut upper mounting nuts	29
Suspension support-to-piston rod nut	34

Rear suspension

No. 1 (front) suspension arm nuts/bolts
1995 and earlier	87
1996 and later	92

No. 2 (rear) suspension arm nuts/bolts
1995 and earlier	87
1996 and later	92
Rear hub and bearing assembly-to-rear axle carrier	59

Rear stabilizer bar
Link nuts	33
Bushing retainer bolts	168 in-lbs

Rear struts
Strut-to-axle carrier nuts/bolts	105
Strut upper mounting nuts	29
Suspension support-to-piston rod nut	36
Strut rod nuts/bolts	67

10

Torque specifications

Ft-lbs (unless otherwise indicated)

Steering

Airbag module Torx screws	48 in-lbs
Steering gear bracket bolts/nuts	43
Steering wheel nut..	25
Tie-rod ends	
Tie-rod end-to-steering knuckle nut	36
Tie-rod end locknut	41
U-joint-to-pinion shaft pinch bolt	26

---

1 General information

Refer to illustrations 1.1 and 1.2

The front suspension **(see illustration)** is a MacPherson strut design. The upper end of each strut/coil spring assembly is attached to the vehicle's body strut support. The lower end of the strut assembly is connected to the upper end of the steering knuckle. The steering knuckle is attached to a balljoint mounted on the outer end of the suspension control arm. A stabilizer bar reduces body roll.

The rear suspension **(see illustration)** also utilizes strut/coil spring assemblies. The upper end of each strut is attached to the vehicle body. The lower end of each strut is attached to an axle carrier. The carrier is located by a pair of suspension arms on each side, and a lon-

gitudinally mounted strut rod between the body and each carrier.

The rack-and-pinion steering gear is located behind the engine/transaxle assembly on the firewall and actuates the tie-rods, which are attached to the steering knuckles. The inner ends of the tie-rods are protected by rubber boots which should be inspected periodically for secure attachment, tears and leaking lubricant.

The power assist system consists of a belt-driven pump and associated lines and hoses. The fluid level in the power steering pump reservoir should be checked periodically (see Chapter 1).

The steering wheel operates the steering shaft, which actuates the steering gear through universal joints. Looseness in the steering can be caused by wear in the steering shaft universal joints, the steering gear, the tie-rod ends and loose retaining bolts.

1.1 Front suspension components

1	*Front stabilizer bar*	*5*	*Strut/coil spring assembly*	*8*	*Rack-and-pinion steering gear*		
2	*Stabilizer bar bushing clamp*	*6*	*Right driveaxle assembly*	*9*	*Support brace*		
3	*Control arm*	*7*	*Left driveaxle assembly*	*10*	*Suspension crossmember*		
4	*Balljoint*						

1.2 Typical rear suspension components

1	Rear lateral arm	5	Stabilizer bushing clamp	8	Strut/coil spring assembly
2	Rear arm toe adjuster	6	Stabilizer link	9	Rear axle carrier
3	Front lateral arm	7	Strut rod	10	Rear suspension crossmember
4	Rear stabilizer bar				

Precautions

Frequently, when working on the suspension or steering system components, you may come across fasteners which seem impossible to loosen. These fasteners on the underside of the vehicle are continually subjected to water, road grime, mud, etc., and can become rusted or "frozen," making them extremely difficult to remove. In order to unscrew these stubborn fasteners without damaging them (or other components), be sure to use lots of penetrating oil and allow it to soak in for a while. Using a wire brush to clean exposed threads will also ease removal of the nut or bolt and prevent damage to the threads. Sometimes a sharp blow with a hammer and punch will break the bond between a nut and bolt threads, but care must be taken to prevent the punch from slipping off the fastener and ruining the threads. Heating the stuck fastener and surrounding area with a torch sometimes helps too, but isn't recommended because of the obvious dangers associated with fire. Long breaker bars and extension, or "cheater," pipes will increase leverage, but never use an extension pipe on a ratchet - the ratcheting mechanism could be damaged. Sometimes tightening the nut or bolt first will help to break it loose. Fasteners that require drastic measures to remove should always be replaced with new ones.

Since most of the procedures dealt with in this Chapter involve jacking up the vehicle and working underneath it, a good pair of jackstands will be needed. A hydraulic floor jack is the preferred type of jack to lift the vehicle, and it can also be used to support certain components during various operations. **Warning:** *Never, under any circumstances, rely on a jack to support the vehicle while working on it. Whenever any of the suspension or steering fasteners are loosened or removed they must be inspected and, if necessary, replaced with new ones of the same part number or of original equipment quality and design. Torque specifications must be followed for proper reassembly and component retention. Never attempt to heat or straighten any suspension or steering components. Instead, replace any bent or damaged part with a new one.*

2   Strut assembly (front) - removal, inspection and installation

Removal

Refer to illustrations 2.3 and 2.5

1   Loosen the wheel lug nuts, raise the vehicle and support it securely on jackstands. Remove the wheel.

2   Unbolt the brake hose bracket from the strut. If the vehicle is equipped with ABS, detach the speed sensor wiring harness from the strut by removing the clamp bracket bolt.

3   Remove the strut-to-knuckle nuts **(see illustration)** and knock the bolts out with a hammer and punch.

2.3 To detach the strut assembly from the steering knuckle, remove the two nuts, then knock out the bolts with a hammer and punch

10

2.5 To detach the upper end of the strut assembly from the body, remove the upper mounting nuts (arrows)

3.3 Install the spring compressor according to the tool manufacturer's instructions and compress the spring until all pressure is relieved from the upper spring seat

3.4 Remove the damper shaft nut

4   Separate the strut from the steering knuckle. Be careful not to overextend the inner CV joint. Also, don't let the steering knuckle fall outward and strain the brake hose.

5   Support the strut and spring assembly with one hand and remove the three strut-to-body nuts **(see illustration)**. Remove the assembly out from the fenderwell.

Inspection

6   Check the strut body for leaking fluid, dents, cracks and other obvious damage which would warrant repair or replacement.

7   Check the coil spring for chips or cracks in the spring coating (this will cause premature spring failure due to corrosion). Inspect the spring seat for cuts, hardness and general deterioration.

8   If any undesirable conditions exist, proceed to the strut disassembly procedure (see Section 3).

Installation

9   Guide the strut assembly up into the fenderwell and insert the upper mounting studs through the holes in the body. Once the studs protrude, install the nuts so the strut won't fall back through. This is most easily accomplished with the help of an assistant, as the strut is quite heavy and awkward.

10   Slide the steering knuckle into the strut flange and insert the two bolts. Install the nuts and tighten them to the torque listed in this Chapter's Specifications.

11   Connect the brake hose bracket to the strut and tighten the bolt

securely. If the vehicle is equipped with ABS, install the speed sensor wiring harness bracket.

12   Install the wheel and lug nuts, then lower the vehicle and tighten the lug nuts to the torque listed in the Chapter 1 Specifications.

13   Tighten the upper mounting nuts to the torque listed in this Chapter's Specifications.

14   Drive the vehicle to an alignment shop to have the front end alignment checked, and if necessary, adjusted.

3   Strut/spring assembly - replacement

1   If the struts or coil springs exhibit the telltale signs of wear (leaking fluid, loss of damping capability, chipped, sagging or cracked coil springs) explore all options before beginning any work. The strut/shock absorber assemblies are not serviceable and must be replaced if a problem develops. However, strut assemblies complete with springs may be available on an exchange basis, which eliminates much time and work. Whichever route you choose to take, check on the cost and availability of parts before disassembling your vehicle. **Warning:** *Disassembling a strut is potentially dangerous and utmost attention must be directed to the job, or serious injury may result. Use only a high-quality spring compressor and carefully follow the manufacturer's instructions furnished with the tool. After removing the coil spring from the strut assembly, set it aside in a safe, isolated area.*

3.5 Lift the suspension support off the damper shaft

3.6 Remove the spring seat from the damper shaft

3.7 Remove the compressed spring assembly - keep the ends of the spring pointed away from your body

Disassembly

Refer to illustrations 3.3, 3.4, 3.5, 3.6 and 3.7

2   Remove the strut assembly following the procedure described in the previous Section. Mount the strut assembly in a vise. Line the vise jaws with wood or rags to prevent damage to the unit and don't tighten the vise excessively.

3   Following the tool manufacturer's instructions, install the spring compressor (which can be obtained at most auto parts stores or equipment yards on a daily rental basis) on the spring and compress it sufficiently to relieve all pressure from the upper spring seat **(see illustration)**. This can be verified by wiggling the spring.

4   Loosen the damper shaft nut with a socket wrench **(see illustration)**.

5   Remove the nut and suspension support **(see illustration)**. Inspect the bearing in the suspension support for smooth operation. If it doesn't turn smoothly, replace the suspension support. Check the rubber portion of the suspension support for cracking and general deterioration. If there is any separation of the rubber, replace it.

6   Lift the spring seat and upper insulator from the damper shaft **(see illustration)**. Check the rubber spring seat for cracking and hardness, replacing it if necessary.

7   Carefully lift the compressed spring from the assembly **(see illustration)** and set it in a safe place. **Warning:** *Never place your head near the end of the spring!*

8   Slide the rubber bumper off the damper shaft.

9   Check the lower insulator (if equipped) for wear, cracking and hardness and replace it if necessary.

Reassembly

Refer to illustrations 3.10, 3.11 and 3.12

10   If the lower insulator is being replaced, set it into position with the dropped portion seated in the lowest part of the seat. Extend the damper rod to its full length and install the rubber bumper **(see illustration)**.

3.10 Typical strut and coil spring assembly details

10

3.11 When installing the spring, make sure the end fits into the recessed portion of the lower seat (arrow)

3.12 The flats on the damper shaft (arrow) must match up with the flats in the spring seat

4.2 To detach the front stabilizer bar from the control arms, remove these two nuts (arrows) from each link

11   Carefully place the coil spring onto the lower insulator, with the end of the spring resting in the lowest part of the insulator **(see illustration)**.

12   Install the upper insulator and spring seat, making sure that the flats in the hole in the seat match up with the flats on the damper shaft **(see illustration)**.

13   Install the dust seal and suspension support to the damper shaft.

14   Install the nut and tighten it to the torque listed in this Chapter's Specifications.

15   Install the strut assembly following the procedure outlined previously (see Section 2).

---

4   Stabilizer bar and bushings (front) - removal and installation

---

Removal

Refer to illustrations 4.2, 4.3 and 4.5

1   Loosen the front wheel lug nuts. Raise the front of the vehicle and support it securely on jackstands. Apply the parking brake and block the rear wheels to keep the vehicle from rolling off the stands. Remove the front wheels.

2   Remove the stabilizer bar link **(see illustration)**. If the ballstud turns with the nut, use an Allen wrench to hold the stud.

3   Unbolt the stabilizer bar bushing clamps **(see illustration)**.

4   Unbolt the front exhaust pipe from the flange in front of the catalytic converter (see Chapter 4) and pull it down far enough to remove the stabilizer bar.

5   While the stabilizer bar is off the vehicle, slide off the retainer bushings and inspect them. If they're cracked, worn or deteriorated, replace them. It's also a good idea to inspect the stabilizer bar link. To check it, flip the balljoint stud side to side five or six times as shown **(see illustration)**, then install the nut. Using an inch-pound torque wrench, turn the nut continuously one turn every two to four seconds and note the torque reading on the fifth turn. It should be about 0.4 to 8.7 in-lbs. If it isn't, replace the link assembly.

6   Clean the bushing area of the stabilizer bar with a stiff wire brush to remove any rust or dirt.

Installation

Refer to illustration 4.8

7   Lubricate the inside and outside of the new bushing with vegetable oil (used in cooking) to simplify reassembly. **Caution:** *Don't use petroleum or mineral-based lubricants or brake fluid - they will lead to deterioration of the bushings.*

8   Installation is the reverse of removal **(see illustration)**.

4.5 To check the balljoint in the stabilizer bar link, flip the balljoint stud side to side five or six times as shown, install the nut and, using an inch-pound torque wrench, turn the nut continuously one turn every two to four seconds, then note the torque reading on the fifth turn. It should be about 0.4 to 8.7 in-lbs; if it isn't, replace the link assembly

4.3 To detach the front stabilizer bar from the vehicle, remove this nut (left arrow) and these two bolts (arrows) from the bushing clamps (left clamp shown, right identical)

4.8 An exploded view of the front stabilizer and control arm assemblies (1993 through 1995 models are as shown; 1996 models use a vertical bolt instead of a nut on the end of a pivot stud for attaching the rear of the control arm to the crossmember)

5.2a To detach the control arm from the steering knuckle balljoint, remove this bolt and these two nuts (arrows) . . .

5 Control arm - removal, inspection and installation

10

Removal

Refer to illustrations 5.2a, 5.2b, 5.3 and 5.4

1   Loosen the wheel lug nuts on the side to be dismantled, raise the front of the vehicle, support it securely on jackstands and remove the wheel.

2   Remove the bolt and two nuts holding the control arm to the steering knuckle. Use a prybar to disconnect the control arm from the steering knuckle **(see illustrations)**.

5.2b . . . and pry the control arm and balljoint apart with a large prybar or screwdriver

5.3 To detach the front of the control arm from the frame, remove this pivot bolt (arrow)

5.4 To detach the rear end of the control arm from the frame on a 1996 model, remove this bolt (arrow); to detach the rear end of the arm on earlier models, remove the nut that attaches the pivot stud to the lower arm bracket and bushing (see illustration 4.8)

3   Remove the control arm front pivot bolt (see illustration).
4   Remove the rear pivot bolt (see illustration). Note: It's not neces-sary to remove the nut and two bolts that retain the control arm bracket unless you're replacing the bushing.
5   Remove the control arm.

Inspection

6   Check the control arm for distortion and the bushings for wear, replacing parts as necessary. Do not attempt to straighten a bent con-trol arm.

Installation

7   Installation is the reverse of removal (see illustration 4.8). Tighten all of the fasteners to the torque values listed in this Chapter's Specifi-cations. Note: Before tightening the pivot bolts, raise the outer end of the control arm with a floor jack to simulate normal ride height.
8   Install the wheel and lug nuts, lower the vehicle and tighten the lug nuts to the torque listed in the Chapter 1 Specifications.
9   It's a good idea to have the front wheel alignment checked, and if necessary, adjusted after this job has been performed.

6   Balljoints - replacement

Refer to illustration 6.3
1   Loosen the wheel lug nuts, raise the vehicle and support it securely on jackstands. Remove the wheel.
2   Remove the cotter pin (if equipped) from the balljoint stud and loosen the nut (but don't remove it yet).
3   Separate the balljoint from the steering knuckle with a picklefork-type balljoint separator (see illustration). Lubricate the rubber boot with grease and work carefully, so as not to tear the boot. Remove the balljoint stud nut. The clearance between the balljoint stud and the CV joint is very tight. To remove the stud nut, you'll have to alternately back off the nut a turn or two, pull down the stud, turn the nut another turn or two, etc. until the nut is off.
4   Remove the bolt and nuts securing the balljoint to the control arm. Separate the balljoint from the control arm with a prybar (see illustration 5.2b).
5   To install the balljoint, insert the balljoint stud through the hole in the steering knuckle and install the nut, but don't tighten it yet. Don't push the balljoint stud all the way up into and through the hole; instead, thread the nut onto the stud as soon as the stud protrudes through the hole, then turn the nut to draw the stud up through the hole.

6.3 Separate the balljoint from the steering knuckle with a picklefork-type balljoint separator

6   Attach the balljoint to the control arm and install the bolt and nuts, tightening them to the torque listed in this Chapter's Specifications.
7   Tighten the balljoint stud nut to the torque listed in this Chapter's Specifications and install a new cotter pin. If the cotter pin hole doesn't line up with the slots on the nut, tighten the nut additionally until it does line up - don't loosen the nut to insert the cotter pin.
8   Install the wheel and lug nuts. Lower the vehicle and tighten the lug nuts to the torque listed in the Chapter 1 Specifications.

7   Steering knuckle and hub - removal and installation

Warning: Dust created by the brake system may contain asbestos, which is harmful to your health. Never blow it out with compressed air and don't inhale any of it. Do not, under any circumstances, use petro-leum-based solvents to clean brake parts. Use brake cleaner or dena-tured alcohol only.

Removal

Refer to illustration 7.8
1   Loosen the wheel lug nuts, raise the vehicle and support it securely on jackstands. Remove the wheel.

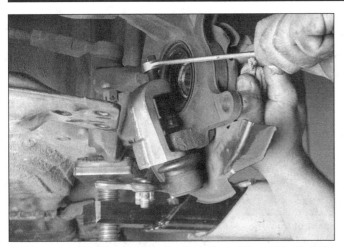

7.8 If you're replacing the steering knuckle but the old balljoint is in good condition, use a balljoint removal tool to remove the balljoint (using a picklefork can damage the balljoint boot)

9.2 To detach the rear stabilizer bar links from the stabilizer bar, remove this nut (arrow) and pivot the link out of the way

2   Remove the brake caliper and the brake disc (see Chapter 9), and disconnect the brake hose from the strut.

3   If the vehicle is equipped with ABS, disconnect and remove the wheel speed sensor.

4   Loosen, but don't remove the strut-to-steering knuckle nuts and bolts (see Section 2).

5   Separate the tie-rod end from the steering knuckle arm (see Section 17).

6   Remove the balljoint-to-lower arm bolt and nuts **(see illustrations 5.2a and 5.2b)**.

7   Push the driveaxle from the hub as described in Chapter 8. Support the end of the driveaxle with a piece of wire.

8   Using a balljoint removal tool **(see illustration)** or a small puller, remove the balljoint from the steering knuckle. Don't use a picklefork unless, of course, you're planning to install a new balljoint on the new knuckle.

9   The strut-to-knuckle bolts can now be removed.

10   Carefully separate the steering knuckle from the strut.

Installation

11   Guide the knuckle and hub assembly into position, inserting the driveaxle into the hub.

12   Push the knuckle into the strut flange and install the bolts and nuts, but don't tighten them yet.

13   If you removed the balljoint from the old knuckle, and are planning to use it with the new knuckle, connect the balljoint to the knuckle and tighten the balljoint stud nut to the torque listed in this Chapter's Specifications.

14   Attach the balljoint to the control arm (see Section 5), but don't tighten the bolt and nuts yet.

15   Attach the tie-rod to the steering knuckle arm (see Section 17). Tighten the strut bolt nuts, the balljoint-to-control arm bolt and nuts and the tie-rod nut to the torque listed in this Chapter's Specifications.

16   Place the brake disc on the hub and install the caliper as outlined in Chapter 9.

17   Install the driveaxle/hub nut and tighten it to the torque listed in the Chapter 8 Specifications.

18   Install the wheel and lug nuts.

19   Lower the vehicle and tighten the lug nuts to the torque listed in the Chapter 1 Specifications.

8   Hub and bearing assembly (front) - removal and installation

Due to the special tools and expertise required to press the hub

and bearing from the steering knuckle, this job should be left to a professional mechanic. However, the steering knuckle and hub may be removed and the assembly taken to a dealer service department or other repair shop. See Section 7 for the steering knuckle and hub removal procedure.

9   Stabilizer bar and bushings (rear) - removal and installation

Refer to illustrations 9.2 and 9.3

1   Loosen the rear wheel lug nuts. Raise the rear of the vehicle and place it securely on jackstands. Remove the rear wheels.

2   Remove the stabilizer bar-to-link nut **(see illustration)**. If the ball-stud turns with the nut, use a hex wrench to hold the stud.

3   Unbolt the stabilizer bar bushing clamps from the body **(see illustration)**.

4   The stabilizer bar can now be removed from the vehicle. Pull the retainers off the stabilizer bar (if they haven't fallen off already) using a rocking motion.

5   Check the bushings for wear, hardness, distortion, cracking and other signs of deterioration, replacing them if necessary. Also check the link bushings for these signs.

9.3 To detach the rear stabilizer bar from the vehicle body, remove the bolts (arrows) from the bushing clamps

10

10.3 Remove the clip (arrow) and pass the hose fitting through the slot in the bracket

10.6 To detach the rear strut from the axle carrier, remove these two nuts (arrows) and drive out the bolts with a hammer and punch

10.7 To detach the upper end of the rear strut from the vehicle, remove these three nuts (arrows)

6   Using a wire brush, clean the areas of the bar where the bushings ride. Installation is the reverse of the removal procedure. If necessary, use a light coat of vegetable oil to ease bushing and U-bracket installation (don't use petroleum-based products or brake fluid, as these will damage the rubber).
7   To inspect the links, refer to Step 5 in Section 4.
8   Installation is the reverse of removal.

---

10   Strut assembly (rear) - removal, inspection and installation

Removal

Refer to illustrations 10.3, 10.6 and 10.7

1   On models with a one-piece rear seat, remove the rear seat back; on models with separate rear seat backs, remove the rear side seat backs; on station wagon models, remove the rear strut cover (the plastic trim piece/cup holder on top of the side trim panel, attached by a single screw) (see Chapter 11).
2   Loosen the rear wheel lug nuts, raise the rear of the vehicle and support it securely on jackstands. Remove the wheel.
3   Remove the clip and detach the brake hose from the bracket on the strut **(see illustration)**. If the vehicle is equipped with ABS, detach the ABS sensor wire from the strut.
4   Disconnect the stabilizer bar link from the strut **(see illustration 9.2)**.

5   Support the axle carrier with a floor jack.
6   Loosen the strut-to-axle carrier bolt nuts **(see illustration)**.
7   Remove the three upper strut-to-body mounting nuts **(see illustration)**.
8   Lower the axle carrier with the jack and remove the two strut-to-axle carrier bolts.
9   Remove the strut assembly.

Inspection

Refer to illustration 10.11

10   Follow the inspection procedures described in Section 3. If you determine that the strut assembly must be disassembled for replacement of the strut or the coil spring, refer to Section 3.
11   When reassembling the strut, make sure the suspension support is aligned as shown **(see illustration)**.

Installation

12   Maneuver the assembly up into the fenderwell and insert the mounting studs through the holes in the body. Install the nuts, but don't tighten them yet.
13   Push the axle carrier into the strut lower bracket and install the bolts and nuts, tightening them to the torque listed in this Chapter's Specifications.
14   Connect the stabilizer bar link to the strut bracket.
15   Attach the brake hose to the strut bracket and install the clip. If the vehicle is equipped with ABS, attach the ABS wire to the strut.
16   Install the wheel and lug nuts, lower the vehicle and tighten the lug nuts to the torque listed in the Chapter 1 Specifications.

10.11 Install the suspension support with the flat side facing forward and the strut-to-axle carrier bracket within 5-degrees of the middle of the distance between the two outer holes

11.2 To disconnect the strut rod from the axle carrier, remove this nut and bolt (arrows)

11.3 To disconnect the strut rod from the body, remove this nut and bolt (arrows)

12.3 To detach the suspension arms from the axle carrier, remove this nut and bolt (if you're only removing the no. 2 arm, it isn't necessary to pull the bolt out)

12.4 To detach the No. 2 (rear) suspension arms from the suspension crossmember, remove the nut and washer; to remove the No. 1 (front) arms, remove the center exhaust pipe and lower the suspension crossmember so the bolt can be pulled out

12.7 An exploded view of the rear suspension arms and the suspension crossmember

17   Tighten the three strut upper mounting nuts to the torque listed in this Chapter's Specifications.
18   Repeat Steps 2 through 17 for the other strut.
19   Install the seat, rear side seat backs or rear strut covers (see Chapter 11).

11   Strut rod - removal and installation

Refer to illustrations 11.2 and 11.3
1   Loosen the wheel lug nuts, raise the vehicle and support it securely on jackstands. Remove the wheel.
2   Remove the strut rod-to-axle carrier bolt **(see illustration).**
3   Remove the strut rod-to-body bracket bolt **(see illustration)** and detach the rod from the vehicle.
4   Installation is the reverse of the removal procedure, but don't tighten the bolts until the suspension is raised by a jack to simulate normal ride height. Be sure to tighten the bolts to the torque listed in this Chapter's Specifications. Tighten the wheel lug nuts to the torque listed in the Chapter 1 Specifications.

12   Suspension arms - removal and installation

Removal

1   Loosen the rear wheel lug nuts, raise the rear of the vehicle and support it securely on jackstands.
2   Block the front wheels and remove the rear wheel.

No. 2 (rear) suspension arms
Refer to illustrations 12.3 and 12.4
3   Remove the nut and washer from the outer end of the suspension arm at the axle carrier **(see illustration)**.
4   Remove the nut and washer from the inner end of the suspension arm at the suspension crossmember **(see illustration)**.
5   Remove the No. 2 suspension arm. **Caution:** *Do NOT loosen the locknuts and turn the adjusting tube; moving this tube will affect the rear wheel toe adjustment.*

No. 1 (front) suspension arms
Refer to illustration 12.7
6   Loosen the nut and bolt securing the inner end of the arms **(see illustration 12.4)**. Also loosen the nut and bolt attaching the outer ends of the arms to the axle carrier **(see illustration 12.3)**. Remove the exhaust system center pipe and the exhaust pipe insulator (see Chapter 4).
7   Support the suspension crossmember with a floor jack. Remove the four bolts retaining the crossmember **(see illustration)**. Lower the crossmember far enough to allow the long through bolt at the inner end of the suspension arm to be pulled forward, out of the crossmember.
8   Remove the front suspension arm-to-rear axle carrier nut and bolt.
9   Remove the front suspension arm-to-suspension crossmember nut and bolt.
10   Remove the No. 1 suspension arm.

Installation

11   Installation is the reverse of removal. Be sure to tighten all sus-

10

pension fasteners to the torque listed in this Chapter's Specifications. If you replaced a No. 2 suspension arm, have the rear wheel toe adjusted by an alignment shop as soon as you're done.

12   Install the wheel and lug nuts, then lower the vehicle to the ground. Tighten the wheel lug nuts to the torque listed in the Chapter 1 Specifications.

13   Have the rear wheel alignment checked by a dealer service department or an alignment shop.

13   Hub and bearing assembly (rear) - removal and installation

Warning: *Dust created by the brake system may contain asbestos, which is harmful to your health. Never blow it out with compressed air and don't inhale any of it. Do not, under any circumstances, use petroleum-based solvents to clean brake parts. Use brake system cleaner only.*

Note: *Due to the special tools required to replace the bearing, the hub and bearing assembly should not be disassembled by the home mechanic. The assembly can be removed, however, and taken to a dealer service department or other repair shop to have the bearing replaced.*

Removal

Refer to illustrations 13.3 and 13.5

1   Loosen the wheel lug nuts, raise the vehicle and support it securely on jackstands. Remove the wheel.

2   Pull the brake drum from the hub (see Chapter 9).

3   Remove the four hub-to-axle carrier bolts, accessible by turning the hub flange so that the large circular cutout exposes each bolt **(see illustration)**.

4   Remove the hub and bearing assembly from its seat, maneuvering it out through the brake assembly.

13.3 To remove the four bolts which attach the hub and bearing assembly to the rear axle carrier, rotate the hub flange and align one of the holes in the flange with each of the bolts

13.5 An exploded view of the rear hub and bearing and rear axle carrier assemblies

5   Remove the old O-ring from the hub seat **(see illustration)**.
6   On models without anti-lock brakes the rear axle hub can be removed from the bearing to allow replacement of the bearing. Due to the special tools required to do this, you'll have to take the hub and bearing assembly to an automotive machine shop and have the old bearing pulled off the hub and a new bearing pressed on (you can re-use the hub itself, as long as it's in good condition). Make sure the hub retaining nut is tightened to the torque listed in this Chapter's Specifications. On models equipped with anti-lock brakes, the hub and bearing must be replaced as an assembly.

Installation

Refer to illustration 13.7

7   Apply a light coat of oil to the new O-ring and install it on the outer circumference of the raised hub in the backing plate **(see illustration)**.
8   Position the hub and bearing assembly on the axle carrier and align the holes in the backing plate. Install the bolts. A magnet is useful in guiding the bolts through the hub flange and into position. After all four bolts have been installed, tighten them to the torque listed in this Chapter's Specifications.
9   Install the brake drum, or disc and caliper, and the wheel. Lower the vehicle and tighten the lug nuts to the torque listed in the Chapter 1 Specifications.

14   Rear axle carrier - removal and installation

Warning: *Dust created by the brake system may contain asbestos, which is harmful to your health. Never blow it out with compressed air and don't inhale any of it. Do not, under any circumstances, use petroleum-based solvents to clean brake parts. Use brake system cleaner only.*

Removal

1   Loosen the wheel lug nuts, raise the vehicle and support it on jackstands. Block the front wheels and remove the rear wheel.
2   Remove the rear brake drum and detach the brake line from the bracket on the strut **(see illustration 10.3)**.
3   Remove the rear hub and bearing assembly (see Section 13).
4   Detach the backing plate and rear brake assembly from the axle carrier. It isn't necessary to disassemble the brake shoe assembly or disconnect the parking brake cable from the backing plate. Suspend the backing plate and brake assembly from the coil spring with a piece of wire. Be careful not to kink the brake line.
5   On models with ABS, remove the wheel speed sensor from the axle carrier **(see illustration 13.5)**.
6   Loosen, but don't remove the strut-to-axle carrier bolts **(see illustration 10.6)**.
7   Remove the suspension arm-to-axle carrier bolt, nut and washers and remove the rear strut rod-to-axle carrier bolt **(see illustrations 11.2 and 12.3)**.
8   Remove the loosened strut-to-axle carrier bolts while supporting the carrier so it doesn't fall and detach the axle carrier from the strut bracket.

Installation

9   Inspect the carrier bushing for cracks, deformation and signs of wear. If it is worn out, take the carrier to a dealer service department or other repair shop to have the old one pressed out and a new one pressed in.
10   Push the axle carrier into the strut bracket, aligning the two bolt holes. Insert the two strut-to-carrier bolts and tighten them to the torque listed in this Chapter's Specifications.
11   Install the suspension arm-to-axle carrier bolt (from the front), washers and nut. Tighten the nut by hand.
12   Connect the strut rod to the axle carrier and tighten the nut and bolt finger tight.
13   Place a jack under the carrier and raise it to simulate normal ride height.

13.7 Apply a light coat of oil to a new O-ring and install it on the raised hub of the backing plate; don't push the O-ring down against the face of the backing plate - when the hub/bearing assembly is installed, the O-ring will seat in its groove around the inside of the hub nut bore as the hub/bearing assembly is tightened

14   Tighten the suspension arm bolt/nut and the strut rod bolt/nut to the torque values listed in this Chapter's Specifications. Remove the floor jack from under the rear axle carrier.
15   On models with ABS, reattach the wheel speed sensor to the axle carrier.
16   Attach the brake backing plate to the axle carrier, install the hub and tighten the four bolts to the torque listed in this Chapter's Specifications.
17   Connect the brake line to the strut bracket and install the clip. Make sure the hose isn't twisted.
18   Install the rear brake drum (see Chapter 9).
19   Install the wheel and lug nuts.
20   Lower the vehicle and tighten the lug nuts to the torque listed in the Chapter 1 Specifications.

15   Steering system - general information

All models are equipped with rack-and-pinion steering. The steering gear is bolted to the engine cradle and operates the steering knuckles via tie-rods. The inner ends of the tie-rods are protected by rubber boots which should be inspected periodically for secure attachment, tears and leaking lubricant.
On models with power steering, the power assist system consists of a belt-driven pump and associated lines and hoses. The fluid level in the power steering pump reservoir should be checked periodically (see Chapter 1).
The steering wheel operates the steering shaft, which actuates the steering gear through universal joints. Looseness in the steering can be caused by wear in the steering shaft universal joints, the steering gear, the tie-rod ends and loose retaining bolts.

10

16   Steering wheel - removal and installation

Warning: *These models are equipped with airbags. The airbag is armed and can deploy (inflate) whenever the battery is connected. To prevent accidental deployment (and possible injury), turn the ignition key to LOCK and disconnect the negative battery cable whenever working near airbag components. After the battery is disconnected, wait at least two minutes before beginning work (the system has a back-up capacitor that must fully discharge). For more information see Chapter 12.*

16.2a To access the airbag module retaining screws, remove the cover on each side of the steering wheel

16.2b There is one T30 Torx retaining screw (shown) on the right side of the steering wheel and there are two T30s on the left side

16.2c Back out the Torx screws until the airbag module is free, but don't try to remove them from the screw case

16.3a Lift the airbag module straight out from the steering wheel . . .

16.3b . . . flip up the locking tab on the electrical connector for the module and unplug the connector

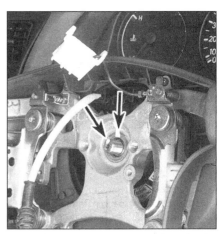

16.5 After removing the steering wheel nut, mark the relationship of the steering wheel to the shaft before removing the wheel

Removal

Refer to illustrations 16.2a, 16.2b, 16.2c, 16.3a, 16.3b, 16.5 and 16.6

1   Turn the ignition key to Off, then disconnect the cable from the negative terminal of the battery. If the vehicle is equipped with an airbag system, wait at least two minutes before proceeding. **Caution:** *If the stereo in your vehicle is equipped with an anti-theft system, make sure you have the correct activation code before disconnecting the battery.*

2   Turn the steering wheel so the wheels are pointing straight ahead, then pry off the small covers on either side of the steering wheel and loosen the T30 Torx screws that attach the airbag module to the steering wheel **(see illustrations)**. Loosen each screw until the groove in the circumference of the screw catches on the screw case **(see illustration)**. Note that there are two screws on the left and one screw on the right; this is normal - there is no missing screw on the right.

3   Pull the airbag module off the steering wheel **(see illustration)** and disconnect the module electrical connector **(see illustration)**. **Warning:** *Set the airbag module down with the trim side facing up.*

4   Unplug the electrical connector for the cruise control (if equipped).

5   Remove the steering wheel retaining nut, then mark the relationship of the steering shaft to the hub (if marks don't already exist or don't line up) to simplify installation and ensure steering wheel alignment **(see illustration)**.

6   Use a puller to disconnect the steering wheel from the shaft **(see illustration)**.

Installation

Refer to illustrations 16.7 and 16.11

7   Make sure that the front wheels are facing straight ahead. Turn the spiral cable counterclockwise by hand until it becomes harder to turn the cable. Rotate the cable clockwise about three turns and align the two red pointers **(see illustration)**.

8   To install the wheel, align the mark on the steering wheel hub with the mark on the shaft and slip the wheel onto the shaft. Install the nut and tighten it to the torque listed in this Chapter's Specifications.

9   Plug in the cruise control connector.

10   Plug in the electrical connector for the airbag module and flip down the locking tab.

11   Make sure the airbag module electrical connector is positioned correctly and that the wires don't interfere with anything **(see illustration)**, then install the airbag module and tighten the Torx retaining screws to the torque listed in this Chapter's Specifications.

12   Connect the negative battery cable.

17   Tie-rod ends - removal and installation

Removal

Refer to illustrations 17.2, 17.3a, 17.3b and 17.4

1   Loosen the wheel lug nuts. Raise the front of the vehicle, support it securely on jackstands, block the rear wheels and set the parking

16.6 If the steering wheel is difficult to remove from the shaft, use a steering wheel puller to remove it

16.7 Verify that the front wheels are pointing straight ahead and turn the spiral cable counterclockwise by hand until it becomes hard to turn the cable, then rotate the spiral cable clockwise three turns and align the red marks (the spiral cable will rotate about three turns to the left or right of center)

16.11 Before installing the airbag module, make sure that no wiring interferes with, or is pinched between, other parts; if you route the airbag harness as shown, it should be fine

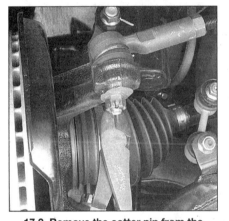

17.2 Remove the cotter pin from the castle nut and loosen - but don't remove - the nut

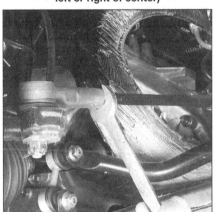

17.3a Loosen the jam nut . . .

17.3b . . . then mark the position of the tie-rod end in relation to the threads

brake. Remove the front wheel.

2   Remove the cotter pin **(see illustration)** and loosen the nut on the tie-rod end stud.

3   Hold the tie rod with a pair of locking pliers or wrench and loosen the jam nut enough to mark the position of the tie-rod end in relation to the threads **(see illustrations)**.

4   Disconnect the tie rod from the steering knuckle arm with a puller **(see illustration)**. Remove the nut and detach the tie-rod.

5   Unscrew the tie-rod end from the tie-rod.

Installation

6   Thread the tie-rod end on to the marked position and insert the tie-rod stud into the steering knuckle arm. Tighten the jam nut securely.

7   Install the castle nut on the stud and tighten it to the torque listed in this Chapter's Specifications. Install a new cotter pin. If the hole for the cotter pin doesn't line up with one of the slots in the nut, turn the nut an additional amount until it does.

8   Install the wheel and lug nuts. Lower the vehicle and tighten the lug nuts to the torque listed in the Chapter 1 Specifications.

9   Have the alignment checked by a dealer service department or an alignment shop.

17.4 Disconnect the tie-rod from the steering knuckle arm with a puller

18   Steering gear boots - replacement

Refer to illustrations 18.3a and 18.3b

1   Loosen the lug nuts, raise the vehicle and support it securely on

jackstands. Remove the wheel.

2   Remove the tie-rod end and jam nut (see Section 17).

3   Remove the outer steering gear boot clamp with a pair of pliers

10

18.3a The outer ends of the steering gear boots are secured by band-type clamps; they're easily released with a pair of pliers

18.3b The inner ends of the steering gear boots are retained by boot clamps which must be cut off and discarded

19.2 Disconnect the power steering line fittings (arrows)

(see illustration). Cut off the inner boot clamp with a pair of diagonal cutters **(see illustration)**. Slide off the boot.

4   Before installing the new boot, wrap the threads and serrations on the end of the steering rod with a layer of tape so the small end of the new boot isn't damaged.

5   Slide the new boot into position on the steering gear until it seats in the groove in the steering rod and install new clamps.

6   Remove the tape and install the tie-rod end (see Section 17).

7   Install the wheel and lug nuts. Lower the vehicle and tighten the lug nuts to the torque listed in the Chapter 1 Specifications.

19   Steering gear - removal and installation

Warning: *These models are equipped with airbags. Make sure the steering shaft is not turned while the steering gear is removed or you could damage the airbag system. To prevent the shaft from turning, turn the ignition key to the lock position before beginning work or run the seat belt through the steering wheel and clip the seat belt into place.*

Removal

Refer to illustrations 19.2, 19.3a, 19.3b and 19.5

1   Loosen the front wheel lug nuts, raise the front of the vehicle and support it securely on jackstands. Apply the parking brake and remove the wheels. Remove the engine splash shields.

2   If equipped with power steering, place a drain pan under the steering gear. Detach the power steering pressure and return lines

(see illustration) and cap the ends to prevent excessive fluid loss and contamination.

3   Remove the universal joint cover **(see illustration)**. Mark the relationship of the lower universal joint to the steering gear input shaft and remove the lower intermediate shaft pinch bolt **(see illustration)**.

4   Separate the tie-rod ends from the steering knuckle arms (see Section 17).

5   Support the steering gear and remove the steering gear bracket-to-firewall mounting bolts **(see illustration)**. Separate the intermediate shaft from the steering gear input shaft and remove the steering gear assembly. **Warning:** *Do NOT turn the steering wheel while the steering gear is removed. If the steering wheel is inadvertently turned, remove the steering wheel and center the spiral cable (see Section 16).*

6   Check the steering gear mounting grommets for excessive wear or deterioration, replacing them if necessary.

Installation

7   Raise the steering gear into position and connect the U-joint, aligning the marks.

8   Install the mounting brackets and bolts and tighten them to the torque listed in this Chapter's Specifications.

9   Connect the tie-rod ends to the steering knuckle arms (see Section 17).

10   Install the U-joint pinch bolt and tighten it to the torque listed in this Chapter's Specifications.

11   If equipped with power steering, connect the power steering pressure and return hoses to the steering gear and fill the power steering pump reservoir with the recommended fluid (see Chapter 1).

12   Lower the vehicle and bleed the steering system (see Section 21).

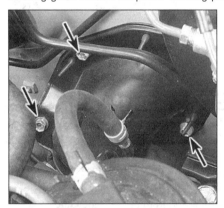

19.3a Remove the universal joint cover bolts (arrows) and remove the cover (only three cover bolts are visible in this photo - there are actually five)

19.3b Mark the relationship of the universal joint to the steering gear input shaft and loosen the U-joint pinch bolt (arrow)

19.5 Remove the lower bolt (arrow) and the upper nut (arrow) from the right steering gear bracket, then remove the nut and bolt from the left bracket (not visible in this photo)

Turn Signals
Manifold Gasket
Power Steering Belt
Oil pan gasket
EGR valve

Oil Leak
Power Steering belt
Screams when cold

20.6 Working from underneath, detach these two vacuum lines (arrows) from the power steering pump

20.7a Besides the pivot bolt, you'll need to remove the adjuster bolt (left arrow) to remove the pump; if you want to remove the pump bracket, remove the two bolts (arrows) at the right as well

...stallation

...y terminal. **Caution:**
...-theft system, make
... disconnecting the

...much fluid out of the
... drain pan under the
... hoses are discon-
nected.

3   Loosen the clamp and disconnect the fluid return hose from the pump **(see illustration)**.
4   Remove the pressure line-to-pump banjo bolt **(see illustration 20.3)**, then detach the line from the pump. Remove and discard the copper sealing washers. They must be replaced when installing the pump.
5   Raise the front of the vehicle and place it securely on jackstands.
6   Working from underneath the vehicle, detach the two vacuum lines from the pump **(see illustration)**.
7   Loosen the pivot bolt (underneath) and adjuster bolt (above) and remove the drivebolt (see Chapter 1). Remove the pivot, adjuster and mounting bolts **(see illustrations)**, then remove the pump from the vehicle.

20.7b An exploded view of the power steering pump and mounting bracket assembly

Union Bolt

Gasket

Pressure Feed Tube

PS Vane Pump Assembly

Clip

Return Hose

Vacuum Hose

Drive Belt

Adjusting Bracket

10

22.1 Metric tire size code

A = Section width   *B = Section height*

23.1 Camber, caster and toe-in angles

Installation

8   Installation is the reverse of removal. Be sure to tighten the pressure line fitting or banjo bolt to the torque listed in this Chapter's Specifications. Adjust the drivebelt tension following the procedure described in Chapter 1.

9   Top up the fluid level in the reservoir (see Chapter 1) and bleed the system (see Section 21).

21 Power steering system - bleeding

1   Following any operation in which the power steering fluid lines have been disconnected, the power steering system must be bled to remove all air and obtain proper steering performance.

2   With the front wheels in the straight ahead position, check the power steering fluid level and, if low, add fluid until it reaches the Cold mark on the dipstick.

3   Start the engine and allow it to run at fast idle. Recheck the fluid level and add more if necessary to reach the Cold mark on the dipstick.

4   Bleed the system by turning the wheels from side to side, without hitting the stops. This will work the air out of the system. Keep the reservoir full of fluid as this is done.

5   When the air is worked out of the system, return the wheels to the straight ahead position and leave the vehicle running for several more minutes before shutting it off.

6   Road test the vehicle to be sure the steering system is functioning normally and noise free.

7   Recheck the fluid level to be sure it is up to the Hot mark on the dipstick while the engine is at normal operating temperature. Add fluid if necessary (see Chapter 1).

22 Wheels and tires - general information

Refer to illustration 22.1

1   All vehicles covered by this manual are equipped with metric-sized fiberglass or steel belted radial tires **(see illustration)**. Use of other size or type of tires may affect the ride and handling of the vehicle. Don't mix different types of tires, such as radials and bias belted, on the same vehicle as handling may be seriously affected. It's recommended that tires be replaced in pairs on the same axle, but if only one tire is being replaced, be sure it's the same size, structure and tread design as the other.

2   Because tire pressure has a substantial effect on handling and wear, the pressure on all tires should be checked at least once a month or before any extended trips (see Chapter 1).

3   Wheels must be replaced if they are bent, dented, leak air, have elongated bolt holes, are heavily rusted, out of vertical symmetry or if the lug nuts won't stay tight. Wheel repairs that use welding or peening are not recommended.

4   Tire and wheel balance is important in the overall handling, braking and performance of the vehicle. Unbalanced wheels can adversely affect handling and ride characteristics as well as tire life. Whenever a tire is installed on a wheel, the tire and wheel should be balanced by a shop with the proper equipment.

23 Wheel alignment - general information

Refer to illustration 23.1

A wheel alignment refers to the adjustments made to the wheels so they are in proper angular relationship to the suspension and the ground. Wheels that are out of proper alignment not only affect vehicle control, but also increase tire wear. The front end angles normally measured are camber, caster and toe-in **(see illustration)**. Camber and toe-in are adjustable on 1996 and later models. Toe-in is the only adjustable angle on 1995 and earlier models. The only adjustment possible on the rear is toe-in. The other angles should be measured to check for bent or worn suspension parts.

Getting the proper wheel alignment is a very exacting process, one in which complicated and expensive machines are necessary to perform the job properly. Because of this, you should have a technician with the proper equipment perform these tasks. We will, however, use this space to give you a basic idea of what is involved with a wheel alignment so you can better understand the process and deal intelligently with the shop that does the work.

Toe-in is the turning in of the wheels. The purpose of a toe specification is to ensure parallel rolling of the wheels. In a vehicle with zero toe-in, the distance between the front edges of the wheels will be the same as the distance between the rear edges of the wheels. The actual amount of toe-in is normally only a fraction of an inch. On the front end, toe-in is controlled by the tie-rod end position on the tie-rod. On the rear end, it's controlled by a cam on the inner end of the rear (number two) suspension arm. Incorrect toe-in will cause the tires to wear improperly by making them scrub against the road surface.

Camber is the tilting of the wheels from vertical when viewed from one end of the vehicle. When the wheels tilt out at the top, the camber is said to be positive (+). When the wheels tilt in at the top the camber is negative (-). The amount of tilt is measured in degrees from vertical and this measurement is called the camber angle. This angle affects the amount of tire tread which contacts the road and compensates for changes in the suspension geometry when the vehicle is cornering or traveling over an undulating surface. It is adjusted using special camber adjusting bolts.

Caster is the tilting of the front steering axis from the vertical. A tilt toward the rear is positive caster and a tilt toward the front is negative caster.

Chapter 11 Body

Contents

1 General information

The models covered by this manual feature a "unibody" construction, using a floor pan with front and rear frame side rails which support the body components, front and rear suspension systems and other mechanical components. Certain components are particularly vulnerable to accident damage and can be unbolted and repaired or replaced. Among these parts are the body moldings, bumpers, hood and trunk lids and all glass.

Only general body maintenance practices and body panel repair procedures within the scope of the do-it-yourselfer are included in this Chapter.

2 Body - maintenance

1   The condition of your vehicle's body is very important, because the resale value depends a great deal on it. It's much more difficult to repair a neglected or damaged body than it is to repair mechanical components. The hidden areas of the body, such as the wheel wells, the frame and the engine compartment, are equally important, although they don't require as frequent attention as the rest of the body.

2   Once a year, or every 12,000 miles, it's a good idea to have the underside of the body steam cleaned. All traces of dirt and oil will be removed and the area can then be inspected carefully for rust, damaged brake lines, frayed electrical wires, damaged cables and other problems. The front suspension components should be greased after completion of this job.

3   At the same time, clean the engine and the engine compartment with a steam cleaner or water soluble degreaser.

4   The wheel wells should be given close attention, since undercoating can peel away and stones and dirt thrown up by the tires can cause the paint to chip and flake, allowing rust to set in. If rust is found, clean down to the bare metal and apply an anti-rust paint.

5   The body should be washed about once a week. Wet the vehicle thoroughly to soften the dirt, then wash it down with a soft sponge and plenty of clean soapy water. If the surplus dirt is not washed off very carefully, it can wear down the paint.

6   Spots of tar or asphalt thrown up from the road should be removed with a cloth soaked in solvent.

7   Once every six months, wax the body and chrome trim. If a chrome cleaner is used to remove rust from any of the vehicle's plated parts, remember that the cleaner also removes part of the chrome, so use it sparingly.

3 Vinyl trim - maintenance

Don't clean vinyl trim with detergents, caustic soap or petroleum-based cleaners. Plain soap and water works just fine, with a soft brush to clean dirt that may be ingrained. Wash the vinyl as frequently as the rest of the vehicle.

After cleaning, application of a high quality rubber and vinyl protectant will help prevent oxidation and cracks. The protectant can also be applied to weatherstripping, vacuum lines and rubber hoses, which often fail as a result of chemical degradation, and to the tires.

These photos illustrate a method of repairing simple dents. They are intended to supplement *Body repair - minor damage* in this Chapter and should not be used as the sole instructions for body repair on these vehicles.

1   If you can't access the backside of the body panel to hammer out the dent, pull it out with a slide-hammer-type dent puller. In the deepest portion of the dent or along the crease line, drill or punch hole(s) at least one inch apart . . .

2   . . . then screw the slide-hammer into the hole and operate it. Tap with a hammer near the edge of the dent to help 'pop' the metal back to its original shape. When you're finished, the dent area should be close to its original contour and about 1/8-inch below the surface of the surrounding metal

3   Using coarse-grit sandpaper, remove the paint down to the bare metal. Hand sanding works fine, but the disc sander shown here makes the job faster. Use finer (about 320-grit) sandpaper to feather-edge the paint at least one inch around the dent area

4   When the paint is removed, touch will probably be more helpful than sight for telling if the metal is straight. Hammer down the high spots or raise the low spots as necessary. Clean the repair area with wax/silicone remover

5   Following label instructions, mix up a batch of plastic filler and hardener. The ratio of filler to hardener is critical, and, if you mix it incorrectly, it will either not cure properly or cure too quickly (you won't have time to file and sand it into shape)

6   Working quickly so the filler doesn't harden, use a plastic applicator to press the body filler firmly into the metal, assuring it bonds completely. Work the filler until it matches the original contour and is slightly above the surrounding metal

7   Let the filler harden until you can just dent it with your fingernail. Use a body file or Surform tool (shown here) to rough-shape the filler

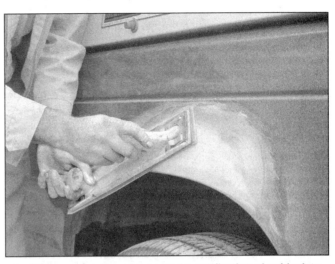

8   Use coarse-grit sandpaper and a sanding board or block to work the filler down until it's smooth and even. Work down to finer grits of sandpaper - always using a board or block - ending up with 360 or 400 grit

9   You shouldn't be able to feel any ridge at the transition from the filler to the bare metal or from the bare metal to the old paint. As soon as the repair is flat and uniform, remove the dust and mask off the adjacent panels or trim pieces

10   Apply several layers of primer to the area. Don't spray the primer on too heavy, so it sags or runs, and make sure each coat is dry before you spray on the next one. A professional-type spray gun is being used here, but aerosol spray primer is available inexpensively from auto parts stores

11   The primer will help reveal imperfections or scratches. Fill these with glazing compound. Follow the label instructions and sand it with 360 or 400-grit sandpaper until it's smooth. Repeat the glazing, sanding and respraying until the primer reveals a perfectly smooth surface

12   Finish sand the primer with very fine sandpaper (400 or 600-grit) to remove the primer overspray. Clean the area with water and allow it to dry. Use a tack rag to remove any dust, then apply the finish coat. Don't attempt to rub out or wax the repair area until the paint has dried completely (at least two weeks)

4   Upholstery and carpets - maintenance

1   Every three months remove the carpets or mats and clean the interior of the vehicle (more frequently if necessary). Vacuum the upholstery and carpets to remove loose dirt and dust.
2   Leather upholstery requires special care. Stains should be removed with warm water and a very mild soap solution. Use a clean, damp cloth to remove the soap, then wipe again with a dry cloth. Never use alcohol, gasoline, nail polish remover or thinner to clean leather upholstery.
3   After cleaning, regularly treat leather upholstery with a leather wax. Never use car wax on leather upholstery.
4   In areas where the interior of the vehicle is subject to bright sunlight, cover leather seats with a sheet if the vehicle is to be left out for any length of time.

5   Body repair - minor damage

See photo sequence

Repair of minor scratches

1   If the scratch is superficial and does not penetrate to the metal of the body, repair is very simple. Lightly rub the scratched area with a fine rubbing compound to remove loose paint and built-up wax. Rinse the area with clean water.
2   Apply touch-up paint to the scratch, using a small brush. Continue to apply thin layers of paint until the surface of the paint in the scratch is level with the surrounding paint. Allow the new paint at least two weeks to harden, then blend it into the surrounding paint by rubbing with a very fine rubbing compound. Finally, apply a coat of wax to the scratch area.
3   If the scratch has penetrated the paint and exposed the metal of the body, causing the metal to rust, a different repair technique is required. Remove all loose rust from the bottom of the scratch with a pocket knife, then apply rust inhibiting paint to prevent the formation of rust in the future. Using a rubber or nylon applicator, coat the scratched area with glaze-type filler. If required, the filler can be mixed with thinner to provide a very thin paste, which is ideal for filling narrow scratches. Before the glaze filler in the scratch hardens, wrap a piece of smooth cotton cloth around the tip of a finger. Dip the cloth in thinner and then quickly wipe it along the surface of the scratch. This will ensure that the surface of the filler is slightly hollow. The scratch can now be painted over as described earlier in this section.

Repair of dents

4   When repairing dents, the first job is to pull the dent out until the affected area is as close as possible to its original shape. There is no point in trying to restore the original shape completely as the metal in the damaged area will have stretched on impact and cannot be restored to its original contours. It is better to bring the level of the dent up to a point which is about 1/8-inch below the level of the surrounding metal. In cases where the dent is very shallow, it is not worth trying to pull it out at all.
5   If the back side of the dent is accessible, it can be hammered out gently from behind using a soft-face hammer. While doing this, hold a block of wood firmly against the opposite side of the metal to absorb the hammer blows and prevent the metal from being stretched.
6   If the dent is in a section of the body which has double layers, or some other factor makes it inaccessible from behind, a different technique is required. Drill several small holes through the metal inside the damaged area, particularly in the deeper sections. Screw long, self-tapping screws into the holes just enough for them to get a good grip in the metal. Now the dent can be pulled out by pulling on the protruding heads of the screws with locking pliers.
7   The next stage of repair is the removal of paint from the damaged area and from an inch or so of the surrounding metal. This is done with a wire brush or sanding disk in a drill motor, although it can be done just as effectively by hand with sandpaper. To complete the preparation for filling, score the surface of the bare metal with a screwdriver or the tang of a file, or drill small holes in the affected area. This will provide a good grip for the filler material. To complete the repair, see the subsection on filling and painting later in this Section.

Repair of rust holes or gashes

8   Remove all paint from the affected area and from an inch or so of the surrounding metal using a sanding disk or wire brush mounted in a drill motor. If these are not available, a few sheets of sandpaper will do the job just as effectively.
9   With the paint removed, you will be able to determine the severity of the corrosion and decide whether to replace the whole panel, if possible, or repair the affected area. New body panels are not as expensive as most people think and it is often quicker to install a new panel than to repair large areas of rust.
10   Remove all trim pieces from the affected area except those which will act as a guide to the original shape of the damaged body, such as headlight shells, etc. Using metal snips or a hacksaw blade, remove all loose metal and any other metal that is badly affected by rust. Hammer the edges of the hole in to create a slight depression for the filler material.
11   Wire brush the affected area to remove the powdery rust from the surface of the metal. If the back of the rusted area is accessible, treat it with rust inhibiting paint.
12   Before filling is done, block the hole in some way. This can be done with sheet metal riveted or screwed into place, or by stuffing the hole with wire mesh.
13   Once the hole is blocked off, the affected area can be filled and painted. See the following subsection on filling and painting.

Filling and painting

14   Many types of body fillers are available, but generally speaking, body repair kits which contain filler paste and a tube of resin hardener are best for this type of repair work. A wide, flexible plastic or nylon applicator will be necessary for imparting a smooth and contoured finish to the surface of the filler material. Mix up a small amount of filler on a clean piece of wood or cardboard (use the hardener sparingly). Follow the manufacturer's instructions on the package, otherwise the filler will set incorrectly.
15   Using the applicator, apply the filler paste to the prepared area. Draw the applicator across the surface of the filler to achieve the desired contour and to level the filler surface. As soon as a contour that approximates the original one is achieved, stop working the paste. If you continue, the paste will begin to stick to the applicator. Continue to add thin layers of paste at 20-minute intervals until the level of the filler is just above the surrounding metal.
16   Once the filler has hardened, the excess can be removed with a body file. From then on, progressively finer grades of sandpaper should be used, starting with a 180-grit paper and finishing with 600-grit wet-or-dry paper. Always wrap the sandpaper around a flat rubber or wooden block, otherwise the surface of the filler will not be completely flat. During the sanding of the filler surface, the wet-or-dry paper should be periodically rinsed in water. This will ensure that a very smooth finish is produced in the final stage.
17   At this point, the repair area should be surrounded by a ring of bare metal, which in turn should be encircled by the finely feathered edge of good paint. Rinse the repair area with clean water until all of the dust produced by the sanding operation is gone.
18   Spray the entire area with a light coat of primer. This will reveal any imperfections in the surface of the filler. Repair the imperfections with fresh filler paste or glaze filler and once more smooth the surface with sandpaper. Repeat this spray-and-repair procedure until you are satisfied that the surface of the filler and the feathered edge of the paint are perfect. Rinse the area with clean water and allow it to dry completely.
19   The repair area is now ready for painting. Spray painting must be carried out in a warm, dry, windless and dust free atmosphere. These conditions can be created if you have access to a large indoor work area, but if you are forced to work in the open, you will have to pick the day very carefully. If you are working indoors, dousing the floor in the

9.1 Before removing the hood, make marks around the hinge plate

9.10 Loosen the hood latch bolts, move the latch and retighten bolts, then close the hood to check the fit - repeat the procedure until the hood is flush with the fenders

9.11 Adjust the hood height by screwing the hood bumpers in-or-out

work area with water will help settle the dust which would otherwise be in the air. If the repair area is confined to one body panel, mask off the surrounding panels. This will help minimize the effects of a slight mis-match in paint color. Trim pieces such as chrome strips, door handles, etc., will also need to be masked off or removed. Use masking tape and several thickness of newspaper for the masking operations.

20   Before spraying, shake the paint can thoroughly, then spray a test area until the spray painting technique is mastered. Cover the repair area with a thick coat of primer. The thickness should be built up using several thin layers of primer rather than one thick one. Using 600-grit wet-or-dry sandpaper, rub down the surface of the primer until it is very smooth. While doing this, the work area should be thoroughly rinsed with water and the wet-or-dry sandpaper periodically rinsed as well. Allow the primer to dry before spraying additional coats.

21   Spray on the top coat, again building up the thickness by using several thin layers of paint. Begin spraying in the center of the repair area and then, using a circular motion, work out until the whole repair area and about two inches of the surrounding original paint is covered. Remove all masking material 10 to 15 minutes after spraying on the final coat of paint. Allow the new paint at least two weeks to harden, then use a very fine rubbing compound to blend the edges of the new paint into the existing paint. Finally, apply a coat of wax.

6   Body repair - major damage

1   Major damage must be repaired by an auto body shop specifi-cally equipped to perform unibody repairs. These shops have the spe-cialized equipment required to do the job properly.

2   If the damage is extensive, the body must be checked for proper alignment or the vehicle's handling characteristics may be adversely affected and other components may wear at an accelerated rate.

3   Due to the fact that all of the major body components (hood, fenders, etc.) are separate and replaceable units, any seriously dam-aged components should be replaced rather than repaired. Sometimes the components can be found in a wrecking yard that specializes in used vehicle components, often at considerable savings over the cost of new parts.

7   Hinges and locks - maintenance

Once every 3000 miles, or every three months, the hinges and latch assemblies on the doors, hood and trunk should be given a few drops of light oil or lock lubricant. The door latch strikers should also be lubricated with a thin coat of grease to reduce wear and ensure free movement. Lubricate the door and trunk locks with spray-on graphite lubricant.

8   Windshield and fixed glass - replacement

Replacement of the windshield and fixed glass requires the use of special fast-setting adhesive/caulk materials and some specialized tools. It is recommended that these operations be left to a dealer or a shop specializing in glass work.

9   Hood - removal, installation and adjustment

Refer to illustrations 9.1, 9.10 and 9.11
Note: *The hood is heavy and somewhat awkward to remove and install - at least two people should perform this procedure.*

Removal and installation

1   Make marks around the bolt heads to ensure proper alignment during installation **(see illustration)**.

2   Use blankets or pads to cover the cowl area of the body and fenders. This will protect the body and paint as the hood is lifted off.

3   Disconnect any cables or wires that will interfere with removal.

4   Have an assistant support the hood. Remove the hinge-to-hood bolts.

5   Lift off the hood.

6   Installation is the reverse of removal.

Adjustment

7   Fore-and-aft and side-to-side adjustment of the hood is done by moving the hinge plate slot after loosening the bolts.

8   Scribe a line around the entire hinge plate so you can judge the amount of movement **(see illustration 9.1)**.

9   Loosen the bolts or nuts and move the hood into correct align-ment. Move it only a little at a time. Tighten the hinge bolts and care-fully lower the hood to check the position.

10   If necessary after installation, the entire hood latch assembly can be adjusted up-and-down as well as from side-to-side on the radiator support so the hood closes securely, flush with the fenders. To make the adjustment, scribe a line around the hood latch mounting bolts to provide a reference point, then loosen them and reposition the latch assembly, as necessary **(see illustration)**. Following adjustment, retighten the mounting bolts.

11   Finally, adjust the hood bumpers on the radiator support so the hood, when closed, is flush with the fenders **(see illustration)**.

12   The hood latch assembly, as well as the hinges, should be period-ically lubricated with white, lithium-base grease to prevent binding and wear.

11

10.2 Unscrew the plastic retainer, then pull it out

10.3 Scribe a mark around the bolt heads to help with lid realignment on installation

10.8 Loosen the bolts, then adjust the latch and striker position

11.3 Draw a line around the hinge plate on the liftgate before removing the bolts

11.9 Adjust the lock striker by loosening the mounting screws slightly and tapping the striker with a soft-faced hammer

12.1 After supporting the liftgate, remove the bolts at each end and detach the support strut

10 Trunk lid - removal, installation and adjustment

Refer to illustrations 10.2, 10.3 and 10.8

1   Open the trunk lid and cover the edges of the trunk compartment with pads or cloths to protect the painted surfaces when the lid is removed.

2   Remove the trunk lid trim cover **(see illustration)**.

3   Make alignment marks around the hinge mounting bolts **(see illustration)**.

4   While an assistant supports the lid, remove the lid-to-hinge bolts on both sides and lift it off.

5   Installation is the reverse of removal. **Note:** *When reinstalling the trunk lid, align the lid-to-hinge bolts with the marks made during removal.*

6   After installation, close the lid and make sure it's in proper alignment with the surrounding panels.

7   Forward-and-backward and side-to-side adjustments are made by loosening the hinge-to-lid bolts and gently moving the lid into correct alignment.

8   To adjust the lid so it is flush with the body when closed, loosen the mounting bolts and move the lock and striker **(see illustration)**.

11 Liftgate (station wagon) - removal, installation and adjustment

Refer to illustrations 11.3 and 11.9

Note: *The rear liftgate is heavy and somewhat awkward to remove and install - at least two people should perform this procedure.*

1   Open the liftgate and cover the edges of the compartment with pads or cloths to protect the painted surfaces when the lid is removed.

2   Disconnect any cables or wire harness connectors attached to the liftgate that would interfere with removal.

3   Use a marking pen to make alignment marks around the hinge mounting flanges **(see illustration)**.

4   Have an assistant support the liftgate and detach the support struts (see Section 12).

5   While an assistant supports the liftgate, remove the lid-to-hinge bolts on both sides and lift it off.

6   Installation is the reverse of removal. **Note:** *When reinstalling the liftgate, align the hinges with the marks made during removal.*

7   After installation, close the liftgate and make sure it's in proper alignment with the surrounding panels.

8   Adjustments to the liftgate position are made by loosening the hinge to liftgate bolts or nuts and gently moving the liftgate into correct alignment.

9   The liftgate latch position can be adjusted by loosening the adjusting bolts and moving the latch. The latch striker can be adjusted by loosening the mounting screws and gently tapping it into position with a plastic hammer **(see illustration)**.

12 Liftgate support strut - replacement

Refer to illustration 12.1

Warning: *The support strut is filled with pressurized gas - do not disassemble this component. If it is faulty replace it with a new one.*

Note: *The rear liftgate is heavy and somewhat awkward to hold securely while replacing the struts - at least two people should perform this procedure.*

1   Open the liftgate and support it in the open position. Remove the bolts at the ends and detach the strut from the liftgate **(see illustration)**.

2   Installation is the reverse of the removal procedure.

13.2a Work a cloth up behind the regulator handle and move it back-and-forth . . .

13.2b . . . until the retainer (arrow) is pushed up so you can remove it

13.2c Pry up on the power window switch and remove it

13.4a Pry the arm rest up with a screwdriver

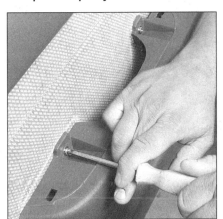

13.4b Remove the armrest screws

13.6 Use a trim panel removal tool to detach the trim panel retaining clips, then pull the door trim up and out to remove it

13   Door trim panel - removal and installation

Refer to illustrations 13.2a, 13.2b, 13.2c, 13.4a, 13.4b, 13.6 and 13.7

Removal

1   Disconnect the negative cable from the battery. **Caution:** *If the stereo in your vehicle is equipped with an anti-theft system, make sure you have the correct activation code before disconnecting the battery.*

13.7 If the plastic watershield is peeled off carefully it can be reused

2   On manual window regulator equipped models, remove the window crank by working a cloth back-and-forth behind the handle to dislodge the retainer **(see illustrations)**. A special tool is available for this purpose but it's not essential. With the retainer removed, pull off the handle. On power window models, pry out the switch assembly, unplug the electrical connector and remove it **(see illustration)**.
3   Remove the outside mirror trim cover (see Section 18).
4   Remove the inside door handle (see Section 15). Remove the door trim panel retaining screws and door pull/armrest assemblies **(see illustrations)**.
5   Insert a wide putty knife, a thin screwdriver or a special trim panel removal tool between the trim panel and door to disengage the retaining clips. Work around the outer edge until the panel is free.
6   Once all of the clips are disengaged, detach the trim panel, unplug any electrical connectors and remove the trim panel from the vehicle by gently pulling it up and out **(see illustration)**.
7   For access to the inner door remove the plastic watershield. Peel back the plastic cover, taking care not to tear it **(see illustration)**. Remove the plastic grommets, if necessary.

Installation

8   To install the trim panel, first press the watershield back into place. If necessary, add more sealant to hold it in place.
9   Prior to installation of the door panel, be sure to reinstall any clips in the panel which may have come out during the removal procedure and stayed in the door.
10   Plug in any electrical connectors and place the panel in position. Press it into place until the clips are seated and install any retaining screws and armrest/door pulls. Install the manual regulator window crank or power switch assembly.

11

14.2 Use two jackstands padded with rags (to protect the paint) to support the door during the removal and installation procedures

14.3 Remove the bolt (arrow) and detach the stop strut

14.4 Before loosening or removing them, mark the door bolt locations (arrows)

14.6a When adjusting the door up-and-down or forward-and-backward a special wrench such as this one will make the job easier

14.6b Adjust the door up-and-down or in-and-out after loosening the hinge to door bolts

14 Door - removal, installation and adjustment

Removal and installation

Refer to illustrations 14.2, 14.3 and 14.4

1   Remove the door trim panel (see Section 13). Disconnect any electrical connectors and push them through the door opening so they won't interfere with removal.

2   Position a jack or jackstands under the door or have an assistant on hand to support the door when the hinge bolts are removed **(see illustration)**. **Note:** *If a jack or stand is used, place a rag between it and*

14.6c Adjust the door lock striker by loosening the mounting screws (arrows) and gently tapping the striker in the desired direction

the door to protect the door's paint.

3   Remove the door stop strut bolt **(see illustration)**.

4   Scribe around the door bolts **(see illustration)**.

5   Remove the hinge-to-door bolts and carefully detach the door. Installation is the reverse of removal.

Adjustment

Refer to illustrations 14.6a, 14.6b and 14.6c

6   Following installation, make sure the door is aligned properly. Adjust it if necessary as follows:

   a) *Up-and-down and forward-and-backward adjustments are made by loosening the hinge-to-body bolts and moving the door, as necessary. A special offset tool may be required to reach some of the bolts* **(see illustration)**.

   b) *In-and-out and up-and-down adjustments are made by loosening the door side hinge bolts and moving the door, as necessary. A special offset tool may be required to reach some of the bolts* **(see illustration)**.

   c) *The door lock striker can also be adjusted both up-and-down and sideways to provide a positive engagement with the locking mechanism. This is done by loosening the screws and moving the striker, as necessary* **(see illustration)**.

15 Door latch, lock cylinder and handles - removal and installation

1   Remove the door trim panel and the plastic watershield (Section 13).

Door latch

Refer to illustration 15.3

2   Reach behind the inside the door panel and disconnect the control links from the latch.

15.3 Remove the latch screws from the end of the door

15.7 The outside handle retention bolts can be reached through access holes in the door frame

15.10 Remove the inside handle screw

3   Remove the latch retaining screws from the end of the door **(see illustration)**.
4   Detach the door latch and (if equipped) the door lock solenoid.
5   Installation is the reverse of removal.

Lock cylinder and outside handle

Refer to illustration 15.7
6   Disconnect the control link from the lock cylinder and outside handle.
7   Remove the outside handle retention bolts and pull the handle and lock cylinder from the door **(see illustration)**.
8   Use a screwdriver to pry the retaining clip off and remove the lock cylinder from the door.
9   Installation is the reverse of removal.

Inside handle

Refer to illustrations 15.10, 15.11a and 15.11b
10   Remove the retaining screw **(see illustration)**.
11   Pull the handle free, disconnect the link from the inside handle control and remove the handle from the door **(see illustrations)**.
12   Installation is the reverse of removal.

16   Door window glass - removal and installation

1   Remove the door trim panel and the plastic watershield (Section 13).
2   Lower the window glass.

3   Carefully pry the inner weatherstrip out of the door window opening.
4   Place a rag inside the door panel to help prevent scratching the glass and remove the two glass mounting bolts.
5   Remove the glass by pulling it up.
6   Installation is the reverse of the removal procedure.

17   Bumpers - removal and installation

Refer to illustrations 17.4a, 17.4b and 17.4c
Warning: *These models are equipped with airbags. The airbag is armed and can deploy (inflate) anytime the battery is connected. To prevent accidental deployment (and possible injury), turn the ignition key to LOCK and disconnect the negative battery cable whenever working near airbag components. After the battery is disconnected, wait at least two minutes before beginning work (the system has a back-up capacitor that must fully discharge). For more information see Chapter 12.*
1   Apply the parking brake, raise the vehicle and support it securely on jackstands.
2   Disconnect the cable from the negative battery terminal and disconnect any wiring that would interfere with bumper removal.
3   Remove the bumper cover if equipped, taking care to avoid damaging the cover and the fender.
4   Working under the vehicle remove the bumper retention bolts **(see illustrations)**.
5   Pull the bumper assembly from the vehicle.
6   Installation is the reverse of the removal procedure.

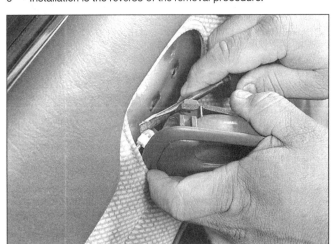

15.11a Rotate the handle out for access to the link

15.11b Detach the control link with a small screwdriver

11

17.4a Typical front bumper details

17.4b Typical sedan rear bumper details

11

17.4c Typical station wagon rear bumper details

Rear Bumper Arm

Rear Bumper Reinforcement

Rear Bumper Energy Absorber

Upper Retainer

Side Support

Side Support

Rear Bumper Cover

18.1a Remove the screw and detach the control handle

18.1b Detach the cover and lift it out (power mirror shown)

18.2a Remove the three bolts securing the outside mirror to the door

18 Outside mirror - removal and installation

Refer to illustrations 18.1a, 18.1b, 18.2a and 18.2b

1   On manually operated mirrors, remove the control handle **(see illustration)**. Detach the mirror cover by using a small screwdriver to pry the retainers free from the door **(see illustration)**.

18.2b Unplug the power mirror electrical connector (arrow)

2   Remove the three retaining nuts and detach the mirror **(see illustration)**. On power mirrors, unplug the electrical connector **(see illustration)**.
3   Installation is the reverse of removal.

19 Seats - removal and installation

Front seats

Refer to illustration 19.1

1   Remove the retaining bolts, unplug any electrical connectors and lift the seats from the vehicle **(see illustration)**.
2   Installation is the reverse of removal.

19.1 Typical front seat details

11

19.3 Typical rear seat details

20.2a Remove the two screws at the top of the bezel

Rear seats

Refer to illustration 19.3

3   On sedan models, lift the front of the cushion up, then pull it out toward the front of the vehicle. Remove the seat back retaining bolts, then lift up on the back to release the seat back from the body.**(see illustration)**.

4   On station wagon models, remove the retaining bolts at the base of the seat cushion, pull the back of the cushion up and remove it from the vehicle. Remove the seat back pivot retaining bolts and remove the seat back from the vehicle.

5   Installation is the reverse of removal.

20   Instrument cluster bezel - removal and installation

Refer to illustrations 20.2a, 20.2b and 20.3

Warning: *These models are equipped with airbags. The airbag is armed and can deploy (inflate) anytime the battery is connected. To prevent accidental deployment (and possible injury), turn the ignition key to LOCK and disconnect the negative battery cable whenever working near airbag components. After the battery is disconnected, wait at least two minutes before beginning work (the system has a back-up capacitor that must fully discharge). For more information see Chapter 12.*

Caution: *If the stereo in your vehicle is equipped with an anti-theft system, make sure you have the correct activation code before disconnecting the battery.*

1   Disconnect the cable from the negative battery terminal.

2   Remove the two screws along the top of the bezel, then detach the two clips at the lower edges by prying with a screwdriver **(see illustrations)**.

3   Grasp the bezel securely and remove it **(see illustration)**.

4   Installation is the reverse of the removal procedure.

21   Glove box - removal and installation

Refer to illustrations 21.1a and 21.1b

Warning: *These models are equipped with airbags. The airbag is armed and can deploy (inflate) anytime the battery is connected. To prevent accidental deployment (and possible injury), turn the ignition key to LOCK and disconnect the negative battery cable whenever working near airbag components. After the battery is disconnected, wait at least two minutes before beginning work (the system has a back-up capacitor that must fully discharge). For more information see Chapter 12.*

Caution: *If the stereo in your vehicle is equipped with an anti-theft system, make sure you have the correct activation code before disconnecting the battery.*

1   Disconnect the cable from the negative battery terminal. Remove the screws, pull the glove box out of the instrument panel and lower it for access to the airbag connector **(see illustration)**. Detach the connector from the clips and remove the glovebox assembly **(see illustration)**.

2   Installation is the reverse of removal.

20.2b   Use a screwdriver to detach the clips at each end of the bezel

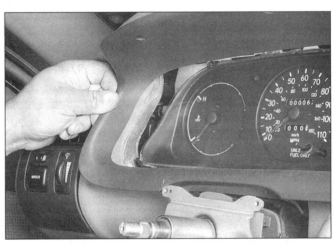

20.3   Detach the bezel and lift it off

21.1a Glove box installation details

21.1b Lower the glove box and detach the airbag connector from the clips (DO NOT unplug the airbag connector unless you plan to remove the airbag module)

22.3a Detach the trim panel, pull it out and turn it over for access to the electrical connectors

22   Center trim panel - removal and installation

Refer to illustrations 22.3a, 22.3b and 22.4

Warning: *These models are equipped with airbags. The airbag is armed and can deploy (inflate) anytime the battery is connected. To prevent accidental deployment (and possible injury), turn the ignition key to LOCK and disconnect the negative battery cable whenever working near airbag components. After the battery is disconnected, wait at least two minutes before beginning work (the system has a back-up capacitor that must fully discharge). For more information see Chapter 12.*

Caution: *If the stereo in your vehicle is equipped with an anti-theft system, make sure you have the correct activation code before disconnecting the battery.*

1   Disconnect the cable from the negative battery terminal.

Upper trim panel

2   Pull off the heater/air conditioning control knobs.
3   Detach the retaining clips at each corner using a small screwdriver, then remove the panel and unplug the electrical connectors **(see illustrations)**.

Lower trim panel

4   Remove the two screws along the upper edge, then pull the panel out and unplug the electrical connectors **(see illustration)**.
5   Installation is the reverse of the removal procedure.

23   Steering column cover - removal and installation

Refer to illustration 23.1

Warning: *These models are equipped with airbags. The airbag is armed and can deploy (inflate) anytime the battery is connected. To prevent accidental deployment (and possible injury), turn the ignition key to LOCK and disconnect the negative battery cable whenever working near airbag components. After the battery is disconnected, wait at least two minutes before beginning work (the system has a back-up capacitor that must fully discharge). For more information see Chapter 12.*

Caution: *If the stereo in your vehicle is equipped with an anti-theft system, make sure you have the correct activation code before disconnecting the battery.*

1   Remove the steering column cover screws **(see illustration)**.
2   Separate the cover halves and detach them from the steering column.
3   Disconnect any electrical connections and the covers.
4   Installation is the reverse of the removal procedure.

24   Steering column lower finish panel - removal and installation

Refer to illustration 24.2

Warning: *These models are equipped with airbags. The airbag is*

22.3b Unplug the connectors

22.4 Remove the screws and pull the lower trim panel out

23.1 Remove the screws and separate the steering column cover halves

11

armed and can deploy (inflate) anytime the battery is connected. To prevent accidental deployment (and possible injury), turn the ignition key to LOCK and disconnect the negative battery cable whenever working near airbag components. After the battery is disconnected, wait at least two minutes before beginning work (the system has a back-up capacitor that must fully discharge). For more information see Chapter 12.

Caution: If the stereo in your vehicle is equipped with an anti-theft system, make sure you have the correct activation code before disconnecting the battery.

1   Remove the two screws and detach the hood release handle.
2   Remove the retaining bolts, disconnect any electrical connections and pull the panel off **(see illustration)**.
3   Installation is the reverse of the removal procedure.

---

25   Console - removal and installation

Refer to illustrations 25.2, 25.4a, 25.4b and 25.5
Warning: These models are equipped with airbags. The airbag is armed and can deploy (inflate) anytime the battery is connected. To prevent accidental deployment (and possible injury), turn the ignition key to LOCK and disconnect the negative battery cable whenever working near airbag components. After the battery is disconnected, wait at least two minutes before beginning work (the system has a back-up capacitor that must fully discharge). For more information see Chapter 12.

Caution: If the stereo in your vehicle is equipped with an anti-theft system, make sure you have the correct activation code before disconnecting the battery.
1   Disconnect the cable from the negative battery terminal.
2   On manual shift models, unscrew the shift knob. On automatic models detach the shift bezel **(see illustration)**.

Rear console

3   Remove the center trim panels (Section 22).
4   Remove retaining screws, lift the console up, detach the clips then remove the console **(see illustrations)**.

Front console

5   Remove the screws retaining the front console to the instrument panel, then lift detach the console **(see illustration)**.
6   Installation is the reverse of the removal procedure.

---

26   Instrument panel - removal and installation

Warning: These models are equipped with airbags. The airbag is armed and can deploy (inflate) anytime the battery is connected. To prevent accidental deployment (and possible injury), turn the ignition key to LOCK and disconnect the negative battery cable whenever working near airbag components. After the battery is disconnected, wait at least two minutes before beginning work (the system has a back-up capacitor that must fully discharge). For more information see Chapter 12.

24.2 Remove the screws (some of which are under covers like this one [arrow]), then detach the finish panel

25.2 On automatic transaxle models, detach the shifter bezel with a screwdriver, then lift it off

25.4a Remove the carpet piece inside the console for access, then remove the retaining screws

25.4b Pull the rear console back to detach the clips

25.5 Remove the screws on each side and detach the front console from the instrument panel

26.3 Passenger airbag module installation details

Caution: *If the stereo in your vehicle is equipped with an anti-theft system, make sure you have the correct activation code before disconnecting the battery.*

Removal

Refer to illustrations 26.3, 26.8, 26.9, 26.10 and 26.12

1   Disconnect the cable from the negative battery terminal.
2   Remove drivers airbag module and the steering wheel (see Chapter 10).
3   Remove the glove box assembly (see section 21), disconnect the passenger airbag module electrical connector and remove the airbag module **(see illustration)**. The electrical connectors used in the airbag system are a twin-lock design; use the proper method for disconnect-ing these connectors or damage to the connector may occur (see Chapter 12). **Warning:** *Store the airbag modules in a safe place with the airbag face (the trim side) pointing up.*

4   Remove the instrument cluster bezel (see Section 20) and remove the instrument cluster (see Chapter 12).
5   Remove the center trim panel (see Section 22), remove the radio (see chapter 12) and the heater and air conditioning control panel (see Chapter 3).
6   Remove the steering column covers (see Section 23) and the lower finish panel (see Section 24).
7   Remove the front and rear console panels (see Section 25).
8   Remove the front door scuff plates and the front-pillar garnish moldings from both sides **(see illustration)**.

26.8 Instrument panel and related components - exploded view

11

26.9 Remove the steering column retaining bolts and lower the column

26.10 Remove the left ventilation duct for access to one of the instrument panel retaining bolts

9   Remove the key lock cylinder (see Chapter 12). Remove the bolts retaining the steering column to the instrument panel and reinforcement brace and lower the steering column **(see illustration)**.

10   Carefully pry out the left ventilation duct, disconnect the electrical connectors and remove the instrument panel retaining bolt behind the duct **(see illustration)**.

11   The main instrument panel wiring harness will remain with the panel when you remove it. Disconnect any remaining connectors. Detach the fuse box from the body and remove it with the panel and harness. Disconnect the electrical connectors from the heater case and remove the ground wire terminals from the center brace.

12   Remove the remaining instrument panel retaining bolts, grasp the instrument panel firmly and pull it sharply to the rear to release the five clips along the base of the windshield **(see illustration)**. Remove the instrument panel from the vehicle.

Installation

13   Carefully remove the wiring harness and the ventilation and defroster ducts and transfer them to the new instrument panel.

14   Guide the instrument panel into position, press the tabs into the five retaining clips and install the retaining bolts.

15   The remainder of installation is the reverse of removal.

---

27   Radiator grille - removal and installation

Refer to illustrations 27.1 and 27.2

1   Remove three screws along the top of the grille **(see illustration)**.

26.12 Instrument panel installation details

2   Pull the top of the grille out for access and disengage the two retaining clips with a screwdriver **(see illustration)**.

3   Once the retaining clips are disengaged, pull the grille out and remove it.

4   Installation is the reverse of removal.

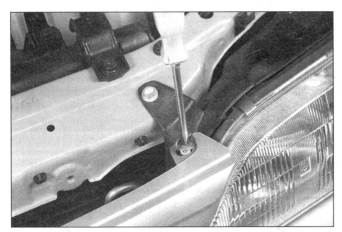

27.1 Remove the three Phillips-head screws along the top of the grille

27.2 Reach behind the grill and detach the clips by squeezing the side together as you pull the grille out

28.3 Cowl louver details

Cowl Louver

Front Pillar
Garnish

Wiper Arm

Seatback

Seat Cushion

Side Seatback

Shoulder Anchor

Inner Seat Belt

ELR

Outer Belt
Anchor

Center Pillar Upper Garnish

Adjustable Anchor

29.4a Typical sedan seat belt details

Front Pillar Garnish

Roof Side Inner Garnish

Front Pillar Lower Garnish

Rear Door Scuff Plate

Center Pillar Lower Garnish

Front Door Scuff Plate

28 Cowl louver - removal and installation

Refer to illustration 28.3

1   Mark the position of the windshield wiper blades on the windshield with a wax marking pen.

2   Remove the wiper arms.

3   Remove the cowl louver retaining screws, disconnect the windshield washer hoses and detach the cowl from the vehicle **(see illustration)**.

4   Installation is the reverse of removal. Make sure to align the wiper blades with the marks made during removal.

w/ Tonneau Cover

Tonneau Cover Hanger

Tonneau Cover

Rear Strut Cover

Rear Strut Cover

Rear Seatback
Lock Striker

Rear Seatback
Lock Striker
Cover

Deck Trim Side Panel

Quarter Trim Jack Cover

Seatback Assembly

Rear Seatback Hinge

Shoulder
Anchor

Deck Board

Rear Floor Finish Plate

Center Belt

Outer Belt Anchor

29.4b Typical station wagon rear seat belt details

29 Seat belts - check

Refer to illustrations 29.4a and 29.4b

1   Check the seat belts, buckles, latch plates and guide loops for any obvious damage or signs of wear.

2   Make sure the seat belt reminder light comes on when the key is turned on.

3   The seat belts are designed to lock up during a sudden stop or impact, yet allow free movement during normal driving. The retractors should hold the belt against your chest while driving and rewind the belt when the buckle is unlatched.

4   If any of the above checks reveal problems with the seat-belt system, replace parts as necessary **(see illustrations)**.

Chapter 12
Chassis electrical system

Contents

1 General information

The electrical system is a 12-volt, negative ground type. Power for the lights and all electrical accessories is supplied by a lead/acid-type battery which is charged by the alternator.

This Chapter covers repair and service procedures for the various electrical components not associated with the engine. Information on the battery, alternator, distributor and starter motor can be found in Chapter 5.

It should be noted that when portions of the electrical system are serviced, the cable should be disconnected from the negative battery terminal to prevent electrical shorts and/or fires. **Caution:** *If the stereo in your vehicle is equipped with an anti-theft system, make sure you have the correct activation code before disconnecting the battery.*

2 Electrical troubleshooting - general information

A typical electrical circuit consists of an electrical component, any switches, relays, motors, fuses, fusible links or circuit breakers related to that component and the wiring and electrical connectors that link the component to both the battery and the chassis. To help you pinpoint an electrical circuit problem, wiring diagrams are included at the end of this book.

Before tackling any troublesome electrical circuit, first study the appropriate wiring diagrams to get a complete understanding of what makes up that individual circuit. Trouble spots, for instance, can often be narrowed down by noting if other components related to the circuit are operating properly. If several components or circuits fail at one time, chances are the problem is in a fuse or ground connection, because several circuits are often routed through the same fuse and ground connections.

Electrical problems usually stem from simple causes, such as loose or corroded connections, a blown fuse, a melted fusible link or a bad relay. Visually inspect the condition of all fuses, wires and connections in a problem circuit before troubleshooting it.

If testing instruments are going to be utilized, use the diagrams to plan ahead of time where you will make the necessary connections in order to accurately pinpoint the trouble spot.

The basic tools needed for electrical troubleshooting include a circuit tester or voltmeter (a 12-volt bulb with a set of test leads can also be used), a continuity tester, which includes a bulb, battery and set of test leads, and a jumper wire, preferably with a circuit breaker incorporated, which can be used to bypass electrical components. Before attempting to locate a problem with test instruments, use the wiring diagram(s) to decide where to make the connections.

Voltage checks

Voltage checks should be performed if a circuit is not functioning properly. Connect one lead of a circuit tester to either the negative battery terminal or a known good ground. Connect the other lead to a electrical connector in the circuit being tested, preferably nearest to the battery or fuse. If the bulb of the tester lights, voltage is present, which means that the part of the circuit between the electrical connector and the battery is problem free. Continue checking the rest of the circuit in the same fashion. When you reach a point at which no voltage is present, the problem lies between that point and the last test point with voltage. Most of the time the problem can be traced to a loose connection. **Note:** *Keep in mind that some circuits receive voltage only when the ignition key is in the Accessory or Run position.*

12

3.1a The main fuse block is located in the driver's side kick panel, under a cover

3.1b A fuse and relay block is located in the engine compartment

3.1c On air-conditioned models, fuse and relay block is located next to the battery

Finding a short

One method of finding shorts in a circuit is to remove the fuse and connect a test light or voltmeter in its place to the fuse terminals. There should be no voltage present in the circuit. Move the wiring harness from side to side while watching the test light. If the bulb goes on, there is a short to ground somewhere in that area, probably where the insulation has rubbed through. The same test can be performed on each component in the circuit, even a switch.

Ground check

Perform a ground test to check whether a component is properly grounded. Disconnect the battery and connect one lead of a self-powered test light, known as a continuity tester, to a known good ground. Connect the other lead to the wire or ground connection being tested. If the bulb goes on, the ground is good. If the bulb does not go on, the ground is not good.

Continuity check

A continuity check is done to determine if there are any breaks in a circuit - if it is passing electricity properly. With the circuit off (no power in the circuit), a self-powered continuity tester can be used to check the circuit. Connect the test leads to both ends of the circuit (or to the "power" end and a good ground), and if the test light comes on the circuit is passing current properly. If the light doesn't come on, there is a break somewhere in the circuit. The same procedure can be used to test a switch, by connecting the continuity tester to the power in and power out sides of the switch. With the switch turned On, the test light should come on.

Finding an open circuit

When diagnosing for possible open circuits, it is often difficult to locate them by sight because oxidation or terminal misalignment are hidden by the electrical connectors. Merely wiggling an electrical connector on a sensor or in the wiring harness may correct the open circuit condition. Remember this when an open circuit is indicated when troubleshooting a circuit. Intermittent problems may also be caused by oxidized or loose connections.

Electrical troubleshooting is simple if you keep in mind that all electrical circuits are basically electricity running from the battery, through the wires, switches, relays, fuses and fusible links to each electrical component (light bulb, motor, etc.) and to ground, from which it is passed back to the battery. Any electrical problem is an interruption in the flow of electricity to and from the battery.

---

3   Fuses - general information

Refer to illustrations 3.1a, 3.1b, 3.1c and 3.3

The electrical circuits of the vehicle are protected by a combination of fuses, circuit breakers and fusible links. The fuse blocks are located under the instrument panel on the left and right (some models) sides of the dashboard, and in the engine compartment next to the battery **(see illustrations)**.

Each of the fuses is designed to protect a specific circuit, and the various circuits are identified on the fuse panel itself.

Three types of miniaturized fuses are employed in the fuse block. These compact fuses, with blade terminal design, allow fingertip removal and replacement. If an electrical component fails, always check the fuse first. A blown fuse is easily identified through the clear plastic body. Visually inspect the element for evidence of damage **(see illustration)**. If a continuity check is called for on the type A fuse, the blade terminal tips are exposed in the fuse body.

Be sure to replace blown fuses with the correct type. Fuses of different ratings are physically interchangeable, but only fuses of the proper rating should be used. Replacing a fuse with one of a higher or lower value than specified is not recommended. Each electrical circuit needs a specific amount of protection. The amperage value of each fuse is molded into the fuse body.

If the replacement fuse immediately fails, don't replace it again until the cause of the problem is isolated and corrected. In most cases, this will be a short circuit in the wiring caused by a broken or deteriorated wire.

3.3 Three types of fuses are used on these models - all can be visually checked

5.2a Insert a pin or paper clip into the circuit breaker reset hole and push it in to reset it

5.2b After resetting, check the circuit breaker for continuity

4   Fusible links - general information

Some circuits are protected by fusible links. The links are used in circuits which are not ordinarily fused, such as the ignition circuit.

The fusible links on these models are similar to fuses in that they can be visually checked to determine if they are melted.

To replace a fusible link, first disconnect the negative cable from the battery. **Caution:** *If the stereo in your vehicle is equipped with an anti-theft system, make sure you have the correct activation code before disconnecting the battery.* Unplug the burned-out link and replace it with a new one (available from your dealer or auto parts store). Always determine the cause for the overload which melted the fusible link before installing a new one.

5   Circuit breakers - general information

Refer to illustrations 5.2a and 5.2b

Because on some models the circuit breaker resets itself auto-

matically, an electrical overload in a circuit breaker protected system will cause the circuit to fail momentarily, then come back on. If the circuit does not come back on, check it immediately. Note, however, that some circuit breakers must be reset manually. Once the condition is corrected, the circuit breaker will resume its normal function.

To reset a manual circuit breaker, first disconnect the cable from the negative battery terminal. **Caution:** *If the stereo in your vehicle is equipped with an anti-theft system, make sure you have the correct activation code before disconnecting the battery.* Remove the circuit breaker, insert a pin into the reset hole and push in until you hear a click **(see illustration)**. Once the circuit breaker is reset, it's a good idea to use an ohmmeter to make sure there is continuity across the terminals before reinstalling it **(see illustration)**.

6   Relays - general information

Refer to illustration 6.2

Several electrical accessories in the vehicle use relays to transmit the electrical signal to the component. If the relay is defective, that component will not operate properly.

The various relays are mounted in several locations throughout the vehicle **(see illustration)**.

If a faulty relay is suspected, it can be removed and tested by a dealer or other qualified shop. Defective relays must be replaced as a unit.

6.2 Typical passenger compartment relay and fuse locations

Light Retainer Relay

Junction Block No. 3

Cruise Control ECU

Daytime Running Light Relay No, 4

Daytime Running Light Relay No. 3

Daytime Running Light Relay (Main)

Theft Deterrent ECU

A/C Amplifier

Door Lock Control Relay

ABS ECU

Junction Block No. 4

Junction Block No. 1

Integration Relay

Shift Lock ECU

Circuit Opening Relay

Engine Control Module (Engine ECU)
Engine and Transmission Control Module (Engine and ECT ECU)

Center Airbag Sensor Assembly

12

8.4 Remove the four combination switch mounting screws (arrows)

8.5 Slip the combination switch off the steering column and unplug the connector (arrow)

7 Turn signal/hazard flashers - check and replacement

Warning: *These models are equipped with airbags. The airbag is armed and can deploy (inflate) anytime the battery is connected. To prevent accidental deployment (and possible injury), turn the ignition key to LOCK and disconnect the negative battery cable whenever working near airbag components. After the battery is disconnected, wait at least two minutes before beginning work (the system has a back-up capacitor that must fully discharge). For more information see Section 27.*

Caution: *If the stereo in your vehicle is equipped with an anti-theft system, make sure you have the correct activation code before disconnecting the battery.*

1   The turn signal/hazard flasher, a small canister shaped unit located in the main fuse block, flashes the turn signals **(see illustration 3.1a)**.

2   When the flasher unit is functioning properly, an audible click can be heard during its operation. If the turn signals fail on one side or the other and the flasher unit does not make its characteristic clicking sound, a faulty turn signal bulb is indicated.

3   If both turn signals fail to blink, the problem may be due to a blown fuse, a faulty flasher unit, a broken switch or a loose or open connection. If a quick check of the fuse box indicates that the turn signal fuse has blown, check the wiring for a short before installing a new fuse.

4   To replace the flasher, simply pull it out of the fuse block.

5   Make sure that the replacement unit is identical to the original. Compare the old one to the new one before installing it.

6   Installation is the reverse of removal.

8 Combination switch - removal and installation

Refer to illustrations 8.4 and 8.5

Warning: *These models are equipped with airbags. The airbag is armed and can deploy (inflate) anytime the battery is connected. To prevent accidental deployment (and possible injury), turn the ignition key to LOCK and disconnect the negative battery cable whenever working near airbag components. After the battery is disconnected, wait at least two minutes before beginning work (the system has a back-up capacitor that must fully discharge). For more information see Section 27.*

Caution: *If the stereo in your vehicle is equipped with an anti-theft system, make sure you have the correct activation code before disconnecting the battery.*

1   Disconnect the negative cable at the battery.

2   Disable the drivers airbag (see Section 27) and remove the steering wheel (see Chapter 10).

3   Remove the steering column cover and the lower finish panel (see Chapter 11).

4   Remove the combination switch retaining screws **(see illustration)**.

Switch position	Tester connection	Specified condition
OFF and Low beam	—	No continuity
OFF and High beam	—	No continuity
OFF and Flash	9 — 12 — 14	Continuity
TAIL and Low beam	2 — 11	Continuity
TAIL and High beam	2 — 11	Continuity
TAIL and Flash	2 — 11 9 — 12 — 14	Continuity
HEAD and Low beam	2 — 11 — 13 3 — 9	Continuity
HEAD and High beam	2 — 11 — 14	Continuity
HEAD and Flash	2 — 11 — 14	Continuity

9.4a Light control switch terminal guide and continuity table

Switch position	Tester connection	Specified condition
Left turn	1 – 5	Continuity
Neutral	–	No continuity
Right turn	1 – 8	Continuity

Turn Signal Switch
(Combination Switch Connector "A")

9.4b Turn signal switch terminal guide continuity table

w/ Mist Wiper Switch

Switch position	Tester connection	Specified condition
MIST	7 – 18	Continuity
OFF	4 – 7	Continuity
LO	7 – 18	Continuity
HI	13 – 18	Continuity

w/ Intermittent Wiper Switch

w/ Intermittent Wiper:

Switch position	Tester connection	Specified condition
OFF	4 – 7	Continuity
INT	4 – 7	Continuity
LO	7 – 18	Continuity
HI	13 – 18	Continuity

Combination Switch
Connector "B"

9.4c Windshield wiper and washer switch terminal guide and continuity table

5   Trace the wiring harness down the steering column to the connector. Release the wiring retainer clamps, if equipped, slide the switch off the column and unplug the connector **(see illustration)**.
6   Installation is the reverse of removal. Refer to Chapter 10 and center the spiral cable before installing the steering wheel.

9   Steering column switches - check and replacement

Refer to illustrations 9.4a, 9.4b, 9.4c, 9.4d, 9.7 and 9.9
Warning: *These models are equipped with airbags. The airbag is armed and can deploy (inflate) anytime the battery is connected. To prevent accidental deployment (and possible injury), turn the ignition key to LOCK and disconnect the negative battery cable whenever working near airbag components. After the battery is disconnected, wait at least two minutes before beginning work (the system has a*

back-up capacitor that must fully discharge). For more information see Section 27.
Caution: *If the stereo in your vehicle is equipped with an anti-theft system, make sure you have the correct activation code before disconnecting the battery.*
1   Disconnect the negative cable at the battery.
2   Remove the steering column cover and lower finish panel (see Chapter 11).
3   Trace the wiring harness from the component to be checked to the harness connector.

Check

4   Unplug the electrical connector and using an ohmmeter, check for continuity between the indicated terminals with the various switches in each of the indicated positions **(see illustrations)**.
5   If the continuity is not as specified, replace the defective switch.

Switch position	Tester connection to terminal number	Specified condition
Washer 1	2 – 16	Continuity
Wiper OFF	–	No continuity
Wiper INT	10 – 16	Continuity
Wiper ON	1 – 16	Continuity
Washer 2	1 – 2 – 16	Continuity

9.4d Rear window wiper and washer switch terminal guide and continuity table

12

9.7 Steering column switch component details

Replacement

6   Remove the combination switch (see Section 8). Remove the four screws retaining the airbag spiral cable and remove the spiral cable from the combination switch.

7   Remove the retaining screws from the switch being replaced and remove the defective switch from the switch body **(see illustration)**.

8   Separate the wiring harness of the switch being replaced from the main wiring harness and remove the terminals from the connector.

9   Release the tabs from the terminal cover at the rear of the connector. From the front of the connector, insert a small screwdriver or pick, pry down on the locking lug and remove the terminal from the rear **(see illustration)**.

10   Insert the terminals from the new switch into the connector, pushing in until they are securely locked in place.

11   The remainder or installation is the reverse of removal. Refer to Chapter 10 and center the spiral cable before installing the steering wheel.

10   Ignition switch and key lock cylinder - check and replacement

Warning: *These models are equipped with airbags. The airbag is armed and can deploy (inflate) anytime the battery is connected. To prevent accidental deployment (and possible injury), turn the ignition key to LOCK and disconnect the negative battery cable whenever working near airbag components. After the battery is disconnected, wait at least two minutes before beginning work (the system has a*

9.9 To remove a terminal from the connector, pry down on the locking lug and pull the terminal out from the rear

back-up capacitor that must fully discharge). For more information see Section 27.
Caution: *If the stereo in your vehicle is equipped with an anti-theft system, make sure you have the correct activation code before disconnecting the battery.*

Ignition switch

1   Disconnect the negative cable at the battery.
2   Remove the steering wheel (see Chapter 10).
3   Remove the steering column cover and lower finish panel (see Chapter 11).

Check

Refer to illustration 10.5
4   Trace the wire from the switch to the connector and unplug the connector.

Terminal / Switch position	1	2	3	4	5	7	8
LOCK							
ACC					O—	—O	
ON	O—	—O		O—	—O—	—O	
START	O—	—O—	—O		O—		O—	—O

If continuity is not as specified, replace the switch.

10.5 Ignition switch terminal guide and continuity table

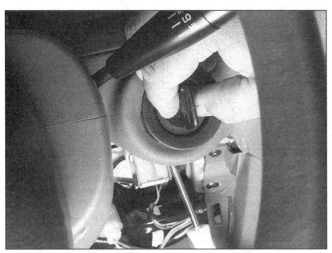

10.9 With the key in the ACC position. push in on the release button and pull the lock cylinder straight out

5   Use an ohmmeter to check for continuity at the indicated terminals with the switch in each indicated position **(see illustration).**
6   Replace the switch if continuity is not as specified.

Replacement

7   Remove the screw(s) retaining the switch to the rear of the lock cylinder housing and remove the switch.
8   Installation is the reverse of removal. Refer to Chapter 10 and center the spiral cable before installing the steering wheel.

Key lock cylinder

Refer to illustration 10.9

9   With the key in the Accessory position, insert a small screwdriver or punch in the hole in the casting and press the release button while pulling the lock cylinder straight out, then remove it from the steering column **(see illustration).**
10   Installation is the reverse of removal. Refer to Chapter 10 and center the spiral cable before installing the steering wheel.

11   Rear window defogger switch - check and replacement

Refer to illustration 11.3

Warning: *These models are equipped with airbags. The airbag is armed and can deploy (inflate) anytime the battery is connected. To prevent accidental deployment (and possible injury), turn the ignition key to LOCK and disconnect the negative battery cable whenever working near airbag components. After the battery is disconnected, wait at least two minutes before beginning work (the system has a back-up capacitor that must fully discharge). For more information see Section 27.*

Caution: *If the stereo in your vehicle is equipped with an anti-theft system, make sure you have the correct activation code before disconnecting the battery.*

1   Detach the cable from the negative battery terminal.
2   Remove the center trim panel and turn it over for access to the defogger switch.
3   Use an ohmmeter to check for continuity at the indicated terminals with the switch in the indicated position **(see illustration).**
4   Replace the switch if the continuity is not as specified.

12   Rear window defogger - check and repair

Refer to illustrations 12.4, 12.5 and 12.7

1   The rear window defogger consists of a number of horizontal elements baked onto the glass surface.
2   Small breaks in the element can be repaired without removing the rear window.

Check

3   Turn the ignition switch and defogger system switches to On.
4   When measuring voltage during the next two tests, wrap a piece of aluminum foil around the tip of the voltmeter negative probe and press the foil against the wire with your finger **(see illustration).**
5   Check the voltage at the center of each heat wire **(see illustration).** If the voltage is 5-volts, the wire is okay (there is no break). If the voltage is 10-volts, the wire is broken between the center of the ele-

11.3 Defogger switch terminal guide and continuity table

Condition	Tester connection to terminal number	Specified condition
Switch OFF	−	No continuity
Switch ON	4 − 6	Continuity
Illumination circuit	1 − 3	Continuity

12.4 When measuring the voltage at the rear window defogger grid, wrap a piece of aluminum foil around the negative probe of the voltmeter and press the foil against the wire with your finger

12.5 To determine if a wire has broken, place the voltmeter positive lead against the defogger positive terminal and check the voltage with the negative lead at the *center* of each wire - if the voltage is 5-volts, the wire is unbroken; if the voltage is 10-volts, the wire is broken between the center of the wire and the positive end; if the voltage is 0-volts, the wire is broken between the center of the wire and ground

12

ment and the positive end. If the voltage is 0-volts the wire is broken between the center of the element and ground.

6   Connect the negative lead to a good body ground. The reading should stay the same.

7   To find the break, place the voltmeter positive lead against the defogger positive terminal. Place the voltmeter negative lead with the foil strip against the heat wire at the positive terminal end and slide it toward the negative terminal end. The point at which the voltmeter deflects from zero to several volts is the point at which the heat element is broken **(see illustration)**. *Note: If the heat element is not broken, the voltmeter will indicate no voltage at the positive end of the heat element but gradually increase to about 12-volts.*

Repair

8   Repair the break in the element using a repair kit specifically recommended for this purpose, such as Dupont paste No. 4817 (or equivalent). Included in this kit is plastic conductive epoxy.

9   Prior to repairing a break, turn off the system and allow it to cool off for a few minutes.

10   Lightly buff the element area with fine steel wool, then clean it thoroughly with rubbing alcohol.

11   Use masking tape to mask off the area being repaired.

12   Thoroughly mix the epoxy, following the instructions provided with the repair kit.

13   Apply the epoxy material to the slit in the masking tape, overlapping the undamaged area about 3/4-inch on either end.

14   Allow the repair to cure for 24 hours before removing the tape and using the system.

13 Radio and speakers - removal and installation

Warning: *These models are equipped with airbags. The airbag is armed and can deploy (inflate) anytime the battery is connected. To prevent accidental deployment (and possible injury), turn the ignition key to LOCK and disconnect the negative battery cable whenever working near airbag components. After the battery is disconnected, wait at least two minutes before beginning work (the system has a back-up capacitor that must fully discharge). For more information see Section 27.*

Caution: *If the stereo in your vehicle is equipped with an anti-theft system, make sure you have the correct activation code before disconnecting the battery.*

Radio

Refer to illustrations 13.3a and 13.3b

1   Disconnect the negative cable at the battery.

2   Remove the center trim panel (see Chapter 11).

3   Remove the mounting screws or bolts and pull the housing out of

12.7 To find the break, place the voltmeter positive lead against the defogger positive terminal, place the voltmeter negative lead with the foil strip against the heat wire at the positive terminal end and slide it toward the negative terminal end - the point at which the voltmeter deflects from zero to several volts is the point at which the wire is broken

the dash **(see illustrations)**.

4   Remove the screws or nuts, pull the radio out, then unplug the electrical connector and the antenna lead and lift the radio out.

5   Installation is the reverse of removal.

Speakers

Refer to illustration 13.7

6   Remove the front door trim panel (see Chapter 11).

7   Remove the speaker retaining screws/nuts. Unplug the electrical connector and remove the speaker **(see illustration)**.

8   Installation is the reverse of removal.

14 Antenna - removal and installation

1   Remove the two Phillips-head screws.

2   Detach the antenna, pull out the cable and unplug it.

3   Installation is the reverse of removal.

15 Headlight bulb - replacement

Refer to illustrations 15.3a, 14.3b, 15.4 and 15.5

Warning: *These models are equipped with halogen gas-filled bulbs which are under pressure and may shatter if the surface is scratched or the bulb is dropped. Wear eye protection and handle the bulbs carefully, grasping only the base whenever possible. Do not touch the surface of the bulb with your fingers because the oil from your skin could cause it to overheat and fail prematurely. If you do touch the bulb surface, clean it with rubbing alcohol.*

13.3a Remove the mounting screws . . .

13.3b . . . pull the radio/bracket unit out, unplug the power connector and disconnect the antenna cable

13.7 Typical front door mounted speaker screws (arrows)

15.3a Use a small screwdriver to pry up on the air intake retainer

15.3b Lift the air intake duct out

15.4 Depress the lever and unplug connector

Caution: *If the stereo in your vehicle is equipped with an anti-theft system, make sure you have the correct activation code before disconnecting the battery.*
1   Open the hood.
2   Disconnect the cable from the negative battery terminal.
3   On the driver's side headlight, remove the air intake duct for access to the back of the housing **(see illustrations)**.
4   Press the lock release and unplug the electrical connector from the bulb assembly **(see illustration)**.
5   Rotate bulb assembly counterclockwise and withdraw it from the headlight housing. Without touching the glass with your bare fingers, insert the new assembly into the headlight housing, install and rotate it clockwise to lock it in place **(see illustration)**.
6   Plug in the electrical connector. Test the headlight operation, then close the hood.

16   Headlights - adjustment

Refer to illustration 16.1
Note: *It is important that the headlights are aimed correctly. If adjusted incorrectly they could blind the driver of an oncoming vehicle and cause a serious accident or seriously reduce your ability to see the road. The headlights should be checked for proper aim every 12 months and any time a new headlight is installed or front end body work is performed. It should be emphasized that the following procedure is only an interim step which will provide temporary adjustment until the headlights can be adjusted by a properly equipped shop.*
1   These models have two adjustment screws, one to the side controlling left-and-right movement and one below the light for up-and-down movement that are accessible from behind the headlight housing **(see illustration)**.

2   There are several methods of adjusting the headlights. The simplest method requires a blank wall, masking tape and a level floor.
3   Position masking tape vertically on the wall in reference to the vehicle centerline and the centerlines of both headlights.
4   Position a horizontal tape line in reference to the centerline of all the headlights. **Note:** *It may be easier to position the tape on the wall with the vehicle parked only a few inches away.*
5   Adjustment should be made with the vehicle parked 25 feet from the wall, sitting level, the gas tank half-full and no unusually heavy load in the vehicle.
6   Starting with the low beam adjustment, position the high intensity zone so it is two inches below the horizontal line and two inches to the right of the headlight vertical line. Twist the adjustment screws until the desired level has been achieved.
7   With the high beams on, the high intensity zone should be vertically centered with the exact center just below the horizontal line. **Note:** *It may not be possible to position the headlight aim exactly for both high and low beams. If a compromise must be made, keep in mind that the low beams are the most used and have the greatest effect on driver safety.*
8   Have the headlights adjusted by a dealer service department at the earliest opportunity.

17   Composite headlight housing - removal and installation

Refer to illustrations 17.4a and 17.4b
1   Disconnect the cable from the negative battery terminal. **Caution:** *If the stereo in your vehicle is equipped with an anti-theft system, make sure you have the correct activation code before disconnecting the battery.*

15.5 Rotate the bulb holder counterclockwise and withdraw it from the housing (when viewed from behind)

16.1 Headlight adjustment screws

12

17.4a Remove the headlight-to-radiator crossmember bolt

17.4b After removing the parking light assembly, the two side retaining nuts (arrows) are accessible

17.4c Pull the headlight straight out to detach the retainer at the lower corner (arrow)

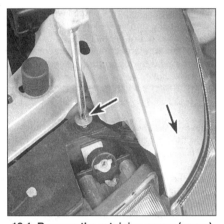

18.1 Remove the retaining screw (arrow) and push the lens housing forward to detach it

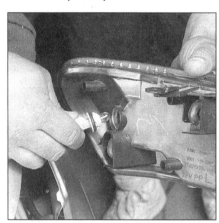

18.2 Unplug the connector and rotate the bulb holders to remove them from the housing

18.3 Remove the turn signal light screw and rotate the housing out of the fender

2   Remove the radiator grille (Chapter 11).
3   Remove the parking light housing (Section 18).
4   Remove the retaining bolts and nuts, detach the housing by pulling it straight out, then withdraw it from the vehicle **(see illustrations)**.
5   Remove the headlight bulb (Section 15).
6   Installation is the reverse of removal.

18.4a Unplug the electrical connector

18   Bulb replacement

Front parking and side marker

Refer to illustrations 18.1 and 18.2

1   Remove the retaining screw and detach the housing by sliding it forward **(see illustration)**.
2   Unplug the electrical connector and rotate the bulb holders counterclockwise to replace the bulbs **(see illustration)**.

Turn signal

Refer to illustrations 18.3, 18.4a and 18.4b

3   Remove the retaining screw and detach the housing by rotating it forward out of the fender **(see illustration)**.
4   Unplug the electrical connector and rotate the bulb holder counterclockwise to remove it **(see illustrations)**.

Rear side marker, turn signal, brake, tail and back-up lights

Refer to illustrations 8.5a, 18.5b, 18.6, 18.7 and 18.8

Sedan

5   Remove the two screws retaining the housing, open the trunk lid and detach the trim cover for access, then remove the nut and pull the housing out **(see illustration)**.
6   Rotate the bulb holders counterclockwise and replace the bulbs **(see illustration)**.

18.4b Rotate the bulb holder counterclockwise and pull it out

Station wagon

7   Remove the retaining screw and lift the housing up to remove **(see illustration)**.
8   Rotate the bulb holders counterclockwise and replace the bulbs **(see illustration)**.

License plate light

Refer to illustrations 18.9, 18.10, 18.11 and 18.12

Sedan

9   Depress the tab and rotate the light housing down for access to the bulb holder **(see illustration)**.
10   Rotate the holder counterclockwise to remove it, the pull the bulb straight out **(see illustration)**.

18.5a Trunk trim panel clip retainer details

18.5b Remove the tail light housing retaining nut (arrow)

18.6 Rotate the bulb holder counterclockwise to remove it

18.7 Remove the station wagon tail light screws and lift the housing straight up

18.8 Station wagon tail light bulb details

18.9 Press the tab in and lower the sedan license plate light housing

12

18.10 Sedan license plate bulb details

18.11 Station wagon license plate housing screws

18.12 Station wagon license plate bulb details

18.13a Use a ball-point pen to push in on the center of the retainers

18.13b Use a screwdriver to pry out the retainers

18.14a Remove the nuts and lift the housing up for access to the bulb holder

Station wagon

11   Remove the screws and lower the housing **(see illustration)**.
12   Remove the bulb holder by turning it counterclockwise, then pull the bulb out of the holder **(see illustration)**.

High mounted brake light

Refer to illustrations 18.13a, 18.13b, 18.14a, 18.14b and 18.15

Sedan

13   Use a ball-point pen to push in the centers of retainers the pry the retainers out with a small screwdriver and remove the light cover **(see illustrations)**.

14   Remove the housing bolts, lift the housing up for access, then rotate the holder counterclockwise to remove it and pull the bulb straight out **(see illustrations)**.

Station wagon

15   Pry the light cover off, remove the bulb holder by turn it counterclockwise, then pull the bulb out of the holder **(see illustration)**.

Interior lights

Refer to illustration 18.17

16   Use a small screwdriver to pry off the lens.
17   Detach the bulb from the terminal. It may be necessary to pry the bulb out, if this is the case, pry only at the end of the bulb (otherwise the glass may shatter **(see illustration)**.

Instrument cluster illumination

Refer to illustration 18.18

18   To gain access to the instrument cluster illumination lights, the instrument cluster will have to be removed (see Section 21). The bulbs can then be removed and replaced from the rear of the cluster **(see illustration)**.

19   Daytime Running Lights (DRL) - general information

The Daytime Running Lights (DRL) system, used on some models, turns the headlights on whenever the engine is started. The only exception is when the engine is on when the parking brake is engaged. Once the parking brake is released, the lights will remain on as long as the ignition switch is on, even if the parking brake is later applied.

The DRL system supplies reduced power to the headlights so they won't be too bright for daytime use while prolonging headlight life.

18.14b Rotate the holder counterclockwise to remove it - the bulb pulls straight out

18.15 Station wagon high mounted brake light details

18.17 Pry carefully at the bulb clip (arrow) and detach the bulb

18.18 Rotate the instrument cluster bulb counterclockwise and lift it out

20.5 Unplug the wiper motor connector (A), remove the bolts (arrows) and detach the motor

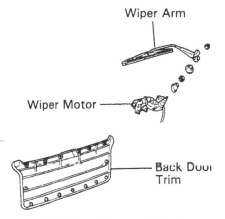

20.7 Rear wiper arm details

20 Wiper motor - check and replacement

Refer to illustrations 20.5 and 20.7

Warning: *These models are equipped with airbags. The airbag is armed and can deploy (inflate) anytime the battery is connected. To prevent accidental deployment (and possible injury), turn the ignition key to LOCK and disconnect the negative battery cable whenever working near airbag components. After the battery is disconnected, wait at least two minutes before beginning work (the system has a back-up capacitor that must fully discharge). For more information see Section 27.*

Caution: *If the stereo in your vehicle is equipped with an anti-theft system, make sure you have the correct activation code before disconnecting the battery.*

1   The windshield wiper motor is located on the right (passenger) side of the underhood compartment and the rear wiper motor is mounted in the liftgate.

Check

Windshield washer/wiper switch

2   Refer to Section 9 for the wiper and washer switch check procedure.

Wiper motor

3   If a motor doesn't work or doesn't park properly and the switch checks out okay, the relay or the motor must be replaced.

Replacement

Windshield wiper motor

4   Disconnect the cable from the negative battery terminal.
5   Unplug the electrical connector, remove the motor bracket retaining bolts, then lower the wiper motor and bracket assembly and remove it from the vehicle **(see illustration)**.
6   Installation is the reverse of removal.

Rear wiper motor

7   Remove the wiper arm, then remove the shaft spindle nuts and washers **(see illustration)**.
8   Unplug the electrical connector, detach the wiper linkage, remove the retaining bolts and lower the motor through the liftgate access hole as an assembly.
9   Installation is the reverse of removal.

21 Instrument cluster - removal and installation

Refer to illustrations 21.3 and 21.4

Warning: *These models are equipped with airbags. The airbag is armed and can deploy (inflate) anytime the battery is connected. To prevent accidental deployment (and possible injury), turn the ignition key to LOCK and disconnect the negative battery cable whenever working near airbag components. After the battery is disconnected, wait at least two minutes before beginning work (the system has a back-up capacitor that must fully discharge). For more information see Section 27.*

12

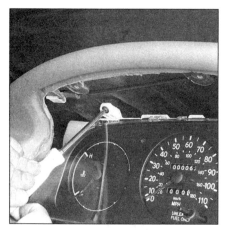

21.3 Remove the instrument cluster screws

21.4 Unplug the electrical connectors and remove the cluster

22.4 Disconnect the electrical connector and remove the bolts (arrows) and detach the horn

Ignition Switch

Cruise Control Switch

Cruise Control ECU

Junction Block No.1
● ECU-B Fuse

Clutch Switch

Stop Light Switch

Parking Brake Switch

Speed Sensor

Actuator

Park/Neutral Position Switch

23.1 Typical cruise control system component layout

Ignition Switch
• Key Unlock Warning Switch

Door Lock Control Relay

Junction Block No.2
• AM1 Fuse

Junction Block No.1
• P/W Fuse
• Gauge Fuse

Door Lock Contol Switch

Door Lock Assembly
• Door Lock Motor
• Door Unlock Detection Switch

24.1 Power door lock system component layout

Caution: *If the stereo in your vehicle is equipped with an anti-theft system, make sure you have the correct activation code before disconnecting the battery.*

1   Disconnect the cable from the negative battery terminal.
2   Remove the instrument cluster bezel (see Chapter 11).
3   Remove the retaining screws and pull the cluster forward **(see illustration)**.
4   Unplug the electrical connectors and remove the cluster **(see illustration)**.
5   Installation is the reverse of the removal procedure.

22 Horn - check and replacement

Refer to illustration 22.4

Check

1   Disconnect the electrical connector from the horn.
2   Test the horn by connecting battery voltage to the two terminals with a pair of jumper wires.
3   If the horn doesn't sound, replace it. If it does sound, the problem lies in the switch, relay or the wiring between components.

Replacement

4   Disconnect the electrical connector and remove the bracket bolt **(see illustration)**.
5   Installation is the reverse of removal.

23 Cruise control system - description and check

Refer to illustration 23.1

1   The cruise control system maintains vehicle speed with an ECU (computer) located in the passenger compartment and actuator located near the battery in the engine compartment. The actuator is connected to the throttle linkage by a cable or rod. Besides the actuator, the system consists of the brake switch, clutch switch, control switches, a relay and associated wiring **(see illustration)**. Some features of the system requires special testers and diagnostic procedures which are beyond the scope of the home mechanic. Listed below are some general procedures that may be used to locate common problems.

2   Locate and check the fuse (see Section 3).
3   Have an assistant operate the brake lights while you check their operation (voltage from the brake light and (if equipped) clutch switch deactivates the cruise control).
4   If the brake lights don't come on or don't shut off, correct the problem and retest the cruise control. Check the clutch switch (Chapter 8).
5   Visually inspect the vacuum hose (if equipped) connected to the servo and check the control linkage between the cruise control servo and the throttle linkage and replace as necessary.
6   Cruise control systems use a variety of speed sensing devices. On these models the speed sensor pickup is located in the transaxle. Remove the bolt and detach the sensor, rotate the sensor and check it with a digital voltmeter while it's rotating (see Chapter 6). If the resistance doesn't vary as the cable rotates, the sensor is defective.
7   Test drive the vehicle to determine if the cruise control is now working. If it isn't, take it to a dealer service department or an automotive electrical specialist for further diagnosis and repair.

24 Power door lock system - description and check

Refer to illustrations 24.1, 24.6a and 24.6b

1   The power door lock system operates the door lock actuators mounted in each door. The system consists of the switches, actuators and associated wiring **(see illustration)**. Diagnosis can usually be limited to simple checks of the wiring connections and actuators for minor faults which can be easily repaired.

12

Terminal Switch position	1 and 2	3	4
LOCK	O————————————O		
OFF			
UNLOCK	O————O		

24.6a Power door lock master switch terminal guide and continuity table

Terminal Switch position	2	3	4
LOCK		O————O	
OFF			
UNLOCK	O————————————O		

24.6b Power door lock switch terminal guide and continuity table

2   Power door lock systems are operated by bi-directional solenoids located in the doors. The lock switches have two operating positions: Lock and Unlock. These switches activate a relay which in turn connects voltage to the door lock solenoids. Depending on which way the relay is activated, it reverses polarity, allowing the two sides of the circuit to be used alternately as the feed (positive) and ground side.

3   Always check the circuit protection first. Some vehicles use a combination of circuit breakers and fuses.

4   Operate the door lock switches in both directions (Lock and Unlock) with the engine off. Listen for the faint click of the relay operating.

5   If there's no click, check for voltage at the switches. If no voltage is present, check the wiring between the fuse panel and the switches for shorts and opens.

6   If voltage is present but no click is heard, test the switch for continuity. Replace the switch if there's no continuity in both switch

25.1 Power window system component layout

Switch position	Tester connection to terminal number	Specified condition
UP	6 — 7 — 8	Continuity
	1 — 2 — 13	
OFF	1 — 2 — 6 — 13	Continuity
DOWN	1 — 2 — 6	Continuity
	7 — 8 — 13	

25.7 Power window master switch terminal guide and continuity table

positions **(see illustrations)**.

7   If the switch has continuity but the relay doesn't click, check the wiring between the switch and relay for continuity. Repair the wiring if there's no continuity.

8   If the relay is receiving voltage from the switch but is not sending voltage to the solenoids, check for a bad ground at the relay case. If the relay case is grounding properly, replace the relay.

9   If all but one lock solenoids operate, remove the trim panel from the affected door (see Chapter 11). and check for voltage at the solenoid while the lock switch is operated. One of the wires should have voltage in the Lock position; the other should have voltage in the unlock position.

10   If the inoperative solenoid is receiving voltage, replace the solenoid.

11   If the inoperative solenoid isn't receiving voltage, check for an open or short in the wire between the lock solenoid and the relay.

Note: *It's common for wires to break in the portion of the harness between the body and door (opening and closing the door fatigues and eventually breaks the wires).*

25   Power window system - description and check

Refer to illustrations 25.1, 25.7 and 25.10

1   The power window system operates the electric motors mounted in the doors which lower and raise the windows. The system consists of the control switches, the motors (regulators), glass mechanisms and associated wiring **(see illustration)**.

2   Power windows are wired so they can be lowered and raised from the master control switch by the driver or by remote switches located at the individual windows. Each window has a separate motor which is reversible. The position of the control switch determines the polarity and therefore the direction of operation. Some systems are equipped with relays that control current flow to the motors.

3   Some vehicles are equipped with a separate circuit breaker for each motor in addition to the fuse or circuit breaker protecting the whole circuit. This prevents one stuck window from disabling the whole system.

4   The power window system will only operate when the ignition switch is ON. In addition, when activated the window lockout switch at the master control switch disables the switches at the passenger's window also. Always check these items before troubleshooting a window problem.

5   These procedures are general in nature, so if you can't find the problem using them, take the vehicle to a dealer service department.

6   If the power windows don't work at all, check the fuse or circuit breaker.

7   If only the rear windows are inoperative, or if the windows only operate from the master control switch, check the rear window lockout switch for continuity in the unlocked position **(see illustration)**. Replace it if it doesn't have continuity.

8   Check the wiring between the switches and fuse panel for continuity. Repair the wiring, if necessary.

9   If only one window is inoperative from the master control switch, try the other control switch at the window. **Note:** *This doesn't apply to the drivers door window.*

10   If the same window works from one switch, but not the other, check the switch for continuity **(see illustration)**.

11   If the switch tests OK, check for a short or open in the wiring between the affected switch and the window motor.

12   If one window is inoperative from both switches, remove the trim panel from the affected door and check for voltage at the motor while the switch is operated.

13   If voltage is reaching the motor, disconnect the glass from the regulator (see Chapter 11). Move the window up and down by hand while checking for binding and damage. Also check for binding and damage to the regulator. If the regulator is not damaged and the window moves up and down smoothly, replace the motor. If there's binding or damage, lubricate, repair or replace parts, as necessary.

14   If voltage isn't reaching the motor, check the wiring in the circuit for continuity between the switches and motors. You'll need to consult the wiring diagram for the vehicle. Some power window circuits are equipped with relays. If equipped, check that the relays are grounded properly and receiving voltage from the switches. Also check that each relay sends voltage to the motor when the switch is turned on. If it doesn't, replace the relay.

15   Test the windows after you are done to confirm proper repairs.

25.10 Door window switch terminal guide and continuity table

Switch position	Tester connection to terminal number	Specified condition
UP	1 — 5	Continuity
	3 — 4	
OFF	1 — 2	Continuity
	3 — 4	
DOWN	1 — 2	Continuity
	4 — 5	

12

Junction Block No.2
- ALT Fuse
- AM1 Fuse

Outer Rear View Mirror

Ignition Switch

26.1 Electric mirror system component layout

Junction Block No.1
- CIG & RADIO Fuse

Mirror Switch

26 Electric rear view mirrors - description and check

Refer to illustrations 26.1, 26.6a and 26.6b

1   The electric rear view mirrors use two motors to move the glass; one for up and down adjustments and one for left-right adjustments **(see illustration)**.

2   The control switch has a selector portion which sends voltage to the left or right side mirror. With the ignition key in the ACC position, roll down the windows and operate the mirror control switch through all functions (left-right and up-down) for both the left and right side mirrors.

3   Listen carefully for the sound of the electric motors running in the mirrors.

4   If the motors can be heard but the mirror glass doesn't move, there's probably a problem with the drive mechanism inside the mirror. Remove and disassemble the mirror to locate the problem.

5   If the mirrors don't operate and no sound comes from the mirrors, check the CIG/Radio fuse in the fuse block located under the left side of the dash (see Section 3).

6   If the fuse is OK, remove the air register/switch panel from the instrument panel for access the back of the mirror control switch without disconnecting the wires attached to it **(see illustration)**. Turn the

ignition ON and check for voltage at the switch. There should be voltage at one terminal. If there's no voltage at the switch, check for an open or short in the wiring between the fuse panel and the switch **(see illustration)**.

7   If there's voltage at the switch, disconnect it. Check the switch for continuity in all its operating positions. If the switch does not have continuity, replace it.

8   Re-connect the switch. Locate the wire going from the switch to ground. Leaving the switch connected, connect a jumper wire between this wire and ground. If the mirror works normally with this wire in place, repair the faulty ground connection.

9   If the mirror still doesn't work, remove the mirror and check the wires at the mirror for voltage. Check with ignition ON and the mirror selector switch on the appropriate side. Operate the mirror switch in all its positions. There should be voltage at one of the switch-to-mirror wires in each switch position (except the neutral "off" position).

10   If there's no voltage in each switch position, check the wiring between the mirror and control switch for opens and shorts.

11   If there's voltage, remove the mirror and test it off the vehicle with jumper wires. Replace the mirror if it fails this test.

27 Airbag - general information

Refer to illustration 27.1

    The models covered by this manual are equipped with a Supplemental Restraint System (SRS), more commonly known as "airbags." This system is designed to protect the driver and front seat passenger from serious injury in the event of a head-on or frontal collision. It consists of airbag modules in the center of the steering wheel and the right side of the instrument panel, two crash sensors mounted at the front of the vehicle (1995 and earlier models) and a center airbag sensor assembly located inside the passenger compartment **(see illustration)**.

Airbag modules

    The airbag modules contain a housing incorporating the cushion (airbag) and inflator unit. The inflator assembly is mounted on the back of the housing over a hole through which gas is expelled, inflating the bag almost instantaneously when an electrical signal is sent from the system. The specially wound wire that carries this signal to the driver's module is called a spiral cable. The spiral cable is a flat, ribbon-like electrically conductive tape which is wound many times so that it can transmit an electrical signal regardless of steering wheel position.

26.6a Use a screwdriver to detach the air register/mirror switch from the instrument panel; press in on the clips and push the mirror switch out

Left/Right
Adjustment

Switch position	Tester connection to terminal number	Specified condition
OFF	—	No continuity
UP	3 – 7 4 – 8	Continuity
DOWN	3 – 4 7 – 8	Continuity
LEFT	1 – 8 3 – 7	Continuity
RIGHT	1 – 3 7 – 8	Continuity

RIGHT SIDE

26.6b Power mirror switch terminal guide and continuity table

Switch position	Tester connection to terminal number	Specified condition
OFF	—	No continuity
UP	3 – 7 6 – 8	Continuity
DOWN	3 – 6 7 – 8	Continuity
LEFT	3 – 7 5 – 8	Continuity
RIGHT	3 – 5 7 – 8	Continuity

Sensors

On 1995 and earlier models, the system has three sensors: two crash sensors at the front of the vehicle behind the bumper and above the wheel arches and a safing sensor in the center airbag sensor assembly located in the center console. On 1996 and later models, all sensors are located in the center airbag sensor assembly.

The front crash sensors are basically pressure sensitive switches that complete an electrical circuit during an impact of sufficient G force. The electrical signal from the crash sensors is sent to the safing sensor in the center airbag sensor assembly, which then completes the circuit and inflates the airbag.

Center airbag sensor assembly

The center airbag sensor contains the safing sensor and an on-board microprocessor which monitors the operation of the system. It checks this system every time the vehicle is started, causing the "AIRBAG" warning light to go on, then off, if the system is operating properly. If there is a fault in the system, the light will go on and stay on and the center airbag sensor assembly will store fault codes indicating the nature of the fault. If the AIRBAG light goes on and stays on, the vehicle should be taken to your dealer immediately for service.

27.1 Typical airbag system component layout

Front Airbag Sensor RH

Front Passenger Airbag Assembly

Spiral Cable

SRS Warning Light

Front Airbag Sensor LH

Steering Wheel Pad (with Airbag)

Center Airbag Sensor Assembly

12

27.8 Each connector used in the airbag system uses a two stage locking system for security purposes - use care when disconnecting the airbag module connectors

• **Primary Lock Incomplete**
  (Secondary Lock Prevented)

• **Primary Lock Complete**
  (Secondary Lock Permitted)

•**Twin-Lock Completed**

27.11 Remove the steering column lower finish panel for access to the driver's airbag module connector

27.13 Remove the access cover inside the glove box for access to the passenger's airbag module connector

Servicing components near the SRS system

Refer to illustration 27.8

8   Nevertheless, there are times when you need to remove the steering wheel, radio or service other components on or near the instrument panel. At these times, you'll be working around components and wiring harnesses for the SRS system. SRS system wiring is easy to identify; they're all covered by a bright yellow conduit. Do not unplug the connectors for the SRS system wiring, except to disable the system **(see illustration)**. And do not use electrical test equipment on the SRS system wiring. **ALWAYS DISABLE THE SRS SYSTEM BEFORE WORKING NEAR THE SRS SYSTEM COMPONENTS OR RELATED WIRING.**

Disabling the SRS system

Refer to illustrations 27.11 and 27.13

9   Turn the steering wheel to the straight ahead position, place the ignition switch in Lock and remove the key. Disconnect the cable from the negative battery terminal. Wait two minutes for the back-up capacitor to discharge.
10   Unplug the yellow connectors at the base of the steering column and under the right side of the instrument panel as described in the following steps.

Driver's side airbag

11   Remove the steering column lower finish panel below the instrument panel (see Chapter 11) and unplug the yellow steering column harness connector **(see illustration)**.

Passenger's side airbag

12   Open the glove box and remove the access cover (see Chapter 11).
13   Unplug the yellow electrical connector from the passenger inflator module **(see illustration)**.

Enabling the SRS system

14   After you've disabled the airbag and performed the necessary service, plug in the steering column (driver's side) and passenger side airbag connectors. Reinstall the lower finish panel and the glove box access cover.

Wire colors are indicated by an alphabetical code.

B	=	Black	L	=	Blue	R	=	Red
BR	=	Brown	LG	=	Light Green	V	=	Violet
G	=	Green	O	=	Orange	W	=	White
GR	=	Gray	P	=	Pink	Y	=	Yellow

The first letter indicates the basic wire color and the second letter indicates the color of the stripe.

Example: L—Y

L   Y
(Blue)   (Yellow)

28.4 Wiring diagram color code chart

15   Connect the cable to the negative battery terminal.
16   Turn the ignition key to On and verify that the "AIRBAG" warning light comes on for approximately six seconds, then goes off.

28   Wiring diagrams - general information

Refer to illustration 28.4

Since it isn't possible to include all wiring diagrams for every year covered by this manual, the following diagrams are those that are typical and most commonly needed.

Prior to troubleshooting any circuits, check the fuse and circuit breakers (if equipped) to make sure they are in good condition. Make sure the battery is properly charged and has clean, tight cable connections (see Chapter 1).

When checking the wiring system, make sure that all electrical connectors are clean, with no broken or loose pins. When unplugging an electrical connector, do not pull on the wires, only on the connector housings themselves.

Refer to the **accompanying illustration** for an explanation of the wiring diagrams applicable to your vehicle.

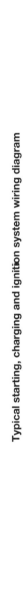

Typical starting, charging and ignition system wiring diagram

Typical engine control system wiring diagram (1 of 2)

Typical engine control system wiring diagram (2 of 2)

Typical electronically-controlled transaxle system wiring diagram

Typical Daytime Running Light (DRL) system wiring diagram

Typical headlight system wiring diagram (without DRL)

Typical backup and stoplight system wiring diagram

12

Typical tail light system wiring diagram

Typical rear window defogger and interior light system wiring diagram

Typical turn signal, hazard warning and horn system wiring diagram

Typical automatic light and seat belt warning system wiring diagram

12

Typical shift lock and airbag system wiring diagram

Typical power window system wiring diagram

Typical wiper and washer system wiring diagram

Typical electric mirror and sun roof system wiring diagram

12

Typical power door lock system wiring diagram (with anti-theft)

Typical power door lock system wiring diagram (without anti-theft)

Typical Anti-Lock Brake System (ABS) wiring diagram

Typical cruise control system wiring diagram

Typical cigarette lighter, clock and audio system wiring diagram

Typical instrument cluster system wiring diagram

Typical 1.8L engine ignition system wiring diagram

Typical radiator cooling fan and air conditioning system wiring diagram

12

Notes

Index

Haynes Automotive Manuals

NOTE: New manuals are added to this list on a periodic basis. If you do not see a listing for your vehicle, consult your local Haynes dealer for the latest product information.

ACURA
*12020 Integra '86 thru '89 & Legend '86 thru '90

AMC
        Jeep CJ - see JEEP (50020)
14020 Concord/Hornet/Gremlin/Spirit '70 thru '83
14025 (Renault) Alliance & Encore '83 thru '87

AUDI
15020 4000 all models '80 thru '87
15025 5000 all models '77 thru '83
15026 5000 all models '84 thru '88

AUSTIN
        Healey Sprite - see MG Midget (66015)

BMW
*18020 3/5 Series '82 thru '92
*18021 3 Series except 325iX models '92 thru '97
18025 320i all 4 cyl models '75 thru '83
18035 528i & 530i all models '75 thru '80
18050 1500 thru 2002 except Turbo '59 thru '77

BUICK
        Century (FWD) - see GM (38005)
*19020 Buick, Oldsmobile & Pontiac Full-size
        (Front wheel drive) '85 thru '98
        Buick Electra, LeSabre and Park Avenue;
        Oldsmobile Delta 88 Royale, Ninety Eight
        and Regency; Pontiac Bonneville
19025 Buick Oldsmobile & Pontiac Full-size
        (Rear wheel drive)
        Buick Estate '70 thru '90, Electra '70 thru '84,
        LeSabre '70 thru '85, Limited '74 thru '79
        Oldsmobile Custom Cruiser '70 thru '90,
        Delta 88 '70 thru '85,Ninety-eight '70 thru '84
        Pontiac Bonneville '70 thru '81,
        Catalina '70 thru '81, Grandville '70 thru '75,
        Parisienne '83 thru '86
19030 Mid-size Regal & Century '74 thru '87
        Regal - see GENERAL MOTORS (38010)
        Skyhawk - see GM (38030)
        Skylark - see GM (38020, 38025)
        Somerset - see GENERAL MOTORS (38025)

CADILLAC
*21030 Cadillac Rear Wheel Drive '70 thru '93
        Cimarron, Eldorado & Seville - see
        GM (38015, 38030)

CHEVROLET
10305 Chevrolet Engine Overhaul Manual
*24010 Astro & GMC Safari Mini-vans '85 thru '93
24015 Camaro V8 all models '70 thru '81
24016 Camaro all models '82 thru '92
        Cavalier - see GM (38015)
        Celebrity - see GM (38005)
24017 Camaro & Firebird '93 thru '97
24020 Chevelle, Malibu, El Camino '69 thru '87
24024 Chevette & Pontiac T1000 '76 thru '87
        Citation - see GENERAL MOTORS (38020)
*24032 Corsica/Beretta all models '87 thru '96
24040 Corvette all V8 models '68 thru '82
*24041 Corvette all models '84 thru '96
24045 Full-size Sedans Caprice, Impala,
        Biscayne, Bel Air & Wagons '69 thru '90
24046 Impala SS & Caprice and
        Buick Roadmaster '91 thru '96
        Lumina '90 thru '94 - see GM (38010)
24048 Lumina & Monte Carlo '95 thru '98
        Lumina APV - see GM (38035)
24050 Luv Pick-up 2WD & 4WD '72 thru '82
24055 Monte Carlo all models '70 thru '88
        Monte Carlo '95 thru '98 - see LUMINA
24059 Nova all V8 models '69 thru '79
*24060 Nova/Geo Prizm '85 thru '92
24064 Pick-ups '67 thru '87 - Chevrolet & GMC,
        all V8 & in-line 6 cyl, 2WD & 4WD '67 thru '87;
        Suburbans, Blazers & Jimmys '67 thru '91
*24065 Pick-ups '88 thru '98 - Chevrolet & GMC,
        all full-size models '88 thru '98; Blazer &
        Jimmy '92 thru '94; Suburban '92 thru '98;
        Tahoe & Yukon '95 thru '98
*24070 S-10 & GMC S-15 Pick-ups '82 thru '93
24071 S-10, Gmc S-15 & Jimmy '94 thru '96
*24075 Sprint & Geo Metro '85 thru '94
*24080 Vans - Chevrolet & GMC '68 thru '96

CHRYSLER
10310 Chrysler Engine Overhaul Manual
*25015 Chrysler Cirrus, Dodge Stratus,
        Plymouth Breeze, '95 thru '98
*25020 Full-size Front-Wheel Drive '88 thru '93
        K-Cars - see DODGE Aries (30008)
        Laser - see DODGE Daytona (30030)
25025 Chrysler LHS, Concorde & New Yorker,
        Dodge Intrepid, Eagle Vision, '93 thru '97
*25030 Chrysler/Plym. Mid-size '82 thru '95
        Rear-wheel Drive - see DODGE (30050)

DATSUN
28005 200SX all models '80 thru '83
28007 B-210 all models '73 thru '78
28009 210 all models '79 thru '82
28012 240Z, 260Z & 280Z Coupe '70 thru '78
28014 280ZX Coupe & 2+2 '79 thru '83
        300ZX - see NISSAN (72010)
28016 310 all models '78 thru '82
28018 510 & PL521 Pick-up '68 thru '73
28020 510 all models '78 thru '81
28022 620 Series Pick-up all models '73 thru '79
        720 Series Pick-up - NISSAN (72030)
28025 810/Maxima all gas models, '77 thru '84

DODGE
        400 & 600 - see CHRYSLER (25030)
*30008 Aries & Plymouth Reliant '81 thru '89
30010 Caravan & Ply. Voyager '84 thru '95
*30011 Caravan & Ply. Voyager '96 thru '98
30012 Challenger/Plymouth Saporro '78 thru '83
        Challenger '67-'76 - see DART (30025)
30016 Colt/Plymouth Champ '78 thru '87
*30020 Dakota Pick-ups all models '87 thru '96
30025 Dart, Challenger/Plymouth Barracuda
        & Valiant 6 cyl models '67 thru '76
*30030 Daytona & Chrysler Laser '84 thru '89
        Intrepid - see CHRYSLER (25025)
*30034 Dodge & Plymouth Neon '95 thru '97
*30035 Omni & Plymouth Horizon '78 thru '90
30040 Pick-ups all full-size models '74 thru '93
*30041 Pick-ups all full-size models '94 thru '96
*30045 Ram 50/D50 Pick-ups & Raider and
        Plymouth Arrow Pick-ups '79 thru '93
30050 Dodge/Ply./Chrysler RWD '71 thru '89
*30055 Shadow/Plymouth Sundance '87 thru '94
*30060 Spirit & Plymouth Acclaim '89 thru '95
*30065 Vans - Dodge & Plymouth '71 thru '96

EAGLE
        Talon - see MITSUBISHI Eclipse (68030)
        Vision - see CHRYSLER (25025)

FIAT
34010 124 Sport Coupe & Spider '68 thru '78
34025 X1/9 all models '74 thru '80

FORD
10355 Ford Automatic Transmission Overhaul
10320 Ford Engine Overhaul Manual
*36004 Aerostar Mini-vans '86 thru '96
        Aspire - see FORD Festiva (36030)
*36006 Contour/Mercury Mystique '95 thru '98
36008 Courier Pick-up all models '72 thru '82
36012 Crown Victoria & Mercury
        Grand Marquis '88 thru '96
36016 Escort/Mercury Lynx '81 thru '90
*36020 Escort/Mercury Tracer '91 thru '96
        Expedition - see FORD Pick-up (36059)
*36024 Explorer & Mazda Navajo '91 thru '95
36028 Fairmont & Mercury Zephyr '78 thru '83
36030 Festiva & Aspire '88 thru '97
36032 Fiesta all models '77 thru '80
36036 Ford & Mercury Full-size,
        Ford LTD & Mercury Marquis ('75 thru '82);
        Ford Custom 500,Country Squire, Crown
        Victoria & Mercury Colony Park ('75 thru '87);
        Ford LTD Crown Victoria &
        Mercury Gran Marquis ('83 thru '87)
36040 Granada & Mercury Monarch '75 thru '80
36044 Ford & Mercury Mid-size,
        Ford Thunderbird & Mercury
        Cougar ('75 thru '82);
        Ford LTD & Mercury Marquis ('83 thru '86);
        Ford Torino,Gran Torino, Elite, Ranchero
        pick-up, LTD II, Mercury Montego, Comet,
        XR-7 & Lincoln Versailles ('75 thru '86)
36048 Mustang V8 all models '64-1/2 thru '73
36049 Mustang II 4 cyl, V6 & V8 '74 thru '78
36050 Mustang & Mercury Capri incl. Turbo
        Mustang, '79 thru '93; Capri, '79 thru '86
*36051 Mustang all models '94 thru '97
36054 Pick-ups and Bronco '73 thru '79
*36058 Pick-ups and Bronco '80 thru '96
*36059 Pick-ups, Expedition &
        Lincoln Navigator '97 thru '98
36062 Pinto & Mercury Bobcat '75 thru '80
36066 Probe all models '89 thru '92
*36070 Ranger/Bronco II gas models '83 thru '92
*36071 Ford Ranger '93 thru '97
        Mazda Pick-ups '94 thru '97
36074 Taurus & Mercury Sable '86 thru '95
*36075 Taurus & Mercury Sable '96 thru '98
36078 Tempo & Mercury Topaz '84 thru '94
36082 Thunderbird/Mercury Cougar '83 thru '88
36086 Thunderbird/Mercury Cougar '89 and '97
36090 Vans all V8 Econoline models '69 thru '91
*36094 Vans full size '92 thru '95
*36097 Windstar Mini-van '95 thru '98

GENERAL MOTORS
*10360 GM Automatic Transmission Overhaul
*38005 Buick Century, Chevrolet Celebrity,
        Olds Cutlass Ciera & Pontiac 6000
        all models '82 thru '96
*38010 Buick Regal, Chevrolet Lumina,
        Oldsmobile Cutlass Supreme & Pontiac
        Grand Prix front wheel drive '88 thru '95
*38015 Buick Skyhawk, Cadillac Cimarron,
        Chevrolet Cavalier, Oldsmobile Firenza
        Pontiac J-2000 & Sunbird '82 thru '94
*38016 Chevrolet Cavalier &
        Pontiac Sunfire '95 thru '98
38020 Buick Skylark, Chevrolet Citation,
        Olds Omega, Pontiac Phoenix '80 thru '85
38025 Buick Skylark & Somerset, Olds Achieva,
        Calais & Pontiac Grand Am '85 thru '95
38030 Cadillac Eldorado & Oldsmobile
        Toronado '71 thru '85, Buick Riviera '79 thru '85
        Buick Riviera '79 thru '85
*38035 Chevrolet Lumina APV, Oldsmobile
        Silhouette & Pontiac Trans Sport '90 thru '95
        General Motors Full-size
        Rear-wheel Drive - see BUICK (19025)

GEO
        Metro - see CHEVROLET Sprint (24075)
        Prizm - see CHEVROLET (24060) or
        TOYOTA (92036)
*40030 Storm all models '90 thru '93
        Tracker - see SUZUKI Samurai (90010)

GMC
        Safari - see CHEVROLET ASTRO (24010)
        Vans & Pick-ups - see CHEVROLET

HONDA
42010 Accord CVCC all models '76 thru '83
42011 Accord all models '84 thru '89
42012 Accord all models '90 thru '93
*42013 Accord all models '94 thru '95
42020 Civic 1200 all models '73 thru '79
42021 Civic 1300 & 1500 CVCC '80 thru '83
42022 Civic 1500 CVCC all models '75 thru '79
42023 Civic all models '84 thru '91
42024 Civic & del Sol '92 thru '95
        Passport - see ISUZU Rodeo (47017)
*42040 Prelude CVCC all models '79 thru '89

HYUNDAI
*43015 Excel all models '86 thru '94

ISUZU
        Hombre - see CHEVROLET S-10 (24071)
*47017 Rodeo '91 thru '97, Amigo '89 thru '94,
        Honda Passport '95 thru '97
*47020 Trooper '84 thru '91, Pick-up '81 thru '93

JAGUAR
*49010 XJ6 all 6 cyl models '68 thru '86
*49011 XJ6 all models '88 thru '94
*49015 XJ12 & XJS all 12 cyl models '72 thru '85

JEEP
*50010 Cherokee, Comanche & Wagoneer
        Limited all models '84 thru '96
50020 CJ all models '49 thru '86
*50025 Grand Cherokee all models '93 thru '98
*50029 Grand Wagoneer & Pick-up '72 thru '91
*50030 Wrangler all models '87 thru '95

LINCOLN
        Navigator - see FORD Pick-up (36059)
59010 Rear Wheel Drive all models '70 thru '96

MAZDA
61010 GLC (rear wheel drive) '77 thru '83
61011 GLC (front wheel drive) '81 thru '85
*61015 323 & Protegé '90 thru '97
*61016 MX-5 Miata '90 thru '97
*61020 MPV all models '89 thru '94
        Navajo - see FORD Explorer (36024)
61030 Pick-ups '72 thru '93
        Pick-ups '94 on - see Ford (36071)
*61035 RX-7 all models '79 thru '85
*61036 RX-7 all models '86 thru '91
*61040 626 (rear wheel drive) '79 thru '82
*61041 626 & MX-6 (front wheel drive) '83 thru '91

MERCEDES-BENZ
63012 123 Series Diesel '76 thru '85
*63015 190 Series 4-cyl gas models, '84 thru '88
63020 230, 250 & 280 6 cyl sohc '68 thru '72
63025 280 123 Series all models '77 thru '81
63030 350 & 450 all models '71 thru '80

MERCURY
        See FORD Listing

MG
66010 MGB Roadster & GT Coupe '62 thru '80
66015 MG Midget & Austin Healey Sprite
        Roadster '58 thru '80

MITSUBISHI
*68020 Cordia, Tredia, Galant, Precis &
        Mirage '83 thru '93
*68030 Eclipse, Eagle Talon &
        Plymouth Laser '90 thru '94
*68040 Pick-up '83 thru '96, Montero '83 thru '93

NISSAN
72010 300ZX all models incl. Turbo '84 thru '89
*72015 Altima all models '93 thru '97
*72020 Maxima all models '85 thru '91
*72030 Pick-ups '80 thru '96, Pathfinder '87 thru '95
72040 Pulsar all models '83 thru '86
72050 Sentra all models '82 thru '94
*72051 Sentra & 200SX '95 thru '98
*72060 Stanza all models '82 thru '90

OLDSMOBILE
*73015 Cutlass '74 thru '88
        For other OLDSMOBILE titles, see
        BUICK, CHEVROLET or
        GENERAL MOTORS listing.

PLYMOUTH
        For PLYMOUTH titles, see DODGE.

PONTIAC
79008 Fiero all models '84 thru '88
79018 Firebird V8 models except Turbo '70 thru '81
79019 Firebird all models '82 thru '92
        For other PONTIAC titles, see
        BUICK, CHEVROLET or
        GENERAL MOTORS listing.

PORSCHE
*80020 911 Coupe & Targa models '65 thru '89
80025 914 all 4 cyl models '69 thru '76
80030 924 all models incl. Turbo '76 thru '82
*80035 944 all models incl. Turbo '83 thru '89

RENAULT
        Alliance, Encore - see AMC (14020)

SAAB
*84010 900 including Turbo '79 thru '88

SATURN
*87010 Saturn all models '91 thru '96

SUBARU
89002 1100, 1300, 1400 & 1600 '71 thru '79
*89003 1600 & 1800 2WD & 4WD '80 thru '94

SUZUKI
*90010 Samurai/Sidekick/Geo Tracker '86 thru '96

TOYOTA
92005 Camry all models '83 thru '91
*92006 Camry all models '92 thru '96
92015 Celica Rear Wheel Drive '71 thru '85
*92020 Celica Front Wheel Drive '86 thru '93
92025 Celica Supra all models '79 thru '92
92030 Corolla all models '75 thru '79
*92032 Corolla rear wheel drive models '80 thru '87
*92035 Corolla front wheel drive models '84 thru '92
*92036 Corolla & Geo Prizm '93 thru '97
92040 Corolla Tercel all models '80 thru '82
92045 Corona all models '74 thru '82
92050 Cressida all models '78 thru '82
92055 Land Cruiser Series FJ40, 43, 45 & 55
        '68 thru '82
*92056 Land Cruiser Series FJ60, 62, 80 &
        FZJ80 '68 thru '82
*92065 MR2 all models '85 thru '87
92070 Pick-up all models '69 thru '78
92075 Pick-up all models '79 thru '95
*92076 Tacoma '95 thru '98,
        4Runner '96 thru '98, T100 '93 thru '98
*92080 Previa all models '91 thru '95
92085 Tercel all models '87 thru '94

TRIUMPH
94007 Spitfire all models '62 thru '81
94010 TR7 all models '75 thru '81

VW
96008 Beetle & Karmann Ghia '54 thru '79
96012 Dasher all gasoline models '74 thru '81
*96016 Rabbit, Jetta, Scirocco, & Pick-up gas
        models '74 thru '91 & Convertible '80 thru '92
*96017 Golf & Jetta '93 thru '97
96020 Rabbit, Jetta, Pick-up diesel '77 thru '84
96030 Transporter 1600 all models '68 thru '79
96035 Transporter 1700, 1800, 2000 '72 thru '79
96040 Type 3 1500 & 1600 '63 thru '73
96045 Vanagon air-cooled models '80 thru '83

VOLVO
97010 120, 130 Series & 1800 Sports '61 thru '73
97015 140 Series all models '66 thru '74
*97020 240 Series all models '76 thru '93
97025 260 Series all models '75 thru '82
*97040 740 & 760 Series all models '82 thru '88

TECHBOOK MANUALS
10205 Automotive Computer Codes
10210 Automotive Emissions Control Manual
10215 Fuel Injection Manual, 1978 thru 1985
10220 Fuel Injection Manual, 1986 thru 1996
10225 Holley Carburetor Manual
10230 Rochester Carburetor Manual
10240 Weber/Zenith/Stromberg/SU Carburetor
10305 Chevrolet Engine Overhaul Manual
10310 Chrysler Engine Overhaul Manual
10320 Ford Engine Overhaul Manual
10330 GM and Ford Diesel Engine Repair
10340 Small Engine Repair Manual
10345 Suspension, Steering & Driveline
10355 Ford Automatic Transmission Overhaul
10360 GM Automatic Transmission Overhaul
10405 Automotive Body Repair & Painting
10410 Automotive Brake Manual
10415 Automotive Detailing Manual
10420 Automotive Eelectrical Manual
10425 Automotive Heating & Air Conditioning
10430 Automotive Reference Dictionary
10435 Automotive Tools Manual
10440 Used Car Buying Guide
10445 Welding Manual
10450 ATV Basics

SPANISH MANUALS
98903 Reparación de Carrocería & Pintura
98905 Códigos Automotrices de la Computadora
98910 Frenos Automotriz
98915 Inyección de Combustible 1986 al 1994
99040 Chevrolet & GMC Camionetas '67 al '87
99041 Chevrolet & GMC Camionetas '88 al '95
99042 Chevrolet Camionetas Cerradas '68 al '95
99055 Dodge Caravan/Ply. Voyager '84 al '95
99075 Ford Camionetas y Bronco '80 al '94
99077 Ford Camionetas Cerradas '69 al '91
99083 Ford Modelos de Tamaño Grande '75 al '87
99088 Ford Modelos de Tamaño Mediano '75 al '86
99091 Ford Taurus & Mercury Sable '86 al '95
99095 GM Modelos de Tamaño Grande '70 al '90
99100 GM Modelos de Tamaño Mediano '70 al '88
99110 Nissan Camionetas '80 al '96,
        Pathfinder '80 al '95
99118 Nissan Sentra '82 al '94
99125 Toyota Camionetas y 4-Runner '79 al '95

Nearly 100 Haynes
motorcycle manuals
also available

5-98

Listings shown with an asterisk (*) indicate model coverage as of this printing. These titles will be periodically updated to include later model years - consult your Haynes dealer for more information.

Haynes North America, Inc., 861 Lawrence Drive, Newbury Park, CA 91320 • (805) 498-6703